IUP

epartment of Nursing & Allie ... ons

TEACHING CIRCLES

Innovative Teaching Strategies in Nursing

Second Edition

Barbara Fuszard, PhD, RN, FAAN

Medical College of Georgia
School of Nursing
Augusta, Georgia

An Aspen Publication®
Aspen Publishers, Inc.
Gaithersburg, Maryland
1995

Library of Congress Cataloging-in-Publication Data

Innovative teaching strategies in nursing/[edited by]
Barbara Fuszard. — 2nd ed.
p. cm.
Rev. ed. of: Innovative teaching strategies in nursing/
Barbara Fuszard, 1989.
Includes bibliographical references and index.
ISBN 0-8342-0609-9
1. Nursing—Study and teaching. I. Fuszard, Barbara.
II. Fuszard, Barbara. Innovative teaching strategies in nursing.
[DNLM: 1. Education, Nursing. 2. Teaching—methods. WY 18 I587
1995]
RT71.F84 1995
610.73'071—dc20
DNLM/DLC
for Library of Congress
94-45369
CIP

Editorial Services: David A. Uffelman

Library of Congress Catalog Card Number: 94-45369
ISBN: 0-8342-0609-9

Printed in the United States of America

3 4 5

In honor of
my teaching colleagues
and those that
showed us the way

Table of Contents

Contributors

Elaine J. Allanach, M.S.N., R.N.
Letterman Army Medical Center
San Francisco, California

Wanda Anderson-Loftin, M.S.N., R.N.
Assistant Professor of Nursing
Georgia Southern University
Statesboro, Georgia, and
Doctoral Student
Medical College of Georgia
Augusta, Georgia

Gayle Bentley, M.S.N.
Instructor
Medical College of Georgia
Augusta, Georgia

Christine Berding, M.S.N., R.N., C.R.R.N.
Instructor
Medical College of Georgia
Augusta, Georgia

Joyce S. Billue, Ed.D., R.N.
Associate Professor
Medical College of Georgia
Augusta, Georgia

Joyce A. Bowie-Guillory, Ph.D., R.N.
Assistant Professor and Director
Cancer Prevention Awareness Program
Morehouse School of Medicine
Community Health/Preventive Medicine
Atlanta, Georgia

Martha J. Bradshaw, Ph.D., R.N.
Assistant Professor
Medical College of Georgia
Augusta, Georgia

Martha H. Bramlett, Ph.D., R.N.
Assistant Professor
Medical College of Georgia
Augusta, Georgia

Kathleen K. Bultman, M.S.N., R.N.
Assistant Professor
Alverno College
Milwaukee, Wisconsin

Patricia Christensen, Ph.D., R.N.
Professor, Parent-Child Nursing
University of South Carolina, Spartanburg
Spartanburg, South Carolina

Susan R. Colgrove, Ph.D., R.N.
Assistant Professor
University of Wisconsin, Oshkosh
Oshkosh, Wisconsin

Marian Lancaster Conway, M.S.N., R.N.
Assistant Professor
Armstrong State College
Savannah, Georgia

Connie F. Cowan, M.S.N., R.N.
Clinical Nurse Specialist, Pediatric Pulmonology
Medical College of Georgia Hospitals and Clinics
Augusta, Georgia

Cynthia L. David, Ph.D.
Instructor, Augusta Technical Institute
Adjunct Assistant Professor
Medical College of Georgia
Augusta, Georgia

Betty Davis, M.S., R.N.
Associate Professor
University of South Carolina, Spartanburg
Spartanburg, South Carolina

Jeffrey S. Dowling, M.S., P.T.
Instructor, Physical Therapy
Medical College of Georgia
Augusta, Georgia

Constance Erpelding, R.N.
Bachelor Completion Student
University of Wisconsin, Oshkosh
Oshkosh, Wisconsin

Nancy Fishback, M.S.N., R.N.
Consultant, Fishback's Augusta Health Alliance, Inc.
Augusta, Georgia

Glenda F. Hanson, M.S., R.N.
Learning Resource Coordinator
Georgia Baptist College of Nursing
Atlanta, Georgia and
Doctoral Student
Medical College of Georgia
Augusta, Georgia

Beverly Henry, Ph.D., R.N., F.A.A.N.
Professor and Head
Department of Administrative Studies in Nursing
University of Illinois at Chicago
Chicago, Illinois

Kathleen Hickman, M.S.N., R.N.
Director of Specialty Nursing
Medical College of Georgia Hospitals and Clinics
Augusta, Georgia

Patricia Shine Hoff, Ed.D., R.N.
Associate Professor
Medical College of Georgia
Augusta, Georgia

Charlotte James Koehler, M.N., R.N., C.C.E., I.B.C.L.C.
Assistant Professor
Medical College of Georgia
Augusta, Georgia

Vickie A. Lambert, D.N.Sc., R.N., F.A.A.N.
Dean and Professor
School of Nursing
Medical College of Georgia
Augusta, Georgia

Pauline M. Loewenhardt, M.S.N., R.N., C.N.A.
Community Nursing Coordinator
James A. Haley Veterans Hospital
Tampa, Florida

Arlene Lowenstein, Ph.D., R.N.
Professor and Chair, Nursing Administration
Medical College of Georgia
Augusta, Georgia

Jerome J. Marcotte, B.S.N.
Senior Community Health Nurse
Rural Outreach Program
Medical College of Georgia
Augusta, Georgia

Jo-Ellen M. McDonough, M.S.N., R.N.C.
Formerly Project Coordinator, Preceptorship in Rural Nursing
Medical College of Georgia
Augusta, Georgia, and
Doctoral Candidate
University of South Carolina
College of Nursing
Columbia, South Carolina

Jean A. Morse, Ph.D.
Professor Emeritus
Health Educational Administration
Medical College of Georgia
Augusta, Georgia

Elizabeth F. Pond, Ed.D., R.N.
Formerly Assistant Professor, Parent-Child Nursing
Certified Childbirth Educator
Medical College of Georgia
Augusta, Georgia

Nancy Schlapman, M.S.N.
Visiting Professor and B.S.N. Coordinator
Division of Nursing
Indiana University, Kokomo
Kokomo, Indiana

Richard L. Sowell, Ph.D., R.N., F.A.A.N.
Director, Division of Research and Program Services
AIDAtlanta, Inc.
Atlanta, Georgia

Russell C. Swansburg, Ph.D., R.N.
Consultant
4917 Ravenswood Drive #1711
San Antonio, Texas

Brenda Talley, M.S.N., R.N.
Assistant Professor
Georgia Southern University
Statesboro, Georgia, and
Doctoral Student
Medical College of Georgia
Augusta, Georgia

Laurie Jowers Taylor, Ph.D., R.N.
Formerly Associate Dean of the Graduate Program
School of Nursing
Valdosta State University
Valdosta, Georgia

Saundra L. Turner, Ed.D., R.N.
Assistant Professor
Medical College of Georgia
Augusta, Georgia

Astrid Hellier Wilson, D.S.N., R.N.
Assistant Professor
College of Health Sciences
Georgia State University
Atlanta, Georgia

Barbara C. Woodring, Ed.D., R.N.
Associate Professor and Chair
Parent-Child Nursing
Medical College of Georgia
Augusta, Georgia

Foreword

There is no practice role in the profession of nursing that does not include the teaching-learning process. Improving competence in both clinical and academic nursing involves the development of improved instructional design and instructional processes. There are advantages for both the teacher and the learner. Students are better served when they understand the purposes and expected outcomes of individual instructional efforts, courses, and curricula. Well-organized educational procedures follow from a clear set of principles. Those individuals engaged in developing or understanding the structure and adequacy of a program will be aided by the concepts, objectives, and procedures included in this volume. The authors have chosen to explain a variety of teaching methods used by nursing educators as well as others that may be adopted in the future. The approach is pragmatic in that explanations are clear and promote implementation. There are also discussions that focus on methodologies to motivate faculty to use innovative methods.

This book presents many structures and procedures important to nursing education. There are descriptions of how to organize and deliver content. The underlying philosophy is that content becomes internalized by the learners only as they understand the structure of the instruction.

The reader may not be inclined to read the entire book in a single sitting. It is more likely that the earnest faculty member will read and contemplate the value of each chapter in the context of a given teaching assignment—designing a course or restructuring existing programs. The potential for application invites critical evaluation by the reader. Questions that may be explored concern the structure presented in the context of the program and the characteristics of the learner. The reader searches for assurances that the proposed structure will increase motivation by improving the quality and character of the learning experiences of those to be taught.

The reader seeks assurances that the proposed structure will increase the amount of content, skills, and values learned. Decisions to adopt or modify structure are based on knowledge of content, educational processes, and desired outcomes. The opportunity to examine several structures increases the probability that decisions about structure will not be made for less desirable reasons: faculty bias, convenience of remaining with the structure already in place, the borrowed prestige of adopting a structure used by a well-regarded university, and non–data-based claims of effectiveness. The decision will occur in a context of knowing how the process of learning is promoted by the structure under consideration.

This book may be used as a textbook for master's programs in nursing for students who are learning the academic role. Its full value will be realized through the thorough discussions of current methods in addition to the exciting examination of structures that have not yet been used for educational nursing programs. The students will have at their fingertips a series of mentors, the authors.

The book should be read by all who are embarking on course or curriculum planning, who have evaluation data indicating that changes are needed, and who are ever vigilant to improve the education of nurses and patients.

Lois Malasanos, Ph.D.
Dean, School of Nursing
University of Florida
Gainesville, Florida

Acknowledgments

I thank the students, who through the years pushed me to seek new teaching strategies to keep pace with their bright minds. Thanks go to the students whose written project offered examples of Co-Consultant: graduate nursing students Roberta Hyde, Gilbert Silbernagel, Maxine Spencer, and Patricia Williams. May they have the joy one day of teaching students just like themselves. Thanks to the colleagues in all the schools at which I have taught. They have been inspirations and supporters, especially those who contributed to this book. Thanks most of all to Sandra Noakes, the most innovative teacher I have met, who spurs me constantly to seek new teaching approaches.

Part I

Introduction

Why are we searching for innovative teaching techniques? Has there been change in the students, the discipline of nursing, technology, or the world, that demands innovative teaching-learning approaches?

The contributors to the chapters in Part I believe there is need for change in the way nurse educators teach. They see changes occurring with ever-increasing rapidity in nursing and in society. Adult learning theory has been chosen as the theoretical rationale for this text, through the approach of experiential learning and demonstrating creativity of approach.

A strong emphasis was sought for creativity, too often stifled by the heavy load of data and rules imposed by the curriculum and tradition. The author of the creative chapter on creativity describes the course that she took as a student that helped reveal her creative potential, and candidly demonstrates the course outcome as evidenced in her poetry.

Thirty-one teaching strategies, a number of which are being introduced for the first time, are offered as being congruent with adult learning principles. The contributors offer their personal experiences with the individual strategies through the examples that expand each chapter.

Chapter 1

Adult Learning and the Nurse

Patricia Shine Hoff

DEFINITION AND ASSUMPTIONS

Andragogy is an important aspect of nursing. Health care organizations assert the need for strategic, sensitive individuals to effectively deliver health care services to the consumer. It then is extremely important to maximize these behaviors among nurses and nursing leadership. Malcolm Knowles initiated the theory of andragogy in his text *The Modern Practice of Adult Education. Andr* comes from the greek word *aner*, meaning man. Andragogy is the art and science of helping adults learn.[1]

Knowles's model of andragogy is a set of assumptions about adult learning, including the following four:

1. Adults desire and enact a tendency toward self-directedness as they mature.
2. Adults' experiences are a rich resource for learning. They learn more effectively through experiential activities such as problem solving.
3. Adults are aware of specific learning needs generated by real life.
4. Adults are competency-based learners who wish to apply knowledge to immediate circumstances.[2]

Knowles believes that a climate of mutual respect is most important for learning—trust, support, and caring are essential components. Learning is pleasant and this should be emphasized.

Andragogy has been influential with practitioners in establishing effective adult learning. Clearly, past experience affects the way in which adults interpret their world. Andralogical approaches urge nursing education leaders to base curricula on learners' experiences and interests.

Adults learn at different rates because of individual differences. The teachers must interact closely with the adult student so that they may see from the student's viewpoint. Thus, learning must be individually based, allowing for individual differences.

Allan Tough suggests that adult learning projects go astray if the learner is unaware of the need for help, is unaware of where and how to get help, or is unable to obtain needed resources because of economic restrictions. To ensure success, the leaders must try to increase learning competence by improving the resources for the learner both in quality and accessibility.[3]

PRINCIPLES OF ADULT LEARNING

Principles derived from learning-process research by Darkenwald and Merriam serve as guidelines for adults. The principles found by the adult leaders are as follows:

- Adults' readiness to learn depends upon their previous learning.
- Intrinsic motivation produces more pervasive and permanent learning.
- Positive reinforcement is effective.
- Material to be learned should be presented in an organized fashion.
- Learning is enhanced by repetition.
- More meaningful tasks and materials are more fully and easily learned.
- Active participation in learning improves retention.
- Environmental factors affect learning.
- Adults learn throughout their lifetime.
- Adults exhibit learning styles, such as
  1. having personal strategies for coding information;
  2. using cognitive procedures—learning in different ways;
  3. liking learning activities to be problem centered and relevant to life;
  4. desiring some immediate appreciation;
  5. having a concept of themselves as learners;
  6. being self-directed.[4]

These principles were identified earlier by Gibb, Kidd, Knox, Brundage, and Macher.[5]

Learning As Change

Brookfield says that we assimilate and integrate ideas, values, and behaviors from others until they actually become parts of *ourselves*. Until some source provides us with alternative thinking and living as well as behaving, we remain with our value systems, beliefs, and behaviors.[6] This statement has tremendous implications for the nurse working with other nurses and/or patients. Nurses and students who have been employing the same behaviors for years are not going to change these practices on their own. The situation requires the intervention of a facilitator who is able to present the nurse with alternatives to current thinking patterns, behavior, and even life style. Adults who are able to reflect critically on their assumptions, then imagine alternatives, are autonomous, self-directed individuals. These adults are much more likely continually to evaluate self, work, personal relationships, and social structures. Verduin et al. suggest that the teacher who wishes to change behavior must modify the way individuals perceive their environment.[7] A major deterrent to this process is threat of change. This pinpoints the need for an open, positive, supportive learning environment.

Motivating Adults

Most individuals have more than one reason for learning. Adults will be motivated by those things that have personal meaning for them. The nurse adult learner is most frequently motivated by a pragmatic desire to use or apply some newly available knowledge.[8]

The learning approach may vary from an awareness of wanting to accomplish something, to a curiosity or puzzlement about an issue, or a commitment to devote time to learn. Each individual reaches a point of questioning whether to settle for the current level of achievement or to strive for new goals that entail risk taking. One might hypothesize that being in a state of transition from one stage of life to another causes many adults to learn. The adult nurse will learn what is needed in order to achieve success in a new state. The true success of learning is the ability to make the needed transition. The nurse never outgrows the need to learn. Each individual, at one time or another, faces the need to change. The learning one undertakes is directly related to the transitions of one's life circumstances.[9]

Wlodkowski, supported by numerous psychological theories, suggests that six major factors have an impact on learner motivation: attitude, need, stimulation, affect, competence, and reinforcement.[10]

Attitudes strongly influence human behavior and learning because they help the individual to receive cues as to the behavior that will be helpful in the world. Attitudes are learned and may be acquired through experience, instructor identification, and role behavior (teacher-student). Attitudes can be modified or changed. They can be helpful in developing positive self-esteem.

A *need* is an internal force that leads the person to move in the direction of a goal. All of us live with a continuing feeling of need. Most psychologists will agree a person can be driven to acquire knowledge, money, or food. These are some compelling needs that motivate the individual.

Stimulation helps to sustain adult learning behavior. Stimulation increases brain activity, keeping one aroused and thus able to deal with the surroundings. The adult who does not find the process of learning stimulating loses attention and becomes bored.

Affect concerns emotional experience—the feelings, concerns, and passions of the individual learning. The feelings one has while learning can motivate behavior. Tomkins accepts that thinking and feeling interact to influence one another and thus change behavior. Affect can serve as an intrinsic motivator. Positive emotions during learning deepen interest in the subject matter.[11]

Competence is the motivation to mold our environment rather than let the environment control us. Wlodkowski states that adults tend to be motivated when effectively learning something valued. Adults who feel a sense of progress and accomplishment are motivated to continue their efforts. This frequently occurs toward the end of the learning process when one has a chance to apply the new learning.[12] The nurse leader who feels assured of her ability to lead another to new learning and achievement feels an overwhelming sense of motivation.

Reinforcement might be defined as learning behavior that occurs spontaneously and thus continues the learning process. The facilitator (nurse) compliments the learner and reinforces the behavior. Penalties, disapproval, and threat often act as negative reinforcers. Adults in our culture do not respond well to coercion. Positive reinforcements such as praise, social approval, and attention are better motivators. These variables should be considered in planning and learning.

The Role of the Facilitator

The term *facilitator* is viewed in adult teaching circles as a more positive term than *teacher.* This does not release the facilitator from teaching. One must assist the nurse to consider alternatives, to reflect and see the self as proactive. However, the learner is always considered as an individual. Ruddock[13] identified these roles for facilitators:

- resource person
- expositor
- demonstrator
- promulgator of values
- taskmaster
- assessor
- helper and group manager

One of the best ways the facilitator can assist the learner is to know the student well. The more known about the student the better he or she can be assisted to perform at full potential. Facilitators should understand and relate to the student and the student's special interests in order to provide positive reinforcement. Assessing the student and knowing his or her needs and environmental influences are essential to preparing for learning.

The facilitator should use discussion groups as a means of encouraging the adult learner to undertake intellectual challenges. Through the utilization of a peer group the adult may experiment with ideas and undertake some special adventures in learning. With peers, many fears may be lost and new approaches may be explored. Through group scrutiny ideas should become more clearly focused and ready for application.

Continuing Professional Development

Most nurses today are involved in working for public agencies; few are in private practice. In their role and practice areas, professionals exhibit a tremendous amount of influence upon society through the identification of key issues *and* problems of considerable consequence to the public, formulation of policy for institutions within society, and the delivery of professional services affecting the quality of life. In essence, because of their expertise, nursing professionals are in a position to serve as leaders in the profession and society.

A major expectation and responsibility of the nurse professionals is continually to improve competencies and performance within their practice area through continuing education and learning. Scheneman[14] believes that continuing professional education is one of facilitation of learning that requires other strategies (coaching, peer mentoring, and team learning) in addition to programmatic and instructional intervention (workshops, seminars, etc.). The new methods will need to be supported and promoted by practitioners.

In summary, adult learners are more motivated, serious, and self-directed than the less mature learner. The effectiveness of adult learning varies with ability but is also affected by the facilitator's approach to learning. Adults approach learning activities in the light of their previous experience, including their education. Most have expectations of gain as a result of the new learning. Learning achievement and persistence in learning can be affected by the educational climate.

The nurse adult learner needs to be recognized as a person with a background in learning. This resource of learning abilities needs to be guided and encouraged to develop. Some ways the nurse facilitator can engender participation are to stimulate thinking, seek ideas, consider learning theories and concepts, and encourage discovery. As a facilitator, one must provide guidance in self-evaluation regardless of the learning skills required. The nurse must be encouraged to be an active participant involved in the learning process. One must remember that even the most independent learner at times needs assistance and/or permission to be the learner.

NOTES

1. M.S. Knowles, *The Modern Practice of Adult Education: From Pedagogy to Andragogy,* 2nd ed. (New York: Cambridge University Press, 1980).

2. *Ibid.,* 43–44.

3. A.M. Tough, *The Adult's Learning Projects* (Ontario: Learning Concepts, 1979), 119–128.

4. G.G. Darkenwald and S.B. Merriam, *Adult Education: Foundations of Practice* (New York: Harper & Row, 1982), 110–111.

5. J.R. Gibb, Learning Theory in Adult Education, in *Handbook of Adult Education in the United States,* ed. Malcolm S. Knowles (Washington, DC: Adult Education Association of the U.S.A., 1960); J.R.Kidd, *How Adults Learn* (New York: Cambridge University Press, 1973); A.B. Knox, ed., *Inservice Education in Adult Basic Education* (Tallahassee, Fla: State University Press, 1971); D.H. Brundage and D. Macher, *Adult Learning Principles and Their Application to Program Planning* (Toronto: Ministry of Education, 1980).

6. S.D. Brookfield, *Understanding and Facilitating Adult Learning,* (San Francisco: Jossey-Bass, Inc. Publishers, 1986).

7. J.R. Verduin, et al., *Adults Teaching Adults: Principles and Strategies* (Austin, Tex: Learning Concepts, 1977), 9–10.

8. Tough, *The Adult's Learning Projects,* 46.

9. R.J. Wlodkowski, *Enhancing Adult Motivation to Learn* (San Francisco: Jossey-Bass, Inc. Publishers, 1985), 60–65.

10. Wlodkowski, *Enhancing Adult Motivation to Learn,* 45.

11. S.S. Tomkins and C.E. Izard, *Affect, Cognition, and Personality* (New York: Springer Publishing Company, 1965), 6.

12. Wlodkowski, *Enhancing Adult Motivation to Learn,* 213–214.

13. R. Ruddock, *Sociological Perspectives on Adult Education,* Monograph 4 (Manchester, England: Department of Adult Education, University of Manchester, 1980).

14. S. Scheneman, Continuing Professional Development, *Adult Learning* 6, no. 4 (1993): 6.

SUGGESTED READING

Caffarella, R.S. 1994. On being a self directed learner. *Adult Learning* 5, no. 5:7.

Davenport, J., III. 1987. A way out of the andragogy morass. Paper presented at the conference of the Georgia Adult Education Association, Savannah, Ga, March 4.

Chapter 2

Experiential Learning

Susan R. Colgrove, Nancy Schlapman, and Constance Erpelding

DEFINITION AND CHARACTERISTICS

The concept of experiential learning is often defined as a series of learning methods that focus on the role of experience in the learning.[1] Distinguishing features of experiential learning include the process of reflection and the transformation of knowledge and meaning that occurs when students reflect on personal experiences. Experiential learning occurs when students reflect on personal experiences, discuss their thoughts with others, and re-evaluate what is known and understood. The interaction of reflection, discussion, and re-evaluation ultimately lead to the transformation of knowledge into new meanings and new ideas.

Specific characteristics distinguish experiential learning from other types of learning. These characteristics include (1) an emphasis on the process of learning as opposed to a focus on the outcomes, (2) knowledge continuously derived from experiences, (3) learning that results from resolving conflicts between concrete experiences and abstract concepts, (4) learning as a holistic activity, (5) transactions that occur between the learner and the environment, and (6) the process of creating knowledge.[2]

Deviating from the traditional model of "feeding" the students "pre-packaged knowledge," experiential learning is an "active process" of learning.[3] Knowledge gained from this active process is subject to the perception and interpretation of the learner and is reality based. Experiential learning allows students to create "personal knowledge" and to make sense of the world around them based on interactive experiences. This type of learning offers nursing students the chance to explore directly many complex health care concepts.

Experiential learning can occur any time the main criteria for learning are focused on personal experiences and active participation by the students in the learning process.[4] Examples of experiential learning include, but are not limited to, group discussions, role-playing, simulations, problem-solving exercises, structured learning activities, games, apprenticeships, internships, clinicals, and laboratory and field studies. Experiential learning methods are not be viewed as replacements for more traditional techniques, but rather as alternate approaches when appropriate.

THEORETICAL RATIONALE

Experiential learning methods have essentially evolved from two sources. One major influence emerged from John Dewey, an American philosopher, who believed that all education processes should be based on students' personal experiences.[5] Combined with Dewey's value of experience was his emphasis on practicality and internal processing. His methods were developed to meet the challenges of coping with change and lifelong learning.

A second major source of influence was contributions from the humanistic psychologists.[6] These theorists believed that persons were not "acted upon" by the environment, but were able to interact with their surroundings to make decisions and choices about life. Humanistic psychology is an optimistic approach to understanding the person as complex, unique, and ever changing. By placing great importance on the variety and interpretation of human experiences, contributions from humanistic psychology positively supported John Dewey's beliefs about education.

Experiential learning reflects both a series of methods by which to learn and an attitude toward learning. In focusing on the process of judgment, decision making, and the value of personal experience, experiential learning closely matches the direction of nursing education. Experiential learning methods such as problem-solving exercises, certain games, simulations, and field activities are excellent methods for teaching critical thinking skills to nursing students of all levels.

CONDITIONS

To plan a nursing course using experiential learning methods, aspects of experiential learning should be combined with andragogy and empowerment. Andragogy is defined as an attitude toward adult education, emphasizing student-centered learning, personal experience, and subjective interpretation.[7] It is grounded in students' prior experience and knowledge, application of that knowledge, and the assumption that education is active and not passive.

Consistent with andragogy and Kolb's experiential learning methods is empowerment.[8] Empowerment is "the interpersonal process of providing the resources, tools and environment to develop, build and increase the ability and effectiveness of others to set and reach goals for individual and social ends."[9] In nursing education, faculty enable students, and as a result of this, students become empowered to learn and are then able to set learning goals. Important to empowerment is a caring and nurturing environment. There must be trust between individuals, open communication and information exchange, acceptance, valuing, and mutual respect. A shared purpose and vision by the faculty and student is necessary, as is shared decision making, for experiential learning to be successful.

To accomplish experiential learning, Burnard believes the following conditions are necessary:

- There is an attitude toward critical thinking and learning among faculty and students, recognizing human experience as a valued source of learning and emphasizing action and reflection on experiences.
- Faculty accept that students as well as educators are knowledgeable.
- Faculty acknowledge the self-worth of the students, encourage students, and respect and value students' thoughts.
- Faculty are the facilitators and listen attentively; faculty allow students to choose the nontraditional method of thinking and questioning. As facilitators, faculty clarify, but do not lecture extensively.
- Faculty empower students and challenge students to develop ideas and to question.
- Faculty take risks with students and with staff, and have competence and humility.
- Faculty model critical thinking ability by being open to new ideas from students. The atmosphere of discussions is conversational; faculty relate to students as people who are interesting and have ideas and knowledge.[10]
- In addition, faculty are willing to relinquish some control, and students are willing to assume control.[11] Assuming control requires personal involvement. A lack of involvement hinders the understanding of theory, whatever the topic.[12]

TYPES OF LEARNERS

Experiential learning methods are appropriate for undergraduate (generic and completion students) and graduate nursing students. For the more experienced nursing student or licensed nurse returning for an advanced degree, experiential learning allows existing knowledge of nursing theory and skills to be utilized in a different way and at a higher level. For inexperienced students, the activities can be at a beginning level depending on the needs of the students and the objectives of the course. However, if there are mixed levels of knowledge and skills within the group, mutual planning of the course with students allows each student to have individualized objectives within overall course objectives. When teaching difficult material, whether it is to beginning or advanced nursing students, students may become apathetic, fail to see important issues, and minimize issues.[13] Increasing opportunities for all levels of students to practice theory through experiential learning methods helps students clarify roles, determine new interests, and understand more deeply a subject area. If learning occurs in a clinical setting the student sees a variety of issues in the natural setting that cannot be seen in readings or lectures.[14]

RESOURCES

No specific resources are necessary. Anything that promotes student activity and empowerment is beneficial.[15] Burnard suggests that large or small groups can be used.[16] However, small groups of less than ten allow for greater trust, increased participation of students, and increased ability to meet objectives.[17] McCaugherty suggests a 1:3 or 1:6 ratio. Adequate time must be allowed for planning, coordinating clinical agencies, orienting students for the experience, postactivity discussions, and evaluation. Outside experts may be appropriate to assist students to meet their objectives.[18]

If clinical agencies are being used, additional time will be needed for planning and observing students. If there is a large group, more than one instructor may be required. It will take time to establish relationships with agencies; develop preceptors, if being utilized; orient agency staff to the objectives of the course, role of the students at the setting, and staff role in student evaluation; coordinate student learning activities; and monitor student progress. Depending on the type of participation by the students at the site, liability issues will need to be explored.[19] In the case of clinical research, proper clearance by human subjects committees will need to be obtained for students participating in data collection. Having a classroom at the clinical agency is important, as student and faculty can have discussion periods on site.

USING THE METHOD

Planning is an important element for the effective use of experiential learning. Because nurse educators must work around a course curriculum and syllabus, it may be difficult to carry out experiential methods in a typical nursing course.[20]

Burnard has proposed a model for combining the principles of andragogy and experiential learning in nursing education.[21] This model emphasizes personal experience, self-/peer evaluation, and a student-centered negotiating approach. In addition, this model allows for planning the course around the course syllabus. Discussions can be dictated by the students, and contracts can be used to further individualize the course for the students.[22] Both students and faculty negotiate the course based on each others' needs; the goal is a balance between the needs of the two groups[23] (Figure 2–1).

In the first stage (self-assessment plus input from the syllabus), students identify their needs and faculty discuss the objectives as described in the course syllabus. It is at this point that the experience of the students can be used to individualize course objectives and determine topics for future discussions.

In stage two a timetable is negotiated with the students. Theory sessions and clinical sessions to develop skills are developed jointly between faculty and students. Skills can include basic or advanced nursing skills, interpersonal skills, computer skills, or other appropriate topics, depending on the course.

In stage three, the learning process, theory can be provided in traditional lecture methods, self-study by students, assigned readings, or student presentations. The skills component uses the experiential learning cycle, emphasizing personal experience, reflection, and transformation of knowledge. The fourth and final stage is self-, peer, and faculty evaluation. All of these stages incorporate student-centered negotiating approaches of andragogy.

Rolfe believes that it is best to begin this type of learning with a gradual approach; initially, content, method, and assignments have more structure; but gradually they become more directed by the students.[24] Basic information is presented to the students that is necessary for them to function in the clinical setting. As time goes on students are encouraged to pursue more complex tasks and areas necessary to develop their own personal interests. Expectations are kept realistic.[25] These activities allow the students to build confidence.

Discussions are directed by student concerns and interests. These discussions can take place in both the classroom and the clinical setting and should emphasize reflection. The relevance of the theory to practice comes together as the student gets more involved in the course and the clinical experience.[26] Students learn not only *by* experience, but *from* experience. The latter complements the former by adding critical thinking and reflecting to the student learning experience.[27]

When using this method it is important to avoid giving too much lecture. The educator remains centered on student reflection and discussion of student experiences. Students have the active role and the educator has the listening role. Good faculty rapport with the students is essential and can be achieved by meeting with students often, and having a balance of 80:20 between experiential and didactic methods.[28]

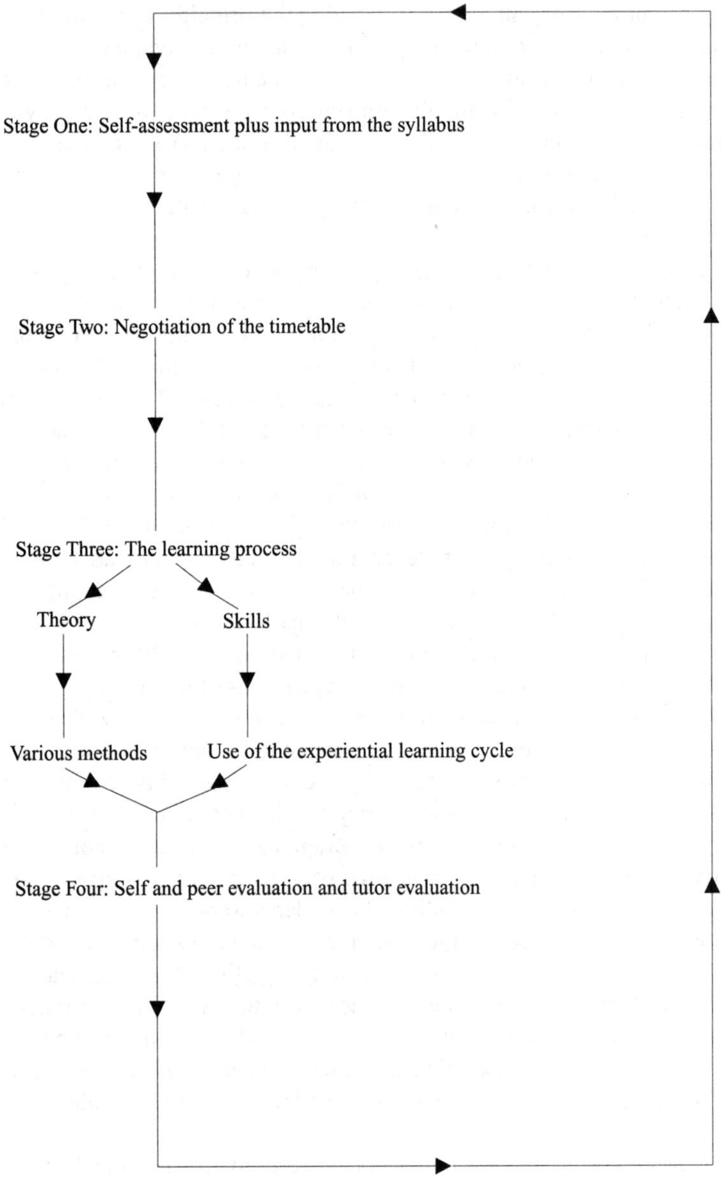

Stage One: Self-assessment plus input from the syllabus

Stage Two: Negotiation of the timetable

Stage Three: The learning process

Theory

Skills

Various methods

Use of the experiential learning cycle

Stage Four: Self and peer evaluation and tutor evaluation

Figure 2–1 A Cycle for Combining Andragogy and Experiential Learning in Nurse Education. *Source:* Reprinted from *Learning Human Skills: An Experiential Guide for Nurses* by P. Burnard, p. 66, with permission of Butterworth Heinemann, © 1990.

At the onset of the course it is important to describe experiential learning to the participants; understanding the roles of the facilitator (educator) and the learner (student) is important. Bayntum-Lee[29] believes that to use this method the educator must emphasize independent autonomous learning in which the educator is a facilitator, enabler, and a joint learner. Essential to this is a trusting environment. This is created by both the psychological climate and the physical environment in which the course takes place.

A psychological climate in which the subject matter has relevance and importance to the student is crucial. To achieve this, it is essential to assess the students' needs, gain knowledge of their work, and involve them in the planning. The environment must also be safe for students to share, in order for the success of learning.[30]

The physical environment can be any setting, a typical classroom or a room at the clinical site. Utilize available opportunities for learning that link theory, curriculum, and practice. Large lecture rooms should be avoided, and the setting should be geared toward adults, without desks, and with chairs placed in a circle. This format prevents barriers, allows for greater movement within the group, and encourages people to participate and speak freely.[31,32] Inviting guests from the community, clinical site, and other faculty to participate in discussion and facilitate experiences can increase concrete experiences.[33]

If a clinical site is being used, it is also important that faculty be at the setting often when students are there, to observe their progress and interact with them during the experience. This requires that faculty be current in the subject area they are teaching.[34]

POTENTIAL PROBLEMS

Experiential learning may be threatening and uncomfortable for some students who do not like group work, classes with clinical labs, or independent learning.[35] However, anxiety with a new method is normal and necessary for students to advance.[36] Experiential learning may not be suitable for all topics. Subjects must be explored on an individual basis.

A great deal of planning is required, coordinating lecture, clinical experience, individual needs, and discussion. This process is time consuming for the faculty. In addition, since the course may not be taught at regular hours, it requires that the student and faculty be more flexible.[37] In groups where there is a mixture of student ages, experience, and educational backgrounds, transfer of learning may be a problem, and a great deal of individual time may have to be spent with the student.

Evaluation is not typical using experiential learning. Verbal feedback, written reports by students, written reports from the clinical area, personal observation, and peer evaluation are just some of the methods utilized. Students may contract with the faculty for the type of evaluation appropriate for the course.

Older students may have difficulty with changing from a teacher-dominated lecture/seminar format to a student-centered, independent-course type of study. Because of curriculum restraints, the course may not truly be student-centered, but techniques and methods that are student centered can be utilized within the confines of the syllabus.[38]

Many of the problems that may be encountered using experimental learning may be unique to the course and may become apparent only after the course has begun. Thus it is difficult to plan for them, and flexibility is necessary on the part of both the faculty and the student.[39]

NOTES

1. P. Burnard, *Self Awareness for Nurses: An Experiential Guide* (Gaithersburg, Md: Aspen Publishers, Inc., 1986), 29–34.

2. D. Kolb, *Experiential Learning: Experiences the Source of Learning and Development* (Englewood Cliffs, NJ: Prentice Hall, 1984), 25–28.

3. Burnard, *Self Awareness for Nurses,* 34–38.

4. Kolb, *Experiential Learning,* 17–38.

5. Burnard, *Self Awareness For Nurses,* 36–38.

6. Ibid.

7. M. Knowles, *Andragogy in Action: Applying Modern Principles of Adult Learning* (San Francisco: Jossey-Bass, Inc. Publishers, 1984).

8. J.H. Hawkes, Empowerment in Nursing Education: Concept Analysis and Application to Philosophy, Learning, and Instruction, *Journal of Advanced Nursing* 17 (1992):609–618.

9. Hawkes, Empowerment in Nursing Education, 610.

10. P. Burnard, *Learning Human Skills. An Experiential Guide for Nurses* (Oxford, England: Heinemann, 1990), 32–74.

11. G. Rolfe, Toward a Theory of Student Centered Nursing Education: Overcoming Constraints of a Professional Curriculum, *Nurse Education Today* 13 (1993):149–154.

12. K. McCluskey-Fawcett and P. Green, Using Community Service to Teach Developmental Psychology, *Teaching Psychology* 19, no. 3 (1992):150–155.

13. McCluskey-Fawcett and Green, Using Community Service.

14. Ibid.

15. Hawkes, Empowerment in Nursing Education, 609–618.

16. Burnard, *Learning Human Skills,* 32–74.

17. D. Bayntum-Lees, Setting the Scene for Experiential Learning, *Nursing Standard* 7, no. 36(1993):28–30.

18. D. McCaughterty, The Use of a Teaching Model to Promote Reflection and the Experiential Integration of Theory and Practice in First-Year Student Nurses: An Action Research Study, *Journal of Advanced Nursing* 16 (1991):534–543.

19. McCluskey-Fawcett and Green, Using Community Service, 150–155.

20. Burnard, *Learning Human Skills,* 32–74.

21. Ibid.
22. Rolfe, Toward a Theory, 149–154.
23. Burnard, *Learning Human Skills,* 32–74.
24. Rolfe, Toward a Theory, 149–154.
25. J.F. Cronin, Four Misconceptions about Authentic Learning, *Educational Leadership* 50, no. 7 (1993):78–80.
26. Burnard, *Learning Human Skills,* 32–74.
27. McCaughterty, The Use of a Teaching Model, 534–543.
28. Ibid.
29. Bayntum-Lees, Setting the Scene, 28–30.
30. Ibid.
31. Ibid.
32. Burnard, *Learning Human Skills,* 32–74.
33. Hawkes, Empowerment in Nursing Education, 609–618.
34. McCaugherty, The Use of a Teaching Model, 534–543.
35. Burnard, *Learning Human Skills,* 32–74.
36. Hawkes, Empowerment in Nursing Education, 609–618.
37. Burnard, *Learning Human Skills,* 32–74.
38. Rolfe, Toward a Theory, 149–154.
39. Ibid.

SUGGESTED READING

Burnard, P. 1992. Learning from experience: Nurse tutors' and student nurses' perceptions of experiential learning in nurse education: Some initial findings, *International Journal of Nursing Studies* 29, no. 2:151–161.

Chapter 3

Creativity in Nursing

Brenda Talley

It is important to explore the concept of creativity in nursing from several perspectives. In a book such as this, one of the more obvious dimensions is the use of creativity in nursing education. However, we should consider creativity not only as a tool to facilitate the teaching-learning process, but as an important part in both the delivery of nursing care and specifically of the healing process, a central concern of nursing. Creativity is also critical in the development of a vision for nursing and the evolvement of nursing as a profession of science and art. We should understand the value of creativity in nursing and examine the process by which creativity can be fostered and supported in nursing.

CREATIVITY IN NURSING PRACTICE

Creativity is the link between science and art. Barrett speaks of the "artistry whereby the science becomes translated into practice"[1] in describing the role of nursing in changing health care dynamics and in expectations of the American public. In nursing, we continually take what we know—that which we have learned—into unique and constantly changing environments. The science is what we know about nursing; the art is what we do with that knowledge. Knowledge does not tell us what to do, it gives us ideas about what to do. There is a creative synthesis of information and knowledge from which come forth caring and healing manifestations. Rogers[2] describes caring as doing, as practice. She saw the world as full of opportunities for using creative thinking in the use of nursing knowledge. "Caring is a way of using knowledge, and we should be using knowledge in all that we do and all that we talk about doing."[3] Creativity allows us to draw upon our "infinite potentials in the service of humankind."[4] It keeps us from being bound to just that which we already know and allows us to continue in the process of becoming.

CREATIVITY AND THE FUTURE OF NURSING

Change seems inevitable in American health care. Historically, humankind has exalted change only in others. Cousins[5] saw the main test before humankind as involving the will to change rather than the ability to change. We cannot expect health care delivery to change and the nursing profession to stay much the same as it is. Change is already happening *to* us. The tragedy would be that the changes instigated by others will take us away from what we want nursing to be. In the mist of confusion and fear, we need a vision of nursing and creative strategies that will direct changes toward the vision.

Johnson[6] describes "visionary pondering" in a story of nursing as it may be in the space age. She visionalizes earthborn and spaceborn humans that are evolving differently and the interactions of those with unique mobility and communication patterns. Creativity, through such techniques as visionary pondering, can assist us in seeing nursing as it should be and reveal paths to our ideal.

CREATIVITY IN NURSING EDUCATION

Gueldner et al.[7] used their creative energy in developing a doctoral-level course for teaching Martha Rogers' Science of Unitary Human Beings. An extensive reading assignment was made for the students that was useful in the study of intellectual knowledge. However, the grasp of the abstract concepts was facilitated by the choice of environment; selection of experiential learning activities, such as meditation, artistic expression, and personal exploration; and the interactions within the group, which included Dr. Rogers. Creative visioning was encouraged and supported.

THE CREATIVE EXPERIENCE: A PERSONAL PERSPECTIVE

As a student participant in this course, I found my life changed. In an environment that made explorations safe and respected, I found my creative energy unbounded by my own expectations of myself and by concerns of the judgments of others. I was aware of the world and of others in ways I have never before experienced. Though always having had a slight creative bent, I had always found my rewards in intellectual and analytical expressions. My early academic focus was in mathematics. Creative endeavors, though perhaps fun and relaxing, had no place in meaningful work. Suddenly I was invited to experience creativity in any way that seemed appropriate to me.

One of the tools we learned about in the course that seemed especially useful to me was meditation. One of the people with us was Carl Brown, outreach coordinator for Drepung Loseling Tibetan University and for Emory University School of Health and Human Ecology, both in Atlanta, Georgia. Carl taught us beginning skills in meditation. Although explaining the relationship of creativity and meditation is beyond the scope of this chapter and of my expertise, I can say that for me the meditation experience enhances creativity. Creativity means seeing things in a new and different way. Expressions of creativity can range from strategies to coax a three-year-old to eat his peas, to the touch of a hand on a troubled brow, or to a sculpture made of stone. But they are not creativity, they are manifestations of creativity. Creativity is the ability to lay aside the way things have always been and explore them in a new way. One of the skills inherent to meditation is that of letting go. It means not only letting go of preconceived notions and ideas, but also letting go of all the distractions around us that cloud our ability to focus on an experience. Meditation frees our energy for reflection and gives us space for new visions. It can give us a calm and beautiful place to create.

My creative energy was directed primarily toward writing poetry. Immediately following this course, actually on the way home, the poems just started coming. My first poem was about the experience of meditation, specifically a form of standing and moving meditation that we began learning as part of the course. Meditation was useful in helping us to begin understanding abstract concepts in a direct, experiential way.

Like a silken cloak
the cool sea wind caresses me,
enfolding me
into the rhythms of the universe.

I sense every grain of sand
beneath my feet
as my consciousness merges
into the essence of unity.

As air through a butterfly net,
the energies of the universe
slip through the space
of my being.

Flowing smoothly, rushing slowly,
vibrant with opalescent energy, serene.
Everywhere, nowhere,
feeling everything and nothing.

Being and nonbeing.
My senses reeling with
the sounds and colors of eternity,
yet not hearing and unseeing

What has been melts
into what is not yet,
like a wax rose
left too long in the sun.

Slowly, I awaken to the
slumber of the present,
to the cry of the gull
and the laughter of children.

I see a purple kite fighting
to reach the clouds,
struggling for freedom, but earth tethered
in the singing winds of now.

I again hear the ocean's rhythm
as waves crash at the shore
and then are not,
but always are.

Source: Reprinted from *Rogers' Scientific Art of Nursing Practice* by M. Madrid and E.A.M. Barrett, eds., with permission of the National League for Nursing, © 1994.

CREATIVITY IN HEALING

We should pay more attention to creativity in healing. Creativity can mean a way of seeing an experience from another's view and can touch that within us from which caring and compassion flow. We do not have to experience each pain to know the hurting.

Poetry and other manifestations of the creative experience can be useful in communicating the essence of an experience. It facilitates sharing of the context, the feelings of the individual, and the meaning an experience has for the individual. It can assist in finding a way to the healing process. The following poem can be considered a distillation of an experience. The writing of this poem began the healing.

Sand in my hands

Invisible tears
rain in my soul.
The remembering
that comes with sleeping
hits my chest
and leaves me breathless
be still, be quiet!
DON'T
HURT
ME
ANYMORE
I try to breathe
the soft night air
but even the cells of my body remember.
With this faint movement
the knife blade presses deeper
into my throat
be still, be quiet!
DON'T
HURT
ME
ANYMORE
His body suffocates me
and the coldness at my back
seems to push me toward him.
His beard is so rough.
Even the smell of him
torments me
I cannot move.
DON'T
HURT
ME
ANYMORE
Pain rages at me
wanting rest.
I reach out my hands
in hope of some defense
reaching, I grasp the earth,
sand in my hands.
Sand, falling through my fingers!
DON'T
HURT
ME

ANYMORE
be still, be quiet!
My voice is silent yet
and my heart forever screams.
Sand in my hands
falling through my fingers
falling through my fingers.
falling through my fingers.

DON'T
HURT
ME
ANY MORE

Healing begins when we can feel compassion for ourselves and for others, even others who have caused injury. It means letting go of anger and pain. It means finding strengths and beauty within ourselves and living a meaningful and useful life.

Let the past be a dim distant star
in the universe of your life,
shining softly in predawn light
with the thousand other stars of who you are.

Let memories be gentle in your heart—
a spider's web caressing your face
on an early morning walk down a wooded trail,
just as the sun comes to show your way.

Let the future be morning's sharp cool air
that enters your body and awakens your soul,
as you walk on from a shadowed still valley
to join the mountain in vivid sunrise.

Let now be the breeze born of light and warmth
that tickles soft new leaves and brings
stars of day to play in a crystal stream.
Dance in it. Live in it. Love in it.

Healing can be viewed as reaching for harmony in all that we are and in our relationships with others and with the world. It is not necessarily regaining health as seen in the traditional sense. We have all seen how the process of death can be healing. "Health," according to Remen, "enables us to find purpose in our life, but it is not the purpose of life. One can serve purpose with impaired health. One might even regain health through serving purpose."[8] Healing can lie in that finding of purpose. The finding of a new path, of a new way of being with one's self, with others, and with one's environment is a creative experience. It is finding a fresh trail through newly fallen snow.

Remen[9] gives an example of a young man who, because of cancer, had lost his leg at the hip. For a long time he was angry and withdrawn, but after a while, he began working with others in their healing. Once he visited a young woman about his own age who had had her breasts removed because of cancer. He purposefully wore shorts so she would see his prosthesis, but she would not even glance at him. Someone had left a radio on. Desperate to get her attention, he unstrapped his prosthesis and began dancing around the room on his one leg, snapping his fingers to the rhythm. She looked at him in amazement and disbelief, but after awhile she laughed and said, "Man, if you can dance, I can sing!" Later Dr. Remen showed this young man drawings she had asked him to do when he first came to the center. One drawing was of a vase with a big crack, a crack so big the vase could never hold water again, never have a purpose. Dr. Remen remembered the young man drawing the crack over and over again with a black crayon, grinding his teeth in anger and frustration. Now, after two years, he looked at it for a moment and said, "Well, it isn't finished" and he drew over the big black crack with bright yellow. "That," he said, "is the light shining through."[10]

CONCLUSION

We should explore creativity in terms of nursing education, in how to set the environment for experiential learning, in the way we share our knowledge, in our expectations of individuals, and in how we measure learning. We should examine the creative experiences that are in our practice of nursing.

It is possible to teach about creativity, but the creative experience is unique to each individual and is a personal discovery. Nursing education can set the environment and can support and value the experiences. Creativity is important in the art of nursing. Creativity enhances our ability to behave in a caring and compassionate manner toward others, and the creative experience can lead us toward a path of healing. Creativity can assist us in defining our ideal in nursing, in developing visions for our future, and in seeing new relationships in health care delivery as the demands and needs of society change.

NOTES

1. E. Barrett, Rogerian Scientists, Artists, and Revolutionaries, in *Rogers' Scientific Art of Nursing Practice,* eds. M. Madrid and E.A.M. Barrett (New York: National League for Nursing, 1994), 61.

2. M. Rogers, Nursing Science Evolves, in *Rogers' Scientific Art of Nursing Practice,* eds. M. Madrid and E.A.M. Barrett (New York: National League for Nursing, 1994), 3–10.

3. Ibid., 7.

4. Ibid.

5. N. Cousins. *Modern Man is Obsolete* (New York: Viking Press, 1945).

6. S. Gueldner, et al., Learning Rogerian Science: An Experimental Process, in *Rogers' Scientific Art of Nursing Practice,* eds. M. Madrid and E.A.M. Barrett (New York: National League for Nursing, 1994), 355–380.

7. Ibid.

8. R.N. Remen, Spirit: Resource for Healing, in *Noetic Sciences Collection* (Special Collection Publication, 1990), 61.

9. Ibid., 61–65.

10. Ibid., 65.

Chapter 4

Strategies for Innovative Teaching

Barbara Fuszard

Changes in the recent past, and those anticipated for the future, are driving the nursing faculty to choose innovative teaching strategies. The restraining forces that might keep the faculty from seeking new strategies arise from what Clark calls an archaic self-image.[1] These primitive aspects of self prevent teachers and students from seeking creative learning environments. Disorganized and undeveloped professional self-images lead people to seek traditional behaviors, to avoid risk. It is the secure adult educator and adult learner who can adapt to creative, intuitive ways of teaching-learning. The mature educators are free to learn with their students, and adult learners are comfortable with differently structured learning settings and approaches.

With ideas for innovative teaching strategies, the adult educator moves from the archaic self-image. With support in the workplace, the educator may risk applying those strategies in the classroom. The adult learner benefits from the new strategies when they are based upon individual learning needs. Benefits of the adoption of appropriate teaching strategies for the adult learner are circular. The teacher risks, and the student has a chance to grow; in growing, the student and teacher are freed from the archaic self-image of what a teacher and what a student should be.

NEW TEACHING-LEARNING STRATEGIES

Educators who developed, used, and wrote about the following teaching-learning strategies risked, and they report that their students grew through the experiences. The strategies discussed here were selected specifically for nursing education, and the examples come from their use with nurses and nursing students. Wolf and Duffy, as discussed in the chapter on gaming, see nursing education as having important differences from education for other fields, which is why this book provides strategies specifically for nursing.[2] The strategies have been used for teaching-learning within nursing, are based upon adult learning principles (especially those of experiential learning), and meet the special learning needs of nurses and nursing students.

King and Gerwig have identified a number of roles for the teacher in humanistic nursing education. The teacher is facilitator, model, observer, participant, and resource.[3] In every teaching-learning strategy offered in the following pages, the role of teacher fits into one or all of those roles.

Feedback Lecture

The *feedback lecture* answers the common query, "But how do you get facts to large groups of students without using the lecture method?" The feedback lecture, again almost unknown in nursing, is the answer *par excellence* for instructing large groups of students. A more complete example is offered to demonstrate the amount of information that can be communicated, reinforced, and tested through a motivating teaching-learning approach that, again, treats the learner as a responsible adult.

Performance-Based Instruction

Performance-based instruction (PBI) is known to the experienced teacher as programmed instruction. It is still alive and well in nursing, and even with the advent of computer-assisted instruction (CAI), has a specially defined role. The PBI booklet has the advantage that it can go everywhere—to the study, the classroom, the clinical setting, wherever it is needed. It also provides a hard-copy record of growth and achievement of the student learners as they progress through the booklet, serving as an evaluation tool.

Role-Play

Role-play is probably one of the most familiar teaching-learning strategies discussed here. With its basis in psychology, its use is well understood and practiced in teaching psychiatric and mental health nursing. Yet it is too valuable to nursing to limit its use to one area of the field. Using role-play, students are permitted to practice behaviors without risk; to get feedback on these behaviors; and to gain understanding of their own reactions, feelings, and perceptions. They develop their own professional value systems as they study and become more accepting of the behaviors and value systems of others.

Debate

Debate was probably introduced to students in high school. In schools of nursing its use continues the developmental process of self-esteem, poise, critical thinking, objective critiquing, and respect for others—characteristics we expect of a professional.

Case Method

Although the *case method* has been around since the Civil War, it is included here to offer a fresh look at the use of an old teaching-learning friend. This method is most appropriate to education because it offers the opportunity to apply and test decisions that would not exist in real practice. For example, a student could apply various medical regimens to a single patient's problem. In its up-to-date form, the importance of expert case development is emphasized.

Nominal Group

The *nominal group* technique is used to teach students to be team players and at the same time independent critical thinkers. The results of this exercise are decisions that demonstrate that "several minds are better than one."

In-Basket

In-basket is familiar primarily to faculty teaching management or staff development courses. The exercise can be fun for students who pretend to sit in a decision maker's chair, where they set priorities and make decisions on all the correspondence that comes to that person's desk during the course of a day. This teaching-learning experience can also be made available to undergraduates.

Gaming

Speaking of fun! *Gaming* can be a light, fun approach to serious learning. Cautions are offered about placement in the curriculum and course, planning, and debriefing.

Portable Patient Problem Pack

The *portable patient problem pack* (P_4) teaching-learning exercise is designed for teaching clinical problem solving. This problem-based approach presents students with real-life problems, even before they necessarily have acquired all the principles and concepts needed to resolve the problem. The P_4 has the ability to teach these concepts and principles as the student works through the problem. In the example included, students work together as a group, sharing experience and knowledge, and learning together. This stimulating teaching-learning method is not extensively reported in the nursing literature, although it was developed for use with medical and nursing students. It involves an initial investment of time, and then provides a supply of material that can be used for a variety of different simulated patient problems.

Computer-Assisted Instruction

Another use of the computer is to teach decision making as it relates to patient problems. Although simulations of *patient management* problems can be achieved with other teaching-learning approaches, today's computers permit "high-fidelity" or true-to-life simulations not possible with other teaching tools. With attachments to the computer, it is even possible to view the "patient" on a screen and hear a taped interview. Again, with products on the market, nursing faculty can quickly learn to develop their own materials. In addition there are many commercially packaged programs already on the market, which, though expensive, would offer the students experts and a polished program.

Video

Video cameras have been available to nursing education for many years, but never to the extent that they are now. Inexpensive sound videos have become commonplace, and are simple for even the inexperienced operator—either teacher or student. This excellent device permits the teachers to learn what happens in a clinical situation when they are not with the students. It permits student and teacher feedback, with excellent results from viewing tapes in a debriefing session. It appears that the accessibility and affordability of video cameras have made possible the expansion of video use in nursing education.

Co-Consultant

Co-consultant teaching strategy has not yet appeared in the literature. Hence references for this chapter come from literature on the consultant role, rather than the use of the consultant role as a teaching strategy. The students in a co-consultant activity work with faculty on a real consultant activity, accepting as much of the responsibility as appropriate to their backgrounds. The purpose of learning is to acquire the professional behaviors that are demonstrated in consulting: facilitating, helping, observing objectively, and offering expert knowledge. It is a unique teaching-learning behavior that brings education and service together in a mutually beneficial relationship, and offers a presently overlooked clinical experience.

Guided Design

Guided design is slowly gaining acceptance from the nursing faculty (Virginia Hageman, University of Missouri-Columbia; Sharron Fromme, Wayne State University; Zina Mirsky, University of California-San Francisco; Marjorie Jackson, University of Michigan; Patricia Diehl, West Virginia University; Charlotte Rappsilber, Corpus Christi State University, etc.).[4] A teaching-learning process that can encompass a class period or an entire course, this unique approach teaches course content by having students work through a real-life problem. In so doing, the students have an opportunity to apply new learning immediately, providing reinforcement and retention with high motivation.

Preceptorial Experience

More common in nursing than some of the previously discussed teaching-learning strategies, *preceptorial experience* is discussed as a formal, highly planned, carefully controlled, and tightly evaluated approach to nursing education. Biculturalism and role socialization are given as theoretical bases for preceptorship, which offers a link between the theory and practice of nursing.

Mentorship

A very individualized, one-on-one teaching strategy offered here is *mentorship.* Over time the mentor takes a personal interest in a protégé, helping this neophyte develop knowledge, skills, and behaviors necessary for a position or level similar to that of the mentor. The mentor offers encouragement, networks, and guided opportunities to function in new roles to which the protégé aspires. Perhaps not thought of as a teaching strategy, this technique rarely enters a classroom, but seems to continue through the professional lives of the two persons concerned when the protégé needs new skills, guidance in values and resources, a model, personal development, or support.

Refocusing the Skills Laboratory

A creative approach to use of the *skills laboratory* is presentation of theory-based practice. Beginning students are given an opportunity after studying nursing theories actually to demonstrate their application in nursing practice. A nursing curriculum based upon a specific theoretical framework can utilize the skills laboratory for developing the student toward increasing complexity and diversity within that framework.

Student-Selected Clinical Experience

One of the treasured adult learning principles requires faculty to "let go" of decisions as students grow into readiness to accept responsibility for them. It is likewise a concept of empowerment, whereby we "plant seeds of leadership, colleagueship, self-respect, and professionalism."[5] It also offers students directed critical thinking, problem solving, and application of knowledge to practice. Its use is related to individual student development.

Teaching Patients with Low Literacy Skills

Low literacy applies to adolescents and adults who have deficits in reading abilities, process, and comprehension. The often-hidden literacy deficits are a special challenge to the health care provider whose practice depends so much upon the ability to convey information to patients and their families. The striking examples of written teaching materials customarily produced for patients and the same material written for those with low skills are offered. The ability to communicate with patients with low literacy skills will be a valuable asset to the professional nurse in our ever-mobile society, and mixing of persons from differing cultures.

Nursing Rounds

Walking rounds call for study of a specific patient's problem, utilizing a preparation of theories, intuition, insight, feelings, patient-family perceptions, and input from other health care personnel, as well as the traditional preparation offered by reading applicable literature. The student learns to problem solve with other classmates, the patient, and the patient's family. The teacher leads through Socratic questioning and role-modeling. Students not only learn facts and procedures, but also practice critical thinking, problem solving, and decision making.

A Community-Based Practicum Experience

An exciting approach to changes in the health care arena is demonstrated as faculty identify a community need and plan a *practicum* that will meet that need for the community while offering a learning experience for the student. Health care service organizations are quickly forming alliances with other agencies of care givers in the health care industry, ensuring themselves of resources and markets. Changes in the health care system will also drastically change opportunities for practica, learning and service areas for faculty and students in schools of nursing. Yet nursing schools have not been equally aggressive in forming alliances and formal agreements that would ensure continuing mutual benefits among schools, agencies, and communities. This prototype deserves careful study by faculty of every educational nursing program.

Nursing Process Mapping

Commonly, students are involved in the learning experience of developing nursing care plans. These plans too often identify only one point in time, and may even be developed after the patient is no longer under the care of the student. *Nursing process mapping,* on the other hand, facilitates creativity; students access their own thinking and experiences, find new associations, and generate a new set of ideas. To create a map the student must think, select important points, relate the information, and then illustrate the information graphically, all of which require the student to think critically.

Clinical Teaching—What Makes the Difference?

Do parent-child faculty teach differently from those in critical care nursing? Faculty members in parent-child nursing, critical care nursing, and research in nursing share their differing techniques based upon the clinical settings, the educational content to be taught, the abilities of the health care staff in the setting, the developmental level of the student, and even the comfort level of the instructor. All approaches speak directly to experiential learning and demonstrate the creative ability of the faculty members.

Delphi

The *Delphi* teaching-learning strategy has not been utilized in nursing because it is seen as a research approach. With this educational strategy, students develop oral and written communication skills to a high level, acquire the ability to critique literature, learn group communication skills, enhance their understanding of research methods, and practice statistical analyses. Beginning- and intermediate-level researchers stand to benefit from the Delphi technique. Of special use in nursing service is the Delphi ability for long-range forecasting of needs and markets.

Scenarios

Scenarios have not been accepted in nursing literature as much as in other planning and decision-making fields. Yet with the changes appearing so rapidly in health care, nurses need to be on the forefront with techniques that permit forecasting and working for the most desirable futures. Written scenarios and the grand scenario, which permit quantification of the probability of occurrence of a future happening, offer the planner and decision maker "facts" or possibilities that otherwise would not be available to them. This technique is more appropriate to the student with more advanced thinking sills. A relatively easy technique to use, it has great benefit to offer the upperclass, the staff development, or the graduate faculty member who teaches strategic planning and decision-making skills.

Tree of Impact

Tree of impact is a kind of scenario that teaches the possible consequences of decisions. It also can show relationships between events and their consequences. It describes possible futures, based upon decisions being made in the present, enabling decision makers to select decisions based upon more "information" than would be available without the tree-of-impact information. It is another technique for the more advanced student, offering a teaching-learning technique in strategic planning and decision making, areas in which limited teaching-learning techniques have been available.

Analogies, Metaphors, and Other Fun Strategies

What better way to end a text than saying, "Learning is fun, see?" This "et cetera" chapter's purpose is to stimulate teachers to find their own teaching-learning materials. They are everywhere—in the comics, in the *Reader's Digest,* in homey sayings, in an old letter in a museum.

Lecture is Not a Four-Letter Word

Well, so we have many alternatives to lecture given in this book. And not much has been said about lecture itself. Is there any place for lecture with the adult learner? One author believes so, and she shares her perceptions with us.

What a delightful special ending to this book is this final chapter. It pulls together various teaching strategies and shows how they can complement/ supplement the lecture.

Most of the teaching strategies described in this text are appropriate for use with undergraduate and graduate students, and for staff development with practicing nurses. The co-consultant strategy, as well as the futuristic techniques, appear more appropriate for the practicing R.N. or the graduate student, as they assume a pre-existing body of knowledge and/or experience upon which the student can draw. Examples in the following chapters are, of necessity, abbreviated. Persons wishing the complete examples, or further information about a teaching strategy, are invited to contact the writer of that section of the book.

NOTES

1. C.C. Clark, *Classroom Skills for Nurse Educators* (New York: Springer Publishing Co., Inc., 1978).
2. M.S. Wolf and M.E. Duffy, *Simulations/Games: A Teaching Strategy for Nursing Education* (New York: National League for Nursing, 1978).
3. V.G. King and N.A. Gerwig, *Humanizing Nursing Education* (Wakefield, Mass: Nursing Resources, 1981).
4. C.E. Wales and R.A. Stager, *Guided Design* (Morgantown, WVa: C.E. Wales and R.A. Stager, 1977).
5. J. Carlson-Catalano, Empowering Nurses for Professional Practice, *Nursing Outlook* 40, no. 3, (1992):140.

Part II

When a Lecture Is Not a Lecture

How does one order 31 diverse teaching strategies into a comprehensible, flowing arrangement? The logic of the following order and classification of teaching-learning strategies is based on grouping interchangeable techniques, or ones with similar rationales, technologies, or student groups. Because of this diversity of approach to various units, constant referral to other techniques and rationale for other groupings is offered.

The chapters in Part II comprise the feedback lecture and performance-based instruction. Both can be used with large groups, and both can convey and repeatedly reinforce facts. Both initially involve a great deal of teacher preparation of materials, and yet place a great deal of responsibility upon individual students for their own learning.

Chapter 5

The Feedback Lecture

Marian Lancaster Conway

DEFINITION AND PURPOSES

The *feedback lecture*, which incorporates principles of performance-based instruction and the conventional lecture, has been used since the early 1970s in the education of various disciplines, ranging from engineering to nursing.[1] It is a teaching method that combines the efficiency of lecture with programmed instruction to provide factual information with active student participation in the teaching-learning process.

As Dean Osterman, pioneer of the feedback lecture, indicated, the emphasis of this strategy is to provide feedback both to students and to faculty. Students receive immediate feedback regarding their acquisition of knowledge through participation in the individual and group learning activities. These same learning activities allow the faculty to evaluate the effectiveness of their teaching.

The feedback lecture tries to improve learning through active student participation in the teaching-learning process. Critical thinking is stimulated through individual and group problem-solving activities presented in the student guide. Students have immediate opportunities to apply new knowledge during the in-class group discussion sessions. Information retention is enhanced by reinforcing learning throughout the feedback lecture unit—before, during, and after the class session. Student involvement is engaged by preclass preparation, in-class participation, and subsequent post-testing. Student progress is evaluated by observing student participation during class activities and their performance on the post-test. Student self-evaluation is encouraged through comparison of pretest and post-test answers with those provided by the faculty.

THEORETICAL RATIONALE

The theoretical background of the feedback-lecture method is an eclectic combination of principles from humanistic and stimulus-response learning theories. Humanistic learning theory asserts that people are active beings with an inherent desire to learn and who will learn in an environment that promotes learning.[2] Some underlying assumptions of humanistic learning theory that are reflected in the feedback lecture method include the following:

- The learner is an active participant in the learning process.
- Learning should involve exploration and discovery.
- Learning proceeds best if it is relevant to the learner.
- Learning should promote the development of insight, judgment, and self-concept.[3]

According to stimulus-response learning theory, all learning consists of a change in behavior. Thus, the learning process is teacher-directed and provides frequent reinforcement to reward student progress toward desired behavior.

CONDITIONS

The feedback lecture is an appropriate method for any teaching situation in which the conventional lecture is used and where increased student participation is desired. It is well suited for large classes—even those of 100 or more students—and those in which the acquisition and application of specific facts are emphasized.

The repetition and frequent reinforcement of learning used in the feedback lecture method enhance knowledge retention. Student involvement in problem-solving activities encourages the use of critical thinking and the application of decision-making skills. Thus the feedback lecture would be an effective teaching method for use at any level of nursing education.

TYPES OF LEARNERS

The feedback lecture is suitable for any type of learner. The linear learner appreciates the specific directions for learning activities and the lecture outline.[4] The adult learner responds well to preclass activities and the group discussion questions.[5] All types of learners value the opportunity to apply newly acquired knowledge in the problem-solving activities.

RESOURCES

The feedback lecture is generally used in a classroom, although it may be used in any formal educational activity. The length of the feedback lecture varies according to length of the class session, but it is recommended that each one-hour session be divided into two 20-minute lecture sessions separated by a six- to eight-minute group discussion session. Equipment and resources needed depend on the faculty member's choice of teaching strategies. Students must have access to adequate resources (library materials, audiovisuals, computers, and so on) to meet the learning objectives. Preparation for the feedback lecture is more time consuming for both faculty and students than the conventional lecture and evaluation method.

USING THE METHOD

The feedback lecture consists of the following ten components as outlined by Osterman[6]:

1. *The Procedural Page:* This page provides information about the feedback lecture and tells the student how to prepare for the lecture.
2. *The Introduction Page:* The purpose of this page is to arouse the student's interest in the topic and to provide an overview of the purpose and goals of the feedback lecture.
3. *The Objective Page:* This page contains the learning objectives for the lecture, stated in behavioral terms. Any new terminology may also be listed on this page.
4. *The Pretest Page:* The purpose of the pretest is to help the student recognize the knowledge obtained from the readings prior to the lecture. The pretest also provides clues to the information that will be covered in the class lecture. The pretest may be taken in or out of class, depending on faculty preference.
5. *The Feedback-Lecture-Outline Page:* The outline provides the student with a detailed overview of the information that will be covered during the lecture. This page should outline the information to be covered during the first 20 minutes of the class. Information should be presented in 15- to 20-minute sessions, followed by activity to reinforce learning.

6. *The Discussion-Questions Page:* This activity separates the first and second sessions of the lecture. Students assemble in pairs or small groups to discuss the questions developed for the feedback lecture. The students write down their answers to the questions and hand them in to the faculty. The student responses may be graded if the faculty chooses to incorporate the feedback lecture activities as part of the overall grade. The correct answers may be given to the students at this time or at the following lecture.
7. *Discussion-Questions-Feedback Page:* This page reinforces the concepts that the students should have applied to answer the discussion questions. Because the student has the opportunity to see the faculty's perception, it provides a model of professional reasoning and application. Even though student and faculty perceptions may differ, they could both be correct. Faculty have the opportunity to evaluate their teaching by circulating among the students as they discuss the discussion questions and by reading students' written responses.
8. *The Lecture-Outline Page:* This page contains the lecture outline for the second 20-minute lecture session.
9. *The Post-Test Page:* This page gives the students immediate feedback about their grasp of the concepts, facts, or information learned in the unit. Again, the test may be taken in or out of class, depending upon faculty preference. Points may be assigned for correct responses, if desired.
10. *The Warm-Up–Activities Page:* Activities the student must complete before the next lecture are listed on this page. Learning activities may include audiovisuals to view, speakers to hear, journal or newspaper articles to read, and numerous other possibilities. This page may be placed after the pretest if warm-up activities are required for the first feedback lecture.

Example
Community Nursing through Feedback Lecture
Marian Lancaster Conway

The focus of community-health nursing practice is the community as a whole. Thus it is important that baccalaureate nursing students learn to identify the health needs of the community in order to plan interventions accurately to meet those needs.

The author of this example, a community-health nursing educator, had used the conventional lecture format, along with group discussion, to present content on community assessment in an undergraduate community-health nursing course. This seemed both appropriate and efficient because the size of the classes ranged from 60 to 120 students. The class met biweekly in three-hour sessions, with the unit on community assessment scheduled for two consecutive class sessions. In addition to mastery of the theoretical concepts, students were required to apply this knowledge in the clinical aspect of the course by conducting an assessment of a community and by planning a hypothetical program based on an identified health need. Needless to say, students came to class with pencils in hand, ready to copy every word. This results in an "I'm teaching, you're learning" situation, with minimal student involvement.

The feedback lecture, "The Community As Client," was developed in an attempt to increase student participation in the learning process. The materials by Osterman were used as a guide to prepare the feedback lecture. All the components outlined by Osterman were included in the lecture packet. However, since the quarter was already underway when it was decided to try out this format for the first time, the students received only the first four components (procedural, introduction, objective, and pretest pages) and the warm-up–activities page before class. The remaining components were distributed on the first day of class.

The pretest and warm-up activities were completed by the students before class. Answers to the pretest and the warm-up activities were distributed to students at the beginning of class so they could check their answers against those of the faculty. The lecture outline was used by the students as a guide for note taking during the lecture. Following the first part of the lecture, students were given the discussion questions and divided into small groups to answer the questions. This seemed to be the most enjoyable part of the feedback lecture for the students, as they became active participants, learning from and with each other. Because the feedback-lecture unit consisted of two three-hour class sessions, three different discussion-questions sessions were interspersed with lecture. The group turned in an answer sheet following each discussion session and collected a discussion-questions-feedback handout for each student. At the end of the second class, there was time to complete the post-test. Students later compared their answers to the post-test with the post-test–answers handout. No grades were assigned to students for the pretests or post-tests, warm-up activities, or discussion questions.

The effectiveness of teaching was evaluated by the faculty member as she mingled among the students during the group activities, and as she reviewed the student responses to the warm-up activities and discussion questions. A more concrete evaluation was provided by student performance on the course midterm and final exams.

The overall student response to the first feedback lecture was positive, especially the discussion-questions session and the lecture outline. The majority of students felt that this format required more preclass preparation on their part than would a conventional lecture. Still they expressed greater satisfaction with the feedback lecture. No difference was noted on test performance when compared with a previous class of the content taught by the author using the conventional lecture format.

Minor modifications were made in the feedback lecture, based on student feedback and faculty evaluation. The feedback lecture has been used by the author four times on two different campuses. Students were provided with the entire feedback-lecture guide two weeks before the unit was scheduled. Only the warm-up activities and discussion-questions feedback were omitted from the packet. The original feedback-lecture format was followed, except that, during the first portion of the class (Warm-up Exercise 1), the students discussed pertinent newspaper and magazine articles that related to the focus on community.

Student and faculty response to the feedback lecture was positive. This is consistent with the findings of Osterman and others who have used the feedback-lecture method.[7] The size of the classes on the second campus averaged 20 students, allowing more contact between faculty and students. Students participated more in the smaller classes.

Although no differences have been noted in test scores, the author plans to expand the use of the feedback lecture to other units in the community-health

---

Exhibit 5–1 Procedure for "The Community As Client"

Procedure

Study and lecture for "The Community As Client" are based upon the feedback-lecture concept. The feedback lecture is designed to increase student participation in the teaching-learning process, to stimulate problem-solving ability, and to promote information retention. This packet is your guide for this unit and includes objectives for this unit, the reading and homework assignments, a pretest and post-test, a lecture outline, and discussion questions that will be used during class. To make the most effective use of this study guide, you should do the following:

1. Read the objectives.
2. Complete the pretest.
3. Read the assigned readings.
4. Check your answers on the pretest with those provided on the page after the pretest.
5. Review the reading materials for those questions that you missed.
6. Complete the warm-up activities before class.
7. Bring this study guide to class and use the lecture outline for note taking.
8. Participate in the discussion sessions in class.
9. Use information provided during class to evaluate your written answers to the discussion questions.
10. Complete the post-test and check your answers.

nursing course in the coming academic year, based on faculty and student satisfaction with the format. Students will be allowed to earn extra credit for some of the assignments. The feedback lecture is highly recommended when more active student involvement in the learning process is desired. Excerpts of handout materials used for the feedback lecture appear as Exhibits 5–1 through 5–8. They demonstrate characteristics of performance-based instruction and the traditional lecture, a combination able to meet the needs of adult learners.

Exhibit 5–2 Introduction to "The Community As Client"

Introduction

Numerous factors in a society influence the people's health. In our country, life styles, technology, and environmental factors—leading causes of illness and death—have affected the focus of health care delivery. While the demand to provide sophisticated technology for diagnosis and treatment of illness continues, the emerging emphasis in health care is on the promotion of health through disease prevention and health maintenance. Continuing assessment of societal changes and their effect on community health is required to meet the challenge of health promotion and disease prevention. How else can we plan for health programs and services that accurately meet the needs of people?

In "The Community As Client," we will be exploring the purposes and methods of community assessment and factors that affect community health. The goal is to provide you with the conceptual skills necessary to apply the nursing process in conducting a community assessment.

Exhibit 5–3 Objectives and Terminology

Objectives

Upon completion of this unit, the learner will be able to

1. define selected basic concepts of community-health nursing practice
2. discuss the purposes of a community assessment
3. discuss at least four methods used in conducting an assessment of a community
4. utilize the community assessment as a tool to identify research needs in community health nursing practice

Terminology

Aggregate	Secondary analysis
Biostatistics	Vital statistics
Community assessment	Windshield survey
Community client	Process evaluation
Informant interviewing	Product evaluation
Participant observation	

Exhibit 5–4 Pretest

Pretest

1. List at least three reasons for conducting a community assessment.
2. List the six basic classifications of data necessary for an accurate community assessment.
3. Match the most appropriate method(s) of data collection with the type of data to be collected. (Data collection methods may be used more than once.)

Type of Data	*Data Collection Method*
____ Environmental hazards	A. Participant observation
____ Population characteristics	B. Informant interviewing
____ Health manpower	C. Review of existing reports
____ Crime patterns	D. Vital statistics
____ Religious influences	E. Windshield survey
____ Protective services	F. Census data
____ Causes of death	
____ Attitudes	

Exhibit 5–5 Activities

Warm-Up Activities
(Alias, Homework)

The following activities are to be completed before the class lecture "The Community As Client."

Read:

- Clark, M.J. (1984). *Community Nursing*. Ch. 10, "The Community as Client," pp. 256–272.
- Ruybal, S.E., E. Bauwens, & M.J. Fasla. (1975). "Community Assessment: An Epidemiological Approach." *Nursing Outlook* 23, June; pp. 365–368.
- Shamanski, S.L. & E. Feszhecker. (1981). A Community is _____, *Nursing Outlook* 29, pp. 182–185.
- Stanhope, M. & J. Lancaster. (1984). *Community Health Nursing*. Ch. 17, "Community as Client," pp. 379–404.

Other Warm-Ups

1. During the week before the lecture, identify articles in newspapers or magazines that illustrate the concepts of community, community client, community health, and partnership for health. Be prepared to share at least one article in class.

Activities

Directions for 2–4.

Complete activities two, three, and four on a sheet of paper titled warm-up activities. The answers may be handwritten or typed—please write legibly! Include your name at the top of the paper. Turn in your answers at the beginning of class and pick up your warm-up activities feedback.

2. Based on your readings, what factor distinguished community-health nursing from other nursing specialties? Give an example . . .

Exhibit 5–6 Lecture Outline—"The Community As Client"

Lecture Outline—Part I

I. The Concept of Community As Client
   A. Community-Health Nursing
      1. Distinguishing features
      2. Aggregate focus
      3. Barriers to aggregate-focused practice
   B. Community
      1. Defined
      2. Characteristics of community
      3. Community functions
      4. Hierarchy of needs
II. Community Assessment
   A. Individual assessment vs. community assessment
   B. Definition of community assessment
   C. Purpose of community assessment
   D. Methods used in community assessment

Discussion Session I: At this point students work in groups of three, completing activities in the first discussion session.

Lecture Outline—Part II

II. Community Assessment (con't)
   E. Data Collection
   F. Sources of data
      1. Local
      2. State
      3. National
   G. Assessment Tools and Guides
   H. Assessment Issues
III. Planning for Community Health
   A. Data Analysis
      1. Examine relationships
      2. Identify and prioritize health problems
      3. Formulate a nursing diagnosis

Discussion Session II: At this point, the students will complete the activities in the second discussion session, again working in groups of three.

   B. Establish Goals and Objectives
      1. Goals
      2. Objectives

Exhibit 5–7 Questions for Discussion

Discussion Questions

The following questions are to be answered in class, in groups of three students.

DISCUSSION SESSION I

Discuss question 1 among yourselves and write your answers on a piece of paper labeled "Discussion Session I." Put all of your names on the answer sheet. When completed (or after eight minutes), turn in your responses and collect one discussion-question-feedback page for each of you. The lecture will begin again after the discussion period.

1. In a routine day, the community-health nurse performs assessments in a child-health clinic, makes a home visit to a pregnant teen who has missed her last two clinic appointments, and plans a nutrition class on infant feeding for new mothers. Does this represent community-aggregate-focused nursing practice? Why or why not?

DISCUSSION SESSION II

Using the Carolton case study (handed out to the class last week), identify the health needs and health problems of that community. List the problems in priority order. Explain why you gave the problem you did top priority and develop a nursing diagnosis for that problem. After five minutes of discussion, be prepared to discuss your problem list, rationale, and nursing diagnosis with the class.

DISCUSSION SESSION III

Using the case study of Carolton, develop a nursing-care plan for one identified problem (to be assigned). Include your nursing diagnosis, an overall goal, and nursing interventions for each objective. After eight to ten minutes, be prepared to discuss your plan with the class.

Exhibit 5–8 Post-Test for "The Community As Client"

Post-Test

1. Which of the following <u>BEST</u> illustrates the definition of community as given by Clark (1984)?
   1. Richmond County
   2. Members of the Georgia Nurses' Association
   3. People who have diabetes
   4. An urban neighborhood of Cambodian immigrants
      A. All of the above
      B. 1 only
      C. 2 and 4
      D. 1, 2, and 4
2. List at least four examples of aggregates in the Carolton case study.
3. Mortality rates for area fifteen in the Carolton case study include which of the following?
   1. Heart disease
   2. Hepatitis
   3. Live births
   4. Homicide
   5. Gonorrhea

   A. All of the above
   B. 1, 2, 4, and 5
   C. 3 only
   D. 1 and 4
   E. 2 and 5

NOTES

1. D.N. Osterman, *Manual for Creating a Feedback Lecture* (Unpublished manuscript, Oregon State University, Corvallis, Oreg, 1981), 3.

2. M.L. Bigge, *Learning Theories for Teachers*, 3rd ed. (New York: Harper & Row, 1976).

3. E.O. Bevis, *Curriculum Building in Nursing*, 3rd ed. (St. Louis: CV Mosby Co., 1982).

4. I.B. Myers, *Introduction to Type* (Swarthmore, Pa: I.B. Myers, 1970).

5. M. Knowles, *The Adult Learner: A Neglected Species*, 2nd ed. (Houston: Gulf Publishing Co., 1976).

6. D.N. Osterman, *Feedback Lecture: The Process and Components* (Corvallis, Oreg, Instructional Development Office, Oregon State University, 1980), 2–11.

7. D.N. Osterman, The Feedback Lecture: Matching Teaching and Learning Styles, *Journal of the American Dietetic Association* 84, no. 10 (October 1984):1221–1222.

SUGGESTED READING

Beard, R., and J. Martley, 1985. The lecture method. In *Teaching and learning in higher education*, 158–173. Scranton, Pa: Harper & Row.

Bowman, J. 1986. Facilitating student involvement in large classroom settings. *Journal of Nursing Education* 25:226–229.

Ehupe, D.S. February 1979. Improving learning efficiency by the lecture method. *Engineering Education* 21:406–408.

Finkava, B.F. September–October 1985. The feedback lecture method: Stimulating active learning. *Nursing Outlook* 33:257, 258.

Osterman, D.N. 1978. Selection and evaluation of alternative teaching methods in higher education. In *Instructional development: The state of the art*, ed. R.N. Bass and D.B. Lumsden. Columbus, Ohio: Collegiate Publishing.

Osterman, D.N. September–October 1982. Classroom lecture management: Increasing individual involvement and learning in the lecture style. *Journal of College and Science Teaching* 18: 77–78.

Osterman, D., et al. January 1985. The feedback lecture. *Idea paper no. 13*. Manhattan, Kans: Kansas State University, Division of Continuing Education.

Chapter 6

Performance-Based Instruction

Saundra L. Turner

DEFINITION AND PURPOSES

Performance-based instruction (PBI) or, the more common term, *programmed instruction* has evolved into many packages since its inception in the late 1950s. The product is, as the current term implies, based on the student's performance. That is, effectiveness increases as feedback is generated by the student's participation in the instruction.[1]

A major benefit of PBI is to validate instruction. It ensures that the student has acquired at least a minimum amount of learning by the completion of the text. This is accomplished through a series of required tests and responses.[2] It also allows for individuality in learning. The student is self-paced and receives immediate feedback in an instructor-free environment, which allows the instructor more time for specific problems. A PBI can be used as a self-contained package or topic of instruction, a supplement to the instruction, a component of the instruction, or as a job aid to the instruction. PBI can be automated as a computer-based instruction or as a programmed text. The focus here is on textual materials.

THEORETICAL RATIONALE

PBI is a cost-effective way of dealing with actual or presumed deficiencies in individual skill or knowledge. The amount of time and talent necessary for the production of the package is not negated by the life expectancy of the material. The instruction should be fairly stable material that can be replicated and reused for a period of time.

The theory base does not differ from that of computer-assisted instruction (CAI), in Chapter 14. Similarities between PBI and CAI are not discussed, only differences.

CONDITIONS

The advantages of PBI over CAI are in cost savings (no computer is needed), convenience (it can be used anywhere, at any time, and with any number of students, without their waiting for a terminal), and portability (it can be taken into the clinical area, the home, or the classroom, wherever it is needed). Students can write directly onto their copies, and there is hard copy for evaluation of their learning. According to research, PBI brings about a higher level of recall—highest when used in conjunction with a good lecture—than the lecture method alone.[3]

TYPES OF LEARNERS

The method is of benefit when learners are at different levels because they can pace the instruction themselves. The feedback makes an expert available to each student.[4]

RESOURCES

This teaching-learning approach relieves the teacher of repetitive-content teaching. The content can be prepared once and updated as needed. The teacher need not remain involved in the implementation, merely the evaluation.

USING THE METHOD

The example that follows was developed as a supplemental text for first-year nursing students. The topic is the practice of universal precautions as an infection control measure. It assesses entry-level knowledge in the pretest with the presumption that all students have a consumer-level knowledge base. The text is designed in an information-mapping format. Other examples of PBI include the familiar text-question-response format that guides the student along a particular track. The intent of this program is to move the student from familiar information to new knowledge and then to the application of the knowledge at a clinical level. The post-test is short and specific, requiring the student to go back to review information, thereby enforcing the concept of using the material as a job aid. The whole program is light and readable to increase its interactivity.

Example
Universal Precautions, Infection Control, and Prevention of Bloodborne Diseases for Health Care Providers
Saundra L. Turner and Gayle Bentley

UNIVERSAL PRECAUTIONS

The practice of universal precautions as an infection control measure has become a standard of practice in all health care settings. Health care providers must be aware of occupational risks for exposure to infections and must use universal precautions practices for care.

Objectives

By the completion of this program the learner will be able to

1. define the term *universal precautions*
2. identify occupational risks inherent in the practice of health care
3. describe methods of reducing risk exposure in the workplace
4. apply universal precautions principles to a workplace scenario

* * * *

UNIVERSAL PRECAUTIONS: INFECTION CONTROL AND PREVENTION OF BLOODBORNE DISEASES FOR HEALTH CARE PROVIDERS

Introduction

The practice of health care carries with it the inherent risk of infection. Health care providers must be constantly aware of the occupational risks involved in health care delivery. Threats to personal well-being are real; therefore, entry into the health care environment must be preceded by intense education on universal precautions measures, as well as frequent updates, to ensure that those at greatest risk are encouraged to practice as safely as possible.

This pretest will give us an entry point into the information to be covered on universal precautions.

Pretest

1. Contamination means exposure of an individual's mucous membranes to
   a. any pathogen
   b. human body fluids
   c. blood-containing or infectious material
   d. mucous secretions, urine, or vomitus
2. The single most effective means of preventing spread of disease involves
   a. wearing protective equipment
   b. avoiding patient contact
   c. using universal precautions only when patients are obviously infectious
   d. careful and frequent handwashing
3. Barrier methods of protection include all of the following EXCEPT
   a. scrub uniforms
   b. latex gloves
   c. masks
   d. eyewear
4. In order to avoid exposure to infected drainage while changing a dressing, the **best** precaution the health care provider should take is to
   a. change the dressing quickly to avoid prolonged contact with the drainage
   b. double-glove, disposing of the first pair after removing the contaminated drainage
   c. irrigate the wound carefully to remove all drainage
   d. wear gloves, gown, and mask when in contact with infected material

Universal Precautions: The Facts

- Guidelines for safe practices in the workplace have been established by the Occupational Safety and Health Administration (OSHA).
- While it is recognized that the exposure to workplace hazards such as bloodborne diseases is a definite risk associated with the health care occupations, it is believed that by making health care providers aware of these hazards and how to protect themselves the risk of transmission of disease can be reduced.

- Transmission involves the mechanisms involved in spreading an infectious agent from a source to a person. Direct contact is the source of transmission for bloodborne diseases such as human immunodeficiency virus infection and hepatitis.
- Prevention of transmission involves the strict use of universal precautions on all patients regardless of their diagnosis or appearance. The goal is to prevent the spread of disease among patients, care givers, and other persons.
- The best means of prevention involves frequent and meticulous washing of hands and other skin surfaces immediately before and after patient contact. It also involves wearing personal protective equipment appropriate to the expected level of exposure to contamination.

Now, for a review of the information covered so far:

- ☐ The governmental agency that has established guidelines giving workers the right to have a safe environment is ______. *(OSHA)*
- ☐ An awareness of the safety standards should reduce the worker's ______ of transmission. *(risk)*
- ☐ Transmission of a bloodborne organism is through ______ contact of the infected or blood-containing material to mucous membranes. *(direct)*

Personal Protective Equipment (PPE)

Health care workers can protect themselves from exposure to bloodborne pathogens through the following precautions:

- Wash hands consistently.
- Wear gloves for direct contact with blood, body fluids, mucous membranes, or nonintact skin for invasive procedures. Wear two sets of gloves when changing dressings, discarding the first set with the soiled dressing and using the second to apply the new dressing. Use gloves when handling any surface that may have been in contact with blood or body fluids. Discard used gloves in a proper receptacle. Wash hands before and after using gloves.
- Wear a mask whenever a procedure is likely to splatter to the membranes of the mouth or nose. Use eyewear or face shields to prevent exposure of the eyes.
- Use gowns to prevent contamination of clothing, because cotton material does not adequately protect the individual from exposure.

Review

- ☐ Personal protective equipment, when used properly, involves barrier protection from exposure to ______. *(bloodborne pathogens)*
- ☐ Consistent use of______ is the single most effective preventive measure. *(handwashing)*
- ☐ Use of equipment such as gloves, masks, and ______ is guided by the anticipated exposure in the procedure to be performed. *(gowns)*

Preventive Measures

The health care provider must not only carefully select the barrier method of protection properly but must also use safe practices in care delivery to prevent transmission of pathogens.

- The most common accidental exposure to bloodborne disease is through a needle-stick injury. Prevention involves single-handed recapping of needles or use of a needleless system.
- Prompt disposal of used needles and sharps in a puncture-resistant container after use is imperative to prevent injury to self and others.
- Primary prevention of exposure to hepatitis B involves having the hepatitis vaccine series of three shots prior to working in a high-risk environment.
- Other preventive measures involve immediately reporting all exposures for prompt testing and treatment and recognizing safe practices in one's personal life outside the workplace.

Summary

We have now covered the essentials of universal precautions. Health care is a high-risk environment, but proper use of protective measures can significantly reduce the risk the health care provider takes. The key is to be aware that there can always be the potential of having exposure to a pathogen; therefore, careful consideration must be given as to how the worker can reduce the chance of transmitting that pathogen from one person to another. And how does one avoid contaminating oneself? Let us move now to a short post-test to see how much has been covered in this short exercise.

Post-Test

1. OSHA has established standards of practice for infection control and prevention of transmission of bloodborne disease because

   a. health care workers are at risk of exposure to infection
   b. bloodborne infections are spread mostly in the workplace
   c. safe practices can eliminate all risk to exposure
   d. OSHA has to monitor unsafe practices
2. Concern for exposure centers around
   a. patients who look infected
   b. any situation where the potential is there for exposure to blood-containing fluids
   c. any time a needle is used
   d. washing hands only after removing gloves
3. Personal protection involves
   a. hepatitis vaccination series prior to working in health care
   b. effective and appropriate use of handwashing and other personal protective equipment
   c. use of barrier methods in sexual activity and other personal exposures
   d. all of the above

NOTES

1. D.H. Bullock, *Programmed Instruction* (Englewood Cliffs, NJ: Educational Technology Publications, 1978).
2. P. Dolphin and B.J. Holtzclaw, *Continuing Education in Nursing: Strategies for Lifelong Learning* (Reston, Va: Reston Publishing Co., 1983).
3. B.J. Brown and P.L. Chinn, *Nursing Education: Practical Methods and Models* (Gaithersburg, Md: Aspen Publishers, Inc., 1982), 3–18.
4. E.K. Austin, *Guidelines for the Development of Continuing Education Offerings for Nurses* (New York: Appleton-Century-Crofts, 1981).

SUGGESTED READING

Bullock, D.H. 1978. *Programmed instruction*. Englewood Cliffs, NJ: Educational Technology Publications.

Clark, C.C. 1978. *Classroom skills for nurse educators.* New York: Springer Publishing Co.

Grimes, D. 1991. *Infectious Disease*. St. Louis: Mosby-Year Book, Inc.

Holland, S., et al. 1976. *The analysis of behavior in planning instruction*. Reading, Mass: Addison-Wesley Publishing, Inc.

Johnson, R. 1973. *Assuring learning with self-instructional packages.* Reading, Mass: Addison-Wesley Publishing, Inc.

Miller, P.J. 1989. Developing self-learning packages. *Journal of Nursing Staff Development* 5: 73–77.

Rice, R. 1993. Principles of universal precautions/body substance isolation. *Home HealthCare Nurse* 11, no. 4:55–59.

Rosenburg, M. 1985. Pick the right self-paced package. *Training and Development Journal* 39: 77–78.

Segall, A.J., et al. 1975. *Systematic course design for the health fields*. New York: John Wiley & Sons, Inc.

Swendsen, L. 1981. Self-instruction: Benefits and problems. *Nurse Educator* 11:6–9.

Tillman, M, et al. 1976. *Learning to teach*. Lexington, Mass: D.C. Heath and Co.

Part III

Simulations

The chapters in Part III contain a mixed bag of teaching-learning strategies, held together by a common "simulation" experience. The great impetus for the nursing faculty to seek simulations is in relation to clinical experiences for students in new roles. Two benefits of simulation over actual clinical experiences are moving faculty to select simulation more frequently than in the past.

Both motivations for selecting simulated experiences over clinical experiences involve economy. The first motivation comes from the health care agencies that have typically provided clinical experiences for students. The many health care students seeking placements in areas for which they have limited experience, and the expense of student instruction in the clinical area, have led health care agencies to be less welcoming to nursing faculty and students.

The second motivation is pressure on the faculty. The nursing faculty is aware of the rapidity with which new knowledge is being produced, and feel the pressure to offer more and more to nursing students in preparation for changing futures. In the past it was felt that during the many clinical nursing hours, students would be exposed to most of the important experiences that faculty thought they needed. Those experiences would be mostly the same for each student. But clinical hours have been shortened, and students may be exposed to very limited and varied experiences. A simulated experience efficiently exposes every student to the same experience, and the faculty member can be present to help reinforce, correct, and evaluate the learning experiences of the students.

The different types of simulations that follow offer a variety of approaches for various purposes. Many are interchangeable for specific class content, and faculty will base decisions on choices upon other characteristics, such as class size, time, and level of student knowledge.

Chapter 7

Role-Play

Arlene Lowenstein

DEFINITION AND PURPOSES

Role-play is a dramatic technique that encourages participants to improvise behaviors that illustrate expected actions of persons involved in defined situations. A scenario is outlined and character roles are assigned. The drama is usually unscripted, relying on spontaneous interplay between characters to provide material about reactions and behaviors for students to analyze after the presentation. Those class members not assigned character roles participate as observers and contribute to the analysis.

Part of the category of simulation, role-play allows participants to explore why people behave as they do. Participants can test behaviors and decisions in an environment that allows experimentation without risk. The scenario and behaviors of the actors are analyzed and discussed to provide opportunity to clarify feelings, increase observational skills, provide rationale for potential behaviors, and anticipate reactions to decisions. New behaviors can be suggested and tried in response to the analysis.

Role-play is used to enable students to practice interacting with others in certain roles, and to afford them an opportunity to experience other people's reactions to actions they have taken. The scenario provides a background for the problem and outlines the constraints that may apply. Defining the important characteristics of the major players establishes role expectations and provides a framework for behaviors and actions to be elicited. The postplay discussion provides opportunity for analysis and new strategy formation.

Although it is a dramatic technique, the focus is on the actions of the characters, and not on acting ability. An actor plays to the audience; the role-player plays to the characters in the scenario. The audience also has a role, that of observing the interplay between characters and analyzing the dynamics occurring. The instructor's role is that of facilitator rather than director. The impetus for the analysis and discussion belongs with the learners. The instructor's role is more passive, clarifying and gently guiding.

Role-play is a particularly effective means for developing decision-making and problem-solving skills.[1] Through role-play the learner can identify the systematic steps in the process of making judgments and decisions. The problem-solving process—identification of the problem, data collection and evaluation of possible outcomes, exploration of alternatives, and arrival at a decision to be implemented—can be analyzed in the context of the role-play situation. The scenario can include reactions to the implementation of the decision as well as the evaluation and reformulation process.

Role-play provides immediate feedback to learners regarding their success in using interpersonal skills as well as decision-making and problem-solving skills. At the same time, role-play offers learners an opportunity to become actively involved in the learning experience, but in a nonthreatening environment.

THEORETICAL RATIONALE

Role-play developed in response to the need to effect attitudinal changes in psychotherapy and counseling.[2] Psychodrama, a forerunner of role-play, was developed by Moreno as a psychotherapy technique. Moreno brought psychodrama to the United States in 1925 and continued to develop it during the 1940s and 1950s.[3] In psychodrama, players may be required to recite specific lines or answer specific questions and may represent themselves; in role-play, players are encouraged to express their thoughts and feelings spontaneously, as if they were the persons whose roles they are playing.[4]

Psychodrama provided a foundation for further development of role-play as an educational technique. Corsini and other psychotherapists and group dynamicists began using role-play to assist patients to clarify people's behavior toward each other.[5] Further development led to the use of role-play in sensitivity training, a technique that became popular in the 1970s. Human-relations and sensitivity-training events share a common educational strategy. The learners in the group are encouraged to become involved in examining their thought patterns, perceptions, feelings, and inadequacies. The training events are also designed to encourage each learner with the support of fellow learners to invent and experiment with different patterns of functioning.[6] Role-play can be used to meet those educational objectives and is frequently used in human-relations and sensitivity training.

CONDITIONS

Role-playing is a versatile technique that can be used in a wide variety of situations. One set of learning objectives might be role-play dealing with the practice of skills and techniques, while another very different group of objectives would use role-play to deal with changes in understanding, feelings, and attitudes. Van Ments points out that role-play is conducted differently for these two sets of learning objectives.[7] The role-play used for the practice of skills may be planned with the emphasis on outcome and overcoming problems. The second type of objectives may be best met with the emphasis on the problems and relationships. This method explores why certain behaviors are exhibited and requires expertise from the instructor in dealing with emotions and human behavior. It is the teacher's responsibility to help the students avoid the negative effects that could come from the exploration of their feelings and behaviors.

Planning and Modifying

Teachers who are new to the technique need to plan before class, but they should monitor the needs of the group as the experience progresses and be able to modify those plans if necessary. The situation developed should be familiar enough so that learners can understand the roles and their potential responses, but it should not have too direct a relationship to students' own personal problems.[8] It may also be effective to use two or more presentations of the same situation with different students in the roles if the objective is to point out different responses or solutions to a given problem. When that method is used, the instructor may choose to keep those students involved in the second presentation away from viewing the first presentation, to avoid biasing their reactions.

Role-play strategy qualifies as an adult learning approach because it presents a real-life situation and tries to stimulate the involvement of the student. It has special value because it uses peer evaluation and involves active participation.

TYPES OF LEARNERS

Role-play is appropriate for undergraduate and graduate students. It is especially effective in staff development programs, because of its association with reality. It is used effectively for reaching of affective outcomes. Role-play can be simple or complex, depending on the learning objectives. Regardless of the simplicity of the play itself, it is important to allow adequate time for planning, preparing the students for the experience, and postplay discussion and analysis. The actual role-play may be as brief as five minutes, although ten to twenty minutes is more common. Van Ments suggests that the technique be broken into three sections: briefing, running, and debriefing. Equal amounts of time may be spent for each session for simple objectives, or a ratio of 1:2:3, with most time spent on the debriefing or analysis, for more complex learning objectives.[9]

RESOURCES

Role-play can be used in most settings, although tiered lecture rooms may inhibit the ability of the players to relate to each other and to the observing students. In that setting the theatricality of the technique is likely to be emphasized over the needed behavioral focus.[10]

Special equipment or props may be simple or not used at all, again depending on the objectives. An instructor may choose to use videotaping or audiotaping. This can be especially helpful to review portions of the action during the debriefing and analysis section. Reviewing tapes may also be helpful for participating students who, because of their roles, were not in the room to hear and see some of the interaction that occurred.

Outside resources are not usually needed for most role-play situations, although additional instructors, trained observers, or specific experts may be used appropriately to meet certain objectives. The technique is best for small groups of students so that those not involved in the character parts can be actively involved in observing and discussing the action in the debriefing or analyzing portion. Van Ments finds role-play increasingly unsatisfactory as a technique in groups with more than 20 to 25 students, although there may be exceptions, depending on objectives and strategies for involving the audience.[11]

USING THE METHOD

Planning is crucial to effective use of role-play as a learning technique. It may be helpful to pilot the exercise before running it in the class situation to allow the instructor to anticipate potential problems and evaluate whether the learning objectives can be met. Discussing critical elements of the role-play with colleagues can be useful if full-scale piloting is not feasible. A small amount of time spent going through the plans with someone else may prevent a critical element from going wrong and disrupting the exercise.[12]

Selecting a scenario and deciding on character roles is an important part of planning. McKeachie cautions that situations involving morals or subjects of high emotional significance, such as sexual taboos, are likely to be traumatic to some students.[13] He has found that the most interesting situations, and those revealing the greatest differences in responses, are those involving some choice or conflict of motives. Student input into planning can also be effective.

To implement the role-play, the scenario and characters need to be described briefly, but with enough information to elicit responses that will meet the learning objectives. It is often helpful to allow students in the character roles to have a few minutes to warm up and relate to the roles they will be playing. Spontaneity should be encouraged, so it is preferable to avoid a script, other than bare outlines of the action. It is extremely important that the observing students be briefed on their role. Enough time must be allotted for discussion and analysis of the action. This debriefing also allows for evaluation of the success in meeting the learning objectives.

In addition to the development of learning objectives and planning, the instructor is responsible for setting the stage for the role-play, monitoring the action, and leading the analysis. Students need a clear understanding of the objectives, the scenario, the characters they are to play, the importance of the role of the observers, and the analysis as a vital part of the process. On occasion the instructor may take a character role, but usually character roles are given to students.

When planning a role-play session the instructor needs to be concerned with the amount of time students may be excluded from the room while waiting their turn to participate. This is especially important when two or more presentations of the same situation are to be used, or the role-play has characters that should not be exposed to the dialogue that occurs before they appear in their roles. It is important to avoid a situation in which excluded students roam the corridors with nothing to do for long periods of time.

In some instances it may be appropriate to have students switch roles during the role-play. This technique can be useful if the group is large and there is a need to involve more students in the action. This also may provide students an opportunity to see and feel different reactions to similar situations. Another example of when to use that technique might be when the objective is to learn how to conduct a group. Students may benefit by playing group member and switching to leader or vice versa during the exercise.

The instructor needs to encourage students to respond to interactions in the role-play in a spontaneous, natural manner, avoiding melodrama and inappropriate laughter or silliness. Effective use of role-play focuses on student participation and interaction. The instructor, as facilitator, channels the discussion to meet the learning objectives, but avoids monopolizing the play or discussion. The instructor must also be able to monitor and control the depth of emotional responses to the situation or interplay as needed, terminating the play when the objective has been met or the emotional climate calls for intervention.

Students need to understand the importance of playing the character roles in ways in which they believe those characters would act in a real-life situation. Students who act as observers must be strongly encouraged to present their observations and contribute to the discussion and analysis. Students can also take part in the development of role-play scenarios, identifying the learning objectives, issues, and problems they feel need to be explored and the scenarios that may provide that exploration.

POTENTIAL PROBLEMS

Van Ments refers to the "hidden agenda"[14] and warns that stereotyping may occur as roles are presented, often reflecting the expectations and values of the students or the teacher. This may lead to unanticipated learning that can reinforce prejudices and preconceptions. Instructors need to be aware of this possibility and avoid writing in stereotypes. They should describe only functions, powers, and constraints of the role described. It is important to rotate roles to avoid overidentification of one student with a specific role. In the debriefing session, the students are invited to question and challenge assumptions.

Students may not always make a distinction between an actor and a role.[15] Criticism of the student playing the role must be avoided, while allowing for critique of the behavior of the role character. The instructor must be aware of the emotional tones involved in the role-play and channel the emotions into activities that will lead to successful attainment of the learning objectives.

Planning and learning objectives should determine the course of the role-play. Students may take the role-play in an unexpected direction, possibly because they have a need to explore another issue or problem. If it is not appropriate to revise the learning objectives to accommodate student needs, the play can be terminated. In that case, the postplay discussion can be used to assist students in recognizing why the technique was not effective. Students should advise how to improve the role-play or develop a different teaching strategy. Repeating a scenario with the same or different characters can sometimes afford a more in-depth examination and add to the experience.

The instructor and students need to be aware that this is not a professional drama. Although at times it may be appropriate to change actors if the role-play does not seem to be going well, it is important not to blame the students. In most cases it will be the teaching strategy that needs changing, rather than the actors. Role-play can be an effective and creative strategy to provide active student participation to meet specific learning objectives.

Example
Role-Playing the Matrix Model
Nancy Fishback, Kathleen Hickman, and Jerome J. Marcotte

The Design of the Matrix Model

The matrix model of organizations was identified by graduate nursing students in an organizational theories class, and three students volunteered to lead the class on the topic. A role-play method was selected for the learning exercise because it allowed all the students to participate and permitted them to experience aspects of management and employment in a matrix.

The matrix design is both an organizational structure and a management philosophy. It is a project organization superimposed on a hierarchical bureaucratic organization.[16] In this hybrid design, a substantial number of people have two bosses, either in a temporary (project) or permanent (functional) basis. Employees, responsible to their functional boss in the hierarchical organization, are assigned to project managers to whom they are responsible until the project is completed (see Figures 7–1 to 7–3). The dual chain of authority enhances the ability of the organization to respond simultaneously to two or more sectors, such as market and technology.

The matrix model serves to combine the philosophy of project management with the functional philosophy of the hierarchical organization. The project viewpoint places emphasis on the horizontal flow of work. There is an emphasis on team effort, participation, decentralized decision making, and open communication.[17] The functional philosophy places emphasis on the vertical communication of superiors to subordinates. Decision making is left to designated experts high in the hierarchical structure.

At the completion of classes in matrix design, the students will be able to

1. identify the basic concepts of a matrix structure
2. organize a matrix organization
3. assess the problems inherent in matrix organizations
4. contrast a matrix with a bureaucratic organizational structure

The Organization of the Class

The class was scheduled to last three hours. The seminar leaders used an overhead projector to present the didactic portion of the material. For about one hour they led discussion on the definition, purpose, and theoretical rationale behind the matrix structure. Then the seminar leaders distributed assignments

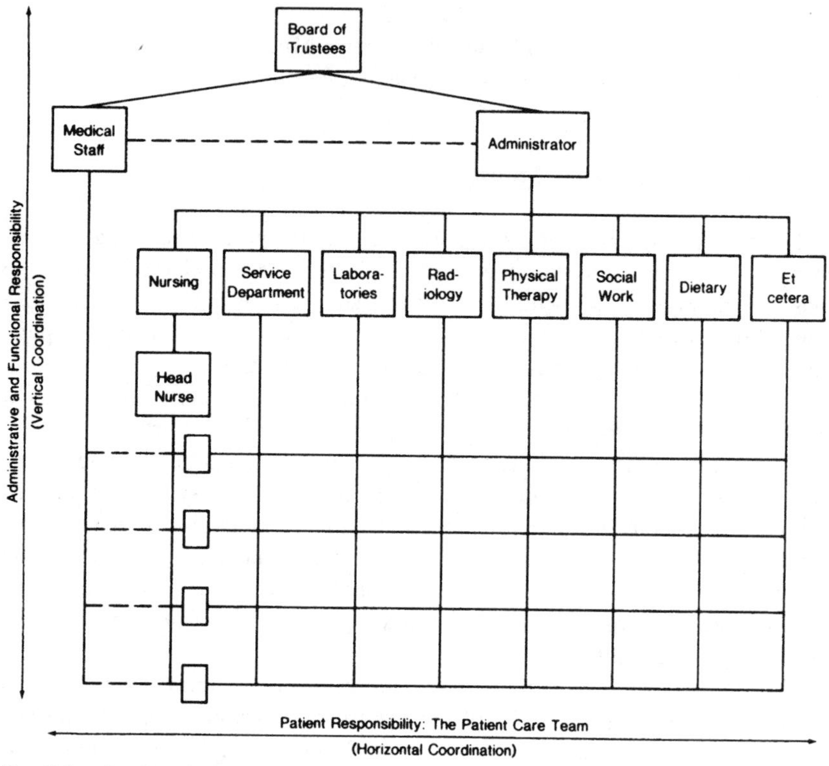

Figure 7–1 Nursing Matrix Model. *Source:* Reprinted from *Hospital and Health Services Administration*, Vol. 22, No. 1, p. 33, with permission of American College of Healthcare Executives, © Winter, 1976.

---

and job descriptions to their classmates. For ten to fifteen minutes, the three functional teams met independently to discuss assignment to the project teams.

Because none of the students had been exposed to the complex structure of matrix in the job situation, a simple example was chosen for the role-play. The leaders established the Molly Meals Deli Service, with the instructor designated as general manager of the firm, and three classmates—Elaine, David, and Lionel—named functional managers (see Figure 7–4). They supervised employees of the salad, dessert, and meat departments, respectively.

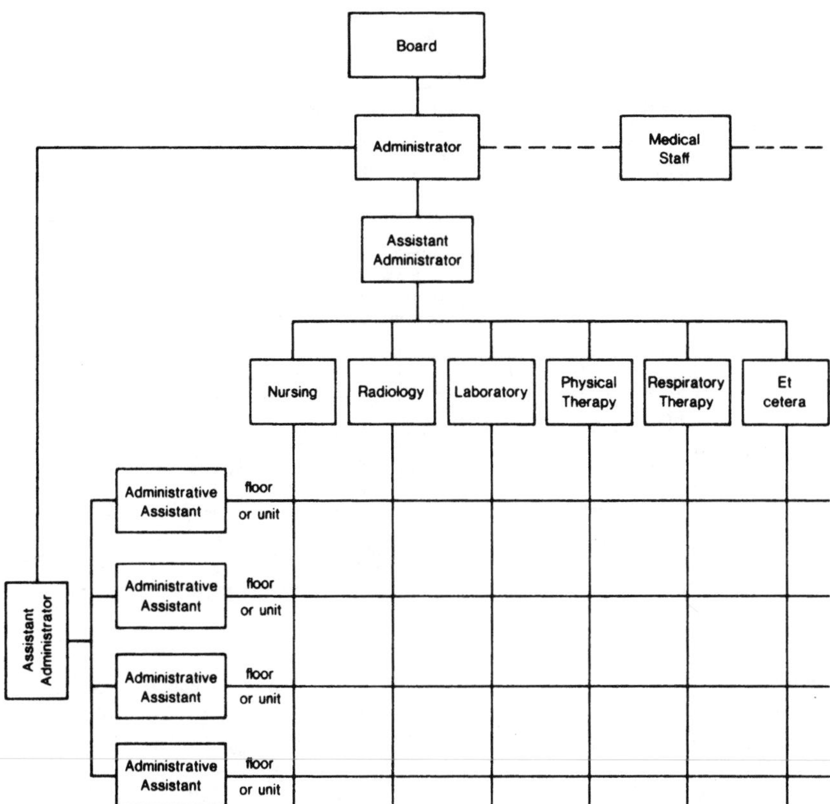

Figure 7–2 Administrative Matrix Model. *Source:* Reprinted from *Nursing Administration Quarterly*, Vol. 3, No. 2, p. 29, Aspen Publishers, Inc., © Winter, 1979.

Three projects were designated: Project A, a snack to be prepared and served in one hour; Project B, a dinner to be planned for the group the following week; and Project C, a banquet for the near future. Three students, Nancy, Kathy, and Jerry, served as project leaders.

Exhibit 7–1 shows the general manager job description and gives a history of the organization. The general manager observed the assignment of personnel by the functional managers to the three projects, and then circulated among the project teams to observe. Exhibits 7–2 and 7–3 are examples of job descriptions for functional leaders and staff. Because an objective of role-play is to demon-

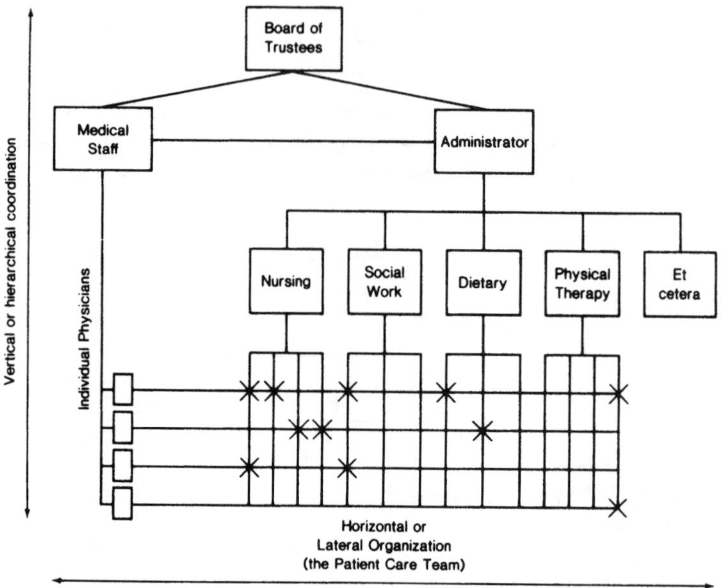

Figure 7–3 Hypothetical Physician Model of the Matrix Organization. *Source:* Reprinted from *Hospital and Health Services Administration*, Vol. 16, No. 4, p. 20, with permission of American College of Healthcare Executives, © Fall, 1972.

strate interactions, managers and staff were all given personal characteristics and personal goals to act out in the project teams.

The project teams worked for 45 minutes. The student leaders had provided supplies to make a snack to make the exercise more realistic, and Project A team actually prepared this snack during their role-play. Project B and C teams worked on their menu planning, while the team members worked through their own private agendas. As an example, salad team member Agnes threatened to quit, dissolving in hysterical tears when criticized by her project team leader. Agnes's specialty was salad bars, and she had been assigned, unfortunately, to the banquet project team. The project team leader, functional team leader, and eventually the general manager were drawn into the conflict. Another salad department worker, Chris, finished her work quickly and efficiently, and even helped others. But her ulterior motives were revealed when she continually sought out the general manager for praise and affirmation of her excellent work. Chris was bucking for a promotion!

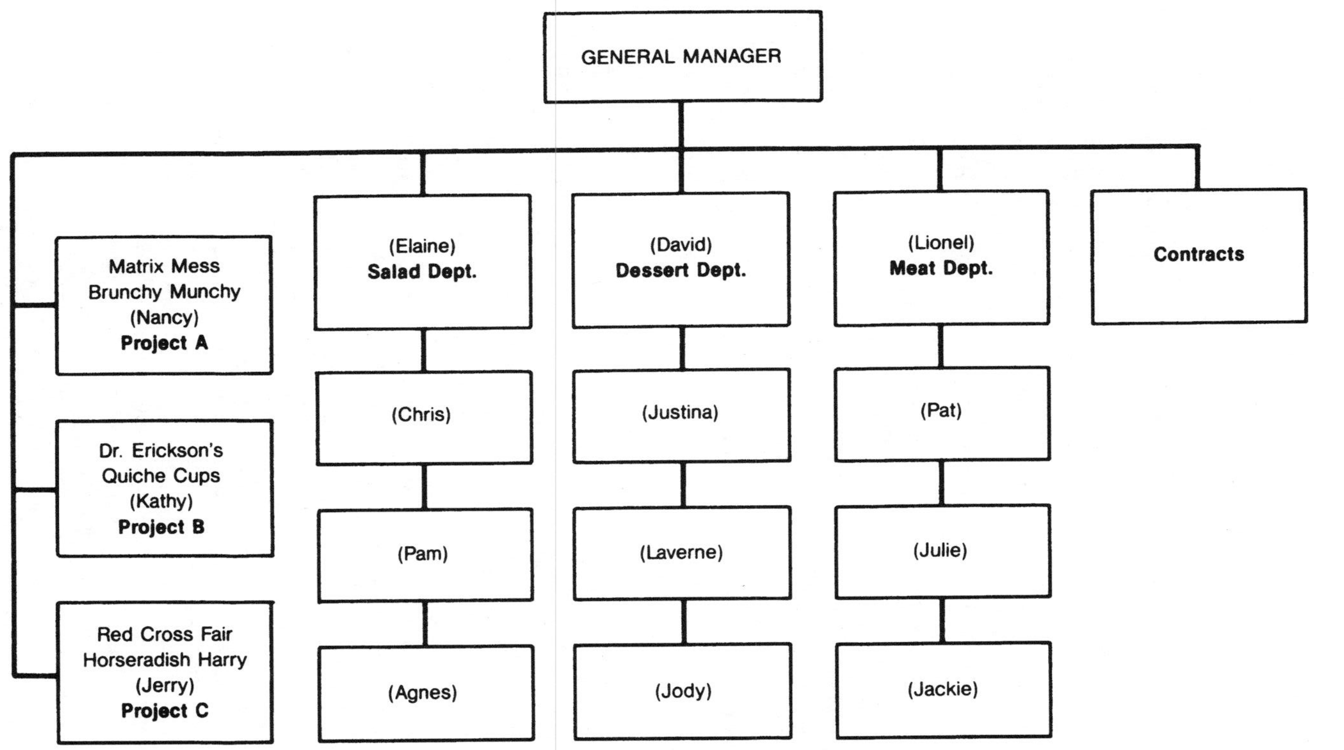

Figure 7–4 Organizational Chart for Molly Meals

Exhibit 7–1 General Manager Role Description for Molly Meals Deli Service

Fricassee Fuszard, you are the general manager of Molly Meals Deli Service. Molly Meals is a 20-year-old business that has catered to the same large-banquet clients for many years. In the past few years two new caterers have been successfully competing for Molly Meals' customers, and the business has been experiencing financial losses.

You were enticed into the business because of your managerial expertise, although the board of directors really would have preferred a male of French nationality. Since your arrival you have reorganized the structure of Molly Meals and diversified your menu lines to include informal banquets, home and office parties, and a 24-hour-notice hors d'oeuvres carry-out service. Your staff functions with fine profit margins, catering to a diverse and demanding clientele. Molly Meals has expanded smartly under your management to meet these new and profitable markets.

You chose the matrix model to organize the service departments because you believed it would be the most responsive to the changing demands of your expanded clientele. While the reorganization has proven financially profitable, constant conflicts between the various departments and product staffs are creating havoc. Personally, you despise the constant bickering and have taken to Excedrin lunches. The word *meal* has become just another four-letter word.

Today you are observing your organization at work. The task for today is to assign the scheduled projects and prepare the menus and/or meals needed.

Exhibit 7–2 Functional Boss Role Description: Desserts

You are an employee of Molly Meals. This organization specializes in planning, preparing, and delivering three-course meals. You are the functional boss of the dessert department. Your employees are specialists in plain and gourmet desserts.

You have three employees who answer directly to you. Employees have résumés with them that describe their special talents. Their weak areas are also highlighted.

Three very important projects have been identified by the general manager of Molly Meals. One project must be completed within the hour, another is due in a week, and a third is due in two weeks. Each project has been assigned a project manager.

You have been nicknamed "Strawberry Shortcake" by your "friends," either because that is your gourmet specialty or because it is what you call all your young female employees. You are confused over the cool response from some of the new employees. The manager of the salad department barely speaks to you. You were just trying to be friendly, but she told you plain enough that her name was Ms. Lettuce.

You want to leave early today because you have a golfing date with one of the other functional managers. You know you could run this business better than that new female. All this coordination business with the project managers just wastes time. You could write down the directions to all your staff in no time and everybody could do what they were told. You did it that way for years and had plenty of time for long lunches and golf. Project managers are just another of life's many sand traps.

After reading the information supplied by the general manager, assign the team members to a project. You may gather more information about the project managers by approaching them and asking questions.

Exhibit 7–3 Team Member Role Description: Desserts

> You are a team member of Molly Meals. Your functional boss is David. He is responsible for your job assignment, work evaluations, and time scheduling.
>
> You are really just working in the dessert department until you can become a functional manager. Managing is your ultimate goal. You always stay under budget and David assigns you to large projects as often as possible.
>
> The project managers are a different story. The desserts you planned for the past several menus were drab and tasteless. All the project managers have informed David that they would rather have someone else next time. The project managers would prefer not to go to the general manager about you, but unless David assigns you elsewhere, or your desserts improve, they will have to find some way to dump you.

The final hour of class was a debriefing, critiquing the interactions that occurred in the new organizational structure. The managers discussed the difficulties they encountered with this double structure and the ways they tried to handle the problems. Employees from the three departments told of the frustration of having two lines of authority and the problem of being evaluated by a manager who was not in contact with their work. Eight specific areas of potential concern were identified by the class leaders, and the class participants related these problem areas to the role-play situation.

The students enjoyed the experience as well as the snack, and all class objectives were met. The seminar leaders, who had met three times for approximately nine hours of planning, said the planning was as rewarding as the actual enactment. A year later, at the graduation party, students remarked that they would never forget the matrix organizational form.

NOTES

1. C.M. Hess and N. Gilgannon, Gaming: A Curriculum Technique for Elementary Counselors (Paper presented at the annual convention of the American Association of Counselors, New York, 1985), 10. ERIC document 267322.
2. J.B.P. Shaffer and M.D. Galinsky, *Models of Group Therapy and Sensitivity Training* (Englewood Cliffs, NJ: Prentice Hall, 1974), 108.
3. J.L. Moreno, *Psychodrama*. Vol. 1. (Boston: Beacon Press, Inc., 1946).
4. S. Sharon and Y. Sharon, *Small Group Teaching* (Englewood Cliffs, NJ: Educational Technology Publications, 1976), 160–161.
5. R.J. Corsini, *Methods of Group Psychotherapy* (New York: McGraw-Hill Publishing Co., 1957).
6. G.K. Gordon, Human Relations—Sensitivity Training, in *Handbook of Adult Education*, ed. R.M. Smith, et al. (New York: Macmillan Publishing Co., Inc., 1970), 427.

7. M. van Ments, *The Effective Use of Role Play: A Handbook for Teachers and Trainers* (London: Kogan Page, 1983).

8. W.J. McKeachie, *Teaching Tips: A Guidebook for the Beginning College Teacher*, 7th ed. (Lexington, Mass: D.C. Heath and Co., 1978), 137–139.

9. van Ments, *The Effective Use of Role Play*, 44–45.

10. Ibid., 45.

11. Ibid., 29.

12. Ibid., 48.

13. McKeachie, *Teaching Tips*, 139.

14. van Ments, *The Effective Use of Role Play*, 98–104.

15. Sharon and Sharon, *Small Group Teaching*, 179.

16. M.P. Charns and M.J. Schaefer, *Health Care Organizations: A Model for Management* (Englewood Cliffs, NJ: Prentice Hall, 1983).

17. P.S. Bruhn and D.H. Howes, Service Line Management: New Opportunities for Nursing Executives, *Journal of Nursing Administration* 16, no. 6 (1986):13–18.

SUGGESTED READING

Bonwell, C.C., and J. Eison. 1991. *Active learning: Creating excitement in the classroom.* Washington, DC: Office of Educational Research and Improvement.

de Tournyay, R., and M.A. Thompson. 1987. *Strategies for teaching nursing.* 3rd ed. New York: John Wiley & Sons, Inc.

Duncombe, S., and M.H. Heikkinen. 1988. Role-playing for different viewpoints. *College Teaching* 36, no. 1:3–5.

Hummel, T.J., and C.M. Batty. 1989. A comparison of computer simulation and videotaped roleplays as instructional methods in the teaching of specific interviewing skills. Paper presented at the annual meeting of the American Educational Research Association. San Francisco, March 27-31.

Kourilsky, M., and L. Quaranti. 1987. *Effective teaching: Principles and practice.* New York: Scott, Foresman & Co.

McKeachie, W.J. 1978. *Teaching tips: A guidebook for the beginning college teacher.* 7th ed. Lexington, Mass: D.C. Heath and Co.

Schomberg, S.F., ed. 1987. *Strategies for active teaching and learning in university classrooms: A handbook of teaching strategies.* St. Paul, Minn: Northwest Area Foundation.

van Ments, M. 1983. *The effective use of role play: A handbook for teachers and trainers.* London: Kogan Page.

Chapter 8

Debate

Martha J. Bradshaw and Arlene Lowenstein

DEFINITION AND PURPOSES

A traditional view of debate may be that of argument for the purpose of persuading the audience toward a clearly identified position. Political debates have been used as opportunities for candidates to make their perspective known on key issues. Debate has been defined as "a systematic contest of speakers in which two points of view of a proposition are advanced with proof."[1] Based upon this definition, debate becomes a useful teaching strategy.

Debate provides opportunities for students to analyze objectively an issue or problem in depth and to reach an informed, unbiased conclusion or resolution. Debate encourages quick identification of the essential nature of the issues as substantiated by the literature, to establish criteria for judging its successful resolution and to weigh, compare, and contrast the merits of alternative strategies for resolution. The process of formulating the debate issue and preparing the arguments enhances critical thinking skills.[2]

> Having to examine and debate an issue brings students to a new level of awareness and helps them to develop the ability to recognize and appreciate the contextual complexities that exist. Although some initial views are adhered to throughout the exercise, others become modified or even changed radically. In either case, students' skills of inquiry are practiced and their world view is broadened by the experience.[3(p.18)]

Source: Adapted from Lowenstein, A. and Bradshaw, M., Seminar Methods for RN to BSN Students, *Nurse Educator,* Vol. 14, No. 5, pp. 27–31, with permission of J.B. Lippincott Company, © 1989.

In addition, presentation of the debate allows students to practice oral communication skills, express professional opinions, and gain experience in speaking to groups.

THEORETICAL RATIONALE

Two important components of the professional role are the analysis of significant issues and the ability to communicate in efficient and effective ways. Professional communication is seen in many forms; scholarly publication, oral presentations, and electronic networking are a few examples. As with other skills, the development of effective communication skills must be fostered by nursing faculty. The ability to communicate one's thoughts clearly and concisely evolves from a formulation of a perspective on a topic, analysis of that perspective as well as other views, and development of sound conclusions. Debate enables students to participate actively in a meaningful communication exercise.

De Young differentiates debate from general discussion by pointing out that general discussion is based upon open-mindedness and a free flow of ideas. Discussion usually aims toward some sort of conclusion, and often is a cooperative compromise. Debate, on the other hand, is argumentative, with each team competing to establish its position as the most correct one or the one that should be upheld.[4]

One of the purposes of debate is for the learner to go beyond merely identifying an issue. Learners must analyze the issue: What are its key elements? What historical precedents have contributed to the issue? Who are the key proponents and opponents of the issue? What is the future of the issue? Analysis on this level leads to powerful learning, calling for the use of reasoning and other forms of higher-order thinking.[5]

CONDITIONS

Debate is most useful as part of a course or seminar in professional and academic settings. Due to the nature of this strategy, it should be employed in a course that centers around issues or topics that raise debatable questions. This strategy can be used to facilitate student ability to implement thinking skills, systematically critique an issue and arrive at salient points, and demonstrate more professional development related to group process.

The learning goals for the debate strategy include improving oral communication and library skills, structuring and presenting an argument, and exercising analytical skills. The process for formulating and presenting the debate should facilitate these goals as much as possible. This means that the faculty should provide as much freedom as possible for the students to reach these learning goals independently. Students should be given enough structure or direction to help them plan and organize their work, but also should understand the responsibility they must take for researching debate positions, analyzing key issues, and practicing speaking skills. In the debate strategy described by Lowenstein and Bradshaw, students were encouraged to take the viewpoint opposite the one they (personally) held. This promoted an understanding of existing oppositional perspectives and enhanced the ability to respond to opposing views.[6]

Preparation for the debate should begin early in the course, to provide adequate opportunity for library research and exploration of issues. Faculty facilitation is an essential part of the learning process. Conditions central to use of debate as an effective strategy include the following:

- Students need to be introduced to key issues in the course, and have been able to identify controversial points suitable for debate.
- Students need to be familiar with one another, in order to form working groups.
- Students need knowledge of existing resources to use in formulating debate. This includes increased familiarity with faculty member(s) as a source of support and information.

TYPES OF LEARNERS

Debate can be used with all levels or types of learners—undergraduate students, graduate students, practitioners—because the learning goals of debate are suitable for all groups. Lowenstein and Bradshaw used debate with R.N. students who were completing the B.S.N.[7] Debate is a particularly successful strategy with this group because these students combine personal experience with actual patient or practice problems with the need to refine communication and analytical skills. Thus, debate provides a true opportunity for professional growth in this type of student.

By creating the need to analyze an issue objectively, debate is useful for a student who is strongly influenced by personal values or certain work experiences. An undergraduate who has not formed a world view about sensitive ethical dilemmas, for example, can have the opportunity to examine the issues and how decisions are made. A practitioner who has been receiving negative influence in the work environment has the opportunity for objective analysis of the situation.

RESOURCES

Faculty serve as an important resource by assuming the role of facilitator. Formal debate questions and positions can emerge from class discussion about important issues. Faculty can assist students in formulating the debate question and can direct them to resources related to the issue.

The library offers many resources for debate preparation. By using the professional literature to support the debate position, students are introduced to a wide range of journals, books, and other printed material. Electronic information systems are extremely helpful to students as they identify debate issues and develop related positions. Database searches enable students to consider related topics, which may generate additional support for a position. Electronic media make available the most current information, which particularly may be helpful for students who have timely political topics. Electronic bulletin boards and other communication networks provide students the opportunity to interact with individuals outside their own institution who are involved with the issue.

The debate can be presented in any planned classroom setting. The environment should be such that the debate teams can be seen and heard by the audience.

USING THE METHOD

In the Lowenstein and Bradshaw method, faculty define broad (topical) areas from the course outline, and identify an advisor for each area. Students choose the general area in which they are interested and form groups of four or five members. At least one group is formed for each topical area, to guarantee that course objectives or topics are addressed. Depending upon student interest and enrollment, a second group may be formed in certain areas. For example, two groups may choose to address the area of professional roles and responsibilities. Specific debate questions are formulated by the group in keeping with the objectives or broad topics of the course and personal interest of group members. Many of the topics are those currently being debated by our colleagues in all levels of nursing: health care reform, nursing care delivery systems, use of restraints, and euthanasia.[8]

Each group should meet with the faculty advisor as needed in order to organize the debate presentation, gain insight into the points being presented, and receive assistance with resources. For each debate group, two students select the affirmative position, two the negative, and the fifth serves as moderator. In groups of four, the faculty advisor serves as moderator. Each group develops a reading list of significant articles related to the issue under debate. The list is circulated to the entire class at least one week prior to the debate. Students not involved in the presentation are expected to be prepared to discuss the issues under consideration.

The debate consists of opening remarks by a moderator, two affirmative and two negative presentations, rebuttal and summary. Following the presentation, the floor is opened to the class for discussion. Questions and comments based upon the presentation and readings are generated by the class. The debate moderator facilitates discussion and provides a final summary of the issues and discussion. With some issues, upon conclusion of the formal debate it may be appropriate to develop a resolution plan. This plan can incorporate some ideas from both positions, to encourage "win-win" negotiation. This gives students experience in developing workable solutions to practice-related issues.

Class members not participating in the debate are asked to evaluate each presenter based upon a rating scale. Students evaluate the analysis of the issue, the evidence presented, supporting resources, organization of the presentation, the argument presented, interaction with the audience and opponents, and response to questions. An overall effectiveness score is given, and the evaluators indicate whether their stand on the issue changed as a result of the debate. All faculty members participating in the seminar also evaluate the presenters. Debate grades are based upon presentation, individual performance, and group efforts that were reflected in the effectiveness of the debate.

To reinforce the learning from the debate, students may be asked to write a formal paper on one of the professional issues discussed in the course. The paper can be evaluated on the presentation of the issue, and on argument for both sides of the issue supported by literature, student position and rationale for selection of the position, application of ideas to practice, and use of references and format.

POTENTIAL PROBLEMS

As with any strategy, potential problems exist. The debate strategy calls for significant student responsibility and preparation, for both debaters and the audience. Thorough research into the issue and the position taken for the argument is required of the debaters. From this they formulate a succinct and effective presentation. Debaters are expected to practice speaking skills and prepare supporting materials for the oral presentation. The debate group provides an appropriate reading list for the other class members. Those students take the responsibility to read about the issue prior to the presentation, in order to understand the issue and participate effectively in discussion. Lack of preparation leads to inadequate presentation of the issue and superficial discussion.

The debate causes students to clearly classify an issue as one that is right or wrong, or answered yes or no. Students may have to defend a position in which they are not clearly committed. Students with strong moral beliefs about an issue may have difficulty defending a specified position or accepting the views of others. At some point during the presentations, it must be made very clear that there are no right or singular answers to most issues.

Nervousness over speaking in public can be a major concern. Some students have had little or no speaking experience, or may have had negative experiences that generated anxiety. Students need encouragement and need to see the debate as an opportunity to speak in an open, receptive group, in order to gain experience. What some students look upon with apprehension often results in being uplifting and beneficial. For example, one student was very timid about speaking in groups and was extremely nervous before and during her debate presentation. Her nervousness was manifested in physical symptoms: sweating, flushed face, tremulous voice, shaking hands, and rapid blinking. She received appropriate support from faculty and students, which encouraged her to work on this problem during the rest of her academic work. Three years later she successfully defended her master's project in a dignified and professional manner. Her public speaking skills have now advanced to the point that she is able to address both groups and individuals effectively in her current employment as a clinical specialist.

The argumentative or confrontational nature of the debate may create anxiety. In addition, debate or public speaking may be a new strategy on which students are graded, thus heightening anxiety. It is important for faculty and students to continually place emphasis on the debate as a **learning experience**. The excitement of defending a position, stressing key points, and deriving a workable solution should be presented as positive outcomes of the debate. Faculty stress that students will not be condemned or inappropriately criticized for taking unpopular viewpoints during the debate. Faculty prepare to handle strong emotional viewpoints and help students understand that there is room for conflicting opinions in our society. Students are encouraged to see the benefit of the opportunity to practice speaking skills, research skills, and group work.

CONCLUSION

Debate is a strategy that promotes student interaction and involvement in course topics. There are many advantages to using this strategy. Debate expands the student's perspective on a given issue, creates doubt about one clear answer, and requires much thought and further evidence before deriving a solution. It increases awareness of opposing viewpoints. As an interactive strategy, debate develops techniques of persuasion, serves as a means by which students confront a controversial issue, and promotes collaborative efforts and negotiation skills among peers. This strategy promotes independence and participation in the decision-making process, as well as enhancing writing and organizational skills. Debate allows for examination of broad issues that influence professional practice. Critical thinking is enhanced by the scrutiny of more than one position on the issue. Debate allows the student a wider forum than writing a paper, and may give a greater sense of accomplishment.[9]

Selection of debate as a teaching strategy requires faculty to make a strong commitment to preparation and guidance. Strong emotions can be elicited by the arguments, and faculty are responsible for monitoring the emotional level and providing guidance to defuse potential problems. Faculty support is needed for students who take minority or unpopular positions and for those who have limited public speaking skills. Following the debate, those students whose ideas are not accepted by the majority are encouraged to recognize those parts of their work that were of value, even if others disagree with their position. It also is important that those students whose ideas reflected the majority view recognize that public consensus can change quickly, and as more information becomes available opinions may be swayed. Finally, faculty help students recognize that the debate is just a start to exploration of professional issues. Students will need to be encouraged to incorporate their newly learned and practiced skills into their professional practice.

NOTES

1. C.L. Barnhart, *The American College Dictionary* (New York: Random House, Inc., 1966).
2. C.S. Green, and H.G. Klug, Teaching Critical Thinking and Writing through Debates: An Experimental Evaluation, *Teaching Sociology* 18 (1990):462–471.
3. N.E. White, et al. Promoting Critical Thinking Skills, *Nurse Educator* 15, no. 5 (1990): 16–19.
4. S. DeYoung, *Teaching Nursing* (Redwood City, Calif: Addison-Wesley Publishing Co., Inc., 1990).
5. M.L. Colucciello, Creating Powerful Learning Environments, *Nursing Connections* 1, no. 2 (1988):23–33.
6. A.J. Lowenstein, and M.J. Bradshaw, Seminar Methods for RN to BSN Students, *Nurse Educator* 14, no. 5 (1989):27–31.
7. Lowenstein and Bradshaw, Seminar Methods.
8. Ibid.
9. DeYoung, *Teaching Nursing*.

SUGGESTED READING

Bonwell, C.C., and J.A. Eison. 1991. *Active learning: Creating excitement in the classroom.* Washington, DC: Office of Educational Research and Improvement.

Cronin, M. 1990. Debating to learn across the curriculum: Implementation and assessment. Paper presented at the Southern States Communication Association convention. Birmingham, Ala. April.

Elliott, L.B. 1993. Using debates to teach the psychology of women. *Teaching of Psychology* 20, no. 1:35–38.

Garland, D.J. 1991. Using controversial issues to encourage active participation and clinical thinking in the classroom. *Community/Junior College Quarterly of Research and Practice* 15, no. 4:447–451.

Green, C.S., III, and H.G. Klug. 1990. Teaching critical thinking and writing through debates: An experimental evaluation. *Teaching Sociology* 18, no. 4:462–471.

Huryn, J.S. 1986. Debating as a teaching technique. *Teaching Sociology* 14, no. 4:266–269.

Leeman, R.W. 1987. Taking perspectives: Teaching critical thinking in the argumentation course. Paper presented at the annual meeting of the Speech Communication Association (73rd). Boston, Mass. November 5–8.

Schomberg, S.F., ed. 1987. *Strategies for active teaching and learning in university classrooms: A handbook of teaching strategies.* St. Paul, Minn: Northwest Area Foundation.

Chapter 9

Case Method

Barbara Fuszard

DEFINITION AND PURPOSES

The *case method* is the use of real-life situations for student analysis and decision making. Students analyze a case problem under the direction of the teacher, reach consensus on the case, and then analyze the implications of their decision. Charles Fisher summarized several types of case methods.

1. *Case problem*—This method presents the facts and the problem itself.
2. *Case report*—Basic elements are included with little supporting information. It does provide the decisions and results.
3. *Case study*—This is a longer, more complete account. Although it may not identify a particular problem, it does contain results and sometimes implications and analysis of actions.
4. *Research case*—This is the most comprehensive method. It includes more on observable events and factors, and offers a complete diagnosis.[1]

This method is appropriate to many types of students and disciplines. It offers application of theory to real-life situations; the cases are taken from real-life situations appropriate to the learning stage of the student and to the discipline. It is especially appropriate for students of the nursing professions, as case studies offer an unequaled practicum for experiencing the real-world situation. The student practices problem solving and decision making within the safety and using the resources of academia.

THEORETICAL RATIONALE

Case method motivates the student with active involvement in the learning process. Cognitive and affective learning take place simultaneously, as the students are required to identify and evaluate their value systems with their colleagues as they deliberate on the case. Theoretical concepts are recalled, tested, and reinforced as the real-life situation is studied. As future professionals who will be working constantly with other human beings, the comprehension of human roles, relationships, and behaviors is critical. The students have a safe atmosphere in which to test various leadership approaches for their appropriateness to the learner and their effectiveness upon others in specific situations—a practice in situational leadership. When this technique is combined with a specific problem-solving and decision-making technique, it gives the student a practical tool for logical decision making.

CONDITIONS

Case method does not offer definite answers—not necessarily even simple or correct solutions to problems. It is not an appropriate vehicle for conveying simple facts. The method's strength is in provoking critical thinking, in testing theoretical learning in the real world—in motivating, and in stimulating retention and recall of learning. It is an appropriate simulation in nursing, when the real practice would involve risk taking that could endanger a patient. Case method also permits development of professional synergy, because students learn to work together with professionals of other disciplines for increased problem-solving and decision-making acumen. As an adult learning strategy, it offers application of knowledge, peer interaction, active involvement, and safe value testing. Students develop respect for their own ability to reason and gain understanding of their dependence upon others for feedback and perspective.[2] Placing this technique at the end of a course permits synthesis of previous learning and application of the theoretical concepts learned throughout the program. Because it is a simulation, it offers efficiency of time, safety, and close supervision not possible in a real-life-practicum experience. A group of five to fifteen students will permit participation of all.

TYPES OF LEARNERS

Case method is appropriate for different types of students. It has been used initially by professional schools, such as social work schools, nursing schools, law schools, business schools, and others. Baccalaureate and graduate students equally benefit from the use of the case method. Staff development students especially enjoy this method for its real-life situations. The method is appropriate when decision-making skills are being taught, rather than facts.

RESOURCES

The different approaches to the case method take different amounts of time. The method demonstrated in this chapter is the *case problem.* Its plan requires some advance preparation on the part of the students as well as the faculty. The group problem-solving task is planned for a one and one-half- to two-hour block of time, and any write-up or evaluation of the decisions reached by the group is outside classtime. A classroom with movable seats is needed so students can form a discussion circle.

The case may be presented in writing, video, or through role-playing. Equipment and resources will be determined by the mode of class presentation. A chalkboard or flip chart is needed to record the group progress through the problem-solving steps.

USING THE METHOD

Students are given the case before classtime, and are encouraged to read current literature on identified issues of the case. The case is then studied according to problem-solving steps like those developed by Bailey and Claus[3] or Sheafor,[4] or by a framework such as the nursing process. The group leader or instructor concludes the case by citing additional readings pertinent to the case.

The teacher can assume the role of group leader, or can, after modeling for the class, have students take turns in assuming this role. Fisher sees the role of the discussion leader as attempting to

- establish an informal, open, and relaxed learning atmosphere
- explain the procedures and anticipated outcomes of the case method

- encourage all participants to enter freely into the discussions
- emphasize that everyone's ideas and experiences are important to share
- draw out the reactions of all participants
- listen carefully to everything that is said
- facilitate the group discussion by providing appropriate guidance and feedback
- offer pertinent, thought-directed questions at times
- help clarify points, comments, or ambiguities
- summarize the discussion, major points, and basic principles
- suggest further references for follow-up
- enjoy the role[5]

Before class, students find and read current articles on important issues of the case. During discussion they offer peer wisdom—thoughtful, risk-taking, value-laden comments and questions on aspects of the case. The student's role includes listening to peers and to the discussion leader, and building on the thoughts of others. The group of students works toward a consensus, by weighing risks and advantages of each alternative action.

Development of the case is a crucial preparation for the case method. Some sources of cases already published are listed at the end of this chapter.

The case presents a brief overview of the incident or situation, often with dialogue. Background facts of settings and other information are provided (in the following technique only to the faculty member, who then shares the information when appropriately questioned). The outcome is unknown, and it is the task of the group to problem solve, to make decisions, and to evaluate how the process functions. A latter step in the process requires the students to turn back to the theoretical issues involved in the case, for benefit of application to future cases.

POTENTIAL PROBLEMS

The case method is not effective for conveying facts. The lecture method is more appropriate to this end. Development of appropriate cases for discussion is a skill that must be developed over time. The neophyte teacher may opt to use already published cases while developing this skill.

Example
Case Method for Pulling the Senior Year Together
Arlene Lowenstein and Richard L. Sowell

Students graduating from a B.S.N. program are expected to have achieved basic competencies in leadership and management. Deciding when and how this material should be integrated into a full clinical curriculum can be problematic. Placement of course content late in the senior year has inherent disadvantages. At this point in their academic preparation, students are looking forward to graduation, are anxious about state board examinations, and are more interested in clinical concepts than managerial ones. They may not appreciate the relevance of the management material to clinical practice. Sustaining interest and enthusiasm can be a major challenge to faculty.

The curriculum at the Medical College of Georgia presents leadership and management as a senior course in the last quarter of study. Course evaluations and student behaviors in class over several years indicated a lack of student enthusiasm for the management content. The nursing administration faculty recognized the need to explore different learning strategies to present the material more creatively and effectively. The challenge was to make leadership and management an integral part of beginning professional practice.

Managerial skills are no longer relegated to administrative levels. In today's milieu, staff nurses are expected to be able to make decisions about care that consider cost effectiveness of interventions, consider outcome measures, and demonstrate accountability in a technically complex environment. Staff nurses must be able to delegate care appropriately and supervise a variety of levels of ancillary personnel. New care delivery systems, such as case management, have evolved. These systems encourage nursing roles that provide continuity of nursing care within both the inpatient and outpatient settings and require nurses to use managerial skills in order to manage patient care effectively.

Recognition of the growing popularity of professional nurses working in the role of case manager presented the faculty with the opportunity to assist students in synthesizing previous knowledge within a holistic framework for practice. The leadership and management course objective was to prepare students for the realities of professional nursing in which they would be expected to demonstrate both clinical and management skills. Faculty selected the strategy of case studies, with case management as a focal point to demonstrate to the students the need for achieving competence in management as well as clinical expertise.

Source: Adapted from Lowenstein, A. and Sowell, R., Clinical Case Studies, *Nurse Educator,* Vol. 17, No. 5, with permission of J.B. Lippincott Company, © 1992.

The strength of the case method as a teaching strategy is in provoking critical thinking, allowing for testing theories in real-world situations, and motivating and stimulating retention and recall of learning. In nursing, case study provides an opportunity for students to apply problem solving and decision making within a safe environment, where actual patients would not be affected. Enhancing the case study discussion with input from faculty and clinical experts can provide a monitoring and feedback mechanism to challenge students to go beyond their own initial responses to the presented situation.

Faculty chose to involve clinical experts in case study preparation and discussion, to provide for student access to role models that combine management and clinical expertise in the practice setting. Since students were at the senior level, faculty chose the teaching strategy of presenting case studies of patients with multiple problems. This approach was selected to reinforce and extend the students' clinical knowledge base and emphasize the importance of appropriate management strategies.

Organizing the Course

A combination of didactic and case study methods were selected to provide a strategy to incorporate both clinical and management principles into the reality of real-life situations that the student might encounter in practice. The didactic portion presented leadership and management principles and theories. The case study presented a clinical problem with both clinical and management data included for analysis. While the didactic portions presented new material and terminology to the students, the case study discussions reinforced synthesis of the new material with previous learning, and promoted application of material to specific nursing situations.

Complex patient case studies from various clinical specialties were selected to challenge clinical reasoning skills, as well as to integrate specific leadership and management principles into the clinical setting, as described in Exhibit 9–1. As shown, the leadership and management content was paired with each clinical case study. An effort was made to emphasize specific didactic content that was an important consideration in each of the clinical case studies. An example of this was the pairing of the care of the patient with acquired immunodeficiency syndrome (AIDS) with didactic content on legal and ethical issues in organizing and managing care delivery. This pairing was chosen to facilitate discussion of the many legal and ethical issues surrounding human immunodeficiency virus infection and AIDS, but also to foster discussion of

Exhibit 9–1 Course Content

Leadership and Management Topic	Clinical Case Study
Introduction to course and management concepts *Introduction to nursing case management*	None
Financial management Fiscal environment and development of resources, budget principles	Care of the obstetrical client with complex problems and care of the premature neonate
Organizing nursing services Care delivery models Staffing	The client with multiple cardiovascular problems and diabetes
Directing nursing services Communication, motivation Delegation, supervision	The client with psychiatric problems
Ethical and legal issues in nursing	The client with AIDS
Controlling/evaluating nursing services Quality assurance The impaired nurse	The client with substance abuse
Problem solving, decision making Managing change	The client with multiple trauma

these principles as commonly encountered in the care of oncologic patients and patients with other terminal illnesses.

A continuing case study approach, as described by Baldwin and Schaffer, was used.[6] One community setting was highlighted for the entire course, avoiding the necessity to re-establish the setting with each case presented. An overall extended family scenario was developed, from which the cases were drawn. This allowed students to become familiar with resources available within a specific community and the families who lived there. The case studies highlighted an extended family that included male and female family members and friends. Profiles of the family and friends included different cultural and educational backgrounds, different ages throughout the life span, and distinct patterns of health decision-making and health activities. Each week a different family member or friends was presented, with a focus on a specific health problem and appropriate managerial implications. Students were expected to approach the case from the perspective of the nursing case manager. This approach was used to facilitate the integration of prehospitalization, inpatient, and rehabilitation phases of an illness-recovery continuum.

Developing the Case Study

An expert panel of both nursing clinicians and faculty was selected to construct each case study. The panel's responsibility included the development of study activities, case materials, and a case study analysis that included critical interventions and key points for discussion. They also served as a resource panel in the actual presentation. The use of academic and clinical experts further facilitated the integration of theoretical and pragmatic perspectives. The use of clinical experts had the added advantage of creating closer ties, and promoted dialogue between the faculty and the staff of the institutions used as clinical sites. A predesigned case study format (Exhibit 9–2) and a sample case were developed by the author and circulated to the case study panels to assist them in providing students with adequate information to facilitate application of the nursing process. Use of the sample study and format as a guide encouraged consistency in the case studies. The background and assessment information focused on data needed by the students to perform a nursing assessment and establish nursing diagnoses. Discussion questions and analyses were formulated to assist the students in developing appropriate interventions and evaluate their potential effectiveness.

Case study selections were made for their relevance to the leadership and management content and to provide the opportunity to work with patients whose care crosses clinical specialties and settings. For example, the case of the patient with complex obstetrical problems included care of an adolescent obstetrical patient with minimal prenatal care and care of her premature infant with residual problems. This case incorporated both maternal and pediatric concepts in relation to clinical care plus a focus on financial considerations for both the

---

Exhibit 9–2 Format for Case Study: Care of the Complex Patient

I. Background
   1. Introduction of patient and clinical problem
   2. Introduction of the health care setting and environment

II. Assessment—Development of patient care plan
   1. Nursing diagnosis
   2. Assessment of setting—resources, managerial diagnosis

III. Discussion questions

IV. Analysis—resolution
   1. Clinical
   2. Managerial

patient and the institution, including the development of resources to address the problems.

Clinical and leadership/management content and problems were introduced into each case study. The nurse was presented as a case manager for the patient. The patient was viewed at different times or staging levels within an illness-recovery continuum: problem onset and development, acute crisis, rehabilitation, ongoing health maintenance, and future health promotion (Exhibit 9–3). The care setting included the acute care hospital and/or care in the community over the course of the described illness episodes. Each case study consisted of up to three sections or levels demonstrating the progress of the case over time.

Discussion questions and a case analysis, emphasizing the important points for discussion, were developed. For the discussion, faculty were also asked to emphasize patient care involving interdisciplinary groups and the inclusion of the patient or family in care planning and decision making. The case analysis

---

Exhibit 9–3 Case Development: Care of the Patient with Complex Obstetrical Problems

This case would be built around a pregnant woman (could be adolescent pregnancy); managerial emphasis would be financial.

	Clinical Concepts	**Managerial Concepts**
Level I:	Pregnancy, lack of adequate prenatal care Psychosocial and ethical concerns	Financial sources available for care
Level II:	Complicated premature labor Cesarean section	Reimbursement issues—cost of diagnostic studies
Level III:	Mom's OK, infant requires neonatal intensive care Psychosocial and ethical concerns	Reimbursement issues—cost of care; financial issues involved in discharge planning
Resolution:	Potential scenarios: Infant recovers and is discharged (to mother or foster care) Infant has severe developmental disabilities Infant dies	

Student is assigned as primary nurse for mother and case manager for both mother and baby.

included dysfunctional patient/family characteristics, prioritized desired outcomes (immediate vs. less immediate and long term), action alternatives and rationales, risks and unintended consequences, theoretical factors, selected reading, and potential research questions. The case analysis was not meant to be distributed to the students, but was developed as a resource to the panel and to the rest of the faculty to identify the important points that were needed in the discussion. The analysis also provided other faculty with an understanding of what had been stressed in a case study other than their own, thereby facilitating integration of content across the course.

Using the Method

Case studies and reading assignments for the didactic and clinical material to be presented were distributed well in advance of the actual presentations. Since the class was very large, attention was given to having students responsible for individual activities to promote individual effort, but also participate in a small group activity. Each student was required to prepare an activity sheet to encourage individual preparation for small-group work and classroom discussion. Each student identified the patient care team that would be appropriate to the patient's care, nursing process components at specific levels of patient acuity, and the related managerial concepts appropriate at those levels. Activity sheets were collected and reviewed by faculty as part of the course grading system and returned to students for feedback.

The course hours were divided into three segments for each case. The first segment was preparation for the case discussion. The students were divided into small work groups to encourage involvement in small group discussion and promote full participation by all students. Two hours of class time were allotted for work group activity. Each group was assigned a small set of discussion questions to prepare for the case discussion. The use of different questions for each group allowed more material to be covered in the discussion. The discussion questions required the students to draw on both clinical knowledge and the corresponding leadership and management material. In the obstetrical case, one group of students were asked to discuss what strategies nurses can use to balance cost containment with the provision of quality care for the patient and her baby.

The second segment utilized a more traditional didactic lecture technique, where the new content was presented, explained, and clarified. Assigned readings included textbook chapters and appropriate articles that presented the leadership and management content and clinically oriented research articles. Examples used in the formal presentation also demonstrated how leadership and management were used in clinical applications as well as administratively.

The final segment was the actual case presentation. With a faculty member serving as moderator, work group reports were presented. Open discussion from other class members was encouraged, and clinical experts serving on the panels contributed responses to the student presentation, answered student questions and identified care delivery options, pointed out issues and resources not identified, and encouraged students to reassess as necessary. The open discussion served as evaluation from the nursing process perspective.

Evaluation

Student evaluation of the course reflected interest in the case studies. This approach resulted in a more positive experience than in previous years. Many students commented favorably on focusing on the complex patient in the case studies, interacting with clinical experts, and focusing management principles on the nursing staff level. The incorporation of the clinical experts enhanced the working relationships between the faculty and the clinical agencies. Students in this course were also involved in the senior clinical practicum experience. During this experience the student is expected to deliver patient care that requires implementation of the management content as they make the transition from student to graduate nurse. Some students were able to identify actual patient care situations in their practicum settings that were very similar to those presented in the case studies, and some had the opportunity to work on the clinical areas with the nurse experts who had participated in class. The use of the combined clinical and management perspective also had the advantage of helping students review patient care decision making in preparation for state boards.

While the overall evaluation of this approach was positive, faculty identified issues that need to be addressed in future course offerings. Since the structure utilizes many faculty and clinical nurses, attention to coordination is essential. To avoid fragmentation and provide consistency, faculty have suggested that one faculty member attend and take responsibility for organizing course activities from week to week. Care needs to be taken to avoid overloading the student with course assignments. Faculty need to prioritize essential content, since the material offered is complex and can be overwhelming to the student if too much is offered. Choosing clinical content is difficult, due to the large number of clinical problems that are commonly seen in health care settings. Our focus was on common problems in which the faculty had clinical expertise and which could be adapted to the application of managerial concepts. Other faculties may find it valuable to develop other case study scenarios that fully utilize their faculty and clinical resources.

The implementation of the clinical case study approach in presenting leadership and management content can be rewarding for faculty and students. As patient acuity continues to increase in hospital and community settings, managing the care of the patient with complex problems is a growing challenge for nurses. Case studies using complex situations can assist in preparing students for the realities of clinical practice.

NOTES

1. C.F. Fisher, Being There Vicariously by Case Studies, in *On College Teaching*, ed. O. Milton (San Francisco: Jossey-Bass, Inc. Publishers, 1978), 260.
2. P.R. Harris, Professional Synergy, *Training and Developmental Journal*, 1, 2 (1981):18–32.
3. J.T. Bailey and K.E. Claus, *Decision Making in Nursing: Tools for Change* (St. Louis: C.V. Mosby Co., 1975).
4. Marian Sheafor, et al., *A Casebook for the Study of Nursing Administration* (Iowa City: College of Nursing, The University of Iowa, 1972), 9–18.
5. Fisher, Being There Vicariously, 279.
6. J. Baldwin and S. Schaffer, The Continuing Case Study, *Nurse Educator* 15, no. 5 (1990):6–9.

SUGGESTED READING

Applegate, M.I., and N.M. Entrekin. 1984. *Case studies for students*. New York: National League for Nursing.

Bailey, M.A. 1992. Developing case studies. *Nurse Educator* 17, no. 5:10–14.

Charns, M.P., and M.J. Schaefer. 1983. *Health care organizations: A model for management*. Englewood Cliffs, NJ: Prentice Hall.

Christensen, C. 1987. *Teaching and the case method.* Boston: Harvard Business School (also *Instructor's guide*).

Hepner, J.O., ed. 1980. *Case studies in health administration: Hospital administrator-physician relationships*. Vol. II. St. Louis: C.V. Mosby Co.

Kazmier, L.J. 1980. *Management: A programmed approach with cases and applications*. New York: McGraw-Hill Publishing Co.

Kemerer, R., and M. Wahlstrom. 1984. How to develop and use in-basket simulations: A case study in the selection of bank managers. *Performance and instruction* 23, no. 4:6–8.

Marks, J.R., et al. 1985. *Handbook of educational supervision: A guide for the practitioner*. 3rd ed. Newton, Mass: Allyn & Bacon, Inc.

Pigors, P., et al. 1967. *Professional nursing practice: Cases and issues*. New York: McGraw-Hill Publishing Co.

Sheafor, M., et al. 1972. *A casebook for the study of nursing administration*. Iowa City: College of Nursing, The University of Iowa.

Sheridan, D.R., et al. 1984. *The new nurse manager: A guide to management development.* Gaithersburg, Md: Aspen Publishers, Inc.

Stevens, B. 1982. *Educating the nurse manager: Case studies and group work*. Gaithersburg, Md: Aspen Publishers, Inc.

Vance, C.M., ed. 1993. *Mastering management education: Innovations in teaching effectiveness.* Newbury Park, Calif: Sage Publications, Inc.

Winstead-Fry, P., ed. 1986. *Case studies in nursing theory*. New York: National League for Nursing.

Chapter 10

Nominal Group Technique

Russell C. Swansburg

DEFINITION AND PURPOSES

The *nominal group* technique is a problem-solving method that avoids development of a self-proclaimed expert by combining independent activity with interacting group structures at specific points in the problem-solving process. The technique produces a decision for a problem that is a solution of a "group of experts."

In using the nominal group technique the problem or task is first defined. Members of the group independently write down ideas about it, making their ideas more problem centered and of higher quality. Each member presents ideas to the group without discussion. The ideas are summarized and listed. Next, the members discuss each recorded idea to clarify and evaluate it. They then vote on and give priority to each decision. The results are averaged, and the final group decision is taken from the pool. The process takes about one and one-half to two hours and results in a sense of accomplishment and closure.[1]

CONDITIONS

The nominal group technique is a method for structuring a group meeting, the purposes of which are to

- obtain a large number of ideas from the group
- order and prioritize those ideas

TYPES OF LEARNERS

Any adult group can make use of these problem-solving steps. Note that it requires both individual and group interaction, under the direction of a facilitator. It is ideal for classroom problem solving.

Scharf suggests a problem-solving team of five to ten persons plus a facilitator to be most effective, because each is assigned a specific responsibility. His effective team has a person who has a real interest in the problem, one who will be implementing the selected alternative, one who will receive output from the alternative, a decision maker with sufficient power to implement, a needed technical expert, a resource controller, an "integrator" or uninvolved party, and a trained workshop team facilitator.[2] In the classroom this technique can be combined with role-play (see Chapter 7), whereas in the work setting appropriate persons would be selected who already fill those roles.

RESOURCES

- Supplies needed
  1. pencils or pens and paper
  2. poster pad or chalkboard
  3. marker pen or chalk
  4. masking tape
- Time required: one and one-half to two hours
- Communication: a technique for individual and group members if they are not in the same setting

POTENTIAL PROBLEMS

Problems with the method can arise with an ineffective group leader and lack of a game plan. Group-think can also arise, if consensus is sought at the expense of critical thinking and realistic consideration of alternative ideas.[3] People are needed who use their feelings, as well as people who think logically and analytically.

USING THE METHOD

The nominal group method proceeds in several stages, as follows:

- Elect a leader or facilitator, who defines the process and assigns the topic to the group.
- Give each member a pencil or pen and a sheet of paper. Ask each member to write down all possible ideas about the assigned topic. Allow five to ten minutes.
- Have each group member present an idea to the group, one at a time, until all lists are exhausted. Do not allow discussion at this point. If an idea occurs to a group member as another is sharing an idea, that member can add it to the bottom of his or her list to be shared later.
- Have the leader or facilitator list all ideas on the poster pad or chalkboard as they are shared and according to the following rules:
    1. There is to be no discussion or evaluation of ideas during the round-robin sharing and listing on the poster pad.
    2. There is to be no debate about equivalency of ideas. All are written on the chart even if they appear to be the same as, or closely related to, another on the chart.
    3. There is to be no rewording of an idea while being listed on the chart.
    4. There is to be no talking out of turn. If the listing suggests a new idea to an individual, he/she can add it to the bottom of the list and give it when his/her turn comes again.
- As pad pages fill up, tear them off and tape them to a wall or other surface so they can be seen by group members.
- Discuss each recorded idea for clarification, elaboration, defense, and evaluation. New items can be added or categories suggested for ideas.
- After all ideas are discussed, have the group vote on and give priority to each decision.
- Average the results. The final group decision is taken from the pool and prescribed to the appropriate entity for implementation.

Example
Using Nominal Group Technique To Teach a Graduate Nursing Course
Russell C. Swansburg

The faculty member teaching a course titled "Advanced Clinical Nursing Concepts for Nursing Service Administrators II"[4] decided to use the nominal group technique to teach a course of three credit hours (class, two hours; clinical, four hours). The course description stated the following:

> This course focuses on the leadership role of nurse administrators in developing and evaluating professional nursing practice in a health care organization. The student engages in analytical thinking about concepts undergirding a professional nursing practice system. Classroom and clinical laboratory experiences are included.

Learning activities included the analysis of a concept for professional nursing practice. The competency-based objectives and assignment for the first two course meetings were as follows:

August 24, 19__

Orientation to the course:

1. Introduce self and describe past education and experience.
2. Discuss the content of the course as defined by the course description, objectives, and assignments.
3. Discuss expectations of knowledge and skills to be gained from this course.
4. Discuss assignments of each student so as to know requirements for course grades.
5. Discuss an evaluation tool for evaluating student assignments and class participation to include frequency of speaking, appropriateness of contribution, courtesy of speaker, substance and depth, and creativity.

August 31, 19__

Develop a working definition of concept analysis. Identify the concepts of nursing administration that are currently important and those that are emerging as increasingly important during the coming decade.

The nominal group technique was first used to analyze the concept of "concept analysis." Each of the six graduate students came to the second class prepared to discuss this concept. They were given five-by-eight-inch note cards and wrote down their ideas as shown in Exhibit 10–1.

All of the ideas in Exhibit 10–1 were written on the chalkboard by the student responsible for leading the class session that day. They were listed in the order stated by the six students during the round robin. The students then discussed and voted on each idea. The final decision as to how each concept would be analyzed as a process is given in Exhibit 10–2, and was derived from discussion of ideas

Exhibit 10–1 Concept Analysis Ideas

- Consider concepts indicative of advanced study and their identification.
- Develop an operational definition by
  1. defining the concept's attributes
  2. identifying the concept's different uses and purpose
- Identify the concept in discussion.
- Define the concepts in discussion according to
  1. types/characteristics
  2. uses
  3. personal perception
  4. applications
  5. evaluation
- Establish why the concept was developed.
- Examine conscious thoughts that are researchable.
- Determine how they are used in the work area and their meanings.
- Define the concept both theoretically and philosophically.
- Determine who is affected—why, where, when, to whom and to what effect the concept has.
- Choose a thought concept that can be researched, a concept with characteristics and traits.
- Scrutinize the concept according to
  1. how it is perceived
  2. its ramifications

The concept must include synergism. Concept analysis may include stages.

in Exhibit 10–1. It should be noted that early in the program students tend not to repeat an idea that is very much like one already listed. They should be encouraged to do so, as any variation may be helpful in constructing the best final list.

It was noted that the group had developed a concept analysis process similar to that of Kemp, who recommended the following six steps:

Exhibit 10–2 Concept Analysis Process

1. Identification and clarification of the concept (definition)—philosophy, content analysis
2. Characteristics and attributes of the concept—whatever the group decides, concrete/abstract, quantity/quality
3. Perception—what people think; interpretation—selling, marketing, determining who the concept affects and what is needed—customers
4. Use of or application—policy, procedure, practice (skills), knowledge
5. Researchability and synergy—evaluation, promotion of change, creation of energy, validation of theory

1. selection of the concept and of the purpose for the analysis
2. identification of the existing definitions and parameters of the concept
3. identification of essential attributes of the concept
4. development of cases
5. identification of antecedents and consequences
6. operationalization of the concept[5]

The students developed the following concept analyses during the course: organizational climate, legal and ethical concepts of nursing practice, a concept analysis of clinical study topics, nursing care delivery systems, theory of nursing management, standards of nursing practice, evaluation of patient care, critical thinking, nursing research, and trends and issues. Exhibit 10–3 shows the many ideas presented by the six students in analyzing the concept of evaluation of patient care.

Exhibit 10–3 Concept Analysis: Evaluation of Patient Care

1. *Identification and clarification*
   a. Program implemented to ensure the excellence of health care
   b. Collaborative effort to evaluate the effectiveness and quality of patient care provided
   c. Process of problem identification and resolution of all aspects of patient care used to maintain or enhance quality
   d. Process by which the effectiveness of health delivery systems (outcomes) is evaluated
   e. Tool that measures and evaluates effective care based on good clinical standards
   f. Program that selectively measures the processes and outcomes of clinical nursing
   g. Ongoing collaborative program designed to measure selectively the effectiveness and quality of processes and outcomes of clinical nursing practice
2. *Characteristics and attributes*
   a. Consistent with mission, philosophy, and goals of organization
   b. Precise standards and indicators
   c. Simple to use and understand
   d. Reliable
   e. Measurable
   f. Meets requirements of accrediting agencies
   g. Integrated with other disciplines
   h. Client oriented
   i. Quality control indicator
   j. Facilitates data analysis
   k. Continuous, ongoing
3. *Perception*
   a. Tedious
   b. Complex

continues

Exhibit 10–3 continued

- c. More paperwork
- d. Doesn't provide information needed
- e. Means to identify opportunity for improvement
- f. Used more often to punish than to reward
- g. Collaborative effort
- h. One-man team vs. collaboration
- i. Monitoring tool (negative)
- j. Promotes accountability

4. *Use/application*
   - a. Maintains quality
   - b. Increases performance
   - c. Promotes decision making
   - d. Promotes improvement of care
   - e. Promotes cost savings
   - f. Enhances compliance with standards of the Joint Commission on Accreditation of Healthcare Organizations
   - g. Assists in trends (identification of)
   - h. Collects statistical data
   - i. Promotes differentiation of practice (strengthens professional practice)
   - j. Identifies training and educational needs
   - k. Promotes client satisfaction
5. *Researchability and synergy*
   - a. Can do research to evaluate effectiveness of care delivery system
   - b. Identifies number of litigations
   - c. Evaluates through assessment of outcomes
   - d. Gives results of satisfaction surveys
   - e. Increases willingness to accept accountability
   - f. Promotes compliance
   - g. Follows Zander's model/variance indicators
   - h. Initiates question-and-answer indicators

NOTES

1. L.L. Northouse and P.G. Northouse, *Health Communication: A Handbook for Health Professionals* (Englewood Cliffs, NJ: Prentice Hall, 1985), 240–241.

2. A. Scharf, Secrets of Problem Solving, *Industrial Management* (Sept-Oct, 1985):7–11.

3. H.J. Brightman and P. Berhoeven, Why Managerial Problem-Solving Groups Fail, *Business* (Jan-Mar, 1986):24–29.

4. Graduate Program, Louisiana State University Medical Center School of Nursing (New Orleans, Fall 1993). The course syllabus.

5. V.H. Kemp, Concept Analysis as a Strategy for Promoting Critical Thinking, *Journal of Nursing Education* 24 (1985):382–384.

SUGGESTED READING

Cawelti, S., et al. 1992. Modeling artistic creativity: An empirical study. *Journal of Creative Behavior* 26, no. 2:83–94.

Dean, P.J., et al. 1992. Identifying a range of performance improvement solutions through evaluation research. *Performance improvement quarterly* 5, no. 4:16–31.

Gallagher, M., et al. 1993. The nominal group technique—A research tool for general practice. *Family Practice* 10, no. 1:76–81.

Gerety, M.B., et al. 1994. The sickness impact profile for nursing homes. *Journal of Gerontology* 49, no. 1:M2–M8.

Hawkins, K.W., et al. 1990. Team development and management. *Library Administration & Management* 4, no. 1:11–26.

Henrich, T.R., and T.J. Greene. 1991. Using the nominal group technique to elicit roadblocks to an MRP II implementation. *Computers & Industrial Engineering* 21, nos. 1–4:335–338.

Hetzel, R.W. 1992. Solving complex problems requires good people, good processes. *NASSP Bulletin* 76, no. 540:49–55.

Mahowald, M.L., et al. 1993. Development of a national core curriculum in rheumatology using a modified nominal group technique. *Arthritis and Rheumatism* 36, no. 9:S143.

Manning, D., et al. 1989. Susceptibility to AIDS: What college students do and don't believe. *Journal of American College Health* 38, no. 2:67–73.

Mercer, D. 1993. Job satisfaction and the headteacher: A nominal group approach. *School Organization* 11, no. 3:153–164.

Mulder, M. 1992. Toward a comprehensive research framework on training and development in business and industry. *International Journal of Lifelong Education* 11, no. 2:139–155.

Neidlinger, S.H., et al. 1993. Defining the major nursing administration issues—Doing more with less. *Journal of Nursing Administration* 23, no. 5:9–10.

Rojewski. J.W., et al. 1992. Preparation for employment in Georgia toward the 21st Century: Developing a vision for secondary vocational education. *Journal of Vocational Education Research* 17, no. 4:41–65.

Swansburg, R.C. 1990. *Management and leadership for nurse managers*. Boston: Jones and Bartlett.

Swansburg, R.C. 1991. *Student workbook and study guide for management and leadership for nurse managers*. Boston: Jones and Bartlett.

Swansburg, R.C., and L.C. Swansburg. 1994. *Staff development: A component of human resource development*. Boston: Jones and Bartlett.

Talbot, R.W. 1992. Directed small group discussions as an evaluation method for improving performance in post-secondary education. *Higher Education Management* 4, no. 3:346–358.

Thiagarajan, S. 1991. Take five for better brainstorming. *Training and Development Journal* 45, no. 2:37–42.

Valacich, J.S., et al. 1993. Communication concurrency and the new media: A new dimension for media richness. *Communication Research* 20, no. 2:249–276.

Woodward, T., ed. 1991. The teacher trainer. *The Teacher Trainer* 5, nos. 1–3.

Zemke, R. 1993. In search of . . . good ideas. *Training* 30, no. 1:46–50, 52.

Chapter 11

In-Basket

Barbara Fuszard

DEFINITION AND PURPOSES

The *in-basket* technique is an exercise for teaching decision making and prioritizing. The technique includes items such as letters, phone calls, and memos of a management or decision-making type that could be expected to come into a manager's in-basket during a time period, such as a day. The student is expected to take action on each piece of correspondence by first prioritizing and then making decisions. The student must provide a rationale for each decision.[1]

There are several purposes or uses for the in-basket. It is used to teach prioritizing and decision making. It can be used as a pretest to determine learning needs,[2] or as a final examination to evaluate learning.[3] It could also be used as a preclass motivator.[4] It is used by the military for teaching decision making and priority setting, but its greatest development and use has been in administrative training in business and education.

THEORETICAL RATIONALE

The roots of the in-basket technique are in simulation or game theory, as discussed in the chapter on gaming, and in decision-making theory. The problems selected are of a wide range and require prioritizing as well as analytical analysis. Students are involved in the instructional process, providing rationale to their peers for their decisions, and receiving feedback from the group and their instructor.

CONDITIONS

This technique is excellent for teaching priority setting and decision making. The themes of the in-basket's contents can be centered around one particular group's problems, such as that of a manager. This would ensure appropriate content as well as process. It is highly motivating, since its problems are real, and it offers an opportunity to examine one's values. It is best utilized with students who already have expertise in the area.

The in-basket exercise starts with pretesting, to determine later improvement made in decision making. Objectives are to motivate and to teach decision-making and prioritizing processes.

Size of overall group of students is immaterial. Group presentation requires a faculty facilitator for each group of five to ten students.

TYPES OF LEARNERS

Typically the in-basket has been utilized with persons who need to make management-type decisions, calling for prioritizing, decision making, and delegating. The example is appropriate to staff development or to graduate education in nursing administration.

RESOURCES

In-basket exercises require a classroom fitted for multifunction use, with desk space for individual work and space for group presentations.

In-baskets are easy to prepare and inexpensive. Each student receives an identical packet, and a way is designated for the student to indicate priority and decision on each item of written correspondence.[5] Content for the correspondence is easily obtained from the contents of a real position-holder's in-basket.[6]

USING THE METHOD

Preparation is done by the instructor. The instructor validates the key to the exercise with knowledgeable colleagues. The materials for the in-basket are gathered and duplicated for each student. Directions for marking the in-basket items and time limits are established. The students work on their individual packets for the designated time and then are called upon to share their decisions. The discussion time provides feedback for the students.

After the instructor's initial preparatory work, students can function without assistance. The teacher participates in the feedback time, directing discussion, asking preplanned questions, and elucidating unclear points.

The student takes the role of a position holder. The student must deal with the tasks that have come before this person during the course of a day, or with what is found in the in-basket after the position holder has been away for a while. As in game theory, the debriefing time is the most important part of the exercise, calling for students to critique their own and others' decisions.

POTENTIAL PROBLEMS

Staropoli and Waltz identify limitations of the in-basket as follows:

- It is not appropriate for analyzing a complex situation.
- It is unreal to the student who is expected to act in reference to a new position, with no experience in it.
- The learner's behavior in the real situation may be quite different from what he or she will indicate in the exercise.
- In-basket may not be appropriate for learners who have never had to make decisions based upon correspondence.[7]

Maybe these limitations are not problems at all. Perhaps the person may behave quite differently in real life from what he or she indicates on the in-basket. Yet the student still has the experience of providing rationale for the decision and receives feedback from peers and instructor on that decision, which is the learning part of the exercise.

An in-basket known to many nurse educators is "You Are Barbara Jordan," developed for the American Hospital Association, and available from the Hospital Research and Education Trust.

Example
Two Hours before My Plane to the Orient
Barbara Fuszard

Graduate students in nursing administration faced the following partial in-basket exercise as Mrs. Lyle. They had one hour of individual work before the debriefing, evaluation period.

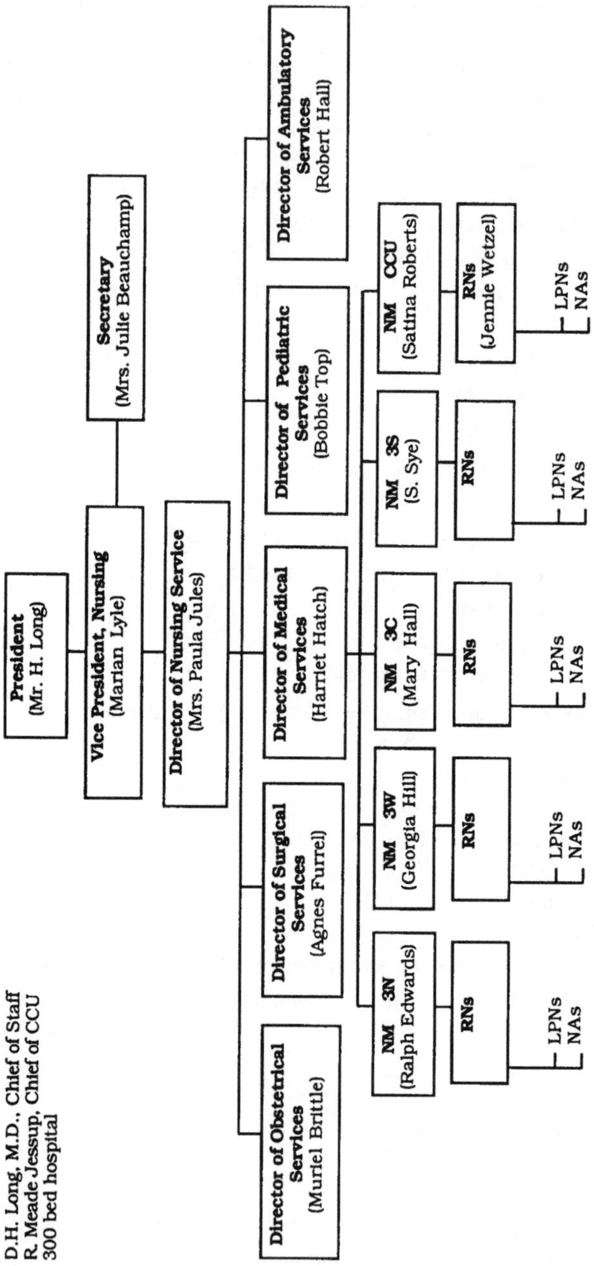

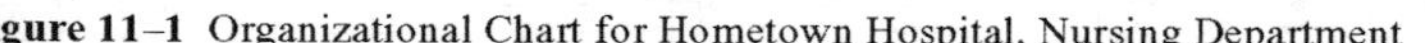

Figure 11–1 Organizational Chart for Hometown Hospital, Nursing Department

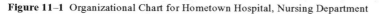

Exhibit 11–1 Letter from Hospital Supply Company

ABBOTT LABORATORIES

North Chicago, IL 30001
Tel. (514) 632-5589

February 10, 19xx

Mrs. Marian Lyle
Vice-President, Nursing
Hometown Hospital
Hometown, ID 53521

Dear Mrs. Lyle:

Thank you for your letter of 5 January. We are happy to be able to meet with your nurses to demonstrate the Abbott intravenous therapy equipment which you will be using beginning 20 February.

Mr. James Willows, our representative, will be able to spend 16–20 February at your hospital. He will bring with him all equipment and supplies necessary for his demonstrations and for the nurses to practice assembling.

As time is at a premium and does not allow for Mr. Willows to communicate with you in writing, we have suggested that he call you on 15 February for final confirmation of these arrangements.

We have also conveyed to Mr. Willows your request for two hundred and fifty (250) copies of our booklet, "Fluid and Electrolytes," so he can bring them with him when he visits your hospital.

It is our pleasure to be of service to you. Please inform us of further ways we may be of help to you.

Yours sincerely,

Ralph Rodgers
Hospital Sales Representative

rr/ph

Mrs. Lyle, vice-president for nursing at Hometown Hospital, has been away from her desk for three days. She took time off to prepare for her trip to the Orient. Her trip is a true honor, for she was selected as one of five nurse executives to visit China, Taiwan, and Japan as consultants in nursing administration. She must leave in one hour to make her plane connection. In this hour she must deal with the contents of her in-basket. She must prioritize and make decisions to defer, delegate, or act herself.

Mrs. Lyle has 15 pieces of correspondence. The instructor interrupts to simulate three phones calls at appropriate times. Figure 11–1 and Exhibits 11–1 through 11–8 show the organization of the nursing department and sample problems with which Mrs. Lyle is faced in her correspondence.

Each student takes the role of Mrs. Lyle for one hour. As they prioritize and make decisions, students are encouraged to make comments on Post-it notes and attach them to the appropriate correspondence.

Exhibit 11–2 Letter from Former Employee

217 Lambert Place
Omaha, NE 23316
January 20, 19xx

Dear Mrs. Lyle,

I am writing as a former employee of your hospital. I used to work at your hospital before I was married. My name then was Sammy Jean Harrington. I worked in the diet kitchen after school and on weekends.

I know you don't know me, but my mother sent me your name so that I could write to you.

You will probably look in the files and the report about me won't be too good, but if you could talk to Miss Goostable, who worked with me then and was the dietitian, she could explain to you about the trouble. Of course I know she is dead now, but the whole thing wasn't my fault and I was young then.

This letter is to let you know that I will be moving back to town since my husband and I decided to get a divorce, and I have to make a living for my three girls (he will keep the boys). I was wondering about positions for practical nurses in your hospital as I am a licensed practical nurse (licensed in New Mexico) and I would like a job in your hospital and I will be living with my mother.

Please let me know about a job there, as I would like to find a job as soon as possible.

Sincerely,

Sammie Gray

Exhibit 11–3 Memo from Distraught Administrator

> Mrs. Lyle:
> Seems to be some friction in CCU. What's going on up there? Three doctors are on my neck!
> H. Long

Exhibit 11–4 Memo from Hospital President

> Inter-Department Correspondence Date: 02/02
>
> To: All Department Heads
> From: Harold Long
> President
>
> RE: Department Head Meeting.
>
> Subsequent to the discussion at our last department head meeting on change of day for our monthly meeting, we shall, beginning in March, meet on the
>
> 2nd Tuesday of the month
>
> at the usual time and place.

Exhibit 11–5 Letter from Wife of Chairman of the Board

57 Coral Heights Place
Hometown, Iowa 53216
February 8, 19xx

My Dear Mrs. Lyle,

Georgie has been telling me about how many poor, dear patients are lying in that hospital, just staring at those awful walls and without a touch of love or home about them. His being on the board, of course, makes their plight a very dear concern of mine as well as his.

I have spoken to my church group about this terrible condition at the hospital, and we thought of asking you, who have the dear patients' concern so close to your heart, if there is something we can do for these dear patients, as our Christian duty. Perhaps we could make some little, gay tray favors. Of course, we would want to deliver them to the poor, dear patients with a little message of good will from our group, so that we could actually share their sorrow and pain with them, and in this way alleviate their burden to some extent.

Please let us know how we may be of service to the suffering.

Sincerely yours,

Exhibit 11–6 Letter from a Nurse Manager

57 Coral Heights Place
Hometown, Iowa 53216
February 28, 19xx

Dear Ms. Lyle,

Jennie Wetzel is threatening to quit. She's really upset about our staffing cutback. I can't get along without her, as everybody else is new. I think we should change the staffing on her shift back to what it was. Please talk to her.

Sincerely yours,

Satina Roberts

Exhibit 11–7 Secretary Receives Bad News

8:35 a.m.

Marian,

Homeville State just called. Jim fell in the swimming pool, and they think he has head injuries. They took him to Tipton Hospital.

I called Mr. Long and he said to use his secretary if you need help.

As soon as I find out something definite, I'll get in touch with Harriet, as she's going to be on this weekend.

Pray for us!

Exhibit 11–8 Chairman of the Board Wants Answers

HOMETOWN BANK AND LOAN COMPANY
HOMETOWN, IDAHO 53521

Wilhelm Vondregrubber President	Wilhelm Vondregrubber II Vice-President

February 6, 19xx

Mrs. Marian Lyle, R.N.
Vice-President, Nursing
Hometown Hospital
Hometown, ID 53521

Dear Mrs. Lyle:

The Board of Trustees of Hometown Hospital, meeting in executive session last Monday, raised the question of the effectiveness of one of the hospital's programs initiated some time ago.

continues

Exhibit 11–8 continued

As you recall, two years ago, at the recommendation of the hospital president, Mr. H. Long, the nursing service department was asked to undertake complete supervision of the housekeeping personnel on the nursing units. Mr. Long felt that this was the only way that cleanliness could be maintained in the patient areas.

Mr. Long continues to hold that housekeeping is a basic nursing responsibility and that cleanliness on the patient areas has been greatly improved since nursing service undertook this responsibility. However, the Board also seeks your evaluation of its previous action and its effects upon your department and the hospital as a whole.

We look forward to receiving your evaluation, observations, and opinions on this topic.

Sincerely yours,

Wilhelm Vondregrubber
Chairman of the Board

WV/dg

The debriefing session involved small groups reviewing and sharing rationale for decisions. Student responses to in-basket exercises have been consistently positive, with more lively critiquing by graduate than by undergraduate students.

NOTES

1. A.B. O'Connor, *Nursing Staff Development and Continuing Education* (Boston: Little, Brown & Co., 1986), 74.
2. B.E. Puetz, *Contemporary Strategies for Continuing Education in Nursing* (Gaithersburg, Md: Aspen Publishers, Inc., 1987), 48.
3. B.E. Puetz, *Evaluation in Nursing Staff Development* (Gaithersburg, Md: Aspen Publishers, Inc., 1985), 95.
4. O'Connor, *Nursing Staff Development.*
5. C.J. Staropoli and C.F. Waltz, *Developing and Evaluating Educational Programs for Health Care Providers* (Philadelphia: F.A. Davis Co., 1978).
6. M.J. Sylvester, Management Games: A Useful Link between Theory and Practice, *Journal of Nursing Administration* 4, no. 7 (July–August, 1974):28–32.
7. Staropoli and Waltz, *Development and Evaluating Educational Programs*, 66.

SUGGESTED READING

Bolton, D.L. 1990. Conceptual changes and their implications for performance assessment: Recent developments in methodology for administrator assessment centers. Paper presented at the annual meeting of the American Educational Research Association. Boston, April 16–20.

Chin, W.H., and S. Scott. 1990. Resistance and co-existence: Should libraries put all their eggs in the technological basket? *Canadian Library Journal* 47, no. 5:323–326.

Collins, E.T. 1990. Finding the right person for the job. *American School Board Journal* 177, no. 7:35–36.

Dukerich, J.M., et al. 1990. In-basket exercises as a methodology for studying information processing. *Simulation and Gaming* 21, no. 4:397–410.

Joesch, J. 1992. Students attempt to find: Do the poor really pay more? *Advancing the Consumer Interest* 4, no. 1:30–32.

Joines, R. C. 1991. Traditional in-baskets vs. the general management in-basket. Paper presented at the annual meeting of the International Personnel Management Association Assessment Council. Chicago, June 23–27.

Keaster, R.D. 1991. The use of in-baskets and small group processes for instruction on characteristics of effective administration. Paper presented at the annual meeting of the Mid-South Educational Research Association. Lexington, Ky, November 13–15.

Kemerer, R., and M. Wahlstrom. 1984. How to develop and use in-basket simulations: A case study in the selection of bank managers. *Performance and Instruction* 23, no. 4:6–8.

Marks, J.R., et al. 1985. *Handbook of educational supervision: A guide for the practitioner.* 3rd ed. Newton, Mass: Allyn and Bacon, Inc.

Nelson, F.H. 1991. Southeast State University: A simulation for higher education administration courses. *Simulation and Gaming* 22, no. 4:490–497.

Penning, N. 1993. A hope for education atop the in-basket. *School Administrator* 50, no. 4:34.

Rist, M.C. 1992. Putting services in one basket. *Executive Educator* 14, no. 4:18–19, 21–24.

Spinrad, P.S. 1989. The in-basket: Real-world teaching for a real-world task. *Journal of Business and Technical Communication* 3, no. 1:89–99.

Sweeney, J., and L. Moeller. 1984. Decision training—The use of a decision curriculum with in-basket simulation. *Education* 104, no. 4:414–418.

Chapter 12

Gaming

Barbara Fuszard

DEFINITION AND PURPOSES

DeTornyay and Thompson define *gaming* as "an activity governed by precise rules that involves varying degrees of chance or luck and one or more players who compete (with self, the game, one another, or a computer) through the use of knowledge or skill in an attempt to reach a specific goal (gain an intrinsic or extrinsic reward.)"[1] They identify overlaps and similarities among simulations, games, and role-play that will be demonstrated in the example at the end of this chapter. Games can range from the very concrete to the very abstract in relation to real life. The example of Alternative Futures Analysis and Review (AFAR) is more concrete, identifying desirable health care for the future.

The game of chess is a representation of the world of two thousand years ago. Monopoly was a creation of the 1930s, the depression years, and reflected how people thought the economy worked (the roll of the dice). War games during World War II offered simulated actions to determine their effects on the real battlefield. Post–World War II management games trained future business leaders. By 1964 two-thirds of all graduate schools of business had included games in their curricula.[2]

Games are used to motivate by involvement, to promote learning and retention by participation in the game, and by immediate feedback.[3] Games are especially valuable in teaching problem solving, an activity that cannot be taught by the lecture method.[4] Games are not intended to present new knowledge, but rather to complement and reinforce present knowledge. Games have a special role in building students' self-confidence and an understanding of the real world. They can reduce the gap between quicker and slower learners, and encourage creative behavior and divergent thought. Research has shown favorable results in the effect of games on affective learning and shaping of student's attitudes.[5]

Wolf and Duffy identify the purpose of gaming in nursing education. It helps nursing students who have difficulty integrating theory and practice. It prepares recent graduates for "reality shock" and disillusionment when they attempt to apply theoretical knowledge at work. In addition to bridging the gap between theory and practice, these conditions make games important to education in nursing.

- *Heterogeneous population*—As nursing students are a heterogeneous group in terms of age, experience, and often culture, games, by encouraging mutual learning, can provide more efficient learning as students learn from one another.
- *Active learner population*—Adult learners are able to assume more responsibility for their own learning, are able to view immediate application of theory, and receive immediate feedback through use of gaming.
- *Affective objectives*—Much of nursing is in the affective realm—valuing, perceiving, commitment. Simulations and simulation games help students deal with the values of clients, other care givers, and themselves in a safe environment.
- *Complex objectives*—No nursing incident is simple. They are made complex by the numbers of persons involved, their values, the clients' various health problems, the institutional norms and regulations, et cetera. Games can help the learner face complex realities. Through games the learning environment can be structured so that the learner can identify the critical variables out of all the variables of an incident. With cost containment and other pressures increasing student-faculty ratios and limiting clinical slots, games offer a group of students the same "clinical" experiences with the supervision of only one instructor.
- *Time compression*—Through gaming, students can receive a number of common, essential "clinical," or growth experiences in a short time. This is not possible when faculty must seek out student experiences in traditional clinical settings.
- *Need for motivation*—Students enjoy games, and are therefore highly motivated. In addition, games offer peer teaching, which is congruent with professional approaches.
- *Need to acquire communication skills*—Games permit students to develop the skill of communication critical to nursing.[6]

THEORETICAL RATIONALE

Gaming, like other simulations, has its origins in psychiatry and psychodrama. Berne says it points out that all people play games with one another.[7] Dewey assigns a moral value to games. He states that games not only fill a basic need for make-believe, but reveal "fresh and deeper meanings to everyday occurrences."[8] The value of games is in their relationship to modeling and analogies. In this relationship they help the student through the gap from theory to practice. Skinner was especially critical of modern education because of the time gap between learning theoretical concepts and applying them to real-life situations. Games bridge this gap by offering immediate application to the real world.[9]

Knowledge is gained from gaming experiences (experiential learning) in a reverse order from knowledge gained from information processing. In information processing, the student is given information, learns the general principles that apply to that information, anticipates particular applications of that knowledge, and finally acts by using the general principle in a specific situation. In gaming, the student first acts, then understands the particular case, generalizes, and applies the knowledge to a new situation.[10]

CONDITIONS

Gaming has been shown to be highly effective for affective as well as cognitive content, including developing value structures along with tolerance and understanding toward others. As this affective education is a part of every course in nursing, gaming is appropriate to any part of the nursing curriculum. Its value, however, does not end with undergraduate education. The graduate nursing student prepares to move to a new role or level within the profession and reassess values, beliefs, and interactions through new parameters. Therefore gaming has a role in advanced education as well. Continuing education and staff development are perfect situations for gaming. With the rapid changes occurring in the profession, the affective strength of gaming can be put to good use in permitting practicing nurses to share perceptions and feelings, and reshape their value systems.

Learning objectives of the game must be congruent with the objectives of the overall course. A spontaneous need or opportunity may arise indicating whether using a game is appropriate. The game most often is homemade. Yet the thought process of a learning objective must be identified to justify the time allotted to the game. For formal games, the instructor needs to ask where in the curriculum a game could be used to greatest effect for affective change or for reinforcement and retention. Carolyn Chambers Clark offers an extensive list of questions in relation to learning objectives, pragmatics, and conditions of gaming. For example, she asks, "How relevant is the simulation-game experience to the real world of the students' clinical experience?" and "How many students can play the simulation game at once?"[11] Her list would be a beneficial checklist for the faculty member developing and/or using a particular game.

TYPES OF LEARNERS

As cited above, undergraduate and graduate nursing students, as well as practicing nurses in staff development or continuing education settings, can benefit from gaming. Because of gaming's real-world orientation, link between theory and practice, and immediate feedback, gaming is viewed by students as a welcome change from traditional teaching.

RESOURCES

Gaming is more time consuming than traditional lecturing. However, research has shown that knowledge and attitudes gained through gaming are longer lasting. As gaming is used for reinforcement, rather than for introduction of new knowledge, however, it is difficult to compare its time needs with those of lecture.

Place, equipment, and resources are determined by the game at hand's space needs and special supplies. Some games need no special supplies, although if games or supplies for the games must be purchased, the cost could be high. Cost of games and space needs are real considerations when planning gaming exercises. The cost is involved, as well as time, when one also considers how many can play the game at one time and the expertise required of the person leading the game.[12]

King states that gaming requires a redefinition of the academic environment. The learning environment for gaming must be open and unstructured. Students are responsible to peers rather than to the instructor for their actions; the teacher is a facilitator. Therefore, the teacher-student relationship must also be unstructured because most of the interaction in gaming is student to student. Learning is heuristic rather than didactic, and can be affective and cognitive simultaneously.[13]

USING THE METHOD

The first step in preparation for use of a game is to identify its purpose. Use of the game must be integrated into course objectives and the sequence of learning activities. Development of the game itself includes the following steps:

1. Define learning objectives.
2. Develop participants' role, materials, and sequence of actions.
3. Develop instructor's manual.
4. Try out the game.
5. Obtain feedback.
6. Revise game based on feedback.
7. Repeat Steps 4, 5, and 6 as needed.[14]

Implementation of the game calls for consideration of such diverse questions as: Can all participants play at the same time? Should they have a preparatory activity? Should materials be distributed in preparation? What preparation of students is needed? How many facilitators will be needed and how are they to be prepared?, and so on. Lists of books are long and can be found in many texts on gaming, including at the end of this chapter. One essential ingredient for the success of even the best-planned game activity is the enthusiasm and enjoyment of the facilitators.

The introduction must identify the game's purpose and the fact that the learning experience should be enjoyable as well as instructive. Rules need to be outlined carefully. It is easier to tell a group essential rules, and how to play a game, than to write them all. Written versions need to cover every exigency of the play, whereas the presence of a facilitator permits instruction only in the incidents that actually arise.

The most difficult part of the teaching-learning strategy of gaming is helping the student see the connection between the game and reality. The student must be able to infer the general principles behind the activity. This is difficult in any experiential learning. Therefore, gaming ends with a debriefing session that reveals the general principles alluded to in the game. Wolf and Duffy state that if the purpose of the game is to offer students synthesis and key factors in a complex situation, more than debriefing is needed. They suggest that either

1. students write an essay about the total process, as soon after completing the game as possible, to determine whether negative learning outcomes have occurred and whether learning objectives have been obtained, or
2. students react to a problem situation similar to the one in the game, which requires application of anticipated learning from the game.[15]

Identifying a place in the curriculum where a game would serve the content well, finding or creating a game, planning how the game will be administered, acting as facilitator during the game, and—most especially—conducting the debriefing are all roles of the teacher with gaming.

The students are expected to be active participants in the game, relating to their peer classmates rather than to the teacher. In debriefing, the students have an opportunity for deep, serious thought about the principles conveyed by the game and how this new experience relates to their values.

POTENTIAL PROBLEMS

Games can get away from one. The group can become boisterous, and it may be difficult to get the students to follow directions and complete all the aspects of the game. It can be thought of as play time because of the relaxed atmosphere of the classroom. The game is also in danger of sabotage if the faculty are not interested in the game or do not value it. Games must be used and directed by faculty who believe in their worth and have carefully assigned them places in the course. Finally, there can be a copyright problem that would prohibit copying commercial games without their owners' approval.

Example
What Future Do You Want?

Barbara Fuszard

Out of the futures' literature comes a delightful outline of a game titled, intimidatingly, Alternative Futures Analysis and Review (AFAR).[16] AFAR has some components of a Delphi game, as it uses small group consensus activity. It differs from Delphi, however, in that Delphi looks at possible futures, and the purpose of AFAR is to find desirable futures. Delphi is a cognitive activity, whereas AFAR is affective. Delphi is anonymous, and AFAR seeks the public domain. AFAR's theme is that there are alterative futures, and AFAR's purpose is to determine which is the most desirable, based on the belief that we have a choice.

AFAR may be used at the beginning of nursing management workshops as an icebreaker. Given the task of identifying the most important characteristics of a leader, participants found themselves jumping on tables, calling "Listen to me! Listen to me!", sending spies to other groups for ideas, and even trying to steal the prizes. Indeed ice was broken at the end of this exercise!

The following example is perhaps more what the author of the game has in mind when developing it. The workshop was entitled "Dollars and $ense," a look at what we can expect from a future that emphasizes cost containment.

The audience was large, so it was divided into eight smaller groups, all seated around tables. (The smallest group with which this author has ever used the game was six persons, and in that case each person acted as a group.) These steps were followed:

1. Each group was asked to develop a list of the ten things it wanted to see in health care in the future. (All group work was done secretly, within the group.)
2. Each group, in turn, was asked for one point from its list. The group was asked to offer an item that had not yet been given by another group. The teacher wrote the items on the board. This listing continued until ten items were on the board.
3. The audience was asked whether it was satisfied with the list, or whether some important point had been overlooked. At this point the game aspect of the exercise was revealed. Groups could win points either for "intelligence" or for "cooperation." Intelligence points were won if an item on the group's list was chosen as one of the final five winning statements. Cooperation points were won if the group voted for an item that was one of the final five winning statements.

   Hearing about points for intelligence gave the groups pause. They realized that they had to have as much of their lists on the board as possible to increase their chance of winning. Yet no point could be substituted on the board unless the group naming it gave permission. Negotiations followed, with lively rationalizations. The final list, agreed to by consensus, was as follows:

   a. optimal health care for all (including affordable and accessible health care)
   b. use of technology as a tool but not replacement for personhood (emphasis should be on personhood)
   c. ability of client to decide which service to use and to go directly to that service without a doctor's referral or order
   d. stress management and mental health built into the system for health care workers
   e. nursing research and utilization of research
   f. preventive health and education
   g. personalized health care with a focus on prevention (holistic approach)
   h. marketability of nursing
   i. equalization of professions, including fees and incomes
   j. increased unification of the profession of nursing
4. Next each group had two minutes to select one item from the list on the board that it felt was the most important point for health care in the future. The group wrote down its decision. When called upon, the group spokesperson announced the choice, and the instructor tallied votes beside each letter above. If the score was tied, for example *a* and *g* each getting three votes with the other votes scattered among the remaining items, a time for debate was allowed. Each group was given two minutes to convince others that its choice was the best. (Time was kept exactly by the instructor.) At

the end of the debate, a revote was taken. When the score was again tied, another period of two-minute debates was offered. When one choice had the majority, a "win" was declared. In this case "g. personalized health care . . ." received most of the votes. The groups that had that item, or one with the same meaning, on their original lists gave themselves five points for intelligence. Those who voted for *g* at the time it received the highest number of votes gave themselves five points for cooperation. Separate scores for intelligence and cooperation were kept by each team.

5. Again the instructor asked, "Which is the most important remaining characteristic of health care that you want in the future?" The groups had two minutes for secret voting, as before. When tallies were counted, those with the winning item on their own group list received four points for intelligence. Those voting for the winning item gave themselves four points for cooperation. Voting continued, with debate and revote used to break ties, until five items had been chosen from the list of ten on the board. Points given for intelligence and cooperation for the third, fourth, and fifth choices were three, two, and one, respectively.
6. The final list of five items showed, in descending order, what the audience selected, through Delphi-like rounds, as the desired health care system of the future.
7. The groups with the highest scores for intelligence and cooperation were given prizes of bags of "penny candy." Then they were told, "Now we will see which groups are the most generous." Suddenly the winners were up, sharing the candy with all the groups.

In this example the AFAR game was used at the end of the workshop. After a short debriefing, the group was able to see indications of learning and some change of attitudes in themselves, revealed through the game.

NOTES

1. R. deTornyay and M.A. Thompson, *Strategies for Teaching Nursing*, 3rd ed. (New York: John Wiley & Sons, Inc., 1987), 27.
2. M.S. Wolf and M.E. Duffy, *Simulations/Games: A Teaching Strategy for Nursing Education* (New York: National League for Nursing, 1978), 3–4.
3. B.E. Puetz, *Contemporary Strategies for Continuing Education in Nursing* (Gaithersburg, Md: Aspen Publishers, Inc., 1987), 145; C.C. Clark, *Classroom Skills for Nurse Educators* (New York: Springer Publishing Co., 1978), 78; E.C. King, *Affective Education in Nursing: A Guide to Teaching and Assessment* (Gaithersburg, Md: Aspen Publishers, Inc., 1984), 114.
4. Clark, *Classroom Skills*, 78.
5. King, *Affective Education in Nursing*, 110, 114–115.
6. Wolf and Duffy, *Simulations/Games*, 9–10.

7. King, *Affective Education in Nursing*, 110, 114–115.
8. Ibid.
9. Ibid., 115–116.
10. Clark, *Classroom Skills*, 128.
11. Ibid., 131–133.
12. Puetz, *Contemporary Strategies*, 148.
13. King, *Affective Education in Nursing*, 110–111.
14. Clark, *Classroom Skills*, 127.
15. Wolf and Duffy, *Simulations/Games*, 26.
16. S. Thiagarjan, Alternative Futures Analysis and Review (AFAR): An Operational Game for Predicting Desirable Futures, *Viewpoints* 52 (March 1976):21–31.

SUGGESTED READING

Alexander, M.A. 1986. Winning with games. *Nurse Educator* 11, no. 5:5.

Clark, H.M. 1986. A health planning simulation game. *Nurse Educator* 11, no. 4:16–19.

Dempsey-Lyle, S., and T.L. Hoffman. 1991. Into aging (game): Understanding issues affecting the later stages of life. 2nd ed. Thorofare, NJ: Slack Inc.

Duke, E.S. 1986. A taxonomy of games and simulations for nursing education. *Journal of Nursing Education* 25, no. 5:197–206.

Duke, R.D. 1978. Simulation gaming. In *Handbook of futures research*, ed. J. Fowles, 353–367. Westport, Conn: Greenwood Press, Inc.

Etzion, D., and E. Segev. Competence and task allocation in a simulated work environment: Its consequences for individual and organizational performance. *Simulation and Games* 15, no. 4:395–413.

Feldman, H.R. 1986. The organization game. *Nursing Management* 16, no. 9:47–49.

Game theory: A management tool. Spring 1986. In *Kellogg World*, 2–5. Evanston, Ill: Kellogg Graduate School of Management.

Horn, R.E., and A. Cleaves, eds. 1980. *The guide to simulations/games for education and training*. 4th ed. Beverly Hills, Calif: Sage Publications, Inc.

Huberman, B.A., and N.S. Glance. 1993. Evolutionary games and computer simulations. *Procedures of the National Academy of Science U.S.A.* 90, no. 16:7716–7718.

National Heart and Lung Institute. 1976. *The hemophilia games: An experiment in health education planning*. Bethesda, Md: U.S. Govt. Printing Office. DHEW Publication no. (NIH) 76-977.

Nowak, M., and K. Sigmund. 1993. A strategy of win-stay, lose-shift that outperforms tit-for-tat in the prisoner's dilemma game. *Nature* 364, no. 6432:56–58.

Smith, H. 1988. *The power game: How Washington works.* New York: Random House, Inc.

Tatano, C. 1986. Strategies for teaching nursing research: Small group games for teaching nursing research. *Western Journal of Nursing Research* 8, no. 2:233–238.

Tenore, E.J., and S.E. Dunbar. 1992. *One step beyond: A systems approach to delivering individualized instruction. A handbook for the Tenore plan.* Pittsfield, Mass: Berkshire Community Press.

Weber, J.R. 1994. Using a gaming-simulation to teach students how to collect data and make clinical judgments. *Nurse Educator* 19, no. 1:5–6.

Chapter 13

The Portable Patient Problem Pack

Jean A. Morse

DEFINITION AND PURPOSES

The *Portable Patient Problem Pack* (P_4) is a teaching-learning method designed to help teach clinical problem solving. P_4 presents simulated patient-management problems in a card-selection format. Each P_4 problem consists of a large deck of color-coded cards from which the user selects—in order—those believed to be relevant to the assessment, treatment, and evaluation of the patient problem being considered.

As developed and used by Barrows and Tamblyn,[1] the face of each *white* card lists a question to be asked of the patient or family. Each *blue* card represents an action to be taken. Each *orange* card lists a laboratory test that might be ordered. *Green* cards list a consultant that students might wish to use to help them assess or evaluate the case. On the back of each card is feedback appropriate to the content that appeared on the card's face. Typically, however, only a small percentage of cards apply to the solution of any particular patient problem. Thus, with little adaptation, a P_4 deck may be used for a variety of different simulated patient problems.

In addition to the informational feedback printed on the back of each card, the student can also be referred to other information sources such as a photograph of the patient or of some relevant data such as an X-ray, or microscopic view; an actual chart or laboratory report; or to a didactic source such as a textbook chapter or a videotape.

Each patient problem begins with a *situation* card, which describes the patient at the point of initial contact and the setting in which the patient is first encountered. On the basis of this information, the student must determine the first step to be taken (that is, what card to select first so that its feedback can be read). Henceforth, the student continues to select cards and attend to their feedback until all relevant questions have been asked and all appropriate actions have been taken. The final step is to read the *closure* card, which provides feedback concerning the optimal path for this patient. A scoring system is provided to allow the student to rate the efficiency and effectiveness of his or her own choices from the card deck.

As with other teaching-learning strategies that use simulated patient-management problems, the P_4 method is a form of *problem-based learning*. The intent is to teach students by presenting them with real-life problems, not necessarily waiting until they have acquired all concepts and principles needed for the problem's solution. P_4 is based on the rationale that, in order to become successful health practitioners, students need to develop effective, efficient skills of inquiry and clinical reasoning.

THEORETICAL RATIONALE

The P_4 concept was developed by Howard Barrows and Robyn Tamblyn for use with medical and nursing students at McMaster University. P_4 is an outgrowth of an earlier teaching-learning format, Barrows and Mitchell's "*problem box*"[2] and of Rimoldi's[3] more limited card-deck version.

By using P_4, Barrows and Tamblyn point out that students *do* learn factual material, but they do so in response to given problems, as the need arises.[4] The result is a learning methodology that students can use relatively independently, at their own pace, and that not only emulates real-life problems, but helps users develop skills of inquiry.

CONDITIONS

Although P_4 decks have probably been most often used by small groups of students, they can also be used by individual students. The decks may be used at the start of the simulation. They can also be used for review, after the content has been presented through other instructional methods. A P_4 problem situation can allow for intensive study from several different content areas or perspectives.

P_4 can be used to teach the adult learner. It utilizes Knowles's assumptions of andragogy—it requires self-directedness, offers experiential activities of real-life situations and problem-solving, and permits immediate application of knowledge to a current situation.[5]

TYPES OF LEARNERS

The P_4 method has many advantages, some of which are shared by other problem-based learning methods, such as the previously presented case method. Students preparing for practice disciplines usually find the P_4 method motivating and inherently interesting. The problems can help them see the relevance of foundational-science content and can assist them to integrate facts and concepts from a broad array of courses. This approach is viewed as especially relevant to their work by nurses in continuing education offerings, such as coronary care or renal dialysis classes. It has also been used successfully with beginning students.

Since students may need to stop and consult various learning materials as they work through their P_4 problem, relevant learning resources should be selected ahead of time and made reasonably accessible to the students. Sufficient time must be allowed for the students to work through the P_4 materials, either in the classroom or laboratory, or as homework. It is also important to allow time for discussion during and debriefing following P_4 use.

In addition to the task of preparing the P_4 deck and integrating it appropriately into the curriculum, another faculty responsibility is to provide consultation as the students carry out their work. The teacher who meets with any given student group may or may not be the developer of the P_4 deck but should be a person who is knowledgeable about the simulated patient problem. The teacher's role is not to direct the students' work, but to guide and facilitate it. This may involve helping them to consider alternatives and inviting them to explain the rationale for their decisions as they select the various cards, thereby helping them assess the logic of their actions. The teacher may also occasionally suggest that a learning resource be consulted, and elicit input from quiescent group members.

Perhaps the greatest temptation for the teacher will be to provide too much explanation for the content that the P_4 problem has been designed to help the students discover on their own. In general, the teacher should avoid directly supplying information unless the students have exhausted all recommended resources and assistance is essential for further progress.

The student group spreads out all the cards so that each one can read the question or action printed on the face of each card. They begin by reading the situation card. Next, they scan all card faces, select the one listing the action they wish to take first, turn the card over to read the feedback for that action, and then continue drawing cards and reading their feedback until either all desired questions have been asked and all relevant actions have been taken, or the students have to stop to locate necessary information that will allow them to proceed further.

As each card is drawn and its feedback read, the card is stacked in order so that the students' "pathway" of actions can later be retraced and evaluated. Once the students believe they have taken all the necessary steps, the closure card is read and they receive information about the appropriateness of the cards selected. The P_4 learning experience may then be followed by classroom or tutorial group discussion.

USING THE METHOD

Several steps are involved in the preparation of a P_4 deck.

1. Decide whether the deck will be used as a regular part of the curriculum or for enrichment. In addition, determine whether it will be used by all students in the class, or only a few. This will help the teacher determine the extent to which the problem should focus on critical content.
2. Select a patient problem by deciding upon
   a. the patient's age,
   b. the patient's health status, and
   c. the setting in which the patient will be seen.
3. Draft the content of the stimulus situation (first card), including a description of the initial contact with the patient.
4. Plan an optimal path that a health professional in your discipline would follow in order to provide care for this patient. (It may be helpful to write a storyboard of the various steps.)
5. List other actions that may or may not be appropriate to the simulated patient case, such as the following:
   a. assessment steps (things to observe or measure, questions to ask, tests to order, or lab results to review)
   b. types of management, treatment, and interventions
   c. titles of other health team members who could be consulted, or to whom the patient could be referred, or to whom selected treatment interventions could be assigned
   d. other data sources that a health professional in your discipline might review in order to gain information, refresh one's memory (for example, as to drug actions), or to verify facts

6. Write each action developed in Steps 5 and 6 on a three-by-five-inch card. (Plan to use different colored cards for different categories of actions. Each action may be printed on colored paper and pasted onto a card.)

NOTE: There are two goals to Steps 4 to 6. The first is to build the correct or pertinent steps (that is, the "optimal pathway" steps developed for Step 4). In addition, the large number of irrelevant, inefficient, or incorrect steps help students learn what not to do. The second goal is to begin a whole series of patient problem decks. The same card fronts can be used for different problems—it is the *feedback* for each card front that is patient-specific. The more complete the first deck is, the easier it is to develop subsequent P_4 decks.

7. On the back of each card, record the feedback (finding, outcome, information, and so on) applicable to this patient's problem. Feedback may also refer students to pertinent information sources such as books, articles, films, charts, videotape, and so on. This would be especially appropriate when the deck is to be used by beginning students and/or as a regular part of the curriculum.
8. Place a different identification number on each card. (This number will be used to help the student evaluate handling of the simulated patient problem.)
9. Draft the closure card and prepare a scoring/feedback sheet. Barrows and Tamblyn suggest a basic scoring model using a range of +2 to –2 points per card.

   +2 = appropriate choice for this patient's problem
   +1 = action is not directly related to the problem, but might be useful if a comprehensive assessment of the patient is desired
   0 = action has no effect one way or the other
   –1 = action is clearly unrelated to effective handling of the patient's problem and may be expensive, uncomfortable, or dangerous to the patient
   –2 = this choice is not only of no value but is excessively expensive, time-consuming, painful, or definitely dangerous to the patient's welfare.[6]

10. Test the deck by asking knowledgeable peers to critique the feedback on the various cards and the path considered as optimal. Revise the deck as needed.
11. Finally, invite a small group of students to try using the deck. Observe them and listen to their discussion. This process will help determine the amount of time students will need to work through the problem, and may also help uncover problems such as
    a. lack of clarity in the wording of card fronts or their feedback,
    b. correct actions that may have been omitted,
    c. ideas for additional cards that represent common errors students tend to make in the handling of this particular problem.
12. Make final revisions in the deck.

POTENTIAL PROBLEMS

When problem-based learning methods such as P_4 constitute the major or sole approach, there is a tendency for learning to be spotty and even haphazard. The solution is to design simulated patient problems that cannot be solved without knowing both essential basic content and clinical skills. One helpful approach is to have an interdisciplinary faculty group review the total set of P_4 problem decks to suggest additional relevant content or significant resources that might be included.

Another problem that may emerge with major or exclusive use of methods such as P_4 is that traditional testing approaches are not appropriate for the evaluation of the students' learning. Further, students may find it difficult to prepare for traditional subject-oriented examinations, particularly those that test isolated facts.

Preparation of a P_4 deck is time-consuming, and typically requires, if not a team effort, at least frequent consultations with knowledgeable peers. While such contacts may well enhance the educational process by making each teacher more aware of the total curriculum content and process, the extensive time demands present a potential problem. One way to help overcome this problem is to develop each P_4 deck to serve as the basis for several different patient problems with only a limited number of case-specific adaptations.

The following abbreviated example of teaching utilizing P_4 closely follows the preceding description.

Example
Juvenile Rheumatoid Arthritis
Jean A. Morse

A simplified P_4 deck was prepared for use in a master's-level course designed to help prospective nursing instructors create innovative teaching materials for beginning students. The simulated-patient situation that was created dealt with an eight-year-old child diagnosed with juvenile rheumatoid arthritis. It focused on nursing assessment and interventions throughout the child's hospitalization and preparation for discharge. The deck was designed for students in a beginning course in pediatric nursing, and was primarily a review of assigned reading material. Because of the limited purposes for its use, this P_4 deck was designed with only three types of cards.

- *blue:* data or information to be gathered
- *pink:* nursing interventions to be carried out
- *green:* consults or contacts to be made with other health professionals

The students for whom this deck was intended had no prior experience with problem-based learning. Therefore, several of the cards were designed with feedback that offered more prompting and immediate knowledge of results than would be desirable in decks for more experienced students.

Presenting Situation

Information on the simulated case was typed on an 8½-by-11-inch sheet and placed in an envelope marked "Presentation of the Situation." The information supplied was as follows:

> You are a nurse in the pediatric ward of an urban hospital. The patient you will consider in this situation is an eight-year-old girl admitted with a diagnosis of juvenile rheumatoid arthritis (JRA), acute onset phase. The little girl's mother is staying with her daughter during the hospitalization, though she had to take sick leave from her job to do so. The other members of this middle-class family include the father, the girl's ten-year-old brother, and her six-month-old baby brother. The boys are being cared for by the father and other relatives. The child's history indicates that she has had chickenpox at the age of six, and roseola at age two. She has had all immunizations plus appropriate booster shots. Her health has been good until recently. The mother reports that the child has seemed whiny and cranky for the past few months.

The Task

Your task in this exercise is to assess, plan, and implement nursing care for this simulated patient. You will do this by selecting appropriate cards, in an appropriate order, from the three rows of cards before you. *Blue* cards are things to investigate, find out, or look up so that you gather information. *Green* cards represent contacts you may wish to make with other professionals. *Pink* cards represent nursing care activities.

You should decide which card to draw first. (Let it be a blue data-gathering card, please!). From there, you should continue drawing any and all cards you think you need or want. (Some of the cards here would not be appropriate to this situation.) Read the feedback on the back of each card before drawing another card. Place each card you draw face down in a stack with the most recent card drawn on top.

Your care for the little girl in this case will continue from shortly after admission until discharge (and beyond if necessary). Therefore, you should draw all the cards you would use during her entire hospitalization, during discharge planning, and beyond, if necessary. When you have finished and wish to draw no more cards, open the "closure" envelope. The information in this envelope will help you evaluate your activities during this simulation. Your work will be evaluated by

1. looking at which cards you drew and the order in which you drew them
2. determining how many inappropriate cards you drew (the fewer the better!)

If you have questions about the task, please ask them before you begin. If you have no questions, you're ready to begin. Good luck!

Samples of the Cards

Some 100 cards were prepared for this P_4 pack, of which approximately 30 were considered essential and relevant to this patient problem. Several examples of blue data-gathering cards (in no particular order) are shown, along with their accompanying feedback.

Card Number and Title	*Feedback*
11. Inquire about child's schedule at school	Child's teacher maintains an orderly, quiet classroom. The children begin at 8:45 A.M. and continue to work in their seats until recess break at 10:15 A.M. Lunch is at noon. The afternoon rest break is at 2:00 P.M. Dismissal is at 3:15 P.M.
29. Take vital signs when initiating contact	VS show: Temp = 104.4°; B.P. = normal; Respiration = somewhat rapid. You also note some rash on her body, and subcutaneous nodules on fingers and toes. Joints are warm, swollen, and tender.
41. Consider actions and side effects of salicylates in preparing plan of care	Review these in your own *PDR*. Note both specific actions and side effects.
71. Check stool	Blood is present.

Even from the limited amount of data shown above, it is obvious that many nursing actions would be necessary in the care of this child. A few examples of the pink (intervention) card titles and associated feedback are shown below.

Card Number and Title	*Feedback*
9. Give salicylates on an empty stomach	Consider potential problems with gastric irritation. If you must administer in this manner, give the salicylates with antacids.

14. Encourage child to reduce food intake	Unless the little girl is undergoing increased appetite as a side effect of steroids, her problem is *more* likely to be anorexia. Why did you choose this card? If it was based on what you know about the effects of steroids, congratulate yourself. If it was just a guess, it would be helpful to review the textbook material on JRA.
34. Place pillows under painful joints	The child prefers flexion, especially during the acute-onset phase. But consider what could happen to muscles from this action. If you are unsure, review your textbook material.
56. Provide warm compresses to affected joints	The effect of this action is the facilitation of joint movement.

Examples of several of the green (consult/contact) cards are shown below.

Card Number and Title	*Feedback*
10. Arrange for parents to meet with genetic counselor	This can be arranged. But, consider: Is there evidence that heredity influences JRA? Please review your text material on this topic.
34. Contact Crippled Children's Agency to obtain access to penicillin on long-term basis	Are you sure this decision is appropriate in the case of rheumatoid arthritis? Are you perhaps thinking of rheumatic fever?
58. Contact (or arrange contact) with child's teacher prior to discharge	Teacher is contacted and informed that child will need more frequent activity breaks than regular schedule permits. If you have already contacted the community health nurse, he or she may prefer to handle this contact.
70. Arrange for, or suggest contact with ophthalmologist	Examination by this health professional on a periodic basis is important, since iridocyclitis is a complication of JRA. If you have already contacted the community health nurse, he or she may handle this contact.

Closure Statement and Scoring Criteria

A short, written discussion of the case, including comments on the order and content of suggested card selections, was placed in an envelope entitled "Closure Statement." This statement also included the explanation of the scoring system, which was devised to take into account the order in which cards were selected. Some of this material is shown below.

Closure Statement

Among your earliest cards selected, you should have chosen to read the chart and review the relevant drugs. Then you should have chosen cards appropriate for your first contact with the child, such as observing her and taking vital signs.

The next group of cards to be selected should have included appropriate means of drug administration, doing checks of urine and stool (and reporting results), and further checking of vital signs. Nursing care should stress use of a flat mattress, warm compresses, splints, warm baths, and so on. Limbs should be kept straight. Range of motion should be carried out (though some authorities feel it should begin in earnest after inflammation has been reduced). The physical therapist, along with the physician, should be consulted.

Numerical Scoring Scheme

Step One: Examine your first ten cards. Give yourself 3 points for each and every one of the following cards that you have: 53, 36, 33, 17, 13, 51, 29, 84, 41, 56.

Step Two: Observe your next 15 cards. Give yourself 3 points for each and every one of the following you have: 53, 84, 21, 19, 17, 43, 47, 22, 29, 39, 56, 49, 41, 71, 33, 62, 36, 26, 16, 79, 13, 35, 81.

Step Three: Beginning with your twenty-sixth card (if you chose that many), give yourself one point for any of the cards listed in steps 2 and 3 and each of the following, if present: 89, 58, 46, 69, 11, 70, 37.

Step Four: Total your points. Now, deduct points as follows: If you have card 86, deduct 15 points. Deduct 7 points for each and every one of the following you selected: 9, 90, 45, 10, 38, 34, 60, 71.

Step Five: Now, total the points you have left after deductions. The maximum possible score is 102. If your overall score is below 60, you should review the section in your textbook on juvenile rheumatoid arthritis.

Outcomes of the Use of the Example

Though less elaborate and complete than those decks developed by the originators of this teaching methodology, the P_4 example just described has been well received both by those it was intended to inspire (the prospective nursing educators), and by the junior-level baccalaureate nursing student groups that have used it. The nursing educators who later attempted to create P_4 decks reported that the process was not only enjoyable, but that it even enhanced their own understanding of the content of the patient cases they chose to consider. The undergraduate students offered comments such as "I wish we could do more of these," "It really made you think," and "I thought I knew that material but I had to go back and review some of it to choose the right cards."

The author found the use of the P_4-deck format for the purposes just described to be a highly positive experience, leading her to agree with Barrows and Tamblyn that:

> Since the P_4 simulates the patient in a very flexible format, it can be adapted easily to meet a variety of student needs at all levels of education in medicine, nursing, and other health professions, as well as in interdisciplinary team learning. Although designed to be used as a unit in a curriculum that features problem-based learning in small groups, it can be used in any educational program.[7]

NOTES

1. H.S. Barrows and R.M. Tamblyn, The Portable Patient Problem Pack (P_4): A Problem-Based Learning Unit, *Journal of Medical Education* 52, no. 12 (1977):1002–1004.
2. H.S. Barrows and R.M. Tamblyn, *Problem-Based Learning: An Approach to Medical Education* (New York: Springer Publisher Co., Inc., 1980).
3. H.S. Barrows and D.L. Mitchell, An Innovative Course in Undergraduate Neuroscience: Experiment in Problem Based Learning with 'Problem Boxes,' *British Journal of Medical Education* 9, no. 4 (1975):223–230.
4. Barrows and Tamblyn, The Portable Patient Problem Pack.
5. M. Knowles, *The Modern Practice of Adult Education: From Pedagogy to Andragogy*, 2nd ed. (New York: Cambridge University Press, 1980).
6. R.M. Tamblyn, et al. An Initial Evaluation of Learning Units to Facilitate Problem-Solving and Self-Directed Study (Portable Patient Problem Pack), *Medical Education* 14, no. 6 (1980):394–400.
7. H.S. Barrows and R.M. Tamblyn, *Instructions on the Use of the P_4 System (Portable Patient Problem Pack)*. (Hamilton, Ontario: Problem Based Learning Systems, McMaster University, 1977), 168.

SUGGESTED READING

Alvarado, A.J., et al. 1990, 1991. Agricultural workers in central California. Vol. 1: In 1989; Vol. 2: Phase II, 1990–1991. *California Agricultural Studies* 90:8, 91:5.

Creedy, D., et al. 1992. Problem-based learning in nurse education: an Australian view. *Journal of Advanced Nursing* 17, no. 6:727–733.

Lucas, C.K. 1988. Toward ecological evaluation. *Quarterly of the National Writing Project and the Center for the Study of Writing* 10, no. 1:1–3, 12–17.

Scheiman, M., and S. Whittaker. 1991. Problem-based learning: Use of the portable patient problem pack (P_4) *Journal of Optometric Education* 16, no. 2:49–56.

Part IV

Technology-Assisted Strategies

The strategies in Part IV need technical equipment for student and faculty use. Yet they would easily have fit with other strategies, such as programmed instruction or even remote faculty/facilitator. These strategies are grouped here so that faculty who do not have access to the necessary technology can easily pass on in the book to more appropriate techniques.

Again, the strategies differ greatly in use. The chapter on computer-assisted instruction (CAI) focuses on development of courseware and integration into the curriculum. The video chapter discusses techniques for feedback and evaluation. Appropriate for any level of nursing education and staff development, the CAI patient management technique may incorporate video and requires the highest level of knowledge from the student for effective use.

Chapter 14

Computer-Assisted Instruction

Cynthia L. David and Jeffrey S. Dowling

DEFINITION AND PURPOSES

Computer-assisted instruction (CAI) is a term that encompasses a variety of teaching situations, the common linkage of which is the use of a computer in the instructional delivery process. The possibilities range from a tutorial program presented on a computer to a complex patient simulation program in which a computer presents and processes information and controls an external videodisc player that presents video sequences of patient diagnosis and treatment. A key feature of CAI that distinguishes it from other modes of learning is *interactivity*. Interactivity promotes active participation by the learner and allows the instructional process to be tailored for each individual.

With the entrance of computer technology into the classroom, some computer language comes with it. *Hardware* refers to physical equipment. It includes the computer and any peripheral devices attached to it, such as a printer or a videodisc player. The computer is composed of a monitor, a keyboard, a hard disk drive, a floppy disk drive, and a central processing unit (the "brains" of the computer). *Software* refers to the programs that run on the computer and associated files. Software programs that are instructional in nature are sometimes referred to as *courseware*.

Individualized instruction is just one of the advantages of CAI. The learner can proceed at his or her own pace and can make mistakes without the fear of public humiliation. A CAI program that is properly designed can teach at a remedial level with extensive review of misunderstood concepts, as well as reinforce the learning of a student who has already mastered the material. Conditional branching based upon a student's interaction with the material allows one program to teach students all across the learning spectrum, from the remedial to the mastery levels. Thus CAI encompasses the best elements of one-on-one tutoring with the ability to meet the needs of large groups of learners.

In the medical fields CAI has some further advantages. Basic factual knowledge presented with CAI can free class time for a human instructor to discuss broader perspectives and issues related to the topic. Also, during any clinical practicum a health care student is necessarily limited to whatever cases are then currently on the unit. With clinical simulations, a variety of patients can be presented to the student and carefully constructed to teach specific concepts. Finally, with CAI a student can practice evaluation and treatment of any patient problem at an intellectual level with no danger to the patient.

Disadvantages of CAI are primarily related to cost and time. The computer equipment itself is expensive if one needs to outfit a learning lab. Also, enough computers need to be available to the students so that everyone can use the CAI during the time period in the curriculum that the material is covered. One way of dealing with cost and availability of computers is to establish a computer lab in the campus library. This sharing of resources spreads the cost of the computers across the entire institution. Also, since libraries are often open in the evenings and on weekends, availability to students can be vastly increased over that of a departmental computer lab. Other cost factors that need to be considered are the prices of software and peripherals and faculty-release time for software development. Careful planning can make the most of resource dollars. Pre-existing software should be evaluated and used when it is sufficient for course needs. Software should be developed only when necessary if financial resources are scarce.

If a decision is made to develop software, there are two options. Courseware can be programmed from scratch with a computer programming language such as PASCAL, C, or BASIC. Another way to generate courseware is with an authoring system. Authoring systems automate the authoring process so that little or no programming experience is required. Another advantage is that usually the programs generated with authoring systems can be revised easily. Authoring systems are available for both of the two major platforms of computer technology in the educational arena, the IBM PC compatible and the Apple Macintosh family.

There are several important considerations in choosing an authoring system, including the following:

- types of computers to which the students have access
- support for a variety of ways to interact with information (such as typing in text from the keyboard, pressing keys, clicking on different areas of the screen, moving objects on the screen)
- importing of color graphics

- ability to branch conditionally to various areas of the program based on a student response
- existence of mechanisms to keep track of a student's responses and to score the student's performance
- multimedia capabilities (i.e., digital video, videodisc, sound, animations)

There are several forms that CAI courseware may take. Drill-and-practice is probably the most simplistic of CAI courseware, the goal of which is the memorization of facts. Tutorials usually present material on a given topic and allow the student to interact with the material to demonstrate understanding before proceeding to the next topic. Simulations (clinical in this context) attempt to create situations that mirror reality so that the student can practice the professional evaluation and treatment skills she or he is trying to acquire. Simulations are the most complex type of courseware because they require the synthesis and application of a wide knowledge base. They can be static or dynamic, depending upon whether the patient's condition changes as a result of student actions. Learning games can encompass any type of design from drill-and-practice to simulations, the key element being competition among players or with the computer.

This chapter focuses on the development of CAI courseware and its integration into the curriculum. The learning theory basis for CAI is discussed, particularly as it relates to the design of effective courseware. Potential problems are also addressed. Illustrated examples are taken from the program *Biomechanics of the Foot and Ankle*, which was created by the authors with the Authorware Professional (Macromedia) authoring system.

THEORETICAL RATIONALE

The theoretical foundation of CAI is eclectic in nature, integrating constructs on learning and instruction from a number of disciplines. Skinner, a renowned behavioral psychologist, believed that operant (voluntary) behavior was the result of conditioning and advocated the use of the principles of operant conditioning in the design of programmed instruction. He was specifically interested in the effects of this reinforcement on the behavior of the organism. He asserted that if certain actions lead to desirable results, those actions would likely be repeated. This important principle and other principles to develop from the work of Skinner include the following:

- providing frequent reinforcement by building in many opportunities for the learner to respond (Each "practice opportunity" is followed by response-specific feedback that helps the learner to check his or her understanding of each content segment.)

- identifying specific outcome behaviors ("learner objectives") that the learner should be capable of at the completion of the lesson, and toward which the instructional content and practice questions are directed
- breaking the content into small bits, that are then carefully sequenced so as to shape the learner's skills into the previously identified outcome behaviors, generally following either a simple-to-complex or part-to-whole pattern[1]

Cognitive psychologists believe that learning is an active constructive process, not just a series of external stimulus-response behaviors. They suggest that a person evaluates a stimulus based on his or her own memories, beliefs, and expectations, and it is this personal internal processing that accounts for varied behavior among individuals to the same external stimulus. Learners need to focus on the learning situation, retrieve previous knowledge bases to accommodate the new information, incorporate (encode) the newly restructured knowledge into memory, and later be able to access the knowledge in order to explain and interpret information.

Dreher and Caputi, from their review of literature, suggest that the integration of the following principles from cognitive psychology be utilized in programmed instructional materials:

- Make the instruction as interactive as possible and require active information processing by the learner.
- Give the learner control and let the learner be self-directed.
- Design an instructional environment similar to the one in which the learner will eventually use the knowledge.
- Provide the appropriate framework needed for organization of the knowledge and skills involved.
- Make the learner aware of the relationships among the concepts and principles being presented.
- Adjust the learning environment to the students' knowledge and skill level.
- Present material in a form consistent with the cognitive developmental stage of the learner.
- Proceed from whole to part, concrete to abstract, familiar to unfamiliar, and practice to theory.
- Build new experiences on old ones.
- Use simulated practice to help the learner experience his or her new role.

- Use problem-solving activities with models prepared by experts available for comparisons.
- Encourage learners to use the knowledge learned to understand and process new information.[2]

Instructional theorists advocate the careful task analysis of each teaching/learning situation. They believe that if this analysis is performed, the specific types of tasks are determined, and the desired outcomes are identified, then principles of learning theory can be used to design the instruction. These theorists also recommend the delineation of objectives in measurable terms and the sequencing of instruction according to the types of learning tasks and skills involved.

Gagne and Briggs, two of the most prominent theorists in this area, contributed greatly to the theoretical base of instructional technology. They discussed the instructional design principles relevant to the preparation of CAI, including the nine "events of instruction," as follows:

1. gaining attention
2. informing learning of the lesson objective
3. stimulating recall of prior learning
4. presenting the stimulus
5. guiding learning
6. eliciting performance
7. providing informative feedback
8. assessing performance
9. enhancing retention and transfer[3]

Learning-theory principles can be applied to CAI that is designed either for the purpose of memorization or for the purpose of critical thinking. Critical thinking skills can be enhanced by questioning, analysis, synthesis, application, problem-solving games, and philosophical discussion.[4]

CONDITIONS

In order to make the best use of CAI, the curriculum is first analyzed to determine what topics may be best taught with CAI. Having completed a needs assessment, available software is surveyed to determine whether there are programs to meet the various needs identified.

For the topics for which one cannot find existing software to meet the needs, one may consider programming original courseware. The authoring system chosen should be compatible with whatever computer platform is available for development and delivery of courseware. Some topics are more suited to CAI than others. Although most authoring systems allow easy revision of courseware, information that changes frequently would be better suited to a different teaching method. A good choice of topic for CAI would be one that remains current, but is difficult for students to grasp.

TYPES OF LEARNERS

CAI can be used effectively by students at any point on the learning spectrum from remedial to mastery levels. Some students are hampered in their efforts to use CAI because of anxiety caused by the use of the computer itself, unrelated to the software being used. Wilson found that 21 percent of a group of 272 undergraduate nursing students had high computer anxiety.[5] However, other research has shown that computer anxiety can be alleviated by hands-on experience.[6]

Designing courseware to be as user friendly as possible is one way to combat computer anxiety. An introduction to general aspects of using a computer during class time, with demonstration and hands-on practice, is another strategy. If further instruction is needed, a manual may be written to accompany the software. It should be written in simple terms so that it can be understood easily by computer novices.

It is possible that the level of computer anxiety seen today is a temporary phenomenon. With the rapid expansion of technology, computers that are already commonplace in society at large will be commonplace in homes as well. We are currently in a transition phase from computers being the province mainly of technology-oriented people to computers being as prevalent as television sets and videocassette recorders. The young people of today who have been exposed to computers at an early age do not seem to suffer from the computer anxiety that affects others. While there will always be a small fraction of people who dislike technology, as a greater number of today's computer-literate youth reach maturity, that fraction will become correspondingly smaller.

RESOURCES

One's CAI efforts may expand to include multimedia solutions. Several optically based technologies presently exist that may be utilized. An interactive videodisc (IVD) generally is a 12-inch disk that stores individual still pictures or motion sequences. The image quality is that of a regular television screen. Videodiscs may be constant linear velocity (CLV) or constant angular velocity (CAV). CLV videodiscs feature linear playback of one hour per side but have few special effects (such as freeze-frame or individual-frame addressing). However, some newer players have digital frame memory that allows freeze frame and frame-by-frame advance. CAV videodiscs can hold 30 minutes of motion video, or approximately 54,000 still images per side, and have the advantage of freeze-frame and independent-frame addressability.

IVD is also described as Level 0 through Level 3, depending on user interaction and computer control. Level 0 is playback only, with no individual-frame addressability. Level 1 adds the ability to do special effects such as slow motion, frame-by-frame advance, and freeze frame. Level 2 disks are encoded with a program that downloads into the player's memory. The student inputs responses via a hand-held remote control, and branching to different sections of the disk can occur, based on student responses. In Level 3 IVD, the player is connected to the computer, which controls all aspects of player operation. Level 3 applications may involve one or two screens. In a two-screen system, the videodisc player is connected to a monitor separate from the computer monitor. A one-screen system requires special hardware but allows the videodisc images to be shown directly on the computer screen.

Compact disk–read-only memory (CD-ROM) is another optical technology that allows storage of data, programs, sounds, movies, or animations on a 4½-inch disk, physically identical to the audio CDs that are now widely available. One CD-ROM disk can store up to 650 megabytes of information. By comparison, a high-density floppy disk can store approximately only 1.2 to 1.4 megabytes of information. CD-ROM, then, is an ideal storage format for large databases of information and reference materials. By definition, CD-ROM can only be read into the computer; the operator cannot write information back to it or erase it, as can be done with magnetic floppy disks. However, erasable CD-ROMs may be on the horizon. Compact disk-interactive (CD-I) is a CD technology that features a special player that combines some functions of a computer and a CD player. It is connected to a television set and stereo and controlled by a remote-control device. It can therefore accept and respond to user input, similar to a Level 2 IVD.

Other equipment that may be useful in multimedia applications include items that translate color graphics, video, and sound into computer-readable files by the process of digitizing. A color scanner is useful for importing color graphics. Video digitizing cards are available that will import video clips and capture still images from a videotape or from a video camera. Sound cards digitize audio sounds either from a microphone or directly via line-level inputs. A variety of software programs exist that allow the user to manipulate color graphics, video sequences, and sounds once they are imported. In order to work with video and sound files, a relatively powerful computer will be necessary with at least 8 megabytes of RAM (random-access memory) for working on the files and a 250- to 500-megabyte hard drive for file storage.

Example
Authoring Courseware on the Foot and Ankle
Cynthia L. David and Jeffrey S. Dowling

The first step in authoring courseware is to assemble the team. The team should consist of a content expert, an instructional designer, a programmer, and an illustrator. Often one person will provide several functions. Using an authoring system may negate the need for a programmer, since most authoring systems are designed to be utilized by nonprogrammers. However, in order to implement complex designs, some knowledge of programming may be necessary to utilize fully the scripting functions that are often part of an authoring system. If budget restrictions prevent hiring an illustrator, graphics may be digitized with a scanner. However, if one intends to sell the courseware, copyrighted images may be used only with permission of the copyright holder.

The next step in the process is to decide on the topic and the content of the courseware. This involves developing the instructional objectives of the program based on an analysis of the curriculum. The instructional objectives should be clearly stated and measurable (Exhibit 14–1). Also, they should be incorporated into the finished courseware as a guide for the student. Farabaugh suggests that objectives can be well written and imaginative, perhaps incorporating elements of a simulation scenario or taking some other unusual approach.[7]

Once the objectives are elucidated, the instruction may be designed. The design process includes deciding on the instructional format and sequencing the instruction. The format chosen may be a tutorial, a game, or a simulation. The instruction is then sequenced appropriately to meet the instructional objectives within the format chosen. The sequencing may be linear with few branch points, or modular with random access to material, or some combination of designs. The sequencing for our tutorial example reflects the content outline (Exhibit 14–2), the points at which the student may interact with the material to demonstrate understanding, and the points at which the student may choose to review previous material. The best way to sequence instruction may be to prepare a flowchart or storyboard showing the various options encountered as one uses the program (Figure 14–1).

The next phase of development involves designing the screens for the introduction and each section of instruction. Screen elements may include text, graphics, animation, or movies. Also, this phase involves planning any audio that will be incorporated into the program. Principles of good screen design should be utilized. Text should be large enough to be readable on the monitor. When

Exhibit 14–1 Objectives

At the conclusion of this program, the student should be able to

1. Describe cardinal plane motion as it relates to the foot and ankle.
2. Differentiate between cardinal plane motion and triplanar motion.
3. Name bony and ligamentous structures of the foot and ankle.
4. Identify the relationship between the bony and ligamentous structures in the foot and ankle.
5. Describe open- and closed-chain functions of the talocrural, subtalar, and midtarsal joints.
6. Determine the effects of open- and closed-chain function on the entire lower extremity.
7. Apply knowledge of structure and function of the foot and ankle to patient problems.

pacing the instruction, keep in mind that text on a monitor is read more slowly than text on a page.[8] Typographical effects (boldface, underlining, etc.) are used sparingly. Generally, one major idea per screen is the rule of thumb in instructional design. Other general considerations include the appropriate use of color and the avoidance of overcrowding the screen. Graphics are chosen

Exhibit 14–2 Content Outline

I. Cardinal planes
    A. Sagittal
    B. Frontal
    C. Traverse
II. Functional anatomy (bones and ligaments)
    A. Talocrural (ankle) joint
    B. Subtalar joint
    C. Midtarsal joint
III. Joint function (joint axis and arthrokinematics)
    A. Talocrural (ankle) joint
    B. Subtalar joint
    C. Midtarsal joint
IV. Application—patient problems
    A. Fracture of right calcaneus
        1. Joint articulation—subtalar
        2. Motion affected—inversion/eversion
    B. Injury to top of foot—bones damaged
    C. Inversion sprain
        1. Anatomical view to show ligaments injured
        2. Identification of ligaments injured

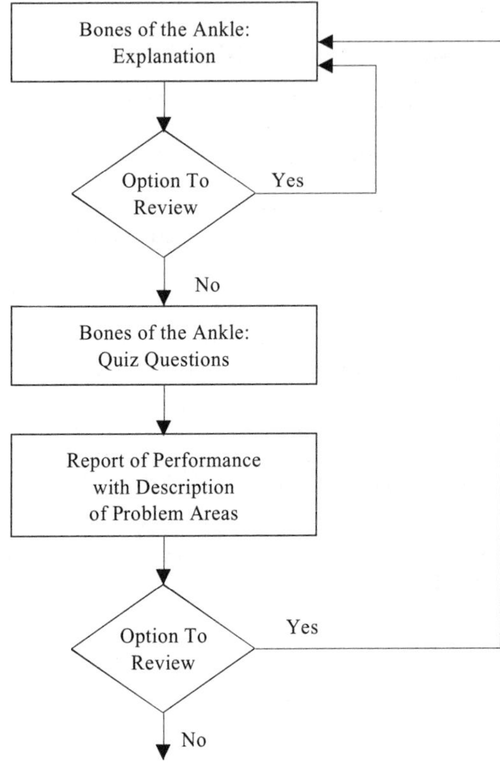

Figure 14–1 Flowchart of a Section

appropriate to the stage of instruction. For example, communications theory research has shown that simple gray-scale or line-art graphics may be better in teaching a new concept in order to focus the student's attention without the distraction of excessive detail.[9,10] However, well-designed color graphics used subsequent to the initial instruction can enhance student interest and learning because the details may be better appreciated.

A key element in quality CAI is the ability of students to interact with information in a number of ways. Active learning is a major principle in facilitating understanding and long-term memory. One level of interaction is the manner in which students input responses. For example, the student may be asked to type answers, click on structures, or move objects on the screen. A higher level of interaction is the way in which students think about the information. French delineated some thought processes related to active student participation:

attending to information, finding answers, generating new ideas, and creating responses that might be reproduced on the screen or on a printer.[11]

Interactions are designed to test the student's understanding and guide his or her thought processes. Reinforcement should be immediate and positive when possible. Correct answers may be rewarded with the option to move more quickly through the program by skipping sections covering topics already mastered. Wrong answers are explained thoroughly in a nonthreatening manner, and hints are given so that the student may try again with her or his thoughts having been directed toward the correct answer. A limit to the number of tries will reduce frustration with the courseware. Exhibit 14–3 shows three sample screens from the patient case section of our tutorial illustrating immediate feedback, explanation for wrong answers, use of scripting functions and variables to provide dynamic feedback and to allow students to identify structures in any order, and a progress report after a quiz section.

Well-designed courseware features not only well-designed content but also a good introduction and a final progress report. The introduction should include a thorough description of the program, what it is designed to do, and how to use it. The final progress report should inform the student of his or her performance and perhaps make suggestions for further study that may be printed for the student to take home after the session. Another important overall design concept is allowing the student to have as much control over the learning process as possible. For example, the student may be allowed the choice of reviewing material or proceeding. Also, enrichment sections may be included that the student may omit or choose to complete.[12]

Once the instruction is designed and programmed, a written manual is prepared. The program is then ready to be tested by other faculty not involved in the project and a few students. Feedback from the faculty and students is solicited concerning both the courseware and the manual and is used in revisions of the program and the manual. This formative evaluation should be scheduled into the development period. After the "beta-testing" phase, the program can be integrated into the curriculum and summatively evaluated, both from a student attitude perspective and also with regard to the learning process. Several evaluation instruments exist in the literature.[13-17] These evaluation instruments could be utilized in evaluating both commercial courseware and faculty-developed courseware.

POTENTIAL PROBLEMS

One potential problem area is poor courseware design. Several studies have shown increased negative attitudes toward CAI at the end of the project. Analyzing the student feedback in these cases reveals elements of CAI design

Exhibit 14–3 Computer-Assisted Instruction: Sample Screens

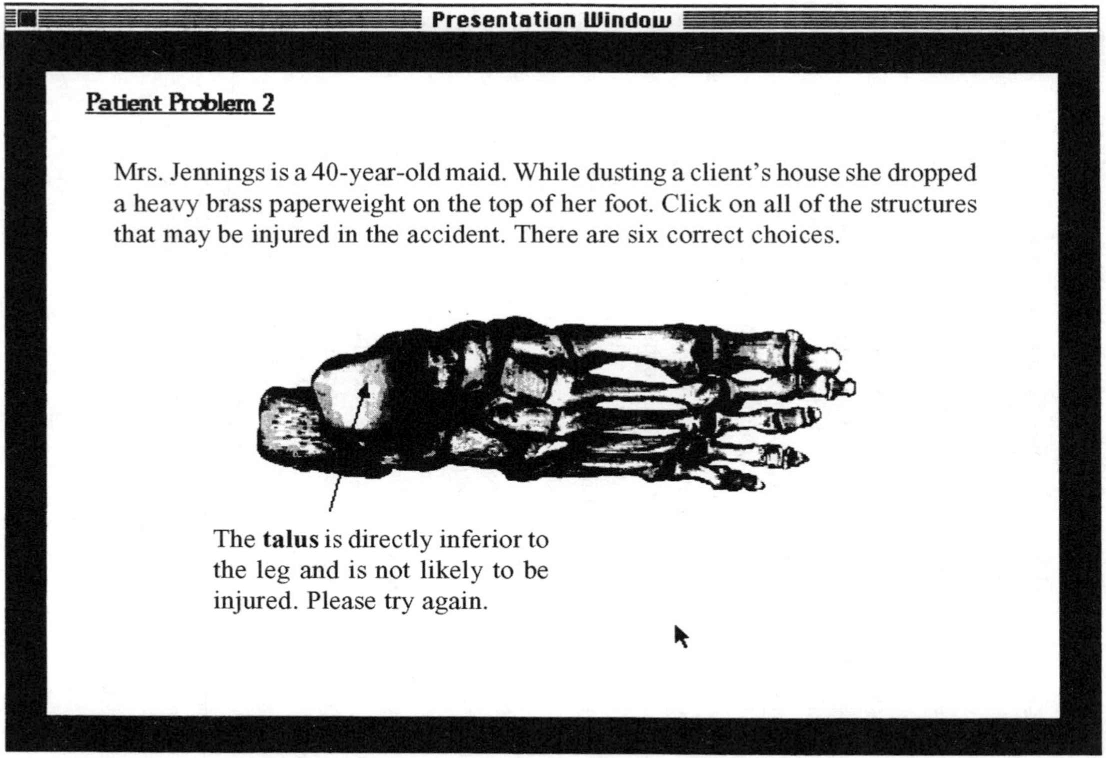

Presentation Window

Patient Problem 2

Mrs. Jennings is a 40-year-old maid. While dusting a client's house she dropped a heavy brass paperweight on the top of her foot. Click on all of the structures that may be injured in the accident. There are six correct choices.

The **talus** is directly inferior to the leg and is not likely to be injured. Please try again.

continues

Exhibit 14–3 continued

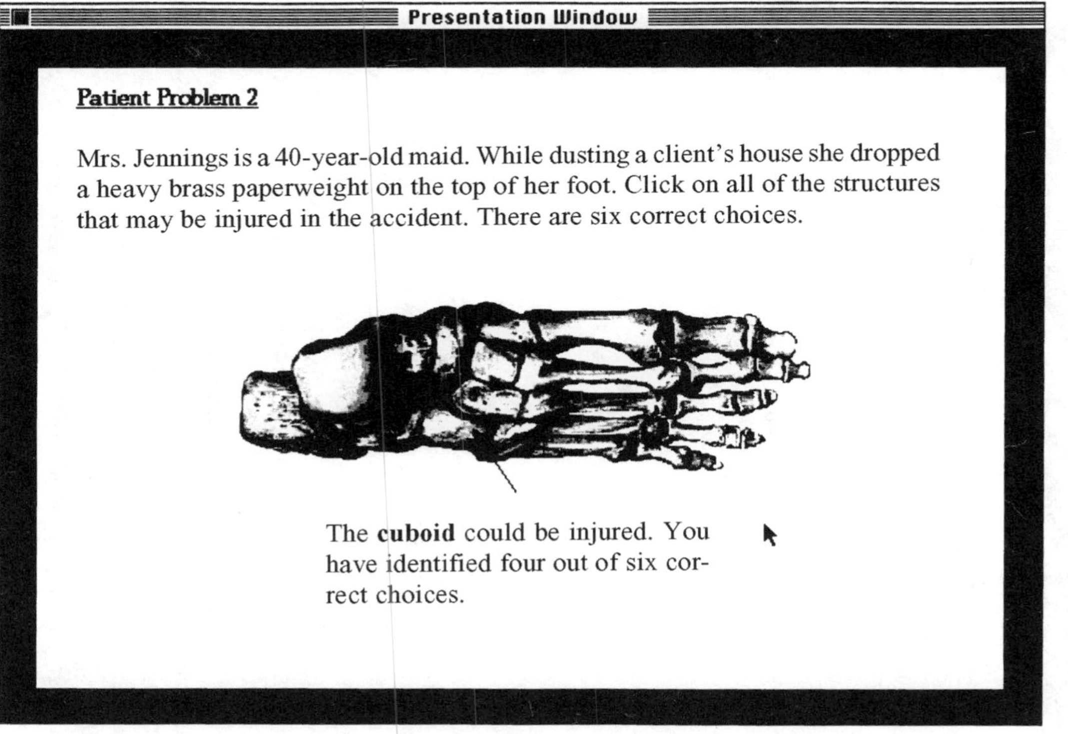
Presentation Window
Patient Problem 2
Mrs. Jennings is a 40-year-old maid. While dusting a client's house she dropped a heavy brass paperweight on the top of her foot. Click on all of the structures that may be injured in the accident. There are six correct choices.
The cuboid could be injured. You have identified four out of six correct choices.

continues

Exhibit 14–3 continued

Presentation Window

Progress Report for the Patient Problems Section:

Out of five questions you identified the correct answer three times.

Recommended areas of review:

Bones of the midtarsal joint
Ligaments of the ankle joint

---

that are important to students, along with designing pitfalls to avoid. Day and Payne had found negative students attitudes associated with lack of feedback for wrong answers, lack of control, lack of interaction of faculty with students, and faulty orientation.[18] More recently Brudenell and Carpenter found that students' negative attitudes resulted from the following: software of limited scope that was not challenging, no feedback for incorrect answers, and no rationale for answers.[19] Research has shown that students respond the best to courseware of appropriate difficulty that is not frustrating, gives quality feedback, and allows the students a great degree of control.[20]

Another potential problem area is the evaluation of CAI. Although Gaston found no significant differences in knowledge or retention between a CAI and a lecture group, advantages other than level of achievement have been demonstrated in other studies.[21] Lyon et al. in a carefully evaluated long-term project found an economy gain, with 96 faculty class hours being eliminated with CAI, as well as an efficiency gain, with the CAI group learning the same material as the class group in 43 percent less time with no loss of achievement.[22] Presumably a proficiency gain also would have been realized if the time saved by using CAI had been spent in continuing the learning process. The Lyon study controlled the evaluation process by eliminating the factors that most often confound research on CAI as defined by Clark.[23] According to this model the experimental and control groups' material should use the same instructional methods (i.e., case based), the same instructional content, and the same level of material. Further, the same teacher should use identical effort in developing both groups' material. Both groups should have equal instructional support. Finally, the study should extend longer than four weeks to control for the novelty effect of CAI. While it may not always be possible to institute all of these requirements in designing the evaluation of CAI, an awareness of these principles and the ability to use some of them may enhance the knowledge base of the actual effects of using CAI.

NOTES

1. B.F. Skinner, *The Technology of Teaching* (New York: Appleton & Lange, 1968), 373–376.
2. M.A. Dreher and L. Caputi, The Integration of Theoretical Constructs into the Design of Computer Assisted Instruction, *Computers in Nursing* 10, no. 5 (1992):219–224.
3. R.M. Gagne, *The Conditions of Learning*, 4th ed. (New York: Holt, Rinehart, & Winston, Inc., 1985), 51–57.
4. E. Pond, et al. Teaching Strategies for Critical Thinking, *Nurse Educator* 16, no. 6 (1991):18–22.
5. B.A. Wilson, Computer Anxiety in Nursing Students, *Journal of Nursing Education* 30, no. 2 (1991):52–56.
6. E. Jordan and D. Stroup, The Behavioral Antecedents of Computer Fear. *Journal of Data Education* 22 (1982):7–8.
7. N. Farabaugh, Maintaining Student Interest in CAI, *Computers in Nursing* 8, no. 6 (1990):249–253.
8. R.S. Kruk and P. Muter, Reading of Continuous Text of Video Screen, *Human Factors* 26 (1984):339–345.
9. F. Dwyer, *Strategies for Improving Visual Learning* (State College, Pa: Learning Services, 1978), 26–27.
10. R. Richey, *The Theoretical and Conceptual Bases of Instructional Design* (New York: Nichols, 1986), 48–49.
11. D. French, Using Learning Theory to Design and Evaluate Computer-Assisted Instruction Software, *Nurse Educator* 11, no. 5 (1986):33–37.
12. Ibid.
13. Ibid.
14. T.B. Jay, The Cognitive Approach to Computer Courseware Design and Evaluation, *Educational Technology* 23, no. 1 (1983):22–26.
15. D. Billings, An instructional design approach to developing CAI courseware, *Computers in Nursing* 3 (1985):217–223.
16. D. Billings, *Computer-assisted Instruction for Health Care Professionals: A Handbook for Designing, Evaluating, and Using CAI Coursework* (Norwalk, Conn: Appleton-Century-Crofts, 1986), 29, 30, 48–50, 103, 104, 139, 140, 161–163, 193.
17. S. Van Ort, Evaluating Audio Visual and Computer Programs for Classroom Use, *Nurse Educator* 14, no. 1 (1989):16–18.

18. R. Day and L. Payne, Comparison of Lecture vs. Computer Managed Instruction, *Computers in Nursing* 2, no. 6:236–240.

19. I. Brudenell and C. Carpenter, Adult Learning Styles and Attitudes toward Computer-Assisted Instruction, *Journal of Nursing Education* 29, no. 2 (1990):79–83.

20. G. Xakellis and C. Gjerde, Evaluation by Second-Year Medical Students of Their Computer-Aided Instruction, *Academic Medicine* 65, no. 1 (1990):23–26.

21. S. Gaston, Knowledge, Retention, and Attitude Effects of Computer-Assisted Instruction, *Journal of Nursing Education* 27, no. 1 (1988):30–34.

22. H. Lyon, et al., PlanAlyzer, an Interactive Computer-Assisted Program to Teach Clinical Problem Solving in Diagnosing Anemia and Coronary Artery Disease, *Academic Medicine* 67, no. 12 (1992):821–828.

23. R. Clark, Confounding in Educational Computing Research, *Journal of Educational Computing Research* 1 (1985):137–148.

SUGGESTED READING

Barron, A., and G. Orwig. 1993. *New technologies for education: A beginner's guide.* Englewood Colo: Libraries Unlimited, Inc.

Clark, R. 1992. Dangers in the evaluation of instructional media. *Academic Medicine* 67, no. 12:819–820.

Frisbie, A. 1993. Potential patterns: Part I: Advances in educational technology—IVD, CD-I, and journeys into virtual reality. *Journal of Allied Health*, Winter.

Software for Health Sciences Education. 1993. A resource catalog. 4th ed. Ann Arbor, Mich: The University of Michigan.

Resources

Organizations

Association for Educational Communications & Technology
1126 16th Street, N.W.
Washington, DC 20036

Society for Applied Learning Technology
50 Culpepper Street
Warrenton, VA 22186

Technology Resources Center
U.S. Department of Education
80 F Street, N.W.
Research Library
Washington, DC 20208-5725

Journals

The Chronicle of Higher Education
Instruction Delivery Systems
T.H.E. Journal
The Videodisc Monitor
Journal of Medical Education Technologies
Educational Technology
Computers in Nursing
Journal of Nursing Education

Chapter 15

Video

Pauline M. Loewenhardt and Kathleen K. Bultman

DEFINITION AND PURPOSES

Use of *video*, according to Clift, "provides a structured stimulus for specific viewer responses—development of skill, change of behavior, or greater self-knowledge."[1] The videotape technique combines some of the aspects of feedback with some of the features of modeling."[2] Videorecording is a magnetic process similar to audiotape recording, and provides an immediate audiovisual recording on a tape that can be erased and used again, much like an audiotape. The use of videotape recording has been standard practice in education of many of the helping professions since the 1960s. Its use in training counselors, teachers, business people, psychologists, psychiatrists, and others is well documented.[3] It was later in the 1970s that this strategy began to be described in the nursing literature.[4] It has been used primarily as a tool for teaching and learning interpersonal communication skills.[5] However, it has the potential for assisting with a wide range of learning experiences.[6]

Videotape may be used to simulate a range of experiences and to promote improved student learning: for faculty development, to demonstrate procedures, to evaluate students, for self-instruction, for student review, to record home visits, to model interviewing techniques, to use with role play, and for peer review.[7] It provides a way to observe growth and development in performance over time, and can help increase students' self-awareness. It can also provide a real yet safe environment in which to practice a wide range of skills, including psychomotor and interpersonal communication skills, and cognitive and affective behaviors.

Because it captures a sequence exactly as it happened, it is available to the student and teacher for use in a variety of ways to motivate behavior change. Depending on the specific learning objectives, type of learner, and setting, it allows individuals to practice specific skills on their own—delivering a speech, for example—or to interact one on one with another person. It is also useful for various kinds of group interactions. In all these instances, if there is a deliberate, careful preparation and orientation, the instructor need not be present during the actual learning experience, yet will have ready access to what happened during the experience. Shaffer and Pfeiffer point out:

> Anyone who guides and directs the behavior of another must inevitably have pertinent information about that person to appraise and give assistance toward improvement. Since student-patient interaction is usually conducted in private, the instructor is not and cannot be aware of the total interaction which takes place between them. Through the use of videotape, the instructor is actually permitted to view the interchange that might transpire between patient and student and can then intelligently guide the student toward individual improvement. It is difficult for most individuals to see themselves accurately and it can be profitable to examine audiovisual accounts and allow the individual to make his/her own critical analysis.[8]

Videotaping technology alone will not lead to improved learning. Results of studies indicate that learner readiness, specific focus, teacher comment, and a supportive, nonthreatening environment are all critical to the success of the experience.[9]

Learning with videotape has potential application for undergraduate and graduate nursing education, but can also assist inservice instructors and continuing education staff. Moran points out that it is a useful tool for self-directed learning efforts, an important aspect of staff development and continuing education. "Videotape has been used successfully in a variety of situations for self-assessment and increased learning."[10]

THEORETICAL RATIONALE

"Until the 1960s, videotape was generally confined to broadcast areas, but the development of portable, low-priced videotaping equipment systems . . . has enabled most institutions and some individuals to acquire them."[11] Fitzgerald, et al. report that they found videotaping so valuable that they purchased their own equipment for their practice laboratory.[12] Research regarding its use is found in the literature of various disciplines, including teacher and counselor education, psychotherapy and mental health, business training, speech education, social work, and nursing education.

Fuller and Baker point out that change theory is one of the underlying principles of videotape feedback. That is, positive reinforcement facilitates goal-directed change and "... the more an individual can effectively utilize feedback ... appropriate to a change project, the more successful he/she will be in attaining his change goal. ..."[13]

Self-cognition or self-confrontation is another theoretical concept forming the framework for videotape use in learning. Self-confrontation, or that situation in which the self is presented to the person, can shape behavior in powerful ways. The capacity to recognize discrepancies between actual behavior and desired behavior and the individual's level of self-esteem, acceptance, and confidence seem to determine the effectiveness of self-cognition. It is clear that self-confrontation is a powerful strategy and can cause disturbances in the viewer. Many questions have been raised as to its effects and many of these are still unanswered. What does seem clear is that this strategy of self-confrontation has the capacity to both help and harm.[14] Dr. Burton Siegal notes succinctly: "Video strips us of our defenses. It casts an impartial eye on us that doesn't lie or subtly distort what we see to fit our own image of ourself as all humans tend to do when they lack the objective view videotape provides."[15]

A third related concept is that of modeling. Modeling uses a standard of appropriate behavior that may be taped or live. The viewer is encouraged to exhibit similar behavior. These imitative attempts may also be videotaped so that feedback may be given. This is termed perceptual modeling to distinguish it from symbolic modeling, which refers to reading how an action is performed.[16] Self-confrontation then allows the learners to compare and subsequently improve their imitative attempts.[17]

In a course on group dynamics, Hardin, et al. offered an experiential learning opportunity that was facilitated by videotaping. The goal of the course was to "help the student learn how they relate to others and some systematic and predictable ways in which groups operate." In a sense, the videotaping provides a double group experience. One group is formed to be videotaped and a second group evolves when the work of analyzing the on-screen dynamic takes place.[18]

The fourth related concept is simulation. Mary Manderino defines simulation as "a deliberate attempt to recreate or simulate 'real-life' situations in a concrete manner. ..." She evaluated two versions of a cardiac arrest simulation for their stress-eliciting capacity. Videotape recordings of the subjects' responses to the simulation were rated by observers. There were no significant differences between the two groups; however, task performance of senior baccalaureate nursing students in cardiopulmonary resuscitation and memory of medications were below expected standards. This study demonstrated one way in which simulation can be combined effectively with videotape recording.[19]

Crowley, et al. used videotaped simulated encounters with families to teach community health. Groups of students acted as families and were thus able to experience both sides of the therapeutic relationship. Faculty and peers reviewed the tapes together, giving each other positive reinforcement and suggestions for changes. Over time faculty using this strategy developed a list of common pitfalls encountered by students. The video simulations also helped prepare the students for real encounters with families.[20]

CONDITIONS

Videotaping for instruction as well as evaluation of learning can be successfully used in a variety of settings and can meet a variety of objectives and outcomes. It is a preferred method of instruction when there is a limited amount of time available to the learner. Through the use of videotape, the learner is able to determine when and for how long to devote time to a particular educational offering.

Video has become almost a staple in many homes; thus more and more students and professionals will have had some exposure to the technology and may be more at ease in using it as a tool for learning.

Videotape is also useful as an instructional aid when distance is a factor. An instructional session can be recorded on video and transmitted to the learner either directly on a television monitor in the class, or by mailing the tape for the learner to use in a playback unit at another location.

As a tool for evaluation and subsequent learning projection, videotaping is without equal in that it provides a visual as well as audio record for the teacher and the learner. The student cannot deny any actions or words. It is thus possible to individualize the learning experiences for the student based on an evaluation of performance. Videotaping is also helpful in recording the motion components of behavior that frequently are missed in the learner's recall of the experience or, at times, by the teacher's direct observation. Having the videotape as a backup helps when the learner, upon reviewing the tape, is aware of errors before they are pointed out by the teacher. This frequently reduces the negative component of thinking that the teacher is "picking on me" or is only aware of the "insignificant."

The videotape record also allows the teacher to support positive behaviors more effectively, especially if a pattern of behavior is noted that can be pointed out to the learner. Finally, as also mentioned previously, videotaping allows the learner to gain an appreciation of the growth that takes place when learning occurs. By keeping "samples" of earlier performances, the learner can have a record of changes that occur as abilities are developed.

Video can be effectively used with all levels of learners. It can be used with beginning students as an introduction to the activities of the professional, and it can also be used as a way to preview clinical environments for the learner as a means to reduce anxiety.[21] It can be used to teach beginning psychomotor skills or beginning-to-advanced communications skills with groups as well as with individuals. Advances in the technology of combining computers and video through the use of interactive disks allow for its use in more cognitive or conceptual activities that teach problem-solving skills.[22]

All topics relevant to professional nursing appear to be appropriate for videotape learning. Frequently videotapes are used to provide discussion stimuli, since they are more able to approximate "real life" through the use of motion as well as sound. They are equally useful for demonstration of skills—both cognitive and psychomotor—by using motion and sound. A sequence of videotaped sessions over time can be used as quick visual reference source for students. One very creative use of videotape was reported by Flynn and DeVoss. They reported on their use of videotaping to record career perspectives from retired professionals in an extended-care facility. They interviewed several elderly nurses and recorded the interviews on videotape in a program they called "I Remember: Nursing." The video was then presented in a preprofessional class and, according to the students, resulted in creative learning.[23]

Learning objectives are as individual as the creativity of the people using the video equipment. In general, objectives should include consideration of the need for introduction or context setting prior to using video as a tool or technique. If the video is to be used for evaluation, appropriate feedback should be planned. This feedback should generally be faculty mediated and should include identification of the positive as well as the negative aspects of the performance. If the video uses emotional stimuli to provoke discussion, then a debriefing session should be included in the planning. Learners of all levels need reinforcement experiences and supporting experiences to ensure that learning will have long-term positive effects on development of ability and knowledge.

Videotaping can provide additional flexibility for faculty and in some cases may save time, thus allowing them to spend time in other ways. Graf describes using video for return demonstrations of psychomotor skills in conjunction with the traditional methods. Video returns required 1.8 hours less per student per semester.[24]

TYPES OF LEARNERS

In addressing the kind of learner who would benefit from this type of instruction, some consideration must be given to the philosophy of learning of both the learner and the teacher. One concept that has been identified in the literature and that deserves consideration is the notion of learning-style preference and learning strategy appropriate to learner preference. Ostmoe and colleagues discuss considerations of learning style in selected learning strategies, maintaining that learning style is considered an "attribute, characteristic, or quality . . . that interacts with instructional circumstances in such a way as to produce differential learning achievement."[25] They further suggest that when learning preference is considered, that instruction is then viewed as an active two-way communication process. Further, when the learner participates in such a way as to have input into the learning, there is a greater probability that the learner will identify the learning as self-relevant and will learn for self-improvement. Burnard describes an approach that is structured to include time for individual reflection as well as peer assessment. His model also allows the learner to choose the type of feedback desired: positive only, negative only, or both.[26]

Finley, et al. used videotape as a means to teach and evaluate interpersonal skills. They identified several factors to consider in maximizing the benefits of videotape. These include consideration of the learner. In addressing the learner, consideration of self-concept was identified as "crucial." In order for the learner to engage in self-evaluation associated with videotaping, thought should be given to the learner's sense of body image and level of self-concept. If these elements are positive, that is, if the learner's self-perception is positive, more benefits can be achieved from the use of videotape to enhance learning. The learner is able more accurately to attend to the positive as well as the negative performance aspects captured by the camera, and with supportive feedback is able to plan actively how the performance and subsequent learning can be enhanced.[27] Carver and Tamlyn supported these findings in their study of sources of stress in videotaping. A majority of the students in their study reported learning had occurred even when they did "not feel comfortable viewing themselves on tape."[28]

Feedback from graduates about the videotaping experience conducted by Hardin, et al. supports the idea that though the process is difficult, it is one of the students' most valuable learning experiences.[29]

To make video a productive learning experience, the student must experience the process in a practice or learning situation before doing it for evaluation. Second, the student must have support during the viewing and subsequently during feedback. This is most frequently a responsibility of the teacher, as is discussed in a later section.

Philip J. McSweeney, addressing video's still-untapped potential, identified some capacities of video technology. Video offers flexibility in terms of production and use, and immediate playback; the user can immediately view the performance after it has been recorded. Video can be conveniently stored, and the equipment required to produce the video (the camera) is becoming more and more compact, thus eliminating some storage problems for equipment as well as facilitating storage of the tape. A great deal of material can be stored on a three-hour tape that is the size of a small sampler box of chocolates!

Another feature of video as identified by McSweeney is the capacity to present reality. Portable equipment can be taken into real health care environments and unobtrusively record material for educational use.

Viewpoint can be controlled in the production of the video by considering camera angle, lighting, distance, and color during the recording. Time can also be manipulated through the use of video. One can shorten time, through editing, or lengthen time by pausing at intervals to ensure that the object of the learning is understood to that point. One can also slow the action so that learners can appreciate detail that is necessary in some procedures.[30]

RESOURCES

Equipment needed to use this technique is increasingly inexpensive and can usually be made available relatively easily. In some instances equipment can be rented until purchase decisions are made.

All decisions on equipment depend on one's need and budget. Minimally, a camera is needed, preferably one with a proven record of dependability. One also needs videotape and a playback unit, called a videocassette recorder (VCR). VCRs are becoming more and more common in both school and health care settings. Thus, for example, students can take a videotape of the procedure with them to the unit or setting and review it immediately prior to performance. If the institution has a media center, there is also the benefit of the availability of editing equipment and studio space to record more professional presentations.

It is a great advantage to have resource people, though explicit written instructions can assist the faculty member and students who have gained some expertise. Knowledgeable technicians are extremely helpful to the novice and do a great deal to reduce anxiety for both the person using the equipment and the individual or individuals being recorded.

USING THE METHOD

An example of how to use the technique follows in some detail. It is important to note that traditionally there has been some resistance to using this method of teaching-learning. At times the teacher may be concerned about accusations of letting TV replace the human component of teacher-learner interaction.

While this potential remains, a teacher who understands the challenge of technology will be delighted at the potential this tool makes available. In the clinical environment, for instance, the teacher frequently experiences the frustration of not being able to be with students all the time. By using the video camera to record some of the student activities, the teacher can indeed have individual time with the student at a time that is more convenient to both. In this way, the teacher can pace the learning and can ascertain how much learning has taken place.

The method is also invaluable as a tool to address the unique and individual learning styles of students. Because the image, the sound, and the motions are recorded permanently, the learner can review material at leisure. The tape can be stopped to review a particular detail, or it can be moved quickly to areas that need more concentration.

The most important thing needed to use video as a teaching-learning strategy in nursing is creativity and a willingness to try. Schuster suggests that "nurse educators often feel that something could be done a better way, yet hesitate to develop a solution." She maintains that "not only must the educator recognize the need for a new approach, the educator must be able to say 'Great, I'll try it.'"[31] It is suggested that a positive attitude and a willingness to experiment with the use of new technologies of video will greatly enhance not only the growth of the learner but also the teacher.

The teaching role in the use of videotape technology is extremely important to a successful outcome. Numerous studies indicate that feedback, teacher attitude, and self-concept of the student are critical factors. "It is not taken for granted that videotape playback of itself will improve performance. Results indicate the primacy of teacher comment in the feedback loop. The feedback alone does not seem to be a good substitute for teacher comment."[32]

Bearing these factors in mind, the teacher should do the following:

- Demonstrate a willingness to accept self-confrontation and agree to be videotaped in some format.
- Know the individual learners and consider their readiness for this type of experience.
- Establish a trusting relationship with the learners.
- Establish a supportive, nonthreatening climate for learning to help allay fear and anxiety.
- Be familiar with the video equipment and comfortable with its use so that the students can make better use of it.
- Provide the student with a comprehensive, careful orientation to the experience that includes specific outcomes, objectives, and detailed procedural information.
- Be available for discussion immediately after the experience and give open, honest, unambiguous, and focused feedback in a psychologically safe setting.
- Assure learners of absolute confidentiality.

There is always a degree of anxiety in people when they are videotaped for the first time, although the inhibiting effects seem to disappear over time.[33] As we approach the end of the twentieth century, however, increasing numbers of nursing students and professional nurses in practice will have had prior experience with video feedback. At the very least, individuals are now becoming more comfortable with telematics, the term applied to new information technologies that bring together video, computers, and satellites in communication systems.[34] "Videotape feedback presupposes a sufficiently strong self-concept and sense of competence so that the learner can take . . . even disagreeable information about himself and use it productively."[35]

In approaching this type of learning experience, then, it is advantageous for students to do the following:

- Assess their own anxiety level with regard to this experience, and choose appropriate ways to alleviate it.
- Try to approach this experience with a relaxed, open, confident attitude.
- Identify individual learning needs related to objectives.
- Conscientiously complete assigned preparatory readings and other assignments given in conjunction with the experience.
- Be prepared to take an active role in the learning experience—the key word is *participation.*
- Express concerns and ask questions—learner input is critical.

POTENTIAL PROBLEMS

If faculty are new to this type of teaching experience, they need to become familiar with it. One or several hands-on practice sessions to allow them to become familiar with the equipment is good preparation.

Avoiding problems with equipment and physical setting also entails careful planning and coordination with technical personnel. A cooperative working relationship with the staff of a resource center is essential.

As literature reveals that many persons are threatened by videotaping, student resistance can be high. If resistance is not overcome by practice sessions, alternate teaching-learning forms should be used.

The following example demonstrates use of videotaping with undergraduate students, although the strategy is appropriate for any student group. The example shows its use to teach interpersonal communication. Students in the example had an opportunity to develop skills throughout their baccalaureate program through recordings on a videotape.

Example
Using Videotaping To Teach Group Dynamics
Pauline M. Loewenhardt

The videotape method was selected as a teaching-learning strategy for junior-level nursing students' introduction to group dynamics. The class in which this method was used met every other week for two hours. During the first hour, the group met as a whole for didactic presentations. During the second hour the students met in small groups with an instructor. These small seminar groups remained together with the same instructor for the entire six quarters of the program. Although this particular example is specific to first-quarter content, this type of learning experience could easily be used as a baseline videotape in an ongoing sequence. This baseline tape would be used as a comparison with later tapes to show development in interpersonal skills.

Course Overview

The course introduces the student to the profession of nursing. Emphasis is placed on the student role in the profession and the responsibility expected as a member of the profession. Through small group participation students are encouraged to recognize the benefit of peer support and critique of their ideas. In order to pass the course, the student must attend all class sessions, demonstrate relevant preparation and participation, and complete all assignments. The videotaping experience is used in the unit on basic group dynamics to help students observe and critique both their own and others' behavior in groups.

Unit objectives related to basic group dynamics include the following:

- Define group dynamics.
- Compare and contrast effective and ineffective groups.
- Identify the components of effective communication.
- Identify the transaction of the decision-making process within a group.

Methodology

Students are given information about the assignment as part of the syllabus for the course (see Exhibit 15–1). As preparation, faculty and students participate in an introductory videotaping session at the beginning of the course. In this initial experience each individual faculty member and student is videotaped while giving a brief (one- to two-minute) self-introduction. Since most of the students

Exhibit 15–1 Videotape Instructions

Students' Instructions for Videotape of Group Interaction

The purpose of this assignment is to

1. provide guided experience for learning group dynamics,
2. demonstrate your ability to participate in a task-oriented small group,
3. assist you in evaluating your own behaviors as well as those of other group members, and
4. demonstrate the ability to accept constructive criticism.

Process

1. Arrangements for videotaping of your seminar group will be made by your instructor through the LRC (Learning Resource Center) at a time convenient for the group.
2. The group task will be assigned by your instructor. Time needed for the actual taping will be 45 to 60 minutes.
3. Once the tape is completed, it will be viewed by your seminar group and instructor during a feedback session.
4. You may also view the tape on your own as often as you like.
5. Strict confidentiality will be maintained; only you and your seminar group and your instructor will view the tape. After the learning experience is finished, the tape will be erased.
6. Write a brief synopsis.

do not know each other and do not know the faculty, this is a way for all to become acquainted. It also familiarizes everyone with the video equipment. The tape is shown during the first class meeting as a way of introducing people, and as an explanation of the videotaping assignment for the unit of group dynamics. This first experience in front of a camera also provides an opportunity for the students to focus on themselves during the viewing without the pressure of learning content.

A typical faculty manual would include the following:

- the videotaping assignment from the syllabus (Exhibit 15–1)
- faculty guidelines (Exhibit 15–2)
- conducting the feedback session (Exhibit 15–3)
- possible problems and concerns, and how to avoid them
- evaluation tools

Technical assistance should be arranged for all taping sessions with staff from the learning resource center at the institution. It is usually not necessary to have

Exhibit 15–2 Videotaping Guidelines

Faculty Guidelines for Using Videotaping

The purpose of these guidelines is to help you and your students use videotape technology. The teaching role is extremely important to a successful outcome. Numerous studies indicate that teacher attitude, honest feedback, and a supportive, nonthreatening climate for learning are critical factors. Bearing these factors in mind, it is helpful to do the following:

- Agree to be videotaped yourself so that you will have first-hand knowledge of what the student experiences.
- Know the individual learners and consider whether they are ready for this type of experience.
- Establish a trusting relationship with the learner.
- Provide a supportive, nonthreatening climate for learning.
- Become familiar with the operation of the video equipment.
- Be knowledgeable about the concept and rationale for use of the technique.
- Be available for discussion immediately after the videotaping session and give open, honest, unambiguous, focused feedback.
- Assure students of absolute confidentiality by erasing tapes after the experience. Obtain written consent for videotaping.

Exhibit 15–3 The Feedback Session

Conducting the Feedback Session

The following seven guidelines are excerpts and not meant to be exhaustive. They are offered as tips culled from broad reading. Please feel free to add your own comments to the list.

1. Keep the feedback session focused on content-related objectives.
2. Conduct the feedback sessions, and for that matter, all seminar meetings, as practice sessions in group dynamics. That is, define the task, look at both content and process, and evaluate the outcome.
3. Guide the group's analysis of its own process, and assist students to examine group and individual dynamics.
4. Point out differences in participatory styles and how they can contribute to the group process.
5. Avoid labels like good/bad, best/worst, but point out how each group is unique, because of variables such as size, values, goals, history, status, and so on.
6. Acknowledge the presence of competition and its effect on the process.
7. Assist students to acknowledge the anxiety associated with self-revelation, and point out that this is what we often expect of patients.

technical staff present for the sessions, but they should be available if there is a problem. It is also helpful to have written instructions for operation of the equipment available to students and faculty.

To summarize, orientation to the videotaping experience should include the following for all those involved.

1. description of videotaping as a teaching-learning strategy
2. rationale for using this strategy
3. role expectations of students, faculty, and technical staff
4. introduction to the equipment and technical staff
5. procedure for the learning experience
6. procedure for the feedback sessions
7. common problems encountered and how to prevent and/or solve them
8. evaluation methods and facilitation of feedback from students

---

NOTES

1. C. Clift, A Synthesis of Research in the Use of Audio-Visual Replay for Instructional Development: A Selected Bibliography of Videotape Utilization (Bethesda, Md: ERIC Document Reproduction Service, 1973), ED-85 785:2.

2. M. O'Connel, Immediate Feedback, Delayed Feedback and Perceptual Cues and Inquiry Verbal Interactions, *Journal of Counseling Psychology* (November 1974):536.

3. Clift, A Synthesis of Research.

4. M.K. Shaffer and I. Pfeiffer, Television Can Improve Instruction, *Journal of Nursing Education* 15, no. 6 (November 1976):3–8; L.L. Eggert, Challenge Exam in Interpersonal Skills, *Nursing Outlook* 23, no. 1 (November 1975):707–710; B. Finley, et al., Maximizing Videotaped Learning of Interpersonal Skills, *Journal of Nursing Education* 18, no. 1 (January 1979):33–41.

5. M.L. Menikheim and M.B. Ryden, Designing Learning to Increase Competency in Interpersonal Communication Skills, *Journal of Nursing Education* 24, no. 5 (May 1985):216–218; M. Anderson and B. Gerrard, A Comprehensive Interpersonal Skills Program for Nurses, *Journal of Nursing Education* 23, no. 8 (October 1984):353–355.

6. M. Manderino, et al. Evaluation of a Cardiac Arrest Simulation, *Journal of Nursing Education* 25, no. 3 (March 1985): 107–111; Shaffer and Pfeiffer, Television Can Improve Instruction.

7. Shaffer and Pfeiffer, Television Can Improve Instruction, 3.

8. Ibid., 7.

9. M. Breen and R. Diehl, Effect of Videotape Playback and Teacher Comment on Anxiety during Subsequent Task Performance (Bethesda, Md: ERIC Document Reproduction Service, 1970), ED 042 333; G. Salomon and F. McDonald, Pre and Post-test Reactions to Self-Viewing One's Performance on Videotape, *Journal of Educational Psychology* (August 1970):280–286; F. Fuller and B.A. Manning, Self-Confrontation Reviewed: A Conceptualization for Video Playback in Teacher Education, *Review of Educational Research* (Fall 1973):469–528; F. Fuller and H. Baker, Counseling Teachers: Using Video Feedback of Their Teaching Behavior (Bethesda, Md: ERIC Document Reproduction Service, 1970), ED 058 760.

10. V. Moran, Facilitating Self-Directed Learning: The Role of the Staff Development Director, in *Self-Directed Learning in Nursing*, ed. S. Cooper (Wakefield, Mass: Nursing Resources, Inc., 1981):71.

11. Clift, A Synthesis of Research.

12. D.C. Fitzgerald, et al., Improving Student Competency via Videotaping, *Nurse Educator* 17, no. 1 (1993):29, 32.

13. Fuller and Baker, Counseling Teachers.

14. Fuller and Manning, Self-Confrontation Reviewed.

15. B. Siegal, VTR In Sales Training, *Training* 4 (1967):39.

16. Clift, A Synthesis of Research, 3.

17. J.A. Sullivan, et al., Video Mediated Self-Cognition and the Amidon-Flanders Interaction Model in the Training of Nurse Practitioners' History Taking Skills, *Journal of Nursing Education* 14, no. 3 (August 1975):39–44.

18. S.B. Hardin, et al., The Video Connection: Group Dynamics on Screen, *Journal of Psychosocial Nursing and Mental Health Services* 21, no. 11 (1983):12–7, 20–1.

19. Manderino, et al., Evaluation of a Cardiac Arrest, 108.

20. C. Crowley, et al., Simulated Encounters Prime Community Health Students for Practice, *Nursing and Health Care* 7, no. 5 (May 1986).

21. S.T. Scheinblum, Film Modeling: Reducing Student Anxiety, *Nurse Educator* 12, no. 1 (January–February, 1987):20–23.

22. B.S. Allen, et al., The Effects of Practice in Detecting Technical Errors on Performance of a Simple Medical Procedure, *Computers in Nursing* 4, no. 1 (January–February 1986):11–16; P. Mitchell and J. Bolles, The Generic Videodisc: An Innovative Technology in Nursing Education, *Journal of Nursing Education* 26, no. 2 (February 1987):74–76.

23. P.T. Flynn and R.A. DeVoss, Using Retired Professionals to Videotape Career Perspectives for Educating University Students, *Educational Gerontology* 9 (1983):187–204.

24. M.A. Graf, Videotaping Return Demonstrations, *Nurse Educator* 18, no. 4 (1993):29, 32.

25. P.M. Ostmoe, et al., Learning Style Preferences and Selection of Learning Strategies: Consideration and Implications for Nurse Educators, *Journal of Nursing Education* 23, no. 1 (1984): 27–30.

26. P. Burnard, Using Video as a Reflective Tool in Interpersonal Skills Training, *Nurse Education Today* 11, no. 2 (1991):143–146.

27. Finley, et al., Maximizing Videotaped Learning.

28. J. Carver and D. Tamlyn, Sources of Stress in Third Year Baccalaureate Nursing Students, *Nursing Papers: Perspectives on Nursing* 17, no. 3 (Fall 1985):7–14.

29. Hardin, et al., The Video Connection.

30. P.J. McSweeney, Sight and Sound . . . Any Use for Video Found? Part 2: A Potential Still Untapped, *Nursing Education Today* 6, no. 5 (November 1986):223–227.

31. S.E. Schuster, Creative Permission: An Unrecognized Need, *Nurse Educator* 12, no. 3 (May–June 1987):16–18.

32. Breen and Diehl, Effect of Videotape Playback, 70.

33. Fuller and Manning, Self-Confrontation Reviewed.

34. M. Aydellote, Nursing's Preferred Future, *Nursing Outlook* 35, no. 3 (May–June 1987): 114–120.

35. Fuller and Baker, Counseling Teachers.

SUGGESTED READING

Anderson, M., and B. Gerrard. October 1984. A comprehensive interpersonal skills program for nurses. *Journal of Nursing Education* 23, no. 8:353–355.

Anderson, B., and N. Hrycak. Spring 1986. Video—A teaching strategy for learning group process. *Nursing Papers* 18, no. 1:5–18.

Bersky, A.K., et al. May 1987. Learning interdisciplinary and assessment skills through videotaped client interviews and collaborative planning. *Journal of Nursing Education* 26, no. 5:202–204.

Goldsmith, J.W. 1984. Effect of learner variables, media attributes, and practice conditions on psychomotor task performance. *Western Journal of Nursing Research* 6, no. 2:229–240.

Hardin, S.B., et al. November 1983. The video connection. *Journal of Psychosocial Nursing* 21, no. 11:12–21.

Menikheim, M., and M. Ryden. May 1985. Designing learning to increase competency in interpersonal communication skills. *Journal of Nursing Education* 24, no. 5:216–218.

Richards, A., et al. 1981. Videotape as an evaluation tool. *Nursing Outlook* 31, no. 1:35–38.

Scheinblum, S.T. January-February 1987. Film modeling: Reducing student anxiety. *Nurse Educator* 12, no. 1:20–23.

Part V

The Remote Faculty

The four strategies of Part V are similar to those of the last in that the faculty member is not as closely involved during the learning process as in some of the other approaches, and therefore a great deal of preplanning is necessary. Yet technology is not required for these approaches. Learning occurs and is reinforced by actually doing, that is, with hands-on experience with real-life events. Knowledge is acquired at the same time the student is involved in problem solving and decision making. All of the strategies are planned for supervised practice in critical thinking.

Chapter 16

Co-Consultant

Barbara Fuszard and Astrid Hellier Wilson

DEFINITION AND PURPOSES

Co-consultant is a teaching-learning technique that uses the consultant process and role for student synthesis and application of knowledge in the practice setting. The *consultation process* can be defined in many ways. It can be applied in most professional activity.[1] "In the pure sense, according to Haveloch, the consultant is a facilitator, helper, objective observer, and specialist in how to diagnose needs, how to identify resources, and how to retrieve from expert sources.... The underlying rationale for consultant is that only the client himself (the user) can determine what is useful for him."[2] The dependent-interdependent relationship between student and faculty member varies with the knowledge level and experience of the student.

The purpose to be achieved by the co-consultant teaching-learning strategy is to help the student become a true professional. The students are to acquire the approach of facilitator, helper, and objective observer—the ideal client-professional relationship. As the students gain knowledge and experience, they will also be able to offer the expert skills of a professional—data-gathering techniques, diagnosis skills, knowledge of resources, and access to expert sources. The co-consultant approach permits the students to learn with a real problem, and with as much support as they need at a particular level of professional development. The range of faculty support is from role-modeling in the clinical setting to remote support through availability in tutorials. The experienced professional, for example, a doctoral nursing student, would be ready to gain practical experience in the entire consultation process.

THEORETICAL RATIONALE

This strategy has roots similar to role-playing, with mental health consultation and role theory forming the structure upon which the strategy is built. Caplan's concept of the consultant-consultee-client relationship is most appropriate for the faculty member-student-client relationship of the co-consultant strategy. The concept of process consultation is especially appropriate for facilitator. It is a collaborative approach in which the consultant facilitates the client's use of his or her own strengths to resolve problems. The role of facilitator implies an egalitarian relationship between consultant and client, rather than that of decision maker to troubled client.

Carl Rogers' humanist approach offers client-centered therapy, where consulting approaches are concerned with client desires and feelings rather than finding an ideal problem solution. The skills that Rogers emphasizes for the first stage (entry) of the consultant-client relationship are the approaches the co-consultant process wishes to teach the young professional—"communication of respect, genuineness, and accurate empathy."

Lewin's force-field-analysis model offers the consultant relationship an analytical approach to description of the environment in which the problem is occurring. This knowledge permits indirect intervention by suggesting change in one part of the environment. McGregor's Theory Y offers a basis for measuring group characteristics such as trust, conflict, communication, and team goals. He suggests the consultant use this information to provide clues to the group on how group effectiveness can be improved. Schein, the father of "process consultation," suggests the consultant's role is to provide "insight" into the interpersonal dynamics involved in the problem, so that they can be structured into a workable frame.[3]

Role theory enters the co-consultant teaching-learning strategy in the relationship of the faculty member to the student. With the young professional the relationship is one of role-modeling for the student, with gradual distancing permitting the student to take over more of the responsibilities as knowledge and skills grow.[4]

CONDITIONS

Co-consultant strategies are valuable for the very young professional student, to inculcate early the professional relationships expected of the graduate. The master's and doctoral students will benefit by developing skill in the complete consultation role.

A special situation can make the co-consultant strategy a method of choice. When there are no professional role models in the setting, it is incumbent upon the faculty member to meet this need. Sister Dorothy Sheehan contends that in hospitals, where most nursing today is practiced, professional nursing services do not exist.[5] If nursing students are learning in these settings, they must have faculty role models to demonstrate the practice of professional nursing.

This method is also ideal for individualizing instruction based upon the student's level of understanding. The faculty member can maintain direct contact with the student, or any level of distancing, depending upon the learning needs of the student.

The co-consultant teaching strategy is an ideal adult learning tool. The student is permitted to work within the existing level of competence and to grow during the experience. The problems are real life, in a real health care setting, offering experiential problem solving. The relationships among facilitator, student, and client evidence mutual respect. This strategy's greatest contribution to adult learning is probably its adaptability to the needs of the individual student. The exercise also permits evaluation of self, work, personal relationships, and social structure in the process of assisting a real client.

A first requirement of the consultation, of course, is a client with a problem. There must be the ability to travel and relatively unstructured time periods for the consultation interaction, both with the client and between co-consultants. Unless group consultation is possible, such as in the example below, there must be more time allotted to the exercise than normal classroom hours. A consultation relationship that can be evaluated, and that can be completed in the time available, must be planned. A co-consultant activity calls for a great deal of planning, and a certain amount of flexibility on the part of all, to meet both client and educational needs. Within the planning, the relationships and responsibilities must be clearly outlined for all parties.

The co-consultant strategy is applicable to almost any content. As the student advances in knowledge and skill and the faculty member begins to withdraw, it becomes increasingly more important that the problem area be in the expertise of the student. The novice nurse will need to learn professional relationships, whereas the advanced student will be involved with the whole consultation process, including expertise in the content area.

TYPES OF LEARNERS

This method is appropriate for the senior undergraduate student, especially the R.N., master's, and doctoral students. Nurses who are experts in their clinical fields are often called upon to offer consultation (formal or informal) to other nurses in nearby institutions. Staff development through co-consultation would prepare them well for the professional aspects of consultation and the entire consultation process, which would enable their expertise in the content area to be put to best use.

RESOURCES

Resources needed emphasize time, especially with beginning professional students, as the relationship is usually a 1:1 faculty-student relationship, and at best calls for an individualized approach to each student. Material resources are not indicated, not even classroom space, as consultations take place within the client agency, and meetings between faculty and student are tutorials.

USING THE METHOD

Frances Lange discusses the five stages of consultation, a logical progression of planned change activities that are followed in the co-consultant method.

1. entry
2. goal setting
3. problem solving
4. decision making
5. termination

Entry is accomplished by the faculty member for the novice professional, as described in the example. With faculty guidance, the more advanced student will be able to negotiate this difficult step. In this stage both consultant and client explore the nature of the problem and negotiate the responsibilities and outcomes of the relationship. In this stage a contract is developed.

Goal setting provides a blueprint for the consultation relationship. It is the beginning of the planning stage, and includes "approaches, objectives, tactics, and possible activities that will achieve the worthwhile goal."[6] Again with the novice professional, the faculty member will role-model the goal-setting activities, with the students contributing to the degree they are able.

Problem solving, and the identification of alternative actions, is the third stage of consultation. Decision making involves analyzing the alternative actions and permitting an informed decision to the problem for the next step. The final step, *termination*, should have been part of the initial plan between client and consultant, and should leave both with feelings of satisfaction and accomplishment.

The example shows a slight change from the five stages outlined by Lange. As outside consultants, faculty and students are contracted to assess, evaluate, and recommend. Other than gathering data from the client, the work of the consultants is to compare findings to a national standard, to report these findings, and to make recommendations of how to meet these standards where deficiencies exist.

The co-consultant teaching-learning method has additional steps added to the consultant role, in which the faculty member and student interact to meet the learning objectives. They include study of the consultant role, objectives of the educational experience, and plans for the first interface between student and client. During the consultant stages, the faculty member maintains contact with the student in the setting or through tutorials. This permits the student to raise concerns and problems, and the faculty member to assess the learning level and learning needs of the student during the process. It also permits immediate planning for each subsequent stage of consultation. Final meetings at the end of the consultation permit faculty-student evaluation of the consultation as a learning experience.

The faculty member's role has been identified in the stages of consultation and elsewhere above, and was identified as changing depending upon the knowledge-skill level and growth of the student. The student role moves quickly from passive to active, and from dependent to interdependent in the process of co-consultation. The student may move at an independent rate through the mentioned roles, and this calls for self-direction and self-motivation to take a more active, interdependent role in the consultation.

POTENTIAL PROBLEMS

There will be confusion of the use of the consultant role as a teaching-learning strategy if the teacher lacks understanding of the consultation process itself. Additional problems will arise if the teacher does not individually assess student readiness for a specific level of dependence-interdependence.

Inappropriate selection of client and/or of student can cause problems in the consultation setting. The faculty member will avoid problems with client selection by spending time and resources to get to know the client well, and to establish a firm contract. The entry stage of the consultation process, therefore, is the critical point for prevention of such problems. Not all students possess the poise and maturity desired for a clinical experience so visible to the public and so dependent on human interaction skills. And not all faculty members have the privilege of choosing the students who will be assigned to this experience. The potential problem student will have to be assigned carefully, after great thought and exploration of client situations available.

A faculty member's expectations for the students and for the agency may be mutually incompatible, causing an ineffectual consultation process and learning process. Again, time and careful study during the entry stage will reduce the chance for such occurrences later in the process. A final limitation of this approach would be in situations offering few consultant opportunities. The faculty member will need to view the catchment area creatively!

The example was modified to offer a group experience to novice consultants, students in master's programs. The group approach with the facilitator co-consultant with the students at all times permits economies of this learning strategy, which otherwise could be prohibitive with novice students.

Example
Consultation for Nursing Service Standards

Barbara Fuszard

The co-consultant method offers the novice student an opportunity to develop professional behaviors. It also serves to replace preceptorships when prepared preceptors are unavailable. Such was the case when the nursing faculty sought practicum experiences for nursing administration students in a rural state where there was only one master's-prepared nurse administrator in the entire state. To the benefit of the hospitals of the state, the rural hospitals obtained free, quality consultation services for their nursing departments through this teaching activity.

In a monthly meeting of the Nursing Service Administrators Group, to which this faculty member was a regular invited guest, the faculty member explored with the nurse administrators their interest in having her and her students offer consultation on nursing service standards. The co-consultant group offered to assess nursing departments on criteria from the Joint Commission on Accreditation of Healthcare Organizations[7] (Joint Commission) and the *Standards for Organized Nursing Services and Responsibilities of Nurse Administrators Across all Settings*[8] by the American Nurses' Association (ANA). This topic was chosen because the rural hospitals had avoided applying for Joint Commission accreditation because of expense, but the nurse administrators wanted to be assured that they were meeting the same standards as Joint Commission hospitals. They also expressed interest in meeting ANA standards.

Before the faculty member had completed her presentation, one of the nurse administrators had already interrupted, saying "First, first!" All of the nurse administrators expressed interest in having the consultant group work with their departments, even those larger hospitals that had Joint Commission accreditation. One nurse administrator said, "The Joint Commission is coming this fall. Help us see if we are ready." And the nursing home nurse administrators said, "Hurry and finish with the hospitals, so that you can help us."

With this reception, the issue of entry for the consultation group was academic. The faculty member took a strong leadership role, because the students were beginning graduate students. Objectives of the student experience were as follows:

- to offer experience of leadership as facilitator, helper, objective observer, and specialist in nursing service standards
- to develop data-gathering skills through skillful interview and observation
- to synthesize the concurrent roles of the consultant.

While students studied from a reading list on the role of the consultant, the faculty member visited the hospital to meet with the nurse administrator and hospital administrator. In lieu of a consultation contract, the faculty member elected to use the introductory forms of a scientific report. The manual utilized was W. Paul Jones, *Writing Scientific Papers and Reports*, 4th ed. (Dubuque, Iowa: Wm. C. Brown Company, 1960) to give the students a format that they could use in the future for varied reports. The acceptance letter written by the faculty member included the following:

> Thank you again for inviting my students and me to serve as volunteer consultants to your hospital for the purpose of developing guidelines for the Joint Commission and ANA standards in your nursing department. We are tentatively planning to come to your hospital for the entire day, Wednesday, 10 November, and to have a written comprehensive report to you by Christmas. Please let me know if 10 November is open for you and your staff.
>
> Our plans at this time will be to ask you to send us certain documents that you have already prepared, so that we may study them before coming. We then plan to spend as much time as you can give us with you, with the nursing personnel, and any patients who "just want to talk" to us. After our visit we will be in touch with you through the mail or by phone for any additional information or will schedule another visit with you as needed.
>
> Our students right now are studying philosophy, purpose and objectives, budgeting, staffing, labor relations, and orientation of the new graduate. They are very excited about the topics. They will cover all the areas outlined by the Joint Commission before coming to you.
>
> Be assured that we will change nothing at your hospital. We will make recommendations and offer standards only in written form, and you are free to do with these materials as you see fit. Our hope is that they will be of real value to you. I will be available after Christmas to personally work with you if you want help in implementing any of the materials.

A large initial task faced by the first group of students was to review the Joint Commission and ANA standards, and to find a way to mesh these criteria for purposes of the consultation visit. The following is an example of ANA and Joint Commission criteria being grouped for purposes of analysis.

ANA Standard II

Organized Nursing Services are Administered by Qualified and Competent Nurse Administrators (p. 3).

ANA Criteria

The nurse executive is a registered nurse who holds a baccalaureate degree in nursing and a graduate degree in nursing or a related field from a program that includes organizational science and management concepts. Certification in nursing administration by a nationally recognized nursing organization is recommended (p. 4).

Joint Commission Standard

Nursing services are directed by a nurse executive who is a registered nurse qualified by advanced education and management experience (p. 145).

Joint Commission Criteria

If the hospital utilizes a decentralized organizational structure there is an identified nurse leader at the executive level to provide authority and accountability for, and coordination of, the nurse executive functions (p. 145).

The criteria were organized under the ANA standards because the Joint Commission standards were in various parts of the manual, and under different services, and would have made organization under the Joint Commission standards more difficult. By the time this lengthy process was completed, the students knew well the Joint Commission and ANA standards for nursing services. Future classes of students had the benefit that the coordinated standards were on the word processor. Their task was to update the standards as they were changed by their sponsoring agencies.

The faculty member had some information to share about the hospital after her visit with the administrators. However, most of the material was yet to be gathered, and this data gathering called upon the observational and interviewing skills of the co-consultants. Three approaches were taken to obtain information for analysis.

First, each co-consultant accepted a section of the standards and determined which interview question to ask of the director of nursing. Second, each co-consultant asked to be attached to a member of the nursing staff for the day of visit, and planned to cover all the questions with this person. Third, each was assigned associated documents and equipment to survey, for final confirmation and information. For example, the student studying the emergency room was responsible for evaluating the classified level of ER service, and the appropriate nurse coverage and equipment appropriate for that level. The sources of information tapped in these ways permitted the co-consultants to verify observations and reporting, and to fill in gaps of information that would not be available from one common source.

Students were also responsible for a level of expertise in the area they would be investigating, such as staffing, budget, philosophy, and organizational charts. Time before the visit permitted these and similar topics to be covered in depth. Students individually searched and organized the literature, providing classmates with a comprehensive bibliography and actual materials that they felt were important for a top position in nursing administration. In addition to reviewing the two sources of criteria that Westwick states are the main criteria for institutional evaluation,[9] they analyzed the standards, using materials such as Cantor's book on the topic.[10] Thus armed with beginning knowledge of the institution, the standards and specific interviewing questions and/or planned observations for gathering data on specific topics, and beginning knowledge of the role of the consultant, the co-consultant experience began.

At the time of the consultation visit, each co-consultant was paired with a member of the nursing staff, and spent the greater share of the consultation visit with that person. Each co-consultant also had interview time with the director of nursing. Questions from the interview schedule, when addressed to the director of nursing, took longer than anticipated, as the director tended to provide richer amounts of data than had been anticipated. Otherwise the day went very much as planned.

The consultants also examined charts and records, and made observations in the specialty areas, such as the emergency room. The director of nursing, the hospital administrator, and the president of the board of trustees met with the entire group of consultants to answer final questions. At the close of the consultation visit the director of nursing was asked to send copies of all policies and procedures of the department for consultant use.

Content of the interviews, observations, and perceptions of the consultants were shared with one another, and then each consultant assumed responsibility for writing one part of the consultation report. Materials copied and forwarded to the group were used to supplement and/or confirm data gathered from the interviews and observations. Findings and recommendations were then developed for each standard and criterion of the two sets of standards.

An example of an ANA standard, and criteria related to that standard from ANA and the Joint Commission, with the student consultant findings and recommendations follows.

ANA Standard I

Organized Nursing Services Have a Philosophy and Structure that Ensure the Delivery of Effective Nursing Care (p. 3).

ANA Criteria

The philosophy of organized nursing services provides to individual nurses the authority and accountability for the clinical management of nursing practice (p. 3).

Joint Commission Criteria

Registered nurses evaluate current nursing practice and patient care delivery models to improve the quality and efficiency of patient care (p. 146).

Findings

The philosophy of nursing or the "authority and accountability for clinical management of nursing practice" (p. 3) statement does not clearly define nursing's role in the participation of the management of the division. At the time of the consultants' visit no committees were functioning. The director of nursing did attend the board of directors' meetings, but did not sit at the table with the administrator and board members.

Recommendations

Committees (such as infection control, pharmacy, medical records, hospital safety, quality assurance) should be established and meetings held on a regular basis. A qualified nurse should be included in the membership of all committees with impact on patient care.

* * * *

Preparing for the consultation visit, and in the classroom analytical period, students discussed how they could, or did, convey respect, genuineness, egalitarianism, and caring—the interpersonal behaviors that are part of the consultation process. This aspect of the co-consultant experience was the chief teaching-learning objective for this group of students. They evaluated their success by the responses and openness of administrators and nursing employees alike, attested to by the volumes of data gathered. They also considered these consultant qualities when writing and rewriting the "findings" and "recommendations" sections of the report, endeavoring to offer pertinent, objective data in a nonthreatening, caring, and appropriate way. A sign of the student success both during the visit and in the written report was evidenced by the director of nursing proudly holding aloft at the next Nursing Service Administrators' Group meeting her inch-thick report, and stating, "You know, we're pretty good!"

The letter of transmittal to the hospital and nursing administrators conveyed qualifiers of the work of this young co-consultant group, and offered further expert help. It read, in part:

> We are indebted to you and your employees for your help in gathering data, both printed and verbal. The candidness of both administration and nursing personnel helped to make the data significant and therefore valuable to you.
>
> Problems can be anticipated in working through some of the long-range suggestions of the report. I will be happy to continue to work with you on these items.
>
> Some of the recommendations will not be of value to you because the suggestions have already been implemented, and the consultants were unaware of the existence of materials or misinterpreted them. Other recommendations may be inappropriate to your institution. You are, of course, under no obligation to implement any of the recommendations of the consultants.
>
> Please feel free to call upon us, through me, if we can be of further assistance. . . .

Several classes of graduate nursing students were treated to a similar approach to the co-consultant teaching strategy. The expected benefits of the interpersonal-relationship part of the consultant process were experienced with each group. As members of future classes also differed in clinical backgrounds, individual applications of the teaching strategy were made with each class. Rural hospitals and nursing homes were found to welcome graduate nursing students in the co-consultant role.

NOTES

1. F. Lange, *The Nurse as an Individual, Group, or Community Consultant* (Norwalk, Conn: Appleton & Lange, 1987).

2. M. Kohnke, *The Case for Consultation in Nursing: Designs for Professional Practice* (New York: John Wiley & Sons, Inc., 1978).

3. Lange, *The Nurse as an Individual*, 34–39.

4. M.E. Hardy and M.E. Conway, *Role Theory: Perspectives for Health Professionals* (New York: Appleton-Century-Crofts, 1978).

5. Lange, *The Nurse as an Individual*, 53.

6. Ibid.

7. *1994 Accreditation Manual for Hospitals* (Oakbrook Terrace, Ill: Joint Commission on Accreditation of Healthcare Organizations, 1993).

8. American Nurses' Association, *Standards for Organized Nursing Services and Responsibilities of Nurse Administrators Across All Settings* (Kansas City, Mo: 1990).

9. C.R. Westwick, Evaluation of Nursing Organization and Structure, in *The Nurse Evaluator in Education and Service*, ed. A.G. Rezler and B.J. Stevens (New York: McGraw-Hill Publishing Co., 1978), 249–263.

10. M.M. Cantor, *Achieving Nursing Care Standards: Internal and External* (Wakefield, Mass: Nursing Resources, 1978).

SUGGESTED READING

(*Note:* Co-consultant as a teaching-learning method does not appear in the literature. Readings here are limited to materials on consultation, especially consultation in nursing.)

Alphabetical list of consultants and consulting firms 1993. *Journal of Nursing Administration* 23, no. 7-8:70–132.

Chamberlain, G. 1994. Women consultants (letter). *British Medical Journal* 308:720.

Clark, M.J. Summer 1986. Factors enhancing the success of a consultation. *Nursing Administration Quarterly* 10, no. 4:1–8.

Clark, M.J. 1986. Planning a successful consultation. *The Facilitator* 12, no. 2:1–2.

Fuszard, B. 1979. Management concepts that work—Consultant in residence. *The Facilitator* 5, no. 6:2.

Grahame-Smith, D.G. 1993. An encounter with Beethoven's cleaning lady. *Lancet* 342:1315.

Kirkbride, M. 1992. A place for infants with HIV. *American Journal of Maternal Child Nursing* 17, no. 5:264.

McKenzie, J. 1983. Basic science department in a government-funded medical school. *Physiologist* 26, no. 5:278–280.

Rosenberg, H., and B. Polonsky. 1990. The role of nonphysician consultants as health-care educators in postgraduate programs of anesthesiology. *Academic Medicine* 65, no. 2:119–122.

Sakauye, K.M., and C.J. Camp. 1992. Introducing psychiatric care into nursing homes. *Gerontologist* 32, no. 6:849–852.

Twardon, C., and M. Gartner. 1992. A strategy for growth in home care: The clinical nurse specialist. *Journal of Nursing Administration* 22, no. 10:49–53.

Chapter 17

Guided Design

Barbara Fuszard

DEFINITION AND PURPOSES

Guided design is a teaching strategy that involves small group problem solving. It is step-by-step practice in guided decision making, with the teacher modeling professional reasoning for real-world problems. It was "invented" by Dr. Charles Wales and Dr. Robert Stager in 1969, with funding by Exxon Educational Foundation under the IMPACT program.[1]

The purposes of guided design are as follows:

- teaching subject matter
- developing the decision-making skills to apply what has been learned to the solution of real-world problems,[2] and proposing to solve basic difficulties in conceptualization, reasoning, abstraction, summarization, interpretation, and problem solving

A byproduct of this education process is increased motivation, which in turn improves the students' retention of subject matter.

In this approach guided design adjusts attitude, reshaping educational approaches so the students learn content by facing real problems that demand the knowledge content they are supposed to learn. An anthropology professor stated: "Don't teach your students anthropology. Teach them to be anthropologists!"[3]

Traditionally, students are taught facts they will need to know in the future. By giving the students real problems to solve, they avoid forgetting and see immediate application to real life of the knowledge they learn. This promotes retention. The authors of guided design feel that the learners who are permitted to work through an ascending order of well-designed problems, actively seeking answers to problems rather than merely memorizing knowledge, will be not only better educated but stronger intellectually.[4] This approach has been shown to raise scores on the Watson-Glaser Critical Thinking Appraisal Instrument.[5] Other research showed a relationship between guided design and graduation grade-point averages (GPAs). Wales noted that regular students and transfer students graduated with similar grade points. After guided design was offered in the freshman year, regular students achieved 25 percent higher on graduating GPAs than the transfer students who did not have the benefit of the guided-design class.[6]

THEORETICAL RATIONALE

Wales and Hageman identified the theoretical foundation of guided design and designed a model to describe it as they compared the technique to the nursing process. They see the basic premise of guided design as the development of a whole person, a self-actualized person. Wales and Stager, originators of the guided design teaching process, saw the self-actualized person as one who could make decisions based on one's own knowledge and values. The goals for guided design (Figure 17–1) include the following:

- acquisition of knowledge
- awareness of values
- ability to make decisions

Wales and Hageman find this model most appropriate for nursing education. As one of the goals of nursing education is to prepare nurses who base decision making upon knowledge and values, guided learning of the decision-making process is vital. This teaching-learning process is based upon the work of educational leaders like Dewey, Bloom, Gagne, Skinner, and Bandura. It frees students to develop their own value system, without merely accepting the teacher's values. It is congruent with adult learning principles, where students work with and learn from peer group relationships, rather than teacher-pupil relationships, and deal with real-life problems.[7]

CONDITIONS

This teaching-learning method is appropriate both for academic nursing education programs and for staff development. It offers the real-world tie to

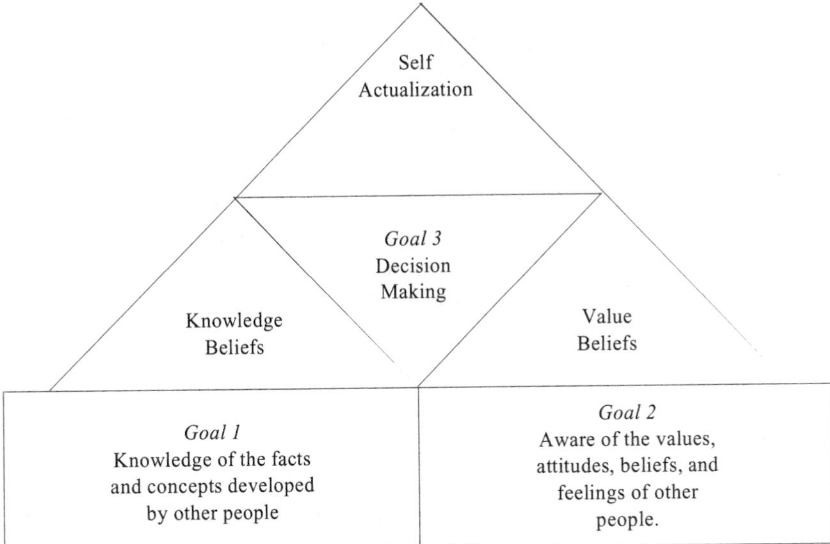

Figure 17–1 Theoretical Foundation of the Guided Design. *Source:* Reprinted from *Journal of Nursing Education,* Vol. 18, No. 3, p. 41, with permission of Charles B. Slack, Inc., © 1979.

theoretical information that motivates the jaded, burned-out student or disillusioned practitioner. It can be used to convey facts, to develop values, to stimulate motivation, and to ensure retention. This method has value in a wide variety of disciplines, and is especially appropriate to professional education because of decision-making and critical thinking benefits.

Although group working may prove difficult to grade, the problem is followed with an independent, similar project that permits individual evaluation of learning. Because of identified theoretical content, also, it is possible to use traditional testing techniques for acquired knowledge. Although like the case method, there is not one solution to any problem, the knowledge base gathered for the solution of the problem is identifiable and can be evaluated.

Size of the student group is not restrictive, but a minimum of five students should be in a group. As a faculty member is available to students as a resource person, multiples of five would limit the number of groups each faculty member could facilitate. Students must be in movable chairs or around tables so that they can face each other. The problem can be one that can be solved in one class period, or in one semester. The longer time periods permit the meeting of secondary objectives, such as learning how to find resources in the library.

The condition that depends exclusively upon the teacher is the time-consuming preparation of a guided-design packet. Preparation is a thoughtful exercise that must precede the classtime. After each problem packet is prepared, it must be tested before classroom use. Often the judgments of experts are necessary for the development of faculty feedback sections.

A number of learning activities take place simultaneously during a guided-design exercise. Students simultaneously develop both cognitive and process skills, are actively involved in their own learning, acquire specific knowledge of the field, learn to organize their knowledge, examine and develop attitudes and values, and incorporate their new knowledge into the lifelong learning they have acquired to date.[8]

TYPES OF LEARNERS

Guided design works at elementary school levels, as well as with college, graduate school, and professional students. Its lock-step approach and reliance on group process may have a stifling effect upon some students. As skills of critical thinking and decision making are sought, along with values development, the process seems ideal for the professional nursing student at the basic and master's levels.

RESOURCES

Resources include a classroom adaptable to small group work, predeveloped problem packets, teachers who know how to facilitate, and copies of the packets for each student.

USING THE METHOD

When the packet is to cover the work of a semester, all the theoretical content of the course must be identified, and that which is to be taught through guided design must be identified. A problem that will tap knowledge as great and diverse as the content for an entire course must be comprehensive and many-faceted.

The guided-design packet itself is a step-by-step slow-motion plan for decision making, with the teacher providing feedback at each step. If this experience is new to the students, it will have to be explained to them.

Wales and Stager offer a practice guided-design project called "The Fishing Trip: An Introduction to the Process of Decision-Making." An initial exercise shows the benefits of group work over individual (independent) work. The format then continues in the usual guided-design pattern of decision-making steps.

- Step A—Introduction.
- Step B—Identify information needs.
- Step C—Gather information.
- Step D—Perform a component analysis and generate possible solutions.
- Step E—Identify constraints.
- Step F—Select the best solution.
- Step G—Analyze possible solutions.
- Step H—Demonstrate synthesis.
- Step I—Evaluate possible solutions.
- Step J—Report the results and make recommendations.
- Step K—Implement the decision.
- Step L—Check the results.[9]

Blocks of class time are needed for the group work, as in all group-discussion techniques. In the example, students need "drop-out" time at Step B to identify information needs before they can continue the decision-making process.

In Step C the teacher can answer critics of the process of guided design who say, "But there is so much content they need to learn!" Any amount of background knowledge can be included here through readings. Additional exercises immediately apply this knowledge to real-world situations.

Step J, reporting results of group work, can become the written project report. The feedback given at this step could be the group grade for the project.

The faculty person develops the problem and the problem packet, and tests the packet before class time.This is the most time-consuming part of this teaching-learning activity. Faculty persons, not necessarily those who developed the packet, must then be available to the student groups as facilitators. They may provide additional questions or suggest resources that the group did not find on its own. Written feedback may be included with the packet, but on a separate page from the step, or can be distributed to the group members when they have completed the step. The writing of the response by the student group ensures a comparison point with the faculty feedback. Finally, the faculty member will evaluate the student work and assign a group grade for the completed packet.

The student is to function as a peer, a group member, sharing knowledge from life experiences as well as from reading the packet. Students also have responsibility for making the group process work—eliciting response from each other group member. Students are responsible for recording group decisions at each step and providing a complete report at the end of the exercise. If the group exercise is followed by an independent assignment drawing upon the same body of knowledge, individual students have the responsibility of completing this assignment independently.

POTENTIAL PROBLEMS

The guided design exercise can be only as good as the problem packet developed by the teacher. Development of the packet can be a time-consuming responsibility. The testing of the packet is an additional responsibility for the teacher. In developing a first problem packet, difficulty may be encountered in writing the feedback responses. Is the teacher/facilitator an expert in the area? Is there enough established documentation for a response, or is there some untapped resource out there that has not been found? What if a graduate student in the class knew more than a teacher/facilitator about the topic? Having to provide expert feedback for every step of the decision-making process forces the faculty member to do extensive class preparation, certainly a plus for the students! A statement may be added to almost every feedback: "Do you agree?" It permits student disagreement, and gives permission for student values to guide the discussion, without the overshadowing of the teacher's value system.

As is the case with all group work, some students may contribute little, and be carried along by their classmates. Thinking may be shallow, without deep value sharing and belief testing. The independent assignment can identify the students who need to test their thinking further, and the facilitator can quickly, through spot-checking, identify groups that are spending insufficient time in peer interaction.

Example

Guided-Design Project in Community Health Nursing

Saundra L. Turner

INSTRUCTION TO THE STUDENT

The following is a self-instruction guided-design project. The object of the guided design is to help you understand the process involved in ethical decision making.

First: The instructor will group students evenly.

Then: Read the instructions together. After each instruction section, stop and decide as a group what you would do at that point in the scenario. Then read what the nurses in the story do.

Written Assignment: Please list the values identified by your group and prioritize them at the end of the lesson.

Please Keep in Mind: The solutions of the nurses in this program should not be considered the BEST solutions, only THEIR solutions. There are no right answers. It is the process that is the object of this instruction.

I hope you enjoy the program.

Step A—Introduction

A community health nurse in a small, private, home health agency has received a referral for home care on a patient discharged from the hospital four days ago.

The discharge planner identified the following priorities: (1) to determine the status of the home situation, (2) to determine the patient's or care giver's ability to care for the patient, and (3) to assess needs for medication administration and dressing changes on a foot ulcer.

As a team member with another nurse they meet together to plan and determine other concerns and priorities before going to the patient's home.

Step B—Identify Information Needs

The nurses decided that since the referral form provided very little significant information and the patient had already been home for four days, they needed to predetermine what must be assessed before entering the home. They then made individual lists of information they needed to obtain.

Step C—Gather Information

Upon making the home visit, further information identified is as follows: The patient is a blind 64-year-old black female with insulin-dependent diabetes mellitus, high blood pressure, and a foot ulcer. The home is a two-room shack. There is a strong stench in the air. There are piles of trash and clothes throughout. The patient is lying on a bed in the front room. She states her son has left with her welfare check to have the heat turned on. She has not eaten today. Her medications are by her bed. She states that her son prepares them for her.

Upon further exploration of the home, one nurse discovers drug paraphernalia in the back room. The other nurse inspects the wound to determine the healing stage. She finds that, while it is granulating well, the dressing has slipped from the site. She rebandages the wound.

The nurses tell the patient they must return to the office to set up her care routine. They tell her to have the son call them when he returns.

They return to the office and ask themselves what are the major issues on which they can have impact and what can be changed in this situation.

Step D—Perform a Component Analysis and Generate Possible Solutions

Upon talking with the social worker, the nurses learn that the son has been a heroin user but currently is in a drug rehab program. The mother is the major source of support for the son, who was quite depressed while she was in the hospital. The social worker has arranged for Meals On Wheels to come daily for a few weeks. This service was to start today. The social worker states that there are no other family members nearby, but the neighbors are very supportive and offer a great deal of encouragement to the family.

Based on this information the nurses must consider what they can do for this family and what outcomes they hope to achieve.

Step E—Identify Constraints

The nurses decided that their next step was to determine what would keep the patient and her son from managing her home care.

Step F—Choose the Best Solution

Based on the identified constraints the nurses determined that they must evaluate and rank their best possible solutions.

Step G—Analyze Possible Solutions

In supporting the family's independence the nurses determined several factors that must be considered. The nurses listed the factors that they wanted to account for.

Step H—Synthesize Pertinent Factors

The nurses' next step was to use the factors they had identified in the development of a plan in the care of this patient.

Step I—Evaluate the Solution

After their contact with the son and the neighbor, the nurses evaluated their solution to determine whether they must choose another alternative or whether this approach could indeed be successful.

They found the son to be willing to learn but needing more instruction than they had anticipated. The neighbor was unwilling to administer the insulin but would provide support by checking on the family and cleaning and cooking for them. The patient was able to administer her own insulin.

Step J—Make Recommendations

The nurses must now decide on follow-up and further involvement with this family. They felt that an important part of that decision depended on their feelings about all that they had discovered. They decided to write down their concerns and identify their values in relation to them. They would then order their values to determine the most important one to them, to determine whether they would be able to deal with the conflicts and then be able to care further for this family.

NOTES

1. C.E. Wales, Data on New Educational Strategy: Guided Design, *Phi Delta Kappan* 60, no. 4 (December 1978):313, 314.
2. P. Ann Redden and R.P. Petriello, A Guided Design Approach to Developmental Science, *Journal of Chemical Education*, 57, no. 10 (October 1980): 712–715.
3. C.E. Wales and R.A. Stager, *Guided Design* (copyright 1977 by the authors), iv.
4. Ibid., 1.
5. Redden and Petriello, A Guided Design Approach.
6. Wales, Data on New Educational Strategy.
7. S.K. Wales and V. Hageman, Guided Design Systems Approach in Nursing Education, *Journal of Nursing Education*, 18, no. 3 (March 1979), 38–45.
8. R. deTornyay and M.A. Thompson, *Strategies for Teaching Nursing*, 3rd ed. (New York: John Wiley & Sons, Inc., 1987), 134, 135.
9. Wales and Stager, *Guided Design*, 4, 16.

SUGGESTED READING

Adams, A.B. May 1983. The guided design strategy in the biochemistry laboratory. *Journal of Dental Education* 47:317–320.

Borchardt, D.A. 1988. Performance and thinking skills: The battle between the conscious and the unconscious. Paper presented at the annual meeting of the Association for Theatre in Higher Education. San Diego, Calif. August. ERIC Document Reproduction Service No. ED298589.

Coscarelli, W.C., and G.P. White. Summer 1982. Applying the ID process to the guided design teaching strategy. *Journal of Instructional Development* 5:2–6.

DeTornyay, R., and M.A. Thompson. 1987. *Strategies for teaching nursing*. 3rd ed. New York: John Wiley & Sons, Inc.

Kneeshaw, S. 1988. Comparative history in the classroom: A lesson plan. *OAH Magazine of History* 3, no. 3–4:43.

Lawrence, D.C. April 1980. Guided design in the basic American government course. *Teaching Political Science* 7:321–328.

Miller, D.I. 1983. Performance-satisfaction theory and attitudes about the guided-design approach to instruction/training. *Psychology: A Quarterly Journal of Human Behavior* 20:31–33.

O'Hanlon, N. 1988. The role of library research instruction in developing teachers' problem solving skills. *Journal of Teacher Education* 39, no. 6:44–49.

Proceedings: A national conference on teaching decision-making. 1980. Morgantown, W.Va: Charles E. Wales.

Redden, P.A., and R.P. Petriello. October 1980. A guided design approach to developmental science. *Journal of Chemical Education* 57:712–715.

Selby, M.L., and D.M. Tuttle. June 1985. Teaching Nursing Research by Guided Design: A Pilot Study. *Journal of Nursing Education* 24:250–252.

Wales, C.E. September 1981. Teaching "process" with guided design. *Journal of College Science Teaching* 11:48, 49.

Wales, C.E., and R.A. Stager. 1978. *The guided design approach*. Englewood Cliffs, NJ: Educational Technology Publications.

Wales, S.K., and V. Hageman. March 1979. Guided design systems approach in nursing education. *Journal of Nursing Education* 18:38–45.

Chapter 18

Preceptorial Experience

Vickie A. Lambert, Jo-Ellen M. McDonough, Elizabeth F. Pond, and Joyce S. Billue

The teaching strategy preceptorial experience allows an opportunity for students to work with clinical experts in a specific health care setting while still under the guidance of a faculty member. This teaching strategy provides socialization into the role of the professional nurse and an opportunity for independent problem solving.

DEFINITION AND PURPOSES

As a method of clinical teaching for nursing students, the preceptorial experience has grown in popularity since the 1960s.[1] Both nurse educators and nurse administrators see such an experience as a means of assisting students in the transition from the idealistic academic setting into the reality-based service arena.[2] The experience tends to enhance clinical performance[3] and to facilitate role socialization.[4]

According to Shamian and Inhaber, a preceptorial experience can be defined as a clinical learning activity that utilizes unit-based nurses who are engaged in a one-to-one teaching experience with nursing students in addition to carrying out their regularly assigned responsibilities.[5] The preceptor serves as a role model and resource person and is immediately available to the student within the clinical setting.[6]

Source: Adapted with permission from Pond, E., McDonough, J.E., and Lambert, V., Preceptors' Perceptions of a Baccalaureate Preceptorial Experience, *Nursing Connections,* Vol. 6, No. 1, pp. 15–25, © 1993.

THEORETICAL RATIONALE

Role socialization provides the theoretical bases for the preceptorial experience. Socialization from a role perspective refers to the "process by which persons acquire the knowledge, skills, and dispositions that make them more or less able members of their society."[7] In the case of the preceptorial experience, society refers to professional nursing practice. The content learned in the process of role socialization encompasses both knowledge and understanding of the structure of the society (professional nursing practice), as well as the behaviors associated with the various positions within the societal structure.

CONDITIONS

The preceptorial experience is helpful in assisting students to take knowledge gained in the academic setting and transfer it to the reality-based service world. The experience provides a learning environment in which the student can become more self-directed and less faculty dependent. Independent problem solving is a primary outcome of a successful preceptorial experience.

TYPES OF LEARNERS

While the preceptorial experience can be used with any student, it appears to be most successful with students who are in the later part of their educational program. The students who appear most comfortable with the experience are self-motivated, self-directed, and challenged by independence. To enhance the success of the experience, the students must be able to identify and deal with their own strengths and limitations, to develop appropriate objectives and strategies for addressing specific learning needs, and to maintain open and appropriate communications with the preceptor and the faculty.

RESOURCES

The preceptorial experience can take place in any health care agency. It can be of any length, as long as adequate time is provided to meet the student's specific learning objectives. A major limitation to the success of a preceptorial experience is the availability and accessibility of qualified individuals to serve in the role of preceptor.

USING THE METHOD

The keys to a successful preceptorial experience are an orientation about the experience for students and preceptors, and the selection of appropriate preceptors. The orientation to the experience needs to focus on the goals and expectations of the experience; the responsibilities of the preceptors, the students, and the faculty; communication procedures; methods of evaluation; possible problems that can occur during the experience and their related solutions; and feelings about the preceptorial experience.

So that the preceptor can successfully fulfill the responsibilities of the role, nurse faculty, nurse administrators, and clinical agency personnel need to be capable of identifying and selecting preceptors who have appropriate characteristics. Characteristics identified as important can be clustered into three distinct groups: clinical nursing characteristics, professional characteristics, and personality characteristics.[8-12] Clinical nursing characteristics consist of one to five years of clinical experience, interest in professional growth, and mastery of clinical skills. Professional characteristics are excellent leadership skills, excellent communication skills, good decision-making ability, advocacy for the learner, and an ability to use resources. Personality characteristics include patience and enthusiasm; a nonthreatening and nonjudgmental attitude toward others; a flexible, open-minded, trustworthy attitude; a sense of humor; self-confidence; willingness mutually to share knowledge and skills; and willingness to commit the time involved in being a preceptor.

It is imperative that each person involved in the preceptorial experience understand his or her respective role and how this role relates to others involved in the experience. Specifically, the role of each of the key players is as follows.

Preceptor

The three primary roles for the preceptor are teacher/role-model, workplace socializer, and co-evaluator. Thus the activities of the preceptor tend to include the following:

- orienting and socializing the preceptee to the health care agency
- teaching, demonstrating, observing, and evaluating the preceptee
- assisting with the development of teaching/learning objectives for the preceptorial experience
- communicating with the faculty on the progress of the preceptee
- working with the faculty member to evaluate the student's progress

Student

The primary roles for the student are learner and collaborator. Thus the activities of the student tend to include the following:

- identifying individual learning needs
- utilizing the expertise and professional wisdom of the preceptor
- preparing for the clinical experience by appropriately reading and by practicing technical skills in the learning laboratory as needed
- communicating learning needs to faculty and the preceptor
- adhering to the policies and procedures of the health care agency
- being accountable for own professional practice
- participating in the evaluation process

Faculty

The primary roles for the faculty are consultant and co-evaluator. Thus the activities of the faculty tend to include the following:

- orienting the preceptor and the student to the preceptorial experience
- meeting with the preceptor and the student on a regular basis to discuss the student's learning needs and progress
- providing consultation to the preceptor
- working with the preceptor to evaluate the student's performance

POTENTIAL PROBLEMS

Most problems involved in the preceptorial experience can be avoided easily with proper planning, an extensive orientation for all participants, careful selection of preceptors, and appropriate assessment of the student's suitability for the experience. On occasion, faculty may encounter some difficulty relinquishing the traditional clinical teaching role. This, however, can be resolved by encouraging faculty to focus on the objectives of the experience and the assets of the teaching modality.

On occasion, personality conflicts may arise between the preceptor and the student. Such conflicts need to be addressed immediately in an open and frank discussion among the preceptor, the student, and the faculty member. If it appears that the conflict cannot be resolved in a timely fashion, then the student needs to be reassigned to another preceptor and possibly to another agency.

The following example demonstrates the preceptorial experience as an appropriate teaching strategy for both baccalaureate and graduate nursing students.

Example
Rural Preceptorial Experience in the Senior Year*

Vickie A. Lambert, Jo-Ellen M. McDonough, Joyce S. Billue, and Elizabeth F. Pond

The rural preceptorial experience, a ten-week course consisting of 160 hours of clinical experience, was designed for senior nursing students who were in the last quarter of their baccalaureate program. This teaching strategy was selected because it provided for professional role socialization, independent problem solving in the clinical arena, and exposure to aspects of health care delivery in a rural setting.

To excite and interest students in a rural preceptorial experience, they were provided information early in the curriculum about the preceptorial experience, given a presentation by graduates of the program who were successfully functioning in a rural health care setting, informed that travel monies would be available to cover the cost of mileage to and from the rural setting, and encouraged to take the rural health elective offered the quarter before the preceptorial experience. The elective provided information that addressed specific issues of culture, health care access, and health care problems as they relate to a rural setting. The elective was done "workshop style," which consisted of two seven-hour class days and one six-hour field trip to a variety of rural health care settings.

A total of 47 students chose to be involved in a rural preceptorial experience and subsequently were placed in rural health care agencies within a 50-mile radius of the university campus. Each student indicated a health care agency preference that was accommodated when possible. Faculty teaching in the rural preceptorial source then worked with nurse administrators in each respective health care agency to identify and select appropriate preceptors based upon predetermined criteria. Once preceptors were selected, each student was appropriately assigned. In turn, each preceptor/student team was assigned to a specific faculty member who monitored between eight and ten preceptor/student teams.

---

*The rural preceptorial experience was funded by the U.S. Department of Health and Human Services (Division of Nursing, Health Resources and Services Administration, Public Health Service, under grant number 5 D10 NU24354-02, "Preceptorship in Rural Hsopitals").

Prior to the start of the preceptorial experience, an orientation was conducted by faculty at the school of nursing for preceptors and students. The orientation included

- the goals of the preceptorial experience
- the role of the health care agency in which the preceptorial experience was being held
- the responsibilities of the preceptor, the faculty, and the student
- the objectives of the rural preceptorial experience
- the evaluation process
- the communication channels to be used
- a discussion of common preceptor concerns

In addition, a manual was provided that contained written information on all of the issues addressed during the formal orientation: the syllabus for the rural preceptorial experience; the goals of the preceptorial experience; the evaluation tools; role descriptions; common preceptor questions and their answers; and the names and phone numbers of the preceptors, faculty, and students. The exhibits below provide information on the goals of the preceptorial experience (Exhibit 18–1); the preceptor qualifications (Exhibit 18–2); and the responsibilities of the health care agency, preceptor, faculty, and student (Exhibits 18–3 through 18–6). Following the exhibits a short situation is provided that demonstrates one possible problem that can occur during the preceptorial experience.

Situation

A faculty member, Dr. J. L. J., visits a senior nursing student, Ms. K., in a rural hospital. The faculty member spends 30 minutes conversing with the student on her progress, but fails to validate the student's assessment with the preceptor. The

---

Exhibit 18–1 Goals of the Preceptorial Experience

The goals of the preceptorial experience are

1. to provide professional role socialization,
2. to allow for independent problem-solving in a clinical arena, and
3. to provide for exposure to aspects of health care delivery in a rural setting.

Exhibit 18–2 Preceptor Qualifications

Required	Highly Recommended
1. Current registered nurse license 2. At least one year of work experience, and with education preferably at the same or higher level than that of the student 3. Ability to facilitate the student's learning 4. Ability to interact with faculty and students and to clarify the preceptor role and the student's learning activities	1. Interest in teaching 2. Ability to facilitate the student's role transition from nursing student to staff nurse 3. Ability to share professional experiences and clinical expertise

Exhibit 18–3 Health Care Agency Responsibilities

The health care agency will

1. provide the preceptor, an R.N. with at least one year of experience, to work with a student throughout the preceptorial experience;
2. ensure that the preceptor and student work within agency guidelines and State Board of Nursing Rules and Regulations;
3. facilitate the accomplishment of student objectives by allowing students access to various health care agency services; and
4. complete all required paperwork, including the State Board of Nursing Preceptor Qualification Record, the agency evaluation, and a photocopy of all preceptor licenses.

Exhibit 18–4 Preceptor Responsibilities

The preceptor will

1. complete the preceptor orientation;
2. orient and socialize the preceptee within the unit and the health care agency, including parking regulations and security measures;
3. collaborate with the student and faculty to develop student learning activities;
4. plan, delegate, and facilitate the student's daily clinical experiences, guided by the objectives of the preceptorial experience;
5. supervise and instruct the student in the clinical area;
6. consult with faculty as needed or desired; and
7. evaluate the student's practice by reviewing the student's objectives, providing ongoing feedback to the student on his or her performance, completing the required course evaluation in collaboration with the faculty and student, discussing the student's progress with faculty during the weekly visit, and notifying the faculty of any serious problems or incidents involving the student.

Exhibit 18–5 Faculty Responsibilities

The faculty will

1. initiate a meeting with the student before the preceptorial experience begins for the purpose of information giving and clarification;
2. meet with preceptor and student to appraise and approve student objectives and learning activities;
3. assist the preceptor by helping to identify learning experiences needed for the individual student, communicating with the preceptor on a weekly basis to discuss student progress, being available by phone for consultation during the student's clinical time, participating in the evaluation process, being a resource and support person, and guiding the preceptor in his or her role; and
4. evaluate the experiences of the preceptorial experience.

preceptor becomes upset and feels that her role is not appropriately acknowledged by the faculty member.

Problem: Lack of understanding of role responsibilities of the preceptor on the part of the faculty.

Expected outcome: Role clarification of the preceptor role on the part of the faculty.

Exhibit 18–6 Student Responsibilities

The student will

1. be on time for clinical, wearing appropriate attire;
2. write personal enabling objectives in collaboration with the faculty and preceptor, revising them as needed;
3. show flexibility and willingness to learn;
4. discuss own strengths and limitations with preceptor and faculty;
5. accept responsibility for own learning in the clinical agency;
6. assume increasing responsibility for clinical activities on the selected unit under the supervision of the preceptor;
7. seek assistance from preceptor with skills as needed, and
8. maintain a daily log for evaluation of objectives.

NOTES

1. F. Myrick, Preceptorship—Is It the Answer of the Problem in Clinical Teaching?, *Journal of Nursing Education* 27, no. 3 (1988):136–138.

2. J. Shamian and R. Inhaber, The Concept and Practice of Preceptorship in Contemporary Nursing: A Review of Pertinent Literature, *International Journal of Nursing Studies* 22, no. 2 (1985):79–87.

3. N. Jairath, et al., The Effect of Preceptorship upon Diploma Program Nursing Students' Transition to the Professional Nursing Role, *Journal of Nursing Education* 30, no. 6 (1991):251–255.

4. G. Clayton, et al., Relationship between a Preceptorship Experience and Role Socialization of Graduate Nurses, *Journal of Nursing Education* 28, no. 2 (1989):72–75.

5. Shamian and Inhaber, The Concept and Practice.

6. B. Chickerella and W. Lutz, Professional Nurturance: Preceptors for Undergraduate Nursing Students, *American Journal of Nursing* 81, no. 1 (1981):107–109.

7. O. Brim, Jr., *Socialization after Childhood: Two Essays*, eds. O. Brim., Jr., and S. Wheeler (New York: John Wiley & Sons, Inc., 1966), 3.

8. J. Taylor and P. Zabawski, Preceptorship Is Alive and Well and Working at BCIT, *Canadian Nurse* 78, no. 6 (1982):19–22.

9. M.L. Murphy and S. Hammerstad, Preparing a Staff Nurse for Precepting, *Nurse Educator* 6 no. 5 (1981):17–20.

10. J. Piemme, et al., Developing the Nurse Preceptor, *Journal of Continuing Education in Nursing* 17, no. 6 (1986):186–189.

11. N. Hsiek and D. Knowles, Instructor Facilitation of the Preceptorship Relationship in Nursing Education, *Journal of Nursing Education* 29, no. 6 (1990): 262–268.

12. M. Amann, et al., Development of a Model for Precepting: The Occupational Health Setting, *AAOHN Journal* 36, no. 1 (1988):25–30.

SUGGESTED READING

Ferguson, L., and B. Calder. 1993. A comparison of preceptor and educator valuing of nursing student clinical performance criteria. *Journal of Nursing Education* 32, no. 1:30–36.

Ferguson, L., and B. Calder. 1993. Educational implications of community health preceptors' practice values. *Nurse Educator* 18, no. 5:20–24.

McDonough, J.E., et al. 1992. A rural nursing practicum: Making it work. *Nurse Educator* 17, no. 4:30–34.

Myrick, F., and C. Barrett. 1994. Selecting clinical preceptors for basic baccalaureate nursing students: A critical issue in clinical teaching. *Journal of Advanced Nursing* 19, no. 1:194–198.

Pond, E., et al. 1993. Preceptors' perceptions of a baccalaureate preceptorial experience. *Nursing Connections* 6, no. 1:15–25.

Williams, J., and S. Rogers. 1993. The multicultural workplace: Preparing preceptors. *Journal of Continuing Education in Nursing* 24, no. 3:101–104.

Chapter 19

Mentorship

Barbara Fuszard and Laurie Jowers Taylor

DEFINITION AND PURPOSES

Mentorship is a form of socialization for professional roles. It entails a relationship in which the mentor works closely with the protégé for purposes of teaching, guiding, supporting, and developing that individual. It is a "teaching strategy in which competencies of a scientific nature are promoted."[1]

A *mentor* is an individual who takes a personal interest in assisting an individual over a period of time to develop the knowledge and skills needed to realize the protégé's full potential and major life goals. A *protégé* is an individual who willingly enters into a relationship with a mentor and accepts the help and support offered by the mentor.

Mentor behaviors are those engaged in by the mentor, which may include some or all of the following: (1) teaching new skills and promoting intellectual development; (2) serving as a guide to acquaint the junior individual with the values, customs, and resources of the profession; (3) being an exemplar for the junior individual to emulate; (4) providing counseling and moral support during times of stress; (5) fostering personal development by believing in the junior person; (6) supporting and facilitating the junior person's life dreams and goals; and (7) sponsoring the person for advancement.[2]

In essence, mentors socialize the neophyte nurses to the norms and expectations of their own role. The mentoring relationship has been referred to as "the gray gorilla syndrome."[3] *Gray gorilla* refers to characteristics of the silverback primate who serves as a leader–teacher–preceptor–role-model for his group.

The richness and value of mentoring relationships are important in the development of young professionals. For example, as the gray gorilla teaches and advises, the neophyte gains knowledge and assessment skills; as the gray gorilla models, the neophyte gains competency and confidence; as the gray gorilla coaches and guides, the neophyte gains problem-solving and decision-making skills; as the gray gorilla facilitates and counsels additionally, the neophyte gains communication and collaborative skills; as the gray gorilla inspires and influences, the neophyte gains humanistic values and creative ideas; and as the gray gorilla motivates and leads, the neophyte gains leadership skills and becomes a gray gorilla.

Obviously the quality of patient care is improved in settings with mentors. Units with a mentor are usually observed to be quieter and more efficiently organized and provide a more therapeutic environment than those without a gray gorilla. In addition, nurses who had the support and guidance of mentors felt greater self-actualization, more job satisfaction, better peer relationships, and less stress than those without mentors.[4]

THEORETICAL RATIONALE

Role theory, including socialization, provides the framework for predicting how individuals will perform in given roles—in this case, the mentor and protégé roles. "Role theory represents a collection of concepts and a variety of hypothetical formulations that predict how actors will perform in a given role, or under what circumstances certain types of behaviors can be expected."[5p.63] Role is viewed as stemming from interaction with actors in a social system. Roles are ongoing processes and are dynamic rather than static.

Roles are learned through the socialization process. Socialization may be viewed as "an interactional and reciprocal process in which the socializee (protégé) and socializer (mentor) are mutually influenced."[6] Socialization is defined by Brim as a "process by which persons acquire the knowledge, skills, and dispositions that make them more or less able members of their society." According to Brim, one learns role expectations and role behavior through the process of socialization.[7] As a primary agent of socialization and as a member of the protégé's support system, the mentor contributes to successful role development.

CONDITIONS

The mentoring system is appropriate in any setting where individuals are exposed to new role expectations. It is also appropriate as a stepping stone for new graduates who have had the opportunity to participate in a preceptorship or internship experience. The mentorship model differs from the preceptorship or internship experiences primarily in intensity, duration, and purpose. While a preceptorship experience may last for a specified length of time (such as an orientation to a particular unit), the mentor-protégé relationship may span several years or even a lifetime. In addition, the mentor-protégé relationship may be more intense than a preceptorship experience. Mentorship is more than guidance. It is a relationship in which the mentor helps the protégé set goals and standards and develop skills; protects the protégé from others in such a way that allows room for risk and failure; facilitates the protégé's successful entry into academic and professional circles; and affords the protégé an opportunity to reach self-actualization in a leadership role.[8]

TYPES OF LEARNERS

This strategy is most appropriate for those individuals assuming new role responsibilities or for those interested in facilitating their professional growth and development.

RESOURCES

Mentoring may occur at any time or in any setting. It may involve time spent in the actual work setting or it may involve collaboration on a project such as a research study or a committee assignment. No specific equipment is necessary. The only requirements are human resources, two individuals committed to working together for the purpose of advancing the development of the protégé.

USING THE METHOD

Many times a mentor-protégé relationship may evolve from a close working relationship with another individual. However, this is not always the case. It is certainly appropriate to ask an individual to serve as a mentor. This may be difficult for people who fear rejection. It is important, however, to remember that most people will be highly flattered to be asked to serve as mentor.

When considering a mentor, it is wise to use criteria as a guideline for selection. Findings from research studies indicate that the ability to master concepts and ideas, as well as possessing integrity, professional values, and trustworthiness are important qualities of the mentor.[9] Mentors are usually selected by the protégé, although the reverse may occur. Only a small number of individuals are lucky enough to fall into a mentor-protégé relationship. Therefore, it is vital that one intentionally seek a mentor who can contribute to one's professional development. It is a voluntary relationship based on trust, compatibility, mutuality, and personal attraction.

In describing the mentor relationship, Bova and Phillips note that "Mentors are those who practice most of the following principles: try to understand, shape and encourage the dreams of their protégés; often give their blessing on the dreams and goals of their protégés; provide opportunities for their protégés to observe and participate in their work by inviting their protégés to work with them; and teach their protégés the policies of 'getting ahead' in the organization."[10] Vance explored mentor relationships among nursing leaders. Specific help provided by the mentors included career advice, guidance, promotion, professional role modeling, intellectual and scholarly stimulation, inspiration and idealism, teaching, advising, and tutoring.[11]

Three major responsibilities of the protégé are (1) initiating—seeking and asking for advice/assistance, (2) sharing—openly sharing goals and needs, and (3) listening.[12] When looking for a mentor, it is vital to make one's goals known and seek high visibility. Asking others for advice or help will let them know that one values their opinions. A potential mentor will respond by commenting on one's work and being appreciative of one's efforts. One can test this potential mentor-protégé relationship by following up with a dialogue with this person. A major consideration when choosing a mentor is to make sure that the mentor fits with one's sense of self. Hall and Sandler offer some helpful suggestions when seeking a mentor:

- Introduce yourself and make the first contact with a professional subject.
- Ask for help regarding the strengths and weaknesses of your work.
- Try to become a research or teaching assistant, junior collaborator, proposal writer, intern, or other type of apprentice. This will provide the opportunity to demonstrate one's abilities and commitment.
- Ask a colleague to mention you or your work to a potential mentor.
- Volunteer to serve on a task force, committee, or project where your potential mentor is also a member.
- Invite your potential mentor to be a guest lecturer in your class or before a campus group.[13]

POTENTIAL PROBLEMS

The mentor-protégé relationship provides the opportunity for both personal and professional growth. As Rogers has noted: "The degree to which I can create relationships which facilitate the growth of others as separate persons is a measure of the growth I have achieved myself."[14]

Although mentoring is perceived as a very positive concept, it has the potential to be deleterious. For example, the mentor may be overprotective or too controlling, stifling creativity and innovation on the part of the protégé. Exploitation is another potential problem related to the mentor-protégé relationship. The mentor may only want a protégé for self-serving reasons.

The mentorship example that follows shows the status of mentorship among nursing faculty, and a faculty member's personal encounter with mentorship.

Example
A Mentoring Relationship
Barbara Fuszard

Every mentor-protégé dyad is unique. This relationship began at the end of the future protégée's master's program in nursing administration. The director of the program made herself available to all students, took a personal interest in them, and had the background to serve as mentor in many roles. She had been an educator, had published extensively, and also had held a variety of administrative roles, so she understood well the positions into which her students were moving.

The protégée accepted a position as nurse administrator in a complex situation, and soon called upon the mentor to offer staff development workshops and personal consultation to her in this new situation. It was given readily, and although no words of mentor-protégée commitment were spoken, a bond began to form.

The protégée returned to school for doctoral study, and the mentor become co-advisor for her doctoral study and dissertation. During the doctoral study, the mentor offered the protégée an opportunity to be graduate teaching assistant, teaching master's students in nursing administration through the case method. The protégée was introduced to group and committee work of graduate faculty, an experience she had not yet had. On occasion both attended national conventions. At a meeting of the Council on Graduate Education for Administration in Nursing (CGEAN) the protégée "rubbed elbows" with educators from all over the country who taught nursing administration at the graduate level. A lifelong interest in nursing administration education began to germinate.

Both protégée and mentor had strong personalities. The relationship had bumpy times when the protégée felt dominated or the mentor felt the protégée was not using her talents. One of the sensitive areas was related to progress on the dissertation. The mentor remembered her own experience of completing her doctorate after age 60 and was determined that this would not occur with the protégée.

Trust was established during a National League for Nursing convention. During a meeting of the House of Delegates, the protégée sat reading handouts she had obtained from salespersons at the exhibits. Her mentor scolded abruptly, saying she should be paying attention to the debates she came to hear. The protégée, normally schooled to respect authority, burst out angrily, "I have heard this debate three times in the last three days and nothing has changed. Their discussion is circular. . . ." The mentor was silent for a short time, and then said, "You're right." After this incident the mentor would ask the protégée why she made a decision before she challenged it, and the protégée felt more comfortable about asking and discussing issues with the mentor.

The mentor-protégée relationship became over the years collegial and friendly. Discussions could be heated, but the protégée always felt a support from her mentor. Positions in service and in education continued over the years for the protégée, and the mentor retired from her formal job. The mentor never stopped caring for or assisting her graduates. She continued her round of consultations and workshops for the benefit of all of them, including this protégée.

The mentor introduced the protégée to the discipline of writing. The mentor was editor of a national newsletter, and permitted the protégée to write a regular column, an activity that continued for eight years. This activity eventually led to the protégée's becoming editor of that newsletter.

After 20 years of the relationship, the mentor permitted the protégée also to become a gray gorilla, mentoring her own graduate students. A typical behavior of the mentor occurred when the protégée was faced with a difficult decision about whether to move to another position. The mentor, though on a fixed income, flew across the country "to be with you and support you while you make your decision." The new gray gorilla has yet to make such a self-sacrificing action for her protégées, but she plans to do so.

NOTES

1. J.J. Fitzpatrick and I.L. Abraham, Toward the Socialization of Scholars and Scientists, *Nurse Educator* 12, no. 3 (May/June 1987):23–25.

2. D.J. Levison, *The Seasons of a Man's Life* (New York: Ballantine Books, Inc., 1978).

3. S.H. Pyles and P.N. Stern, Discovery of Nursing Gestalt in Critical Care Nursing: The Importance of the Gray Gorilla Syndrome, *Image: The Journal of Nursing Scholarship* 15, no. 2 (1983):51–57.

4. Ibid.

5. M.E. Conway, Theoretical Approaches to the Study of Roles, in *Role Theory: Perspectives for Health Professionals*, ed., M.E. Hardy and M.E. Conway (Norwalk, Conn: Appleton & Lange, 1988), 63–72.

6. B.A. Hurley, Socialization for Roles, in *Role Theory: Perspectives for Health Professionals*, ed. M.E. Hardy and M.E. Conway (New York: Appleton-Century-Crofts, 1978), 29–72.

7. O.G. Brim. Jr., Socialization through the Life Cycle, in *Socialization after Childhood: Two Essays*, ed. O.G. Brim and S. Wheeler (New York: John Wiley & Sons, Inc., 1966), 3–49.

8. A.M. Valadez and C.A. Lund, Mentorship, Maslow and Me, *Journal of Continuing Education in Nursing* 24, no. 6 (1993):259–263.

9. L.T. Jowers, Mentoring: Correlates with Role Conflict and Role Ambiguity (Unpublished doctoral dissertation, University of Texas at Austin, 1987).

10. B.M. Bova and R.R. Phillips, The Mentoring Relationship as an Educational Experience, *ED*, 224–244.

11. C. Vance, The Mentor Connection, *The Journal of Nursing Education*, 12, no. 4 (1973):7–13.

12. R. Klaus, Formalized Mentor Relationships for Management and Executive Development Programs in the Federal Government, *Public Administration Review* 41, no. 4 (1981):489–496.

13. R.M. Hall and B.R. Sandler, Academic Mentoring for Women Students and Faculty: A New Look at an Old Way to Get Ahead, *ED*, 240–291.

14. C. Rogers, The Characteristics of a Helping Relationship, *Personnel and Guidance Journal* 37 (1958):6–16.

SUGGESTED READING

Alvarez, A., and K. Abriam-Yago. 1993. Mentoring undergraduate ethnic-minority students: A strategy for retention. *Journal of Nursing Education* 32, no. 5:230–232.

Arnoldussen, B. 1990. The mentor perspective. *Nursing Administration Quarterly* 15, no. 1:28–31.

Baldwin, D., and J. Wold. 1993. Students from disadvantaged backgrounds: Satisfaction with a mentor-protege relationship. *Journal of Nursing Education* 32, no. 5:225–226.

Banoub-Baddour, S., and L.T. Gien. 1991. Student-faculty joint authorship: Mentorship in publication. *Canadian Journal of Nursing Research* 23, no. 1:5–14.

Boyle, C., and S.K. James. 1994. Nursing leaders as mentors: How are we doing? *Nursing Administration Quarterly* 15, no. 1:44–48.

Caine, R.M. 1994. Empowering nurses through mentoring. *MedSurg Nursing* 3, no. 1:59–61.

Caine, R.M. 1990. Mentoring: Nurturing the critical care nurse. *Focus on Critical Care* 17, no. 6:452–456.

Carlson, K. 1993. Evolutions: Open doors. *Journal of Post Anesthesia Nursing* 8, no. 6:435–436.

Chandler, G.E. 1993. The RN mentor program: An exercise in leadership. *NLN Publications* (14-2511):339–354.

Cooper, M.D. 1990. Mentorship: The key to the future of professionalism in nursing. *Journal of Perinatal and Neonatal Nursing* 4, no. 3:71–77.

Davidhizer, R. 1993. Mentoring nursing students to write. *Journal of Nursing Education* 32, no. 6:280–282.

Davidhizer, R. 1993. Self-care and mentors to reduce stress and enhance administrative ability. *Geriatric Nursing* 14, no. 3:146–149.

Davies, E. 1993. Clinical role modelling: Uncovering hidden knowledge. *Journal of Advanced Nursing* 18, no. 4:627–636.

DeMarco, R. 1993. Mentorship: A feminist critique of current research. *Journal of Advanced Nursing* 18, no. 8:1242–1250.

deTournyay, R. 1990. Setting limits (editorial). *Journal of Nursing Education* 29, no. 3:101.

Ellis, H. 1993. Teaching roles in critical care—The mentor and preceptor. *Intensive and Critical Care Nursing* 9, no. 3:152–156.

Fields, W.L. 1991. Mentoring in nursing: A historical approach. *Nursing Outlook* 39, no. 6:257–261.

Fox, W.J., et al., 1992. The mentoring relationship. *AORN Journal* 56, no. 5:858–867.

Grossman, M. 1993. Mentorship: Bonds that strengthen professions (editorial). *Canadian Journal of Nursing Research* 25, no. 3:7–13.

Haas, S.A. 1992. Coaching: Developing key players. *Journal of Nursing Administration* 22, no. 6:54–58.

Hockenberry-Eaton, M. 1992. Nursing research—Moving forward through networking, collaboration and mentorship. *Journal of Pediatric Oncology Nursing* 9, no. 3:132–135.

Holloran, S.D. 1993. Mentoring: The experience of nursing service executives. *Journal of Nursing Administration* 23, no. 2:49–54.

Jowers, L.T., and K. Herr. 1992. A review of literature on mentor-protege relationships. Review. *NLN Publications* (15-2339):49–77.

Lenkman, S. 1992. Mentoring in nursing administration. *Aspen's Advisor for Nurse Executives* 7, no. 11:5–8.

Levi, P.C., and A. Marriner-Tomey. 1991. Visiting professor mentorship. *Nurse Educator* 16, no. 3:11, 22, 30.

Mansour, M. 1991. Multiple mentoring strategy in the academic preparation of quality assurance directors. *Nursing Connections* 4, no. 2:53–61.

Marshall, C. 1993. Mentorship in critical care. *British Journal of Theatre Nursing* 2, no. 11:22–23.

Mills, J. 1991. The nurse manager as mentor. *Pediatric Nursing* 17, no. 5:493.

Orth, C.D., at al. 1990. The manager's role as coach and mentor. *Journal of Nursing Administration* 20, no. 9:11–15.

Parker, D. 1992. Mentoring concepts applied to clinical practice. Review. *Gastroenterology Nursing* 15, no. 1:35–39.

Phippen, M.L. 1993. My orthopedic mentor. Editorial. *Seminars in Perioperative Nursing* 2, no. 2:vi–viii.

Prestholdt, C.O. 1990. Modern mentoring: Strategies for developing contemporary nursing leadership. Review. *Nursing Administration Quarterly* 15, no. 1:20–27.

Rankin, E.A. 1991. Mentor, mentee, mentoring: Building career development relationships. *Nursing Connections* 4, no. 4:49–57.

Rawl, S.M., and L.M. Peterson. 1992. Nursing education administrators: Level of career development and mentoring. *Journal of Professional Nursing* 8, no. 3:161–169.

Rempusheski, V.F. 1992. A researcher as resource, mentor, and preceptor. *Applied Nursing Research* 5, no. 2:105–107.

Sidani, S. 1991. Mentoring the novice nurse researcher. *Journal of Pediatric Nursing* 6, no. 1:57–59.

Simpson, R.L. 1990. Contemporary leadership begins with mentoring. Editorial. *Nursing Administration Quarterly* 15, no. 1:ix–xi.

Sorrell, J.M. 1992. Ethics of writing in nursing: Responsible mentorship. *Nursing Connections* 5, no. 4:67–71.

Sorrell, J.M., and H.N. Brown. 1991. Mentoring students in writing: "Gourmet express" versus "fast food service." *Journal of Nursing Education* 30, no. 6:284–286.

Stachura, L.M., and J. Hoff. 1990. Toward achievement of mentoring for nurses. *Nursing Administration Quarterly* 15, no. 1:56–62.

Sundwick, K. 1993. It could make a difference. *Gastroenterology Nursing* 16, no. 3:97–98.

Taylor, L.J. 1992. A survey of mentor relationships in academe. *Journal of Professional Nursing* 8, no. 1:48–55.

White, L.M. 1990. The mentee perspective. *Nursing Administration Quarterly* 15, no. 1:32–35.

Yoder, L. 1990. Mentoring: A concept analysis. *Nursing Administration Quarterly* 15, no. 1:9–19.

Part VI

Clinical Teaching

A large number of the new chapters in this second edition of *Innovative Teaching Strategies in Nursing* address clinical teaching. Philosophical underpinnings and cautions for the faculty member open and close this section.

Content of the chapters then begins with the learning laboratory, where students are first introduced to the clinical side of their courses. The remainder of the chapters address either specific strategies, such as nursing rounds, or the holistic approach of an entire course. Some of the strategies are developed more fully than others, where elaboration is needed for clarification.

Chapter 20

Philosophical Approaches to Clinical Instruction

Martha J. Bradshaw

INTRODUCTION

The purpose of clinical instruction is to give the student opportunities to bridge didactic information with the realities of nursing practice. In guided situations, students blend theoretical knowledge with experiential learning, in order to bring about a synthesis and understanding of those endeavors known collectively as *nursing*. Clinical learning is directed by a nurse educator who is operationalizing his or her practical knowledge about teaching. Through use of this practical knowledge, the instructor translates a formal curriculum into active engagement with students.[1]

ROLE OF THE CLINICAL INSTRUCTOR

In the clinical setting, the teacher guides the students in applying theory to patient care. The faculty role in clinical instruction is diverse and demanding. The instructor is expected to be competent, experienced, knowledgeable, flexible, patient, and energetic. The instructor should be capable of balancing structure with spontaneity.

The successful student clinical experience—measured in terms of learning outcomes and an internalized sense of fulfillment—is largely influenced by the types of assignments the instructor provides. The planning and selection of these assignments, as well as actual teaching, are value-laden and reflect the faculty member's philosophical approach to clinical learning. Furthermore, the role or roles the instructor chooses to fulfill influence selection of student activities. The roles in which individual instructors see themselves may include interaction with students, serving as a role-model, or functioning as an expert reference. Roles that students see as important ones for clinical instructors to hold have been identified as resource, evaluator, encourager, promoter of patient care, and benevolent presence.[2] Once this image of self is determined, teachers consciously or subconsciously shape situations that will enable them to enact their various roles. This enhances teacher effectiveness, since the instructor is most comfortable in fulfilling preselected roles.

In addition to image of self, other personal attributes influence the instructor's thinking regarding student assignments. There is some indication that teachers' background knowledge and preferences for orientation to practice strongly influence planning and decision making by teachers.[3] Therefore, an instructor with a concrete, structured practice background (such as surgical nursing) may select or plan patient assignments that are more structured than those selected by an instructor from a less structured background (such as psychiatric nursing). The potential conflict exists between teacher and student regarding learning and practice preferences. With careful planning and collaboration with the students the clinical instructor can best shape the learning situations to meet students' needs.[4]

FOUNDATIONS FOR SELECTION OF CLINICAL ACTIVITIES

Another philosophical perspective that governs clinical learning is the instructor's view of the *purpose* of the clinical learning experience. The three most common purposes are for students to (1) apply theoretical concepts, (2) experience actual patient situations, and (3) see and implement professional roles. Based upon the chosen perspective, the instructor selects the agency or unit and plans the type of clinical assignment best suited for the identified purpose. The realism of clinical activities brings added benefit to any of the three types of experiences.

The planning and supervising of clinical learning calls for the instructor's own philosophical stance to be blended with the selected goal(s) of the clinical experience. Student assignments may have one of the following goals:

Learn the **patient:** Provide one-to-one total care.
Learn the **content area:** Practice a variety of care activities in one setting.
Learn **role(s):** Function as a staff or team member or as a practitioner, administrator, or other selected roles.

Assignments can be based upon theories of action:

People-centered: interpersonal interaction systems
Health: promotion, maintenance, functioning
Nature of practice milieu: decision making, leadership, collaboration[5]

The instructor who selects a student focus for clinical assignments may value empowerment as part of his or her philosophical approach to teaching. The aims of this approach are the cultivation of responsibility, authority, and accountability in novice practitioners.[6] Selected clinical activities directed toward empowerment could include:

Analytical nursing: use of actual experiences (instructor or student based) to define and solve problems
Change activities: development of planned change and identification of resources to bring about this change
Collegiality: professional interactions (instructor-student, student-student, student-staff) to solve problems, promote optimal care
Sponsorship: collaboration and interaction with preceptors, administration; analysis of bureaucratic system[7]

Within the framework of the assignment, the instructor then makes decisions about which activities will enhance learning outcomes. This again reflects the values of the teacher, beliefs about how learning should take place and how teacher role fulfillment will influence this learning. For example, the instructor who values participatory learning and role modeling will be actively involved in many aspects of the student's activities, and his or her presence will be felt by the student—at the bedside or in interaction with staff members. Purdon points out that such role-modeling has positive benefits for students, such as reducing fears and seeing effective communications.[8] The instructor who wishes to foster independence in students may take on the role of resource person and become centrally available to students as needed. The instructor who places emphasis on organization and task accomplishment will oversee numerous student activities and facilitate completion of the assignments within a designated period of time. Many instructors value all of these activities as a part of student learning. To accomplish all of these calls for a great deal of diversity and planning on the part of the teacher.

Some philosophical approaches to teaching and role assumption by educators are more subtle, yet promote more complex, higher-order learning. More specifically, the teacher who values empowerment and accountability in students will take on a less directive role and assume one that is more enabling. The instructor who wishes to promote independence in students must be willing to release a certain amount of control, in order to give freedom for students to learn and grow.

CLINICAL ACTIVITIES AND PROBLEM SOLVING

The instructor who promotes problem-solving abilities in students is one who fashions clinical activities to meet this goal. Discovery learning is one way in which student autonomy and problem solving can be enhanced. Students can have experiences where they can realize, or discover, patient responses to certain aspects of care, or how structuring an activity differently is more time saving. These discoveries boost self-esteem when students see what they have learned on their own, or that they have the ability to resolve certain problematic situations. Discovery learning also has been found to increase student motivation, interest, and retention of learned material.[9] The instructor then is rewarded by seeing growth take place in the students.

Another approach to promoting problem-solving abilities is by placing emphasis on the clinical, or patient, problem, rather than the clinical setting. Student assignments that take place in familiar, repetitive settings enable students to deal with patients *in that setting*. As Reilly and Oermann point out, nursing practice settings are moving away from acute care environments, and students should be equipped to work with clinical problems in diverse settings. In addition to learning how to deal with clinical problems, students also experience professional socialization through role discontinuity. In making the transition from instructor-directed, structured, familiar assignments to empowering, unstructured, undefined patient problems, students experience new ways of defining their own roles and responsibilities as practitioners.[10]

STUDENT DEVELOPMENT

The strategy of reciprocal learning is one that not only meets clinical learning needs but promotes collegiality as well.[11] Reciprocal learning usually takes the form of peer teaching, or student-to-student instruction. This learning informally occurs within most clinical groups and can become more purposeful and goal directed through instructor planning. By pairing students for specific learning activities, the student learner gains information, experience, and insight in new ways. Learners receive individualized, empathetic instruction and may feel more relaxed with a peer than with a faculty teacher. The student teacher also learns about instruction, helping, and working with others. Student teachers also assume the responsibility of role-models and collaborators.[12]

FACULTY DEVELOPMENT

The powerful influence of the instructor as a person should not be overlooked. Development of an effective clinical instructor and the evolution of a meaningful, positive, clinical learning experience are based upon insight, planning, and implementation by the faculty member. Therefore, individual teachers need to cultivate an appropriate image of self as a teacher. In addition, the clinical instructor should indulge in periodic self-reflection: Is my own clinical competence being maintained? Are my own views on nursing and the teaching-learning process congruent with student perspectives and needs? Should teaching strategies, types of assignments, or communication skills be revised? The effective faculty member may need to reshape his or her own teaching perspectives to better blend with those perspectives held by the clinical students.

CONCLUSION

The philosophical approach to teaching is the foundation by which the instructor operationalizes his or her own practical knowledge. Carlson-Catalano has pointed out that much of the instruction that takes place is related to how the instructor has internalized professional values and developed an image of self as a practitioner and role model.[13] The clinical instructor is a pivotal person for developing positive or negative self-concepts in students.[14] The instructor who wishes to promote empowerment in students must see his or her own self empowered to do so. Only then can needed socialization and empowerment take place. The empowered instructor is able to visualize the potential learning opportunities in the clinical environment.[15] Effective clinical instruction emerges from conscious efforts on the part of the instructor. These efforts should be based upon background knowledge, strongly formed values, and a well-defined image of self as a nurse teacher. Applying these personal resources enables the teacher to bring about effective clinical instruction. Formal and personal learning outcomes then are achieved.

NOTES

1. M. Johnson, Review of Teacher Thinking: A Study of Practical Knowledge, *Curriculum Inquiry* 14, no. 4 (1984):465–468.

2. S. Flagler, et al., Clinical Teaching Is More Than Evaluation Alone!, *Journal of Nursing Education* 27, no. 8 (1988):342–348.

3. D. Yaakobi and S. Sharan, Teacher Beliefs for Practices: The Discipline Carries the Message, *Journal of Education for Teaching* 11, no. 2 (1985):187–199.

4. L. Sutcliffe, An Investigation into Whether Nurses Change Their Learning Style According to Subject Area Studied, *Journal of Advanced Nursing* 18, no. 7 (1993):647–658.

5. D.E. Reilly and M.H. Oermann, *The Clinical Field: Its Use in Nursing Education* (Norwalk, Conn: Appleton-Century-Crofts, 1985).

6. M. Manthey, Empowerment for Teachers and Students, *Nurse Educator* 17, no. 4 (1992):6–7.

7. J. Carlson-Catalano, Empowering Nurses for Professional Practice, *Nursing Outlook* 40, no. 3 (1992):139–142.

8. J.E. Purdon, Fear of Persons with HIV Infection: Teaching Strategies for Helping Students Cope, *Journal of Nursing Education* 31, no. 13 (1992):138–139.

9. S. DeYoung, *Teaching Nursing* (Redwood City, Calif: Addison-Wesley, 1990).

10. Reilly and Oermann, *The Clinical Field.*

11. D. Goldenberg and C. Iwasiw, Reciprocal Learning among Students in the Clinical Area, *Nursing Outlook* 17, no. 1 (1992):27–29.

12. Goldenberg and Iwasiw, Reciprocal Learning, 28.

13. Carlson-Catalano, Empowering Nurses, 139.

14. B. Kelly, The Professional Self-Concepts of Nursing Undergraduates and Their Perceptions of Influential Forces, *Journal of Nursing Education* 31, no. 3 (1992):121–125.

15. P.S. Chally, Empowerment through Teaching, *Journal of Nursing Education* 31, no. 3 (1992): 117–120.

Chapter 21

Refocusing the Nursing Skills Laboratory

Glenda F. Hanson

DEFINITION AND PURPOSES

Theory-based practice is recognized as a key element in the development of nursing science.[1,2] Yet, in searching for ways to establish the connections between theory and practice for the undergraduate baccalaureate nursing student, the educator has been both challenged and frustrated.[3,4] Beginning students are generally given an introductory overview of nursing theories. However, application of these theories in clinical practice is often neglected due to emphasis on communication, client comfort, client safety, and other areas of immediate concern during early clinical experiences. This situation may lead to the belief that theory is abstract and disconnected from reality and not essential to nursing practice.[5] Additionally, like most forms of learning, the meaningfulness of the theoretical information is diminished as the time between introduction and application is prolonged.

The purpose of this chapter is to explore ways to facilitate an early foundation of theory-based practice in the nursing curriculum.

THEORETICAL RATIONALE

Knowles's[6] model for adult learning provides a framework for education that incorporates principles that value the individual's life experiences. The model

---

Source: Adapted from Hanson, G., Refocusing the Skills Laboratory, *Nurse Educator*, Vol. 18, No. 2, with permission of J.B. Lippincott Company, © 1993.

promotes a climate that requires openness, collaboration, competence, creativity, and success. Kolb's[7] experiential learning model bases learning on the premise that humans move from concrete experience to abstract conceptualization by a process of experience and experimentation. These educational theories are judged by this author to have common elements that make them compatible with the science of unitary human beings, as described by Martha E. Rogers,[8,9] which provides an example of a nursing theory later in this discussion.

It is the responsibility of nurse educators to structure the learning environment so as to provide students with experiences that move them to higher levels of cognition. By grounding these experiences in nursing theory, the educator is able to promote the concept of theory-based practice.

CONDITIONS

A theory-based education derives from a theory-based curriculum. The first step in curriculum development is to define and articulate the faculty's beliefs. Nursing theories such as Martha Rogers' Science of Unitary Human Beings provide a basis by which this process may unfold. It is the beliefs (or conceptual framework) gleaned from the theory that provide faculty with the basis from which the curriculum is constructed.[10] The school's philosophy flows from the broad beliefs of the framework and should reflect the views of the faculty regarding the purpose of nursing and its relationship to the universe, world, and society. Bevis[11] states that a philosophy should be general enough to support the specifics of the framework as well as give direction for research. The philosophy provides answers to the following questions: (1) what is the nature of the client?; (2) what is the nature of nursing?; (3) what is health?; and (4) what are the basic commitments of this program? Once this is established, the curriculum specifics unfold from this perspective.

Many schools of nursing provide nursing skills laboratory experiences early in the curriculum. As described by Infante,[12] the purpose of a nursing skills laboratory is to provide a simulation of reality so that "the reality can be better understood, controlled, and practiced." The laboratory allows the student to rehearse the wide range of psychomotor activities used to engage in nursing practice. The contained setting of the campus laboratory thus provides the teacher and learner with early opportunities to apply the ideals of the nursing theories in a low-risk, custom-designed environment. It is the role of the faculty to examine the curriculum content and search for specific strategies to illustrate the flow of practice from its conceptual systems.

TYPES OF LEARNERS

The typical undergraduate nursing student in skills laboratory experience is beginning or about to begin the first clinical sequence. The student at this point has usually had some exposure to nursing theory but little or no opportunity to apply the theory to nursing practice activities. The focused laboratory atmosphere is ordered so that the student understands the focus and the objectives of the experience, and is able to relate the experience to the overall curriculum objectives. The student is given the freedom and the motivation to set his or her own goals and to assume responsibility for moving from concrete knowledge to the more abstract applications of the knowledge. Structure, guidance, and direction are provided by the educator and accepted by the learner in the spirit of collaboration.

RESOURCES

The practice of skills in the nursing laboratory often focuses on subjects such as comfort, safety, management of personal hygiene, administration of medications, or health assessment. Skills are practiced in a controlled, simulated setting that allows the student the opportunity to focus on learning without the environmental distractions or constraints of a clinical setting. Resources provide a sense of realism, since the more the experience approximates the client situation, the more likely it is to bridge the gap between classroom and clinical. Environment is a key concept in nursing practice, and its importance is demonstrated in the educational setting. The laboratory environment may be as simple or as sophisticated as the budget allows. Laboratory faculty are grounded in the theoretical framework that they are seeking to apply. They are committed to promoting the beliefs and values of the framework in the students and to providing opportunities for developing or patterning of the students toward the identified objectives. This may include allowing the student to set individual goals, to experiment with various techniques, to work in groups, to imitate the performance of others, to assemble and handle applicable equipment, to question freely, and/or to practice for proficiency.

USING THE METHOD

Once the decision is made to use the skills lab as a focal point for nursing theory, the educator begins by examining the environment for congruency with the framework. For example, self-directed learning is not well represented in a lecture hall with a podium and rows of desks. Neither is holistic nursing care reflected by the use of plastic body parts such as pelvic models to demonstrate urinary catheterization. Attention is given to such aspects as general atmosphere, colors, lighting, ventilation, sounds, sights, teacher-learner ratio, and flow of movement.

Next, the overall structure of the laboratory experience is examined. Freedom and self-direction are impaired by activities that are overstructured and tightly monitored. Strict adherence to criteria and emphasis on testing hamper learners from experimentation, creativity, and setting of individual goals. While standards of client comfort and safety must be maintained, students and educators realize that a variety of methods and circumstances may lead to the accomplishment of the stated objectives. One need only examine several nursing textbooks to realize the range of options and interpretations that make up nursing practice.

All lab activities are framed within the theoretical perspective. While interventions may remain constant between theories, perspectives will vary. Client immobility, for example, may be perceived as a self-care deficit or an impairment of human field motion, depending on the view and circumstances. Students are constantly encouraged to explore and articulate these connections as they move through lab experiences.

POTENTIAL PROBLEMS

The methods described in this chapter only work when students and faculty collaborate together toward the common goal of excellence in nursing practice. Some students are ready to flourish in an atmosphere of openness and collaboration. Other students may be more comfortable with structure and rigid criteria. Likewise, some faculty may find it difficult to relinquish some of their control over the student experience. The educator remains sensitive and responsive to the differences in readiness that participants bring to the laboratory setting. Faculty learn that this type of teaching often requires more rather than less energy on their part as compared with the more traditional teaching roles. Included in the choices available to the students may be the choice of more structure and more prescribed learning. This structure may be in forms such as optional computer activities, additional laboratory time, individual appointments with faculty, supplemental projects, or structured group activities.

Discussion

The nursing skills laboratory is an environment rich with potential. It is in this setting that educators may find an early focus point to model and articulate theoretical applications through their teaching styles and strategies. Likewise, students may take risks and experiment in ways that might not be appropriate in the clinical setting. Implications are plentiful for any and all activities taking place in the lab, including leadership/management role-playing, research, problem solving, decision-making exercises, computer-assisted instruction activities, and specifics of care for clients in various stages of living and dying. Limitations exist only in the minds of the participants.

The visionary nurse educator has a responsibility to facilitate the student's transition to the role of professional nurse. Education may be conceptualized as the bridge between the science and the practice of nursing. The professional nurse whose practice of nursing flows naturally from a theoretical perspective will be better prepared to meet the challenges of twenty-first century nursing on earth and beyond. Preparing this professional is the challenge facing the nurse educators of today. The following example illustrates how theory-based practice can be used as a basis for nursing skills laboratory activities.

Example
Toward Theory-Based Practice
Glenda F. Hanson

Martha Rogers's[13] science of unitary human beings is used to illustrate how the nursing skills laboratory can facilitate the transfer of theory to practice. A nursing curriculum based on Rogers's theoretical framework would include an emphasis on the following elements of nursing practice: "the whole person, continuous innovative pattern changes, increasing complexity and diversity, continuous mutual process with the environment, complex and diverse evolution, [and] manifestations of change" (M. E. Rogers, personal communication, August 19, 1989). The school using this framework would be philosophically committed to promoting these beliefs and values in students, to providing opportunities for developing or patterning of the student toward increasing complexity and diversity, and to fulfilling the role of the professionally educated nurse.

Ways of changing or modifying the environment to meet specific situations have been investigated by researchers within the Rogerian conceptual system. Environmental factors such as motion,[14] color,[15] sound,[16] lighting,[17] and activities[18] have been studied by Rogerian researchers and been shown to be associated with a positive direction of human energy flow. It follows that the Rogerian-based laboratory would use this information to create a learning environment that is a pleasant, dynamic, and creative activity center. Research within the framework dictates that the surrounding be colorful, with a predominance of hues from the high end of the color spectrum (blues and violets). Freedom of choice is the hallmark of the system, with students being allowed to select from and move through a variety of activities that would promote achievement of their perceived goals. Guidance from faculty is an available option, and learning in groups is encouraged. Faculty should consciously maintain their own high-energy level, using mutual process to promote student empowerment. Students are encouraged by verbal and nonverbal cues to develop their own creative and diverse characteristics.

Management of alteration in respiratory pattern manifestations, such as airway obstruction, is an aspect of nursing practice that frequently provides a basis for simulated laboratory activities. This focus may be used to provide specific examples using the nursing process approach in a Rogerian-based skills laboratory.

Assessment

Although "true Rogerian scholars would view physical assessment techniques as particulate and not holistic" (M. E. Rogers, personal communication, August 19, 1989), we have maintained that professional nurses should be able to gather information regarding the health of the client in any way possible, including the use of physical assessment skills. The presentation of the physical assessment content provides the educator with an opportunity to articulate the concept of holism, leading into a presentation of unified field pattern. This can be applied to all body systems, but assessment of the respiratory system provides an example for illustration.

Students may be led in a discussion of the ways in which data collected about the respiratory system are manifestations of the irreducible human being, and not just a physiological function of the lung tissue. The meaninglessness of examining a single lung, separate from the human organism, illustrates this point. When led in discussion, students commonly will describe how changes in respiratory patterns may reflect agitation or biochemical changes stemming from processes in other body systems, such as diabetes. Integrality (oneness with the environment) is a key principle with the Rogerian framework, and this may be illustrated by providing audio reproduction or peer simulation of various lung sounds. Invariably, students will report personal discomfort when listening to or auscultating sounds associated with respiratory distress, such as wheezes or stridor, thus demonstrating their own continuous mutual process with the environment.

To the typical assessment techniques of inspection, palpation, percussion, and auscultation, the Rogerian educator would add smell, language patterns, and posturing as important manifestations of the client's field wave. Scanning or fragmentation of the assessment process are rejected in favor of a holistic and intuitive exchange with the client in a continuous mutual process.

Planning

Students selecting strategies for those clients with an alteration in respiratory pattern may be led in conceptualizing the situation in terms of an alteration or obstruction of typical motion and energy flow. Information gathered from the assessment process is used to formulate nursing plans for creative and therapeutic interventions. Goals are articulated to reflect the movement of the client toward increasing diversity and actualization. Short-term goals focus on immediate needs, and long-term goals seek to maximize the potential for restoration of health. The client with an obstructed airway typically will have short-term needs for a sense of well-being, healing or optimal functioning, actualization, and creative adjustments to change.

Intervention

Interventions are selected to meet the appropriately stated, desired outcome of transforming the client's presentation of blocked motion. The student caring for this simulated client with an airway obstruction would consider interventions designed to pattern the client's environment in a way promoting normal air flow. These techniques may include imposed motion, positioning, or altering the environmental field with the strategic introduction of humidity, coolness, sounds, touch, etc. It should be pointed out that none of these interventions involve a direct manipulation of the anatomically defined respiratory system.

The art of nursing may be presented in case study performance based on client perceptions, with attention to the goals of healing and actualization. Suctioning of the respiratory passages by introduction of a catheter may be selected by the student as an appropriate intervention under a given set of circumstances, in which case the performance of the procedure would be guided by the scientific principles of motion, sterility, anatomy and physiology, and physics. The technical aspects of the procedure skill and the care of the client with a respiratory obstruction should evolve naturally and logically, with faculty guidance offered as necessary. The client's comfort and relaxation would be emphasized through the awareness that the procedure involves the unitary human field, and not just the respiratory tree. Therapeutic touch, imagery, and other techniques to promote client relaxation should be incorporated into the study of this and other appropriately selected nursing skills.

Evaluation

Continuous evaluation is vital to both nursing and education processes. Within the Rogerian framework, evaluation is emphasized in the context of the continuous process of change and diversity. As with assessment, evaluation is directed toward the whole or unitary human being. Using the goals as a guide, the nurse focuses on the process of patterning of the human and environmental fields. Subjectively, the client's report of greater comfort, awareness, sense of well-being, and harmony with the environmental field would indicate new pattern development. Objectively, additional data may be gathered by using the techniques of human environmental field assessment.

Evaluation of student learning and performance should be a mutual process between student and faculty, and based on the student's goals. Faculty are guided by the principles of the selected nursing theory, educational principles, and their own expertise in the standards of practice in nursing. Students completing the process should feel secure both in their technical clinical preparation and their ability to practice grounded in theory.

NOTES

1. A.I. Meleis, *Theoretical Nursing: Development and Progress* (Philadelphia: J.B. Lippincott Co., 1985).
2. V.A. Kemp, Themes in Theory Development, in *The Nursing Profession: Turning Points*, ed. N.L. Chaska (St. Louis: Mosby-Year Book, Inc., 1990), 608–616.
3. B.E. Smith, Linking Theory and Practice in Teaching Basic Nursing Skills, *Journal of Nursing Education* 31 (1992):16–23.
4. P.D. Ashworth, Theory and Practice: Beyond the Dichotomy, *Nurse Education Today* 13 (1993):321–327.
5. R.B. Harris, Introduction of a Conceptual Nursing Model into a Fundamental Baccalaureate Course, *Journal of Nursing Education* 2 (1986):66–69.
6. M.S. Knowles, *The Modern Practice of Adult Education* (New York: John Wiley & Sons, Inc., 1980).
7. D.A. Kolb, *Experimental Learning: Experience as the Source of Learning and Development* (Englewood Cliffs, NJ: Prentice Hall, 1984).
8. M.E. Rogers, Nursing Science and Art: A Prospective, *Nursing Science Quarterly* 1 (1988): 99–102.
9. M.E. Rogers, Nursing Science and the Space Age, *Nursing Science Quarterly* 1 (1992):27–34.
10. E.O. Bevis, *Curriculum Building in Nursing: A Process* (New York: National League for Nursing, 1989).
11. Ibid.
12. M.S. Infante, *The Clinical Laboratory* (New York: John Wiley & Sons, Inc., 1985).
13. Rogers, Nursing Science and Art; Nursing Science and the Space Age.
14. H.M. Ferrence, The Relationship of Time Experience, Creativity Traits, Differentiation, and Human Field Motion, in *Explorations on Martha Rogers' Science of Unitary Human Beings*, ed. V. Malinski (Norwalk, Conn: Appleton-Century-Crofts, 1986), 95–104.
15. B. Ludomirski-Kalmanson, The Relationship between the Environmental Energy Wave Frequency Pattern Manifest in Red and Blue Light and Human Field Motion in Adults with Visual Sensory Perception and Total Blindness (Unpublished dissertation, New York University, 1984).

16. M.J. Smith, Human Environment Process: A Test of Rogers' Principle of Integrality, *Advances in Nursing Science* 9 (1986):21–28.

17. S. Thomas, Modeling the Human Environment Encounter (Paper presented at the meeting of the Society for Rogerian Scholars, Southeast Region, Augusta, Georgia, August 17, 1989).

18. S.H. Gueldner, The Relationship between Imposed Motion and Human Field Motion in Elderly Individuals Living in Nursing Homes, in *Explorations on Martha Rogers' Science of Unitary Human Beings*, ed. V. Malinski (Norwalk, Conn: Appleton-Century-Crofts, 1986), 161–172.

SUGGESTED READING

Meleis, A.I. 1991. *Theoretical nursing: Development and progress*. 2nd ed. Philadelphia: J.B. Lippincott Co.

Oerman, M. 1994. Reforming nursing education for future practice. *Journal of Nursing Education* 33:215–219.

Wilson, M.E. 1994. Nursing student perspective of learning in a clinical setting. *Journal of Nursing Education* 33:81–86.

Chapter 22

Student-Selected Clinical Experiences

Elizabeth F. Pond

DEFINITION AND PURPOSES

Student-selected clinical experiences help to satisfy adult learning needs and empower nursing students to practice professional nursing. This teaching strategy is used to encourage students to select a clinical experience that will meet their individual learning needs, satisfy their curiosity about a different area of nursing practice, and provide some choice and control within their educational program. It also allows the student to interact with a seasoned professional in a preceptorial or mentoring relationship for a short period of time.

Most clinical experiences are determined by program goals and outcomes, accrediting organizations' criteria, health care trends, and resources. Within this framework, faculty can plan for student-selected clinical experiences, whether it is once or several times during a course or for an entire course, such as the final practice course.

THEORETICAL RATIONALE

The theoretical rationale for student-selected clinical experiences comes from two areas: adult learning theory and empowerment strategies. Several of Knowles's assumptions about adult learning[1,2] relate specifically to this teaching strategy. These are that adults tend to be self-directed, that they learn more from experiential activities, and that they are aware of their own learning needs based on their life experiences. Nursing students are adult learners at various levels of maturity, and most will benefit from a strategy that allows them to choose the learning environment and conditions based on their own needs.

According to Carlson-Catalano, empowerment strategies are needed to "plant seeds of leadership, colleagueship, self-respect, and professionalism; encourage critical thinking, problem solving, and application of knowledge to practice; free students from mechanistic learning; and counteract learned isolation, passivity, and confinement."[3] She states that empowering strategies "can prepare students to implement professional nursing practice,"[4] and may include activities in the categories of analytical nursing, change activities, collegiality, and sponsorship. The teaching strategy of student-selected clinical experiences is an empowering strategy, in that it allows for student analysis of clinical experiences, interaction of instructor and students as colleagues, and mentor relationships with practicing professionals in clinical settings.

CONDITIONS

The use of student-selected clinical experiences depends upon program goals and outcomes, and flexibility that faculty and students have within the nursing program. Use of this teaching strategy also depends upon the availability of professional nurses in a variety of clinical settings who are willing and have the time and resources to work with students.

TYPES OF LEARNERS

This teaching strategy can be adapted to meet the needs of undergraduate and graduate students. Undergraduate students in the latter part of their program and graduate students probably have the most flexibility for use of this strategy over a longer period of time. However, use of this strategy in the earlier part of an undergraduate program can assist students to meet their learning needs and begin "practicing" as professional nurses.

RESOURCES

Nursing professionals within a variety of clinical settings are needed to meet student needs; thus faculty must have a network of contacts in the health care community. Faculty must be able to communicate the objectives of such an experience and follow up on the process and outcomes of the experience. Using this teaching strategy, innovative and creative faculty can help students meet numerous learning needs and can help students grow professionally.

USING THE METHOD

At the beginning of the course in which this strategy is to be used, faculty discuss the purpose and process of the strategy with students, and assess student learning needs and ideas about possible clinical experiences. Once student needs, objectives, and clinical sites are clarified, faculty collaborate with appropriate nursing professionals to plan the experiences. A variety of methods can be used for students to share their experiences: group discussion, written reports, and oral presentations. Evaluation of the experiences by students, the nursing professionals in the clinical settings, and faculty is essential in identifying the benefits of the experiences and any problems encountered.

POTENTIAL PROBLEMS

Problems may be encountered when student learning needs and objectives are not clear and when unanticipated problems with scheduling and other concerns occur in the clinical setting with the nursing professional. Careful planning with clarification of specific student needs and appropriate selection of nursing professionals and clinical sites will prevent most problems. Follow-up discussion and analysis of the experiences will help students to think critically about issues encountered.

The following example illustrates a student-selected clinical experience as a successful teaching strategy for undergraduate students.

Example

"TBA" Clinical Activity

Elizabeth F. Pond

Students enrolled in a clinical course that included five weeks of twice-weekly experiences in perinatal or obstetrical settings had the opportunity for one "to be announced" (TBA) clinical activity. At the beginning of the quarter, the instructor explained the activity and provided the following information:

- *Purpose of activity*—to provide an "extra-special" experience based on student learning needs
- *Required activity*—present a 15- to 30-minute clinical postconference related to the student's experience

- *Other possible activities*
  1. Observe nurse in advanced practice in perinatal nursing or other field.
  2. Plan, implement, and evaluate teaching or other project on nursing unit.
  3. Develop own ideas for activities.
  4. Supplement clinical experiences in labor and delivery unit, newborn nursery, or postpartum unit.
- *Directions*—Submit objectives and plan to instructor for approval at least 24 hours in advance. In some cases, a week may be needed to make arrangements for the clinical experience. Write up outcome and submit to instructor.

Over a two-year period, approximately 32 students selected a variety of clinical experiences. These included working with a lactation consultant, pediatric oncology clinical nurse specialists, neonatal intensive care nurses, nurse anesthetists, and nurses implementing special projects. One student chose to work in a private physician's office. Another chose to work with a nurse who performed fetal assessment procedures, such as biophysical profiles. A few chose to supplement their experiences in the regularly scheduled clinical areas. Interestingly, none of the students chose to plan, implement, and evaluate a teaching or other project on the nursing unit. This was probably because they were already doing a teaching project with mothers on the unit.

Feedback from all students was positive. They enjoyed being able to choose a clinical experience—one in which they were really interested and one that they would not have been able to experience otherwise. Comments from students included the following:

- "I was able to get both theory and practical experience . . . I learned a great deal." (lactation consultant)
- "We feel very fortunate that we were given the opportunity to follow these two very wonderful nurses. It takes a special person to fill the shoes of a pediatric oncology clinical specialist."
- "I really enjoyed my experience. I learned so much about childhood cancer, and the success stories that go along with it. I got to talk with children suffering from these terrible diseases, and see how their families deal with it on a day-to-day basis. I not only saw the physical aspects, but the psychosocial, emotional, and financial aspects also. I really got a good view of holistic nursing care . . . it was very worthwhile."
- "I think these TBA days are a wonderful way to get some exposure to an area we are particularly interested in."
- "I had a wonderful experience in the NICU [neonatal intensive care unit]. I was hooked up with an excellent nurse who really showed me around and

explained what she did . . . . The worst part of the day was near the end when a baby passed away . . . . It was touching to see how much they [the nurses] cared."

- I really enjoyed the clinical experience because it tied what we are learning in class into the real world." (NICU)
- The nurse anesthetist "was very helpful and willing to answer any and all questions I had . . . I was completely satisfied with the experience. . . ."
- "I had a terrific day!" The nurse anesthetist "was great! . . . I had thought that I wanted to become an OR nurse, but this experience has strongly made me consider pursuing nursing anesthesia."

NOTES

1. M.S. Knowles, The Modern Practice of Adult Education: from Pedagogy to Andragogy, 2nd ed (New York: Cambridge University Press, 1980).
2. P.S. Hoff, Adult Learning and the Nurse, in *Innovative Teaching Strategies in Nursing*, ed. B. Fuszard (Gaithersburg, Md: Aspen Publishers, Inc., 1989), 7–11.
3. J. Carlson-Catalano, Empowering Nurses for Professional Practice, *Nursing Outlook* 40, no. 3 (1992):140.
4. Ibid., 139.

Chapter 23

Teaching Patients with Low Literacy Skills

Connie F. Cowan and Joyce A. Bowie-Guillory

DEFINITION AND PURPOSES

America's literacy problems have been a concern for years, prompting many communities to institute literacy programs and classes for their citizens. In the 1980s, 20 percent—or one out of five—of adults were estimated as being functionally illiterate and having difficulty reading at or below a fifth-grade level or low-literacy level.[1] However, a more recent study by the National Center for Educational Statistics indicates that approximately 50 percent of America's adults fall in the lowest two levels (out of five levels) of literacy when tested, which categorizes them as being functionally illiterate.[2] A reading level this low negatively influences one's ability to function effectively in society. Everyday skills such as reading a menu, filling out a job application, or addressing an envelope properly become matters of difficulty for the person with low literacy skills (LLS). Understandably, difficulties evolve when trying to teach these people about complex health care matters. As the primary patient educators for health care matters, these statistics affect nurses greatly. It requires us to plan and implement our patient education strategically and to choose carefully the written materials utilized.

Multiple studies have evaluated low literacy levels as they relate to patient education and written materials. Doak et al. studied 100 common patient education materials (i.e., diet instructions, patient Bill of Rights, etc.) and found the mean reading level needed to comprehend them was the tenth grade.[3] They studied a corresponding patient population and found their reading ability to be at a seventh-grade level despite most being high school graduates. This study was replicated by the South Carolina Diabetes Control Project in 1984, resulting in similar data. An expansion of the Doak study tested 300 common patient education materials from around the United States and found the reading level needed for these materials was 11th grade.[4]

Grimm evaluated the reading levels of 100 diabetic patients in a large teaching hospital.[5] Of this population, 60 percent read at a fifth-grade level or below (42 percent of this group were reading at the level of third grade). Grimm also evaluated the reading level of 40 of the most commonly used national diabetes educational materials. The average readability level of these materials was tenth grade.

Meade and Byrd studied 258 subjects from a primary care clinic in Milwaukee as part of a smoking cessation program.[6] Their study revealed a median reading level of sixth grade and a median educational level completion of tenth grade. Most of the patient education booklets that they evaluated for their study were written above the ninth-grade level.

Dixon and Park studied the reading difficulty and overall comprehensibility of various booklets and consent forms utilized in an 830-bed, private, Midwest hospital. The materials all scored at reading levels between grades 9.5 and 13.8.[7]

Streiff reported similar results when she studied 28 patient education materials and 106 patients in an ambulatory care setting. The mean readability level for the materials was the 11th grade. Five of the pamphlets specific to the topic of contraception required a reading level of grade 13.2. The patients had a mean completed grade level of 9.9, but a reading skill level of grade 6.8.[8]

A review of the literature reveals that the majority of written patient education materials, relating to a variety of health topics, require at least a tenth-grade reading level.[9-12] Yet a person's reading level does not necessarily correlate with the number of years they have attended school. Several studies have revealed a two- to four-grade level disparity between the level of schooling completed and one's reading level.[13-18] In Grimm's study, however, the statistics were more disturbing. The mean of one half of the study population completed the tenth grade, yet read at a sixth-grade level, while the mean of the other half completed the 11th grade, and read at a fourth grade level![19] This disparity between the reading level of educational materials and the patient's reading level suggests that much of the written patient education information is being poorly understood or misunderstood. Ultimately, the use of high-level written materials as the primary method of patient education negatively affects learning, comprehension, and adherence.

THEORETICAL RATIONALE

Orem's theory of self-care is utilized as the framework for the integration of self-care concepts into patient education and adherence. Self-care as explained by Orem is the behavior from life situations that persons direct to themselves or their environment to regulate factors affecting their own development, health, or well-being.[20] She further describes them as learned and goal-oriented activities.

Hill and Smith add to Orem's theory by describing specific conditions that they deem essential for meeting self-care needs.[21]

- specific knowledge, skills, and the responsibility for health care needs
- motivation and energy to initiate and persevere in the self-care process
- placing a high value on health
- the belief that the health behaviors involved in self-care will reduce vulnerability to illness

Hill and Smith also relate that in Orem's theory, education is the primary means used to correct self-care deficits or problems in providing for one's own health care needs.[22] Inherent in Orem's theory is the premise that when a self-care need is not met, a self-care demand is present. Self-care deficits exist when people are unable to meet their self-care demands. Education/learning is extremely important in influencing one's self-care practices and ultimately the motivation to comply with health regimens. Education (formal and informal) can influence how they may utilize specific information to direct or improve their lives. Patients cannot be expected to follow treatment instructions when they lack a basic understanding of the rationale, procedures, and requirements of their regimen.[23] If a self-care deficit evolves, then patient education may be required as an intervention. Thus, a nurse or other provider may be involved in an educative or consultative relationship to help alleviate or correct the self-care deficit.[24]

According to Hussey and Gilliland, low literacy and illiteracy are major contributing factors to nonadherence. Though a person may possess adequate reading skills, understanding and interpretation are not guaranteed.[25] The idea of being able to function or act on content after reading it has led to the development of functional literacy. Poor reading skills have an impact on understanding and interpretation of meaning, but also on the client's organization of thought, perception, and vocabulary development. All of these factors can cause confusion and misunderstanding so that instructions are misinterpreted.[26] Without comprehension, adherence is by chance rather than by choice."[27]

CONDITIONS

In order to teach people with LLS, it is essential for us to understand the difficulties and obstacles they may encounter. Doak, et al. explain that people with LLS experience several areas of difficulty in addition to reading: reading ability, comprehension, process, organization of perceptions or thoughts, and problem-solving skills.[28]

Reading ability relates to one's actual ability and level of reading. It involves letter and word recognition. Persons with LLS often read letter by letter to derive each word, and thus read in a slow, halting manner. This method also negatively affects comprehension. These persons recognize typed or printed words more easily than handwritten, cursive words.

Comprehension involves understanding the meaning of what is read, not just recognizing the words. It includes listening comprehension (understanding what is being read or verbally instructed). Comprehension is usually lower and less complete for the person with LLS, often due to reading as well as language deficits. Thus, poor vocabulary and listening skills make it more difficult for persons with LLS to express themselves or to fully understand others who have greater fluency. However, Grimm notes that this is not always the case. In that study, many patients were found to be articulate and able to communicate quite effectively, yet had LLS when tested. Grimm states that often these patients have dealt with their deficit for many years and have learned to cope with and conceal their deficits.[29]

Inherent in comprehension is cultural literacy. Cultural literacy means that an individual possesses the background information and perspective necessary to read with understanding. The individual must understand the undertones of a comment or conversation, the intonation of voice, and in what context the comment is being used, whether it be slang, terminology, or custom. Cultural literacy involves knowing how to communicate without having to explain.

Process is one's ability to utilize reading, language, and comprehension skills to develop a whole picture—being able to utilize one's resources, internal and external (i.e., life experiences) to derive a logical connection (comprehension) of a concept, situation, or instructions. It involves the *organization of perceptions or thoughts*, which is one's ability to formulate a logical sequence to thoughts, ideas, events, etc., which in turn helps to organize data into a whole, logical, sequential picture. This is a sophisticated cognitive process and often causes difficulty for the patient with low literacy skills. It requires that information be taught in small increments for better understanding and for the sequence to be remembered. *Problem-solving skills* are often delayed for a person with LLS. Many times, because of a deficit in this area, directions (verbal or written) are taken quite literally, with no understanding as to why, and with no room for adaptation of thoughts or actions based on circumstances.

Thus, with the above conditions possible, the conditions for learning must include time for demonstration, questions, repeat demonstration, and further questions. The environment should be quiet, structured, and conducive to learning, as for any adult learner. Teaching patients with LLS requires patience on the part of the teacher, as well as astuteness in determining whether the patient is really understanding the instruction.

TYPES OF LEARNERS

Low literacy applies to adolescents and adults who have deficits in reading abilities, process, and comprehension. Low literacy affects people of all races. Socioeconomic status does not determine illiteracy, because illiteracy is found in all levels of society.[30] The point must be made here that although a person may not be able to read or to read well enough to understand or interpret meaning does not mean that he or she is lacking intelligence. Illiteracy does not equate to low IQ or low intelligence.[31] And as stated previously, the number of years one has completed in school does not necessarily predict one's literacy abilities. Unskilled and poorly skilled readers have several characteristics in common:

- They usually agree with everything. If you ask whether they understand, the answer will usually be yes.
- They are well defended. They are not easy to distinguish, and they try hard to maintain their dignity.
- They tend to be literal and concrete. This causes them difficulty with conceptualization because their databases are limited (normally, data are usually acquired through reading). Comprehension is slow and usually incomplete. They also have difficulty in classifying information.
- They may not view words or pictures from left to right and may not be good at sounding out words. They also may not be able to recognize signs, symbols, abbreviations, or synonyms.
- Their perspective is usually limited to direct personal experiences; thus they operate on a more restricted information base.
- They are usually restless in teaching-learning environments because of the threat of exposing their poor literacy or illiteracy.
- They usually will not volunteer to answer questions when in a group setting.

RESOURCES

Multiple resources are available to assist the person with LLS and the professional trying to teach these people. There are national, regional, and local literacy programs designed to assist the person with LLS. The professional may consult with the National Institutes of Health Literacy Program in Bethesda, Maryland; Patient Learning Associates, Inc. (Cecelia and Leonard Doak) in Potomac, Maryland; regional, statewide or local literacy programs; teaching facilities in local or regional colleges; health education institutions/hospitals; libraries; and local audiovisual services. In addition, if local resources are limited, the development of one's own materials may be warranted. Several references at the end of this chapter should assist in the creation of materials.

USING THE METHOD

Successful methods of teaching patients with LLS include verbal instruction, repetition or review of the instructions, demonstration and return demonstration, and teaching in small increments to allow for process and comprehension. Focus the instruction on the desired patient behavior(s), eliminating information that is extraneous or not directly relevant to achieving those behaviors.[32] Repeatedly reviewing the information and procedures is important.[33] Seek consensual validation by having the patient repeat the instructions as they were interpreted. When giving verbal instructions, make sure the client comprehends, since medical jargon can be confusing.[34] Verbal instructions should include the patient's own terminology, and key instructions should be concise, ordered, and as vivid and explicit as possible. Each idea or topic should be taught one step at a time, and information and teaching sessions should be limited. Instructions being given should be broken down into segments or components. Breaks should be provided at the end of each segment/component to provide time for review, feedback, and questions.[35] Use as many visual aids as possible. Slide/tape programs are excellent for those who are illiterate.[36] Video programs are equally good.

Written materials should be used only if they are written on a level that correlates with (or near) the patient's reading level. These materials should be printed or typed with lowercase and uppercase letters, and not handwritten, especially not in cursive writing. The type size should be large, for ease in distinguishing letters.[37-40] The use of all capitalized letters should be avoided because it is harder to read. Educational materials should include a few key points and should include graphics or pictures, which add to the understanding of the concept being taught.[41-43] The utilization of subheadings assists the patient in sifting through information to find the topic of interest or need.[44,45] "Chunking" words or ideas together in a meaningful context assists patients in understanding and remembering the intended educational message.[46] Only one idea should be conveyed in each sentence or paragraph.[47,48] The use of active voice (conversational style) makes materials easier to read and comprehend, and also makes it more personal.[49-51]

POTENTIAL PROBLEMS

The term *simplified* should not be misinterpreted to mean simplistic or intended for a simpleton. When this occurs, materials for the patient with LLS end up being childlike, or childlike associations are made. Pictures may be "silly" or cartoonlike despite trying to convey adult concepts. This is insulting and demeaning to the patient. "Talking down" to the patient defeats the collaborative educator/learner role and places the learner in a more subservient role.

Careful attention must be paid to the patient's actual capabilities and understanding; otherwise incorrect assumptions may ensue. There is a danger in making assumptions because the clients may have received additional education or they may be quiet in normal circumstances. When low literacy is suspected, one must use extreme caution and avoid any hint of disapproval, impatience, or judgment.

Example
Teaching Reflux
Connie F. Cowan and Joyce A. Bowie-Guillory

The following is a portion of a patient instruction handout formerly utilized in a clinic in a large teaching hospital. The revised version of these instructions is currently in use at that clinic. Portions of those instructions are used here to illustrate how instructions may be revised for use with patients with LLS.

Example #1
<u>(ORIGINAL TEXT):</u>
REFLUX

> Many children and adults have regurgitation of food, liquids, and/or acid from the stomach back into the esophagus and throat. Sometimes it causes no problems, but it may cause heartburn, chest pains, vomiting, wheezing, coughing or even pneumonia or sinusitis. Some respiratory symptoms may be related to or precipitated by gastroesophogeal reflux. When this is the case, our recommended approach to treatment is as follows: Avoid high acid foods such as licorice, mint, tea, coffee, cokes, chocolate, ketchup and alcoholic beverages. Smoking may worsen the condition, and thus patients must be encouraged to eliminate smoking behaviors. Elevation of the head of the bed approximately 2-4 inches on a brick or block assists in reducing reflux by means of gravity.

(7 sentences; 118 words; 22 polysyllabic words; written in passive voice; 10-point print; uses capital letters for emphasis; there is no order to the instructions).

Using the SMOG method[52] of evaluating written materials for literacy levels, the original text, in its entirety, scored at an 11th-grade reading level.

Example #2
(REVISED, SIMPLIFIED VERSION):

Reflux

Reflux is when food, liquid or acid backs up from the stomach into the throat. It may cause "heartburn," chest pains, vomiting (throwing up), wheezing in the lungs, or coughing. It may even cause infections in the lungs or sinuses. If your doctor thinks reflux is causing some of your lung problems, here are some things which may help you.

1. Do not eat licorice, mint, chocolate, or ketchup.
2. Do not drink tea, coffee, cokes or sodas.
3. Do not drink beer, wine, or liquor.
4. Stop Smoking!!
5. Raise up the head of your bed on a brick or block (about 2–4 inches)

(9 sentences; 99 words; 5 polysyllabic words; written in active voice; 14-point print; title is enlarged and points are underlined for emphasis; instructions are ordered; print is block letters for ease in distinguishing letters).

Using the SMOG method[53] of evaluating written materials for literacy levels, the revised text, in its entirety, scored at an eighth-grade reading level.

CONCLUSION

There are many people in the United States today with LLS. The condition is cross-cultural and is not dependent on social class. Adherence is often a problem for these clients, since written instructions on their level are not available for reference and because they often will not ask questions.

Patients with LLS usually learn best from verbal and demonstrative teaching, supplemented with written materials tailored to their level. It becomes the educator's responsibility to be certain that the client has every opportunity to learn by whatever means necessary. A person's educational level does not necessarily correlate with his or her reading level or abilities. Therefore, to maximize comprehensibility, foster self-care practices, and facilitate adherence, the level of written materials must be properly matched to the intended target audience.[54] Teaching in increments works well with patients with low literacy, because their ability to comprehend and process information is delayed. Therefore, one must tailor patient education to the patient's actual needs and abilities rather than the nurses' perceptions of such. This requires an accurate and ongoing assessment of each individual and of all materials utilized for patient education.

NOTES

1. C.C. Doak, et al., *Teaching Patients with Low Literacy Skills* (Philadelphia: J.B. Lippincott Co., 1985).

2. Educational Testing Service and National Center for Educational Statistics, *Adult Literacy in America: National Adult Literacy Survey* (Washington, DC: Office of Education Research and Improvement, U.S. Department of Education, 1993).

3. Doak, et al., *Teaching Patients with Low Literacy Skills.*

4. L.G. Doak and C.C. Doak, Lowering the Silent Barriers to Compliance for Patients with Low Literacy Skills, *Promoting Health* 8, (1987):6–8.

5. J. Grimm, The Development of Diabetes Footcare Pamphlets for Patients with Low Literacy Skills (Master's thesis, Medical College of Georgia, 1990).

6. C.D. Meade and J.C. Byrd, Patient Literacy and Readability of Smoking Education Literature, *American Journal of Public Health* 79, no. 2 (1989):204–206.

7. E. Dixon and R. Park, Do Patients Understand Written Health Information?, *Nursing Outlook* 38, no. 6 (1990):278–281.

8. L.D. Streiff, Can Clients Understand Our Instructions?, *Image: Journal of Nursing Scholarship* 18, (1986):48–52.

9. Doak, et al., *Teaching Patients with Low Literacy Skills.*

10. Doak and Doak, Lowering the Silent Barriers.

11. Dixon and Park, Do Patients Understand?

12. Streiff, Can Clients Understand?

13. Doak, et al., *Teaching Patients with Low Literacy Skills.*

14. Grimm, The Development of Diabetes Footcare Pamphlets.

15. Meade and Byrd, Patient Literacy and Readability.

16. Streiff, Can Clients Understand?

17. M.D. Boyd and R.H.L. Feldman, Health Information Seeking and Reading and Comprehension Abilities of Cardiac Rehabilitation Patients, *Journal of Cardiac Rehabilitation* 4, no. 8 (1984): 343–347.

18. J.M. Swanson, et al., Readability of Commercial and Generic Contraceptive Instructions, *Image: Journal of Nursing Scholarship* 22, no. 2 (1990):96–100.

19. Grimm, The Development of Diabetes Footcare Pamphlets.

20. D.E. Orem, *Nursing: Concepts of Practice*, 4th ed. (St. Louis: Mosby-Year Book, Inc., 1991).

21. L. Hill and N. Smith, *Self-Care Nursing: Promotion of Health*, 2nd ed. (Norwalk, Conn: Appleton & Lange, 1990).

22. Hill and Smith, *Self-Care Nursing.*

23. A.G. Taylor, et al., Do Patients Understand Patient Education Brochures?, *Nursing & Health Care* 3, no. 6 (1982):305–310.

24. Hill and Smith, *Self-Care Nursing.*

25. L.C. Hussey and K. Gilliland, Compliance, Low Literacy and Locus of Control, *Nursing Clinics of North America* 24, no. 3 (1989):605–611.

26. Ibid.

27. Doak and Doak, Lowering the Silent Barriers to Compliance, 8.

28. Doak, et al., *Teaching Patients with Low Literacy Skills.*

29. Grimm, The Development of Diabetes Footcare Pamphlets.

30. A. Haggard, *Handbook of Patient Education* (Gaithersburg, Md: Aspen Publishers, Inc., 1989).

31. Haggard, *Handbook of Patient Education.*

32. Doak and Doak, Lowering the Silent Barriers.

33. A. Walker, Teaching the Illiterate Patient, *Journal of Enterostomal Therapy* 14, no. 2 (1987):85.

34. J. Guillory, Ethnic Perspectives of Cancer Nursing: The Black American, *Oncology Nursing Forum* 14, no. 3 (1987):66–69.

35. Doak and Doak, Lowering the Silent Barriers.

36. J. Guillory, Relationships of Selected Physiological, Psychosocial, and Spiritual Variables Associated with Survivorship in Socioeconomically Disadvantaged African American Women with Breast Cancer (Dissertation, Medical College of Georgia, 1992).

37. Doak, et al., *Teaching Patients with Low Literacy Skills.*

38. Doak and Doak, Lowering the Silent Barriers.

39. P. Farrell-Miller and P. Gentry. How Effective Are Your Patient Education Materials? Guidelines for Development and Evaluation of Written Educational Materials, *The Diabetes Educator* 15, no. 5 (1989):418–422.

40. M.D. Boyd, A Guide to Writing Effective Patient Education Materials, *Nursing Management* 18, no. 7 (1987):56–57.

41. Doak, et al., *Teaching Patients with Low Literacy Skills.*

42. Doak and Doak, Lowering the Silent Barriers.

43. Farrell-Miller and Gentry, How Effective Are Your Patient Education Materials?

44. Dixon and Clark, Do Patients Understand?

45. Boyd, A Guide to Writing Effective Patient Education Materials.

46. Doak, et al., *Teaching Patients with Low Literacy Skills.*

47. Boyd, A Guide to Writing Effective Patient Education Materials.

48. C.D. Meade and D.M. Howser, Consent Forms: How to Determine and Improve their Readability, *Oncology Nursing Forum* 19, no. 10 (1992):1523–1528.

49. Doak, et al., *Teaching Patients with Low Literacy Skills*.

50. Farrell-Miller and Gentry, How Effective Are Your Patient Education Materials?

51. Boyd, A Guide to Writing Effective Patient Education Materials.

52. H.G. McLaughlin, SMOG-Grading: A New Readability Formula, *Journal of Reading* 12 (1969):639–646.

53. McLaughlin, SMOG-Grading.

54. Taylor, et al., Do Patients Understand?

Chapter 24

Nursing Rounds

Wanda Anderson-Loftin

DEFINITION AND PURPOSES

Nursing rounds offer an interactive, patient-centered strategy in which students utilize bedside teaching of a concept grounded in the reality of the practice world. The teacher provides the student with a tool for nursing rounds, directions for accomplishing the learning activity, and criteria for peer evaluation. Students select a concept or patient problem that has meaning for them and is specific to the nursing care of an individual patient. Theories, intuition, insight, feelings, patient-family perceptions, and input from other health care personnel are used in preparing for nursing rounds. During walking rounds, each student presents the chosen topic at the patient's bedside for immediate discussion with the patient and family and for a later analysis by the clinical group. Students not conducting nursing rounds listen, ask questions, and contribute to the analysis by sharing their own observations, insights, and experiences. The teacher maintains the focus on nursing, facilitates group process, and assists students in acquiring critical thinking skills by use of Socratic questioning, which leads students through the critical thinking process.

Nursing rounds are used to develop the clinical reasoning skills of critical thinking, problem solving, and decision making in students while they learn basic concepts in nursing. By preparing oral presentations for nursing rounds and participating in rounds presented by others, students learn the rules and rationales for such things as new nursing procedures, nursing care of patients with highly technical equipment, physical assessment techniques, implications of abnormal laboratory findings for nursing care, and application of basic scientific principles to nursing situations.

Although the content of nursing rounds may be the procedural lists of things that all nursing students must learn, the focus is on syntactical learning, which helps students see meaningful wholes, patterns, and relationships; crystallize insights; recognize significant clues, exercise intuition; and find meaning.[1] In this way, the critical thinking skills of cue sensing, hypothesis testing, and interpretation of data for problem identification are stimulated and encouraged.

Nursing rounds place the patient at the center of the learning experience and socialize students into the art of caring, compassionate nursing. The tool for nursing rounds structures patient-centered nursing, and the teacher maintains the focus throughout the learning activity. Students learn caring, compassionate nursing from the modeling of care by caring, compassionate teachers. The teachers' philosophy, ethics, and values are powerful socialization tools and foster the enculturation of students into the norms, values, and mores of the profession.

Students are prepared for the real world of nursing in nursing rounds because nursing rounds are based on the reality of the practice world. This reality base makes the course aligned and meaningful for the student.

Finally, nursing rounds facilitate the development of mature, independent learners who can think as well as do. One of the most important aspects of facilitating learner independence is creating an environment that requires learners to be actively involved and to accept responsibility for their own learning. Of equal importance is a change in the role of the teacher to one of a more egalitarian nature.

THEORETICAL RATIONALE

The strategy of nursing rounds is based on Bevis's typology of learning.[2] Bevis proposed that the goal of all education is to graduate students who are independent, self-directed, internally motivated, lifelong learners who are familiar with inquiry approaches to learning.[3] Learners are moved along a continuum from immaturity to maturity by use of facilitative learning styles and by carefully chosen student-teacher interactions and learning activities.

Bevis states that individuals learn content in many different ways and that training can be differentiated from education by the type of learning involved.[4] The typology of learning[5] (see Exhibit 24–1) groups learning into six different types. The first three types are described as training and the last three are designated as educative. The oral presentations that students prepare in nursing rounds are classified as "training" and encompass the first three types of learning: item, directive, and rationale. However, the uniqueness of nursing rounds is on the increased focus on syntactical learning, the increased dialogue, and the change in the role of the teacher.

Exhibit 24–1 Typology of Learning

1. Item Learning involves learning of separate pieces of information, simple relationships, and objective measurements such as temperature and blood pressure. Students list, relate single factors, describe, and complete tasks by rote learning and following given step-by-step procedures.
2. Directive Learning means learning the rules, prohibitions, and injunctions and when to apply them and when not to apply them. It is the development of protocol or safe set of directions for assembling items or tasks. Directive learning must follow or be learned concurrently with item learning.
3. Rationale Learning is the application of theory and research to practice. It is characterized by the rational use of formal properties of theories and activities, logical sequencing of items and directions, and relating skills and interventions to items and directions. It permits reality-based practice of classical and known patterns.
4. Contextual Learning is the socialization of nurses into nursing. It involves learning the culture, mores and folkways, values, ethics, and general philosophy of nursing. This category deals with learning the jargon and work-role relationships of coordination, collaboration, and colleagueship and developing a view of nursing as a caring, compassionate, human science.
5. Syntactical Learning means seeing meaningful wholes, patterns, and relationships. It is exercising intuition, recognizing significance, finding meaning, and expressing insights. Contextual aspects of the situation are considered and influence the departure from general rules or common nursing behaviors. Paradigms are developed to guide practice, and informal properties such as feeling and intuition are used in their development. Student learning in this category involves interpreting, evaluating, projecting, and predicting, using both data and intuition. It grasps the real essence of things as opposed to the classical, rule-driven models of practice.
6. Inquiry Learning involves using standard tools, such as research, in creative and visionary ways to identify and solve the problems of nursing. It is the generation of new ideas, theories, and ways of using old ideas in new and innovative ways. In this category learners pose questions, fantasize about new possibilities, and create ways to make those possibilities reality. They are questing and enjoy the quest.

Source: Adapted from *Toward a Caring Curriculum: A New Pedagogy for Nursing* by E.O. Bevis and J. Watson, eds., pp. 91–94, with permission of the National League for Nursing, © 1989.

TYPES OF LEARNERS

Nursing rounds are appropriate for undergraduate, graduate, and staff development programs and all levels of students and staff. As learners progress toward independence and self-direction, they seek more complex concepts and multiproblem situations. Staff development programs may be structured around case presentations of client care by nurses from novice to expert.[6] The reality base of nursing rounds makes this an excellent learning activity for staff development.

RESOURCES

Nursing rounds are best used in an inpatient setting that provides the opportunity for patient-family-student interactions. Patient-family-student dialogue provides the contextual aspects of the situation, such as the meaning of the illness to the patient and its impact on his or her family. It is through this type of dialogue that learners develop empathetic understanding of the patient's/family's viewpoint and incorporate these contextual elements into the formulation of the nursing problem.

Videotaping or audiotaping may be used at the teacher's discretion. Replay during the analysis session often stimulates insights by which hidden meanings are understood and parts become a whole.

Technical equipment, supplies, surgical prostheses, and other material resources used are specific to the patient problem or nursing concept presented. These resources are generally already in use in the patient environment.

Learners are also encouraged to consult with other health care personnel identified as experts in the area being researched. In this way, learners are given the opportunity to scan the environment for available human resources and to incorporate the consultation process into practice.

Time is one of the most critical resources needed for nursing rounds. This learning activity is best accomplished at intermittent intervals toward the end of the time frame set for the learning experience, and with small groups of learners. A group of six to eight learners is ideal, although a group of eight to ten is possible. One- to one-and-a-half-hour intermittent sessions over a three- or four-week period are generally adequate for this number of learners.

APPLICATION

Careful planning is necessary to ensure that students are structured for success and that sufficient time is available for dialogue. The teacher provides learners with objectives; a tool for nursing rounds, which includes patient identification data, medical information, and directions for presentation of concept (see Exhibit 24–2); and criteria for peer evaluation.

The timing of nursing rounds is also a responsibility of the teacher and a crucial part of planning. In an eight-week clinical rotation, nursing rounds are begun the fifth or sixth week. Two to four learners present at nursing rounds on each of these weeks. Twenty minutes is allowed for each presentation. After completion of this portion of nursing rounds, the group meets for 20 minutes to dialogue about the problems and concepts presented and to search for commonalities, patterns,

Exhibit 24–2 Presentation of the Nursing Concept

Directions:

This part of Nursing Rounds is performed inside the patient's room. Time allowed is twenty minutes.

Choose a single concept to present. This may be a new nursing procedure, nursing care involved with an unfamiliar piece of equipment, or a physical assessment technique and implications of findings for nursing care, or you may present one of the patient's nursing problems and nursing care relevant to the problem. You may elect to present an analysis of the patient's laboratory data, the relationship of the data to the patient's physical condition, and implications for nursing care. In essence, you may choose any nursing concept or patient problem that you desire as long as it relates to nursing and is relevant to the care of your patient.

Consult your teacher about your choice of concepts. She may be able to suggest ideas, approaches, or resources.

What meaning does your selected concept hold for you?

What significance does your chosen concept have for the rest of your nursing career?

Support your presentation with relevant theories or scientific rationale.

This part of the presentation is to be demonstrated at the patient's bedside. Include the patient in the discussion and direct your presentation to him or her also. Do not "talk over" the patient. If technical language is a necessary part of your presentation, explain to the patient that you are going to "talk to the nurses now" and afterward paraphrase what was said in lay terms for the patient. If your patient is unable to comprehend, offer a simple explanation while attempting to establish eye contact. Gentle touch and a soothing voice often reassure these patients even though they may not understand what you are saying.

Be prepared to share any insights ("Ah, Ha!") that you have gained through this presentation.

relationships, significance, meanings, and insights. A critique of the presentations is also given at this time through a process of peer evaluation, and completes nursing rounds.

Thoughtful planning of patient assignments provides learners with fruitful choices of concepts for analysis. A tactic that is particularly productive is use of a grand rounds format wherein all the patients presented have a problem in common. If one of the curriculum concepts is pain, then patients with a patient-controlled analgesia (PCA) pump, an epidural pump, and PRN intramuscular narcotics may be assigned. Presentation of different case examples of patients with pain facilitates concept analysis when students analyze the commonalities, differences, assumptions, and meanings.

Planning by the learner entails selecting a concept or patient problem that is relative to some aspect of the patient's care, is meaningful to the learner, and has some significance to the learner's nursing education. The teacher acts as a consultant to assist the learner in identifying the salient aspects of the situation, maintaining the focus on nursing, and guiding the learner in selection of meaningful and significant patient problems. The learner then researches the chosen topic and prepares an oral presentation according to directions and criteria.

Nursing rounds are implemented by bedside presentation of the nursing concepts. The patients' participation is incorporated into nursing rounds, thereby reinforcing meaningful, realistic, patient-centered learning.

During the bedside presentation, the learner focuses on rationale learning. The teacher focuses on syntactical learning. The learner uses rationale learning in theological sequencing of items and directions and by the application of relevant theories. For example, if a student has demonstrated the use of a PCA pump, the presentation logically includes procedures for use of equipment (directive learning); pain theory, such as the gate control theory (rationale learning); patient teaching (rationale learning); and use of the nursing process in assessment, diagnosis, intervention, and evaluation of pain (rationale learning).

The teacher seizes the opportunity for syntactical learning as it occurs. Learners are taught to attend to feelings—their's, the patient's, and the family's—and to use them just as they would use objective cues. Hunches and best guesses (intuition) are recognized as legitimate sources of information and are used in diagnosis and care. The teacher uses spontaneous and issue-specific Socratic questioning[7] to focus on meaningful wholes, patterns, and relationships; significance, intuition, and insights; and the context of the situation. Socratic questions are those that help students clarify information; probe assumptions, reasons, and evidence; enter empathetically into viewpoints of others; and discover implications and consequences.

The teacher models how to obtain patient participation in care while facilitating critical thinking and analysis of concepts by posing questions relating to the patient's viewpoint on care. Questions such as, "What do you think about this machine [PCA], Mr. Smith?" "Have you experienced other pain relief measures that work better for you?" "Tell us about them." "How is Mr. Smith's PCA like Mr. Jones's epidural pump?" "How is it different?"

During the bedside presentation, the teacher must be ready tactfully and spontaneously to correct situations in which values are being betrayed or norms are not being met. A common problem is that students, in their anxiety over group presentation, speak primarily to the teacher or to their classmates in rapid, technological, and medical terminology. In this situation, the teacher may turn to the patient, establish eye contact while gently touching the patient, and say, "Mr. Smith, Mary was explaining to the other learners about how this PCA machine controls your pain and what nursing care you require while you're using it. What she said was . . . ." In this way, attention is refocused on the patient, patient interaction and communication are role-modeled, learner self-esteem is preserved, and the value of patient-centered nursing is communicated. Learners assimilate the modeling of caring, compassionate, nursing care through contextual learning.

After the bedside presentation, the group meets in a conference room for the analysis session. The teacher facilitates a search for commonalities, relationships, patterns, meanings, significance, and insights. Typical questions at this point are: "What nursing problems do these patients have in common?" "Which ones are different?" "What makes their responses alike or different?" "What is the rationale for your answer?" "What are you assuming?" "What effect will the nursing care have?" This is also a time for spontaneous Socratic discussions when the teacher notes that students are interested in a topic or raise an important issue.

Evaluation is the final component of nursing rounds. Peer evaluation is used in assigning a grade to the oral presentation. A criterion-referenced evaluation tool is provided to each learner in the course syllabus along with the objectives, directions, and tool for nursing rounds. The teacher participates in the grading as a peer: teacher-assigned grades are of equal weight with student-assigned grades. In addition, the teacher also evaluates how well each learner uses the peer evaluation process according to the criteria developed for that purpose. Consequently, learners receive two grades of equal weight for nursing rounds, one for the learning activity and one for peer evaluation. The averages of these grades account for a percentage of the learner's clinical grades.

INCREASED DIALOGUE

An increase in the number and types of interactions is a key to the overall success of nursing rounds. Not only is there teacher-learner dialogue, but also dialogue is encouraged between learners and learners and between learners and patients. If dialogue is allowed to lapse into the old teacher-learner "drill and grill," nursing rounds lose some of their dynamism and their power to foster critical thinking skills, inquiry modes of learning, and learner maturity.

Teacher-learner dialogue helps students identify cues that only an experienced nurse would know. For instance, the learner may have little prior experience in knowing that an incision that is well approximated, with no drainage, but slightly "boggy" to the touch, is most likely to break down—particularly if the patient is a smoker. Learner-teacher dialogue helps the student see it as a primary problem.

Learners are taught to assess the meaning, significance, and relevance of cues with questions that help clarify the nursing diagnoses and probe for supporting evidence and consequences. Examples of questions that help differentiate nursing diagnoses are those such as, "Is the patient presenting with symptoms that do not fit the patterns of the primary or secondary diagnoses?" "What are they?" "What do you think is causing these symptoms?" "What evidence do you have to support your thinking?" This type of learner-teacher dialogue leads the student through the critical thinking process and reinforces it through practice.

Often, it is learner-learner dialogue that pulls the pieces of the puzzle into a composite picture so that the relationship of the parts to the whole may be seen. Learner questions often point out missing pieces of information, a correlation essential to understanding at their particular level that may have been made and forgotten years ago by the teacher. Learners' observations and comments bring their diverse and rich experiences and their values to the situation and lend a multifaceted view that lends to negotiation of meanings.

ROLE OF THE TEACHER

The change in the role set of the teacher[8] is essential to the success of the type of learning attempted here and deserves closer scrutiny. In nursing rounds, the teacher adopts a more egalitarian role than traditionally assumed, fostering the role of teacher as consultant and expert-fellow-learner. In this way, teacher-structure is decreased as students learn to self-structure, and students are moved toward independence and self-direction as they strive toward learner maturity.

One important aspect of facilitating learner independence is creating an environment that requires learners to be actively involved. The teacher provides the structure for nursing rounds. Active participation is built in by providing the learner with the freedom and the responsibility for choosing a concept or patient problem to present. The teacher acts as a consultant in selection of meaningful and significant topics and in identifying and using resources appropriately. To conduct nursing rounds, the learner must actively prepare and perform. Discussion and analysis also require active participation.

During nursing rounds, the teacher assumes the role of facilitator of group process and expert-fellow-learner. In this role, the teacher stimulates discussion and critical thinking with Socratic questioning. While individuals present, other learners question and share their observations, experiences, and insights. The teacher helps learners search for meaning and significance, trust their intuition, and crystallize insights.

Finally, in peer evaluation, the teacher provides the initial structure and then shares in the critique of the learners' work as a peer. The idea here is to reinforce that a mutual critique is more important than the concept of grading.[9] This fosters the egalitarian and liberating learner-teacher relationship that is the key to the role change described here.

POTENTIAL PROBLEMS

Maintaining the focus on nursing is a frequently encountered difficulty in nursing rounds. This problem stems partly from the fact that learners have difficulty differentiating nursing from medicine and may choose concepts such as disease process or operative procedures. The teacher uses consultation skills to redirect and maintain the focus on nursing.

Learner anxiety is a serious issue for only an occasional learner; however, most learners will experience mild anxiety. Anxiety may be diminished by demonstrating what is expected in mini-nursing rounds. In place of postconference, the teacher may conduct ten-minute, bedside teaching demonstrations of patient problems encountered in the care of assigned patients. Modeling nursing rounds provides learners with a gestalt of what is expected and takes away fear of the unknown. During the analysis session, learners will become familiar with the technique of Socratic questioning and thus will be better prepared for this method of teaching. Modeling is a good way to structure for learner success in nursing rounds.

Fatigue will decrease the number and quality of interactions among participants of nursing rounds. Without a sufficient quantity and quality of interactions, the bedside demonstration is rendered training as opposed to education. Careful timing and adherence to the schedule will prevent fatigue and thus facilitate a productive learning experience.

Example
Care of the Patient with Altered Nutrition
Wanda Anderson-Loftin

A general surgical floor of an acute care hospital was the setting for this nursing rounds session. Learners were junior nursing students enrolled in their first adult nursing practicum course.

Organization of the Nursing Rounds

Students were introduced to nursing rounds on the first clinical practicum day. The objectives, directions, and evaluation criteria, provided in the course syllabus, were explained, and examples of nursing rounds conducted in the past were offered. A tentative time schedule was proposed, and volunteers for the first nursing rounds were requested. It was also suggested that students develop an awareness of concepts or patient problems that had some significance for the rest of their nursing careers and that held some meaning for them.

At the beginning of the practicum and before beginning nursing rounds, the teacher conducted several mini-nursing rounds on the concept of pain. The patients selected were controlling pain by use of a PCA pump, transcutaneous electrical nerve stimulation (TENS), or an epidural pump.

The schedule for nursing rounds allowed for nine students to complete the learning activity during the last four weeks of an eight-week practicum. On each of the first three weeks, two students conducted nursing rounds during the last hour and 15 minutes of clinical. On the last week, three students conducted nursing grand rounds during the last one and one-half hours of the practicum.

The grand nursing rounds were on care of the patient with altered nutrition. The patients selected were receiving total parenteral nutrition (TPN), continuous enteral feeding by Dobbhoff feeding tube, and intermittent tube feeding through a gastrostomy tube. A ten-minute lecture-demonstration was given on each of the feeding methods and focused on feeding procedure and rationales, care of feeding tubes and central lines, and precautions. Ten minutes was allowed for questions, comments, and interactions with the patient. These patients were generally debilitated and uncommunicative, and learner-patient interaction was unproductive in this instance. No family was present, nor had any family been noticed visiting.

During the analysis session, commonalities and differences were discussed. Students discovered that all of the patients were elderly and lived alone or in a nursing home, and the pattern of the complete blood count (CBC) indicated an anemia that was present to some degree on admission. Major differences were found in the etiology of alteration in nutrition. Mrs. P. was being given intermittent bolus feedings for a stage IV decubitus ulcer. Mr. R. was receiving TPN for nutritional deficiency related to alcoholism. Mrs. J. had dysphagia and was being fed by continuous enteral feedings.

Students were unsure of what evidence of improved nutritional status existed, so measures of nutritional status were reviewed by the teacher. The group then evaluated the patients for improved nutrition by weight, hair texture, muscle mass, color of mucous membrane, and improved lab results.

During the discussion, the interrelationships of age, nutrition, wound healing, alcoholism, and lab data became clearer to students. A pattern of age, disability, social isolation, and decreased red blood cells, hemoglobin, and hematocrit, among others, were recognized as significant in altered nutrition. This is an example of successful nursing rounds in which a significant amount of learning occurred at both training and educative levels.

CONCLUSION

Nursing rounds are based on the reality of the practice world. The reality base makes the content course-aligned and have meaning for the student. Because of their basis in reality, nursing rounds prepare students for the real world of nursing practice and are responsive to the demands of the practice environment. Use of nursing rounds serves as an exemplar for a different way to develop clinical judgment and expertise. Finally, nursing rounds place the patient at the center of the learning experience and socialize the learner into the art of caring, compassionate nursing.

NOTES

1. E.O. Bevis, Nursing Curriculum as Professional: Some Underlying Theoretical Models, in *Toward a Caring Curriculum: A New Pedagogy for Nursing*, ed. E.O. Bevis and J. Watson (New York: National League for Nursing, 1989), 67–106.
2. Ibid., 91–94.
3. Ibid., 81–89.
4. Ibid., 91.
5. Ibid., 91–95.
6. S.C. Cobb and M.E. Cooley, Nursing Rounds: Idea to Reality, *Oncology Nursing Forum* 15, no. 1 (1988):23–27.
7. R. Paul and A.J.A. Binker, Socratic Questioning, in *Critical Thinking: How to Prepare Students for a Rapidly Changing World* (Sonoma, Calif: Foundation for Critical Thinking, 1993), 269–278.
8. E.O. Bevis and J. Murray, The Essence of the Curriculum Revolution: Emancipatory Teaching, *Journal of Nursing Education* 29, no. 7 (1990):326–331.
9. E.O. Bevis and J. Watson, eds., *Toward a Caring Curriculum: A New Pedagogy for Nursing* (New York: National League for Nursing, 1989).

SUGGESTED READING

Benner, P. 1984. *From novice to expert: Excellence and power in clinical nursing practice*. Menlo Park, Calif: Addison Wesley Publishing Co., Inc.

Benner, P., and C.A. Tanner. 1987. Clinical judgment: How expert nurses use intuition. *American Journal of Nursing* 87:23–31.

Bevis, E.O. 1988. New directions for a new age. In *Curriculum revolution: Mandate for change*, ed. National League for Nursing, 27–52. New York: National League for Nursing.

Corcoran, S.A., and C. Tanner. 1988. Implications of clinical judgment research for teaching. In *Curriculum revolution: Mandate for change*, ed. National League for Nursing, 159–175. New York: National League for Nursing.

National League for Nursing, ed. 1989. *Curriculum revolution: Reconceptualizing nursing education*. New York.

Tanner, C. 1988. Curriculum revolution: The practice mandate. *Nursing and Health Care* 9, no. 8:427–430.

Chapter 25

A Community-Based Practicum Experience

Betty Davis and Patricia Christensen

DEFINITION AND PURPOSES

Health screening involves the identification of unrecognized problems or potential problems in individuals or populations. Health screenings can also provide opportunities for unique partnerships between schools of nursing and agencies that provide services to clients. These partnerships can be mutually very beneficial. The screening experience contributes to student learning while providing invaluable health professional services to the community.

In the experience described in this chapter, the health screenings involved the assessment of head and neck, hearing, vision, development, skin integrity, height and weight, and nutritional status of groups of high-risk, school-aged children in an after-school program sponsored by the Salvation Army. The purpose of the practicum experience was twofold—to provide an opportunity for nursing students to learn about children's health, and second, to provide the children with skilled observations about their health status. In anticipation of the practicum experience, the students did extensive reading in child physical, social, and cognitive development. The groups of children screened consisted mainly of children who, by virtue of their low socioeconomic status, were considered to be at high risk for unidentified and untreated problems that could impair their health and learning.

THEORETICAL RATIONALE

The theoretical framework for this experience was a synthesis of the primary care model of prevention and learning theory. The relationships among poor health, delayed childhood development, learning problems, inadequate academic achievement, and socially inappropriate coping skills have been well documented.[1-3] Additionally, as health care moves from acute care to community-based settings, nursing faculty members need to provide a wider range of community-based experiences for students. Nursing education needs to be client-centered and take place where the population is available, in order to provide opportunities for students to learn the necessary skills.[4-6] Child health activities, in particular, are increasingly community-based in schools, day-care settings, after-school programs, and family homes. According to Elders, some of the greatest problems of delivering primary care to children are that a large percentage of children are not covered by health insurance, and 70 percent of mothers work and cannot transport their children to a doctor or clinic.[7]

An essential component of primary health care, according to the World Health Organization, is participation of communities and health care organizations.[8] The relationships forged by these partnerships are reciprocal in that "communities express their needs and contribute to their own well-being, and health and human service professionals help them achieve their goals."[9] Thus, the screening of vulnerable populations by nursing students is an expression of a mutually supportive relationship whereby the students can learn and the community can be served by them.

CONDITIONS

Health screenings can be used in a wide variety of settings with diverse populations. In the example discussed here, the population was school-aged children. The screens were promoted as "Healthy Kids Program." Other situations could include screenings of the elderly for hypertension, stress, medication effects, cholesterol, and so forth. College students could be screened for hearing, vision, scoliosis, nutritional status, height, weight, knowledge of birth control methods, and a myriad of other age-appropriate data. Almost any group of individuals could be utilized for health screenings. The settings for the screenings can vary from schools, senior citizen centers, stores, shopping malls, and anywhere that groups of people frequent.

Since the objectives for each group screened is different, the learning opportunities for the students are diverse. The careful planning, implementation, and evaluation of the screenings provide a full spectrum of learning experiences for nursing students. Students are expected to explore human development very thoroughly, to communicate effectively with diverse groups, to utilize their observational skills, and to evaluate essential client data. The reporting and follow-up activities of those persons with identified problems provide invaluable links to health care providers for the clients and students alike.

Planning

The screening activities require a great deal of advance planning, which can involve students as well as faculty and community agencies. The degree of student involvement in planning will vary depending on the time frame for the practicum and the focus of the learning objectives. Where the time frame is short and the focus for student learning is primarily implementation and evaluation, students' involvement in planning may be limited to individual preparation. However, students' participation in planning may be extensive. At the onset of the course, students can identify the population and settings as part of the clinical experience. After contracting with the agency (school, community center, and so forth), the faculty provide the students with the opportunity to write the objectives, identify resources, provide the materials, publicize the event, and implement and evaluate the experience. This clinical practicum can be offered on a select basis (one time) or can be a major project that can span several weeks or a whole semester. The whole class is divided into work groups, each of which is assigned a certain responsibility for the activity. After the assignment of groups, students can work independently of each other (with consultation and assistance from faculty) to accomplish their particular objectives. The hours spent in planning are counted as part of the required clinical time.

It has been gratifying to observe that, given an explanation of the screening and its value to children and students, business organizations and other community agencies often will donate materials and resources to help defray any expenses. The cooperation and support of these organizations further promote the community/school partnership.

Modifying

It may be necessary for faculty members to do some of the advanced planning, especially when agency contracts for student experiences are negotiated several months in advance. In addition, permissions from school officials and parents can likewise be very time consuming. The system for these permissions may have to be put in place before students can begin the screening activities. Although the authors have not had problems with parental permissions, it is advisable to plan well ahead for any eventualities. A careful explanation of the screening activities (including statements that the students will not be undressed) may forestall any hesitation on the parents' part to grant permission.

An additional outcome of the screening process may be a continuing relationship between the school and the community agency, based on clients' needs. The school of nursing participants (faculty and students), in every case, will need to anticipate the need for follow-up sessions and plan for them. For example, in the experience of screening the school-aged child, the students assessed that many of the children had nutritional deficiencies. As a follow-up activity, the students presented a teaching/learning project on healthy snacks. Other such activities have included brushing and flossing teeth and safety issues.

TYPES OF LEARNERS

Health screenings are appropriate learning activities for undergraduate and graduate students. Screening activities can be simple (only assessing height and weight) or quite complex (multisystem assessments) and can include various groups in a wide range of settings. The amount of faculty supervision can vary, depending on the skill level of the student. Obviously, graduate students and senior nursing students would be able to perform more independently and participate in more extensive planning.

The health screening described in this chapter was placed in the junior-level, parent-child course; however, other screenings have been part of the senior-level community health course. Regardless of the level of student, health screenings can provide an enriching clinical experience. The objectives can be adjusted to the skill level of the students and advanced as the students become more proficient.

RESOURCES

Health screening is an excellent teaching strategy for parent-child community-based practicums, because screenings can be performed in a variety of settings and most schools of nursing already have the needed resources and personnel for implementation. The type and amount of room space and the equipment needed are determined by the particular health assessment components to be performed and numbers of children or other clients to be screened.

The Salvation Army after-school programs used as examples here were excellent settings for child health screenings, since approximately 60 to 100 children participate in the after-school programs at the two sites utilized. Child health assessments were performed in a general-purpose room separate from the recreational area, which provided privacy. Tables and chairs were located in the rooms and sinks for handwashing were located nearby.

Two different types of screenings were performed on separate days. The first screening included client history and physical assessment relative to height and weight; blood pressure, pulse, and respiration; skin and nails; vision, hearing (Weber and Rinne tests) and developmental assessment (Goodenough Draw a Person) (see Exhibit 25–1). A second screening included physical assessment relative to head and neck, eyes, ears, nose, sinuses, mouth and throat, and client history relative to diet and exercise. These assessments are typical of screenings for the school-age population.[10]

Exhibit 25–1 Child Health Assessment: School-Age Child

HEIGHT, WEIGHT, VITAL SIGNS, SKIN, VISION, HEARING, DEVELOPMENT

DATE: ____________________

NAME: ______________ AGE: ___ BIRTHDATE: ____________ M ___ F ___

Ht. __________ Percentile ________ P __________ BP (Arm Used):

Wt. __________ Percentile ________ R __________ R ______________

L ______________

SKIN: (Circle all findings)

ROS: pruritus, rashes, bruising, lesions, excessive dryness, oiliness, acne

PA: (Circle all findings)

	Normal	*Variations*
Color	light, dark, pink undertone	pallor, cyanosis, erythema, jaundice, ecchymosis, petechiae
Texture	smooth, soft	uneven, rough
Temperature	warm	cool, very warm
Moisture	slightly dry	oily, clammy, excessive dryness
Turgor	elastic	suspended (tented) swelling (edema)

Additional Comments:

NAILS: (Circle all findings)

ROS: injury, deformities

PA: (Circle all findings)

continues

Exhibit 25–1 continued

	Normal	*Variations*
Color	pink, deeply pigmented nail beds (in dark skin)	blue (cyanosis), blue-black (hemorrhage), yellow, white
Shape	convex	concave (spoon nails) clubbing
Texture	smooth, hard but flexible	soft, brittle, pitting
Quality	smooth/even edges	short/ragged, uncut/dirty

Additional Comments:

VISION: (Circle all findings)

ROS: blurred vision (bumping into objects, sitting very close to television, sitting close to blackboard, holding book close to face, writing with head near desk, squinting, rubbing eyes, excessive tearing, "burning"/irritation), use of glasses/contact lenses

Date of last optic examination: ____________________

PA:

	Normal	*Variations*
Alignment (Corneal Light Reflex)	Orthophoria	Esotropia (inward deviation) R ________ L ________ Exotrophia (outward deviation) R ________ L ________

Visual Acuity (Snellen Chart)	R	L
with glasses/contacts	________	________
without glasses/contacts	________	________

Behavioral observations:

Additional Comments:

continues

Exhibit 25–1 continued

HEARING: (Circle all findings)
ROS: difficulty hearing, hearing loss

PA:		*Normal*	*Variations*
	Weber	midline or equally both ears	Lateralization: R _________ L _________
	Rinne	AC > BC bilaterally	AC = BC BC > AC
	Whisper Test:		

Additional Comments:

DEVELOPMENTAL ASSESSMENT:

Goodenough Draw A Person Test:

General Description of Development:

REFERENCES:

Jarvis, C. (1992). *Physical Examination and Health Assessment* (1st ed.), Saunders.
Whaley, L.F., & Wong, D.L. (1991). *Nursing Care of Infants and Children* (4th ed.), Mosby.

Eight to ten students and one faculty member were present for each screening. All equipment and assessment materials were provided by the school of nursing. Equipment and materials included vision charts (Snellen alphabet and Snellen E), portable scales, a measuring tape (for measuring distance from the eye chart and for use as a height measurement), sphygmomanometers, stethoscopes, tuning forks, penlights, tongue blades, alcohol swabs, flavored chewing gum and chocolate candy for assessing cranial nerve I (CNI), alcohol swabs, white paper and pencils (for developmental assessment), assessment forms, and pens for documentation. Rewards (prizes) were offered as incentives for the children to participate in the screenings and follow-up sessions (rescreening and mini–health teaching as needed). These rewards were donated by faculty, students, and outside sources such as dentists, businesses, and church groups.

The reward items included pencils, pens, erasers, toothbrushes, toothpaste, sample-size soaps, stickers, sugarless gum, raisins, and apples. An effort was made to give rewards that were useful, safe, and appealing to the school-age group. Rewards might also include items such as coloring sheets, crossword puzzles, health-related booklets, and so forth. Many of these items are available at no cost through community agencies such as health departments, law-enforcement agencies, fire departments, and American Red Cross chapters.

The costs for some materials may be appropriated in the school of nursing budget if planned for in advance. Additionally, seeking sponsorship from businesses and organizations in the community can be an effective strategy for promoting community and school partnerships.

USING THE METHOD

The success of health screening in a community setting as a teaching strategy is highly dependent upon planning and collaboration with the community agency personnel. Extensive planning and collaboration were used in the example described in this chapter. In an initial meeting at the Salvation Army facility, agency directors and faculty identified (1) unmet needs of the high-risk school-age population to be served, (2) experiences needed for student learning—practice of assessment skills and related follow-up care (rescreening and referrals for abnormal findings and mini-teaching sessions based on identified needs), and (3) services to be provided by school of nursing faculty and students and dates and times for the screenings and follow-up care. Faculty members elicited information about the children who attended the after-school program, including a general description, special needs of any of the children (handicaps, allergies, and so forth), and the schedule of a typical day's activities at the facility.

During this initial meeting there was discussion and agreement concerning specific resources to be provided by the Salvation Army and those to be provided by the school of nursing. Also, there was agreement that the children's participation would be voluntary. Faculty agreed to provide promotional materials such as a poster for the agency's bulletin board and fliers for distribution to children and families. The Salvation Army staff agreed to promote the screenings by verbally supporting the screenings in their communications with children and their families, listing the screening activities on their printed calendar of events, displaying the poster on a prominent bulletin board, and distributing the promotional fliers. Meeting at the community agency facility provided faculty the opportunity to observe the physical environment and anticipate needs relative to setup and implementation.

Neither a formal written contract nor a parental consent form was deemed necessary, based on the community agency's policy, and therefore was not used. It was determined that a consent form was not needed since the screenings were common ones that did not require removal of clothing, the parents would be well informed through promotional efforts, and the children's participation would be strictly voluntary. Both the contract and consent form could easily be established as policy, and in many settings would be essential.

The faculty's role in physical preparation for the screenings was critical for successful implementation of screenings and enhancement of student learning. Students were not involved in the planning and physical preparation because of a limited time frame and focus for the students. Faculty responsibilities were as follows:

- developing specific student learning objectives (see Exhibit 25–1)
- developing clinical preparatory assignments for students (see Exhibit 25–2)
- developing assessment forms for each type of screening (see Exhibit 25–1)
- obtaining outside sources and funding for promotional materials and incentive rewards, as well as purchasing or collecting the items to be used as rewards
- creating, printing, and distributing promotional materials that clearly delineated the screenings and incentive awards
- planning the number of assessments to be performed during each screening
- reserving equipment and supplies from the learning resource center in the school of nursing
- transporting equipment and supplies to and from the screening site
- identifying resources for referrals.

While students came to the course with prior knowledge and competency in performance of physical assessment skills, including an overview of physical assessment skills for children, they were expected to prepare extensively for the screenings. Their preparation included review of physical, developmental, and nutritional assessment and child health textbooks. Also, prior to the screenings, students participated in a campus laboratory exercise that addressed developmental assessment and communication strategies for children.

During a preconference (30 to 45 minutes), the faculty member served as a facilitator for the student discussion of general expectations, the physical setup, and operations of the screening. Faculty members reviewed and clarified procedures, skills, normal findings for school-age children, assessment form content, and documentation based on student questions and input. Other topics

Exhibit 25–2 Health Screening for High-Risk School-Age Children

Learning Objectives

During the health screening the student will:

1. Perform selected aspects of physical, nutritional, and developmental assessment including client history and physical exam components. (Selected aspects will be designated by instructor. Students should be prepared to perform comprehensive assessments.)
2. Document assessment findings on child health assessment forms.
3. Identify normal findings for physical, nutritional, and developmental assessment of the school-age child.
4. Utilize effective techniques in communicating with children.
5. Identify techniques that can be utilized to encourage cooperation and participation of children.
6. Identify characteristics of high-risk school-age children.
7. Analyze assessment findings, including comparison of actual findings for individual children to normal findings.
8. Identify specific needs for follow-up care (rescreening, referrals) for individual children.
9. Identify an action plan for a mini-health teaching session based on a common health need of high-risk children.

Clinical Preparation

1. Required Readings:
   Whaley, L.F., & Wong, D.L. (1991). *Nursing Care of Infants and Children* (4th ed.), Mosby, pp. 32–42, 185–218, 222–294, 761–800.
2. Review of Content:
   a. Information covered in prior courses relative to physical assessment and nutrition for school-age children.
   b. Information covered in campus lab relative to developmental assessment and communication strategies for children.

discussed were characteristics of high-risk populations, sociocultural values and practices, the impact of socioeconomics on health practices, and the importance of confidentiality. Faculty guided students through a brainstorming session to identify ways to encourage children to participate in the screenings—for example, interacting with children in the recreational areas, explaining and demonstrating equipment and procedures, giving compliments and praise to the children, and thanking the children for their cooperation and participation. Faculty assisted students to identify informal teaching opportunities within the screenings, such as the purpose of equipment, hygiene measures, proper way to cleanse the ear canal, and nutritional snacks.

Students were directed by faculty to observe for and document any unusual findings or outstanding characteristics (signs of abuse, hyperactivity, etc.) and to observe social interactions (what children talk about—their fears, interests, likes, and dislikes).

There are several ways to operationalize health screenings. At the Salvation Army sites, two different methods were used, with only one method in operation on a given day. In the first one, which is most typical of health fair screenings, the participants moved from one station to another, in sequence. This method is especially beneficial when screening large numbers of children and when equipment is limited (for example, scales, sphygmomanometers, eye charts). Students organized themselves into several small groups, with two or three students per group and one group at each station. Students established a rotation schedule that provided opportunities for all students to perform each type of assessment. An advantage of this method was that student learning was enhanced through the active participation in organization and team efforts.

In the second type of screening, each student completed all of the assessments for one child at a given time. Forty-six children were assessed during the practicum experience. With both types of screenings, children received incentive rewards at several intervals. Throughout the screenings, faculty members facilitated student learning by being available for consultation, demonstrating assessment techniques as needed, assisting with students' performance of skills, and role-modeling effective communication techniques.

EVALUATION

The evaluation component of health screenings has multidimensional importance as a teaching-learning strategy. The evaluation process for the example cited here included (1) an analysis of assessment findings and identification of any needed follow-up measures, (2) an evaluation of the screenings process and identification of areas for change, and (3) an evaluation of students' learning.

Much of the evaluation occurred during a postconference (45 to 60 minutes in length), which immediately followed the screenings. Students compared assessment findings for each child to normal findings, using their textbook as a reference. Abnormal findings and potential health problems were highlighted and discussed by the entire group of students, with the faculty member serving as a facilitator. Specific plans were made for follow-up as needed based on three action plans.

1. rescreening—for example, blood pressure, vision, hearing

2. referral of parents to other health care sources—for example, school nurses, free medical clinics, health departments (If a school of nursing has a nursing practice center, this would be an ideal place for referral.)
3. mini-teaching sessions based on an overall need of the high-risk children in the after-school program

All assessment forms have been placed in the school of nursing office by faculty to maintain confidentiality. Total assessment findings for individual children were not shared with Salvation Army staff. However, the staff did assist faculty and students in scheduling rescreenings for children who had abnormal findings and in communication with parents regarding the need for additional follow-up.

Evaluation of the health screening by students, faculty, and agency staff involved stating an overall impression of the effectiveness of the screenings, as well as specific identification of the positive aspects and areas for change. Request for an oral evaluation was initiated in postconference discussions by the faculty member. Discussion provided valuable insight into problems, feelings, frustrations, enthusiasm, and successes experienced during the screenings. Students and faculty evaluated the screenings in relation to types and sequence of assessments performed; the organization, time frame, and clinical site (physical environment and cooperation of agency staff); adequacy of equipment and supplies; use of incentive rewards; availability of faculty; and workability of the assessment forms. Discussion of these factors provided valuable information for future screenings, especially delineation of components that might need change. The faculty members asked questions and shared personal observations to guide the discussion. Most of the areas identified for change related to the short time frame for students to organize themselves at the assessment stations and some improvements as to the flow of traffic. On a few occasions, students felt overwhelmed with the large number of students who wanted to participate, and thus felt rushed to complete the screenings. Also, during the postconference, students compared their actual observations of growth and development and the characteristics and behaviors of high-risk children to expected findings.

Feedback from the Salvation Army staff indicated that the screenings definitely had been seen as a service to the agency and to the children in the after-school program. In addition, the children had very much enjoyed the individual attention and had looked forward to the subsequent visits of the students and faculty.

Evaluation of students' learning was based on stated learning objectives for the health screening experience. Discussion in postconference, students' comments on a written self-evaluation of clinical performance, and faculty observations of student performance during pre- and postconferences and during the screenings were the vehicles for evaluation. All findings indicated that health screening was a very positive teaching strategy for teaching students about child health because it provided an opportunity for students to

- practice child health assessment (hands-on experience) for multiple clients
- practice communication skills with school-age children
- assess growth and development
- provide informal health teaching for children
- develop professionalism through accountability and service to the community
- introduce and/or reinforce the importance of healthy behaviors
- increase personal awareness of the impact of cultural and socioeconomic factors on health status
- assess the characteristics and health needs of a high-risk population
- plan strategies for illness prevention and health promotion
- participate in critical thinking through analysis of data and planning strategies for follow-up care

POTENTIAL PROBLEMS

There are several potential problems that may have an impact on the effectiveness of health screening as a teaching-learning strategy. A primary concern is that inadequate planning and preparation may result in insufficient resources, lack of organization, and ineffective implementation. Another concern is uncertainty of client numbers in a setting where clients are strictly volunteers. Having either too many or too few volunteers to participate could prevent achievement of students' learning objectives. Guidelines were established for limiting the number of volunteers in the after-school programs but were sometimes difficult to implement because of the desire to accommodate the many children who wanted to participate. Limiting the number of participants was necessary but frustrating to students, faculty, and the children themselves.

Professional liability is another significant concern. While a formal written contract and a parental consent form were not used in screenings for the after-school program, it would be prudent to consider them. Questions of liability relative to referrals should also be explored. Should there be a mechanism to determine whether parents follow up on suggested referrals? Should the school of nursing seek formal contracts with other health care providers for follow-up care? These are among the questions that will need to be considered in the planning phase. Consultation with legal professionals or the state board of nursing may be indicated (See Chapter 28, "Issues in Clinical Teaching.")

CONCLUSION

Health screenings can be excellent opportunities for mutually beneficial partnerships between schools of nursing and agencies that provide services to clients. The screening experience contributes to student learning while providing invaluable health professional services to the community.

In the experience described in this chapter, the health screenings involved school-age children. The groups of children screened consisted mainly of children who, by virtue of their low socioeconomic status, were considered to be at high risk for unidentified and untreated problems that could impair their health and learning. It is hoped that the screening activities described here can contribute significantly to the well-being of these vulnerable children.

NOTES

1. C. Malloy, Children and Poverty: America's Future at Risk, *Pediatric Nursing* 18, no. 6 (November/December, 1992):563–567.
2. J.B. Igoe, A Blueprint for Health Promotion: Children's Rights and Community Action, *Pediatric Nursing* 16, no. 4 (July/August 1990):410–411.
3. J.A. Vessey and M.N. Swanson, School-Based Clinics and the Pediatric Nurse: An Interview with Surgeon General M. Joycelyn Elders, *Pediatric Nursing* 19, no. 4 (July/August, 1993):359–362.
4. Ibid., 359.
5. S.E. Barger and P.M. Kline, Community Health Service Programs in Academe: Unique Learning Opportunities for Students, *Nurse Educator* 18, no. 6 (November/December 1993):22–26.
6. Vessey and Swanson, School-Based Clinics and the Pediatric Nurse, 359.
7. Ibid.
8. S. Farley, The Community as Partner in Primary Health Care, *Nursing & Health Care* 14, no. 5 (May 1993):244–249.
9. Ibid., 244.
10. L.F. Whaley, and D.L. Wong, *Nursing Care of Infants and Children*, 4th ed. (St. Louis: Mosby-Year Book, Inc., 1991).

SUGGESTED READING

Barger, S., and P.M. Kline. 1992. Community health service programs in academe: Unique learning opportunities for students. *Nurse Educator* 18, no. 6:22–26.

Burback, C.A.L., and P. Baldwin. 1992. Linking community needs with student research experiences. *Nurse Educator* 17, no. 3:37–42.

Collando, C.B. 1992. Primary health care: A continuing challenge. *Nursing & Health Care* 13, no. 8:408–413.

Farley, S. 1993. The community as partner in primary health care. *Nursing & Health Care* 14, no. 5:244–249.

Haussler, S.C., and B.S. Cherry. 1993. The community: A primary site for students in pediatric nursing. *Journal of Education* 32, no. 4:183–184.

Igoe, J.B. 1991. Beyond green beans and oat bran: A health agenda for the 1990s for school-age youth. *Pediatric Nursing* 16, no. 3:289–292.

Igoe, J.B. 1991. An update on student health fairs. *Pediatric Nursing* 17, no. 2:170–172.

Igoe, J.B. 1993. School-linked family health centers in health care reform. *Pediatric Nursing* 19, no. 1:67–68.

Malloy, C. 1992. Children and poverty: America's future at risk. *Pediatric Nursing* 18, no. 6: 553–557.

Moccia, P. 1993. Nursing education in the public's trust. A faculty of the community: No unreal loyalties for us. *Nursing & Health Care* 14, no. 9:472–474.

Pruitt, R.H., and B.F. Campbell. 1994. Educating for health care reform and the community. *Nursing & Health Care* 15, no. 6:308–311.

Shalala, D.E. 1993. Nursing and society: The unfinished agenda for the 21st century. *Nursing & Health Care* 18, no. 6:289–291.

Whaley, L.F., and D.L. Wong. 1991. *Nursing Care of Infants and Children*. 4th ed. St. Louis: Mosby-Year Book, Inc.

Wood, C.H. 1994. We must explore a middle course between the extremes. *World Health Forum* 5:308.

Chapter 26

Nursing Process Mapping Replaces Nursing Care Plans

Charlotte James Koehler

DEFINITION AND PURPOSES

The *nursing process mapping* format is a tool to assist nursing students to organize their thoughts and actions and to communicate these to their clinical instructor. It can be used in conjunction with an in-depth assessment database and is used instead of a traditional nursing care plan.

Traditional nursing care plans have been with us for a long time and have served a much-needed purpose, but with the growth of nursing knowledge and the continuous reassessment of the role of the nurse comes evaluation of tools and ways of accomplishing tasks. In evaluating the traditional nursing care plan, as used by students, several problems come to mind. To begin with, it is rarely used as a plan, but is frequently used in retrospect and developed almost completely after the care has taken place. To call it a care plan is a misnomer. Format rather than substance is often emphasized. For example, we spend many hours ensuring that the student knows what column the information goes in and how to phrase the information correctly, rather than the thought processes that the student used in developing the "plan."

Another problem with the traditional nursing care plan is the use of documenting rationale that often becomes an all-consuming task. In the early stages of nursing care plans this was important. The profession was building a scientific base, and nursing textbooks provided very little nursing care documentation. Today nursing care is in all textbooks and is covered thoroughly in nursing education programs. Students know to use ice to reduce swelling of an incision—it is common knowledge—but they spend time finding the correct page and line when this time could be spent thinking about what is happening with the patient, selecting important information, and relating the material. Another situation that often occurs with students is the ready access of care plans from texts and hospital computers. It is not unusual for the student to select a few appropriate aspects and then use them with very little thought.

The purpose of mapping nursing practice in nursing education is to have the student develop critical thinking skills, that is, assess the patient, gather information from the literature, select relevant points, relate all of this information to the care of the patient, and illustrate the information graphically. It helps the student establish priorities, seek relationships among information, and build on previous knowledge.[1]

THEORETICAL RATIONALE

Concept mapping is well documented in education literature, especially in the fields of math and science. It has been used to analyze changes in the development of concept understanding held by students and to promote meaningful learning.[2] Mapping has been given various labels, depending upon the intended use. It has been called cognitive mapping, idea mapping, patterned mapping, patterned note taking and flow charting.[3] Jones and Sims state that mapping facilitates creativity; students are able to access their own thinking and experiences, find new associations, and generate a new set of ideas.[4]

Miccinati states that to create a map the student must think, select important points, relate the information, and then illustrate the information graphically, all of which require the student to think critically.[5] In the literature, concept mapping is defined as a method of organizing information in graphic form.[6] Heinz-Frye and Novak define concept mapping as a tool to enhance meaningful learning.[7]

CONDITIONS

Mapping is a versatile technique that can be used in a variety of situations. The process requires instructor flexibility and students whose anxiety level is low enough to be introduced to something new and different. Since mapping is a process, it can be used in a variety of ways and can be very simplistic or developed to a very complex format. Because this process is so adaptable, it can be used with a learner of almost any age and in a variety of situations. The application is limited only by the imagination of the user.

Planning and Modifying

Teachers who are new to this technique can become more familiar and comfortable with it by using it in lecture. Mapping can be used to represent a concept or idea in lecture, such as the relationships among information, psychomotor skills, cognitive skills, and attitude as they relate to competence in giving nursing care (see Figure 26–1).[8] It can also be used more informally to organize thoughts for a classroom presentation. Teachers can also devise interesting but familiar ideas for students to map as a classroom activity to introduce the mapping process.

TYPES OF LEARNERS

Mapping is appropriate for undergraduate and graduate students. The student can use it as an independent process; it can be used for small group work or in

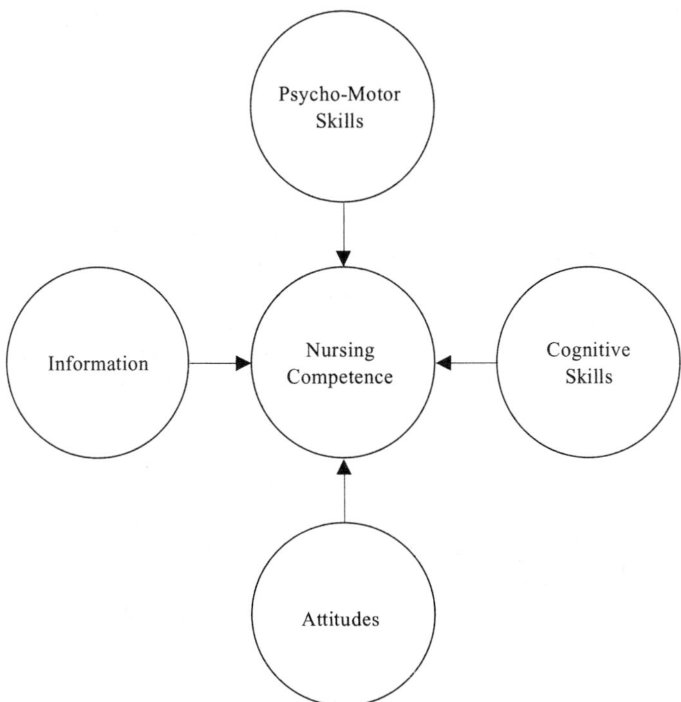

Figure 26–1 Development of Nursing Competency. *Source:* Adapted with permission from Wager, W., Teaching/Learning Process, paper presented at Teaching Skills for Health Professions Educators, St. Simons Island, GA, August 1994.

a very large classroom situation. It is especially useful in assisting students to think critically about the inter-relatedness of new information, as well as to look at old information and relate it in different ways. Mapping can be simple or complex and can be varied widely to suit many learning situations. It is important to introduce this process in a way that students with a variety of experiences and knowledge can relate to it and see its usefulness.

RESOURCES

Mapping can be used in almost any setting and requires few resources. A paper and pencil are the only necessary supplies. Wycoff states that color activates the brain and helps us think better; adding colored pens and paper could help the student be more creative and enjoy the exercise.[9] Wycoff also states that music increases right brain activity and helps turn on our thinking process, which assists the development of mapping. Using one or both of these strategies would be helpful if it is appropriate to the setting.

USING THE METHOD

Becoming familiar with the process and planning how it can be used in individual situations is most important to overall effectiveness. Using mapping in visual aids in class and in handouts is an effective way to introduce the concept of mapping. This can be done without labeling it or calling attention to the method, but just as a way of graphically representing information that one wants the student to comprehend. Figure 26–1 is an example of mapping that could be used in an introductory nursing class to help the student understand how information, skills, and attitudes learned from life, prenursing courses, and nursing courses are all necessary and important in reaching the aspiration of nursing competence.

A way of further involving the students is to have them use the technique personally and in a nonthreatening way. Wycoff suggests that the students be provided selected background music, colored pens, and paper,[10] and then asked to write a specific word or draw a representation of the word on the center of the paper. Starting with something as concrete as "desk" or "chair" and moving to something more related to nursing, such as "injection" or "bed bath," can be easy for students to relate to. The students are to spend no more than five minutes on any one map. They should be instructed to write down all thoughts and words that come to mind and to write as fast as they can. These ideas should flow from the central word or picture with ideas that generally relate to each other on branches. Remind the students that this is a process and that whatever they put on their map is OK. There are no right or wrong answers.

Once students become familiar with the concept of mapping, they can be directed to specific uses for communicating nursing assessment, care, and evaluation. This is a creative process, and giving the students a great deal of direction stifles this creativity; the process once again will become focused on form rather than substance. Giving this type of guidance without structure allows the student to think critically about the patient, focus on important assessment information, choose appropriate nursing interventions, and visualize the inter-relatedness of the process that is nursing care.

Student examples of mapping (see Figures 26–2 through Figure 26–5) varied tremendously in format and terminology, but the thought and insight needed to care for patients is evident much more so than in traditional nursing care plans. These maps were used with a comprehensive database. On the reverse side the students included a brief (two or three sentences) evaluation of the care that they gave during the clinical, a brief evaluation of how they are meeting course objectives, and a general reference statement (i.e. author or lecturer). They were also required to attach a copy of a nursing journal article. They were encouraged to use a nursing research article, but a clinical article was accepted. They underlined how their article helped them to better care for their patient.

EVALUATION

When asked a few simple questions about this process, students were overwhelmingly positive. They stated that this process made them think through things on their own, and they didn't just copy out of the book. They felt that they were better able to see the inter-relatedness of the entire process. It was easy for them to use and generally less time consuming.

Faculty using the form assessed that it communicated more succinctly what care was given and what thought process was used by the student. It was easier to read and evaluate, as well as being interesting.

Anytime something new is used there is a potential for problems. Questions to ask those involved are: "Will all students be able to use and feel comfortable with a non-guided format?" "Will faculty feel comfortable with the evaluation?" The most important question to ask about mapping is: "Will mapping facilitate the learning process?" These questions will be answered as the mapping process is used. Perhaps the most important question of all is: "Does our current method facilitate learning?"

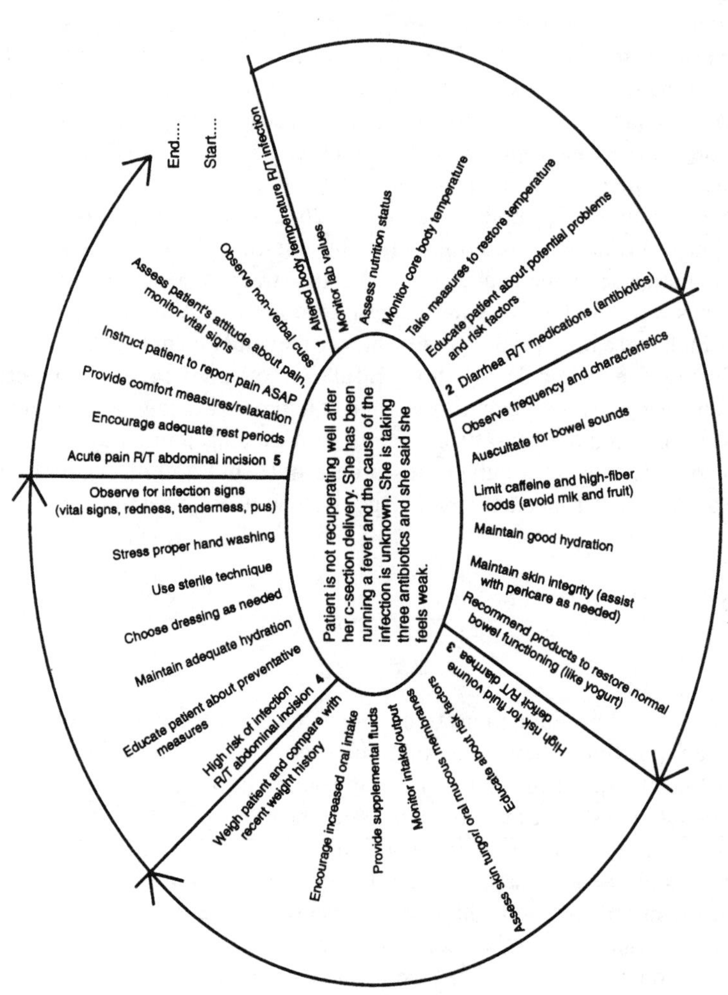

Figure 26–2 Student Example of Mapping

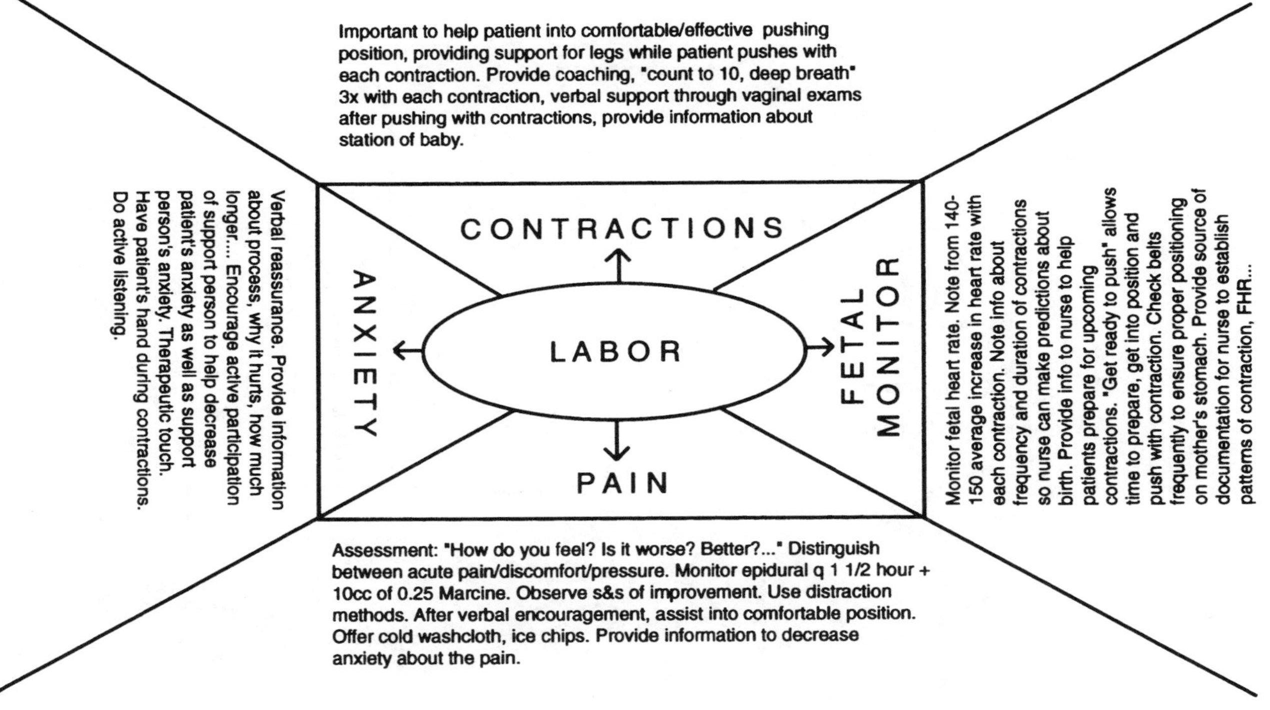

LABOR
CONTRACTIONS
FETAL MONITOR
PAIN
ANXIETY
Important to help patient into comfortable/effective pushing position, providing support for legs while patient pushes with each contraction. Provide coaching, "count to 10, deep breath" 3x with each contraction, verbal support through vaginal exams after pushing with contractions, provide information about station of baby.
Monitor fetal heart rate. Note from 140-150 average increase in heart rate with each contraction. Note info about frequency and duration of contractions so nurse can make predictions about birth. Provide info to nurse to help patients prepare for upcoming contractions. "Get ready to push" allows time to prepare, get into position and push with contraction. Check belts frequently to ensure proper positioning on mother's stomach. Provide source of documentation for nurse to establish patterns of contraction, FHR...
Assessment: "How do you feel? Is it worse? Better?..." Distinguish between acute pain/discomfort/pressure. Monitor epidural q 1 1/2 hour + 10cc of 0.25 Marcine. Observe s&s of improvement. Use distraction methods. After verbal encouragement, assist into comfortable position. Offer cold washcloth, ice chips. Provide information to decrease anxiety about the pain.
Verbal reassurance. Provide information about process, why it hurts, how much longer.... Encourage active participation of support person to help decrease patient's anxiety as well as support person's anxiety. Therapeutic touch. Have patient's hand during contractions. Do active listening.

Figure 26–3 Student Example of Mapping

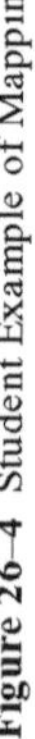

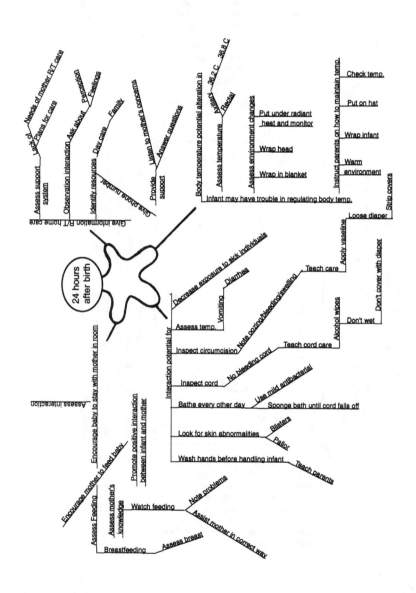

Figure 26–4 Student Example of Mapping

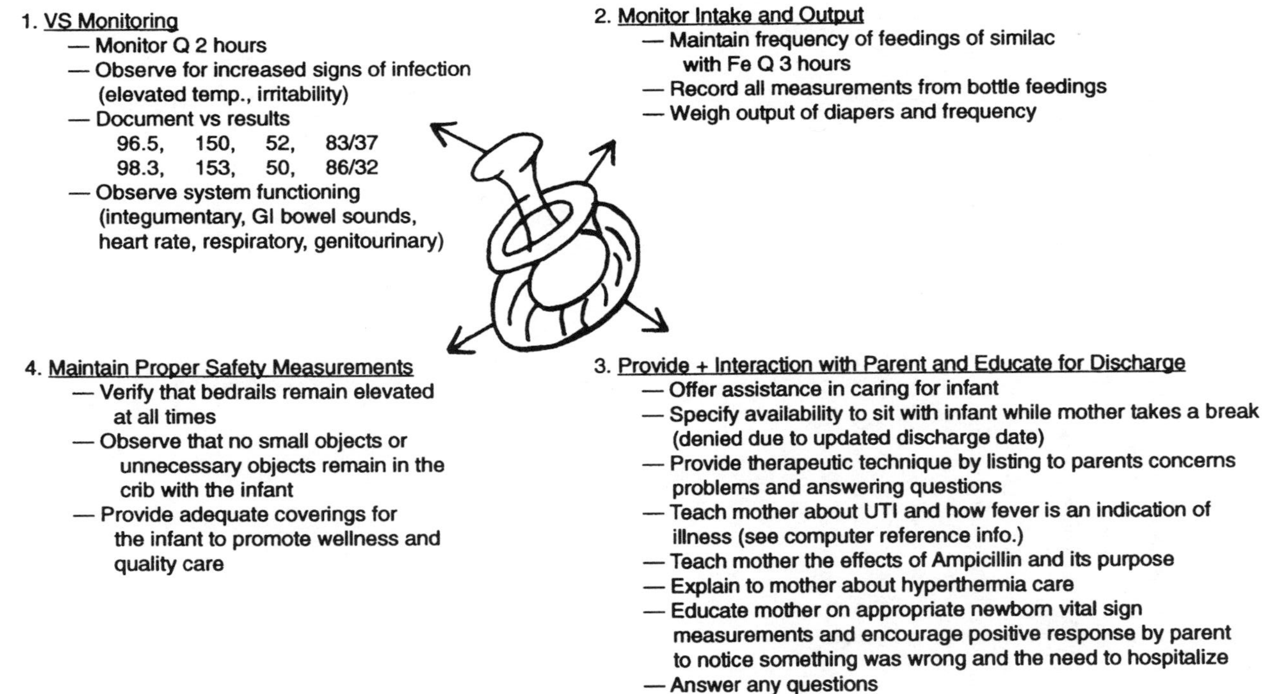

Clinical Task Performed on 25-Day Old Patient
1. VS Monitoring
— Monitor Q 2 hours
— Observe for increased signs of infection (elevated temp., irritability)
— Document vs results
96.5, 150, 52, 83/37
98.3, 153, 50, 86/32
— Observe system functioning (integumentary, GI bowel sounds, heart rate, respiratory, genitourinary)
2. Monitor Intake and Output
— Maintain frequency of feedings of similac with Fe Q 3 hours
— Record all measurements from bottle feedings
— Weigh output of diapers and frequency
3. Provide + Interaction with Parent and Educate for Discharge
— Offer assistance in caring for infant
— Specify availability to sit with infant while mother takes a break (denied due to updated discharge date)
— Provide therapeutic technique by listing to parents concerns problems and answering questions
— Teach mother about UTI and how fever is an indication of illness (see computer reference info.)
— Teach mother the effects of Ampicillin and its purpose
— Explain to mother about hyperthermia care
— Educate mother on appropriate newborn vital sign measurements and encourage positive response by parent to notice something was wrong and the need to hospitalize
— Answer any questions
4. Maintain Proper Safety Measurements
— Verify that bedrails remain elevated at all times
— Observe that no small objects or unnecessary objects remain in the crib with the infant
— Provide adequate coverings for the infant to promote wellness and quality care

Figure 26–5 Student Example of Mapping

NOTES

1. J. Miccinati, Mapping the Terrain: Connecting Reading with Academic Writing, *Journal of Reading* (March 1988):542–552.

2. P. Horton, An Investigation of the Effectiveness of Concept Mapping as an Instructional Tool, *Science Education* 77, no. 1 (1991):95–111.

3. Miccinati, Mapping the Terrain.

4. S. Jones and D. Sims, Mapping as an Aid to Creativity, *Journal of Management Development* 4, no. 1 (1985):47–60.

5. Miccinati, Mapping the Terrain.

6. P. Gold, Cognitive Mapping, *Academic Therapy* 19, no. 3 (1984):277–284.

7. J. Heinz-Frye and J. Novak, Concept Mapping Brings Long-Term Movement toward Meaningful Learning, *Science Education* 74, no. 4 (1990):461–472.

8. W. Wager, Teaching/Learning Process (Paper presented at Teaching Skills for Health Professions Educators, St. Simons Island, Ga, August, 1994).

9. J. Wycoff, *Mindmapping: Your Personal Guide to Exploring Creativity and Problem Solving* (New York: Berkeley Books, 1991).

10. J. Wycoff, *Mindmapping.*

Chapter 27

Clinical Teaching—What Makes the Difference?

Barbara Fuszard

Is clinical teaching one style? One strategy? What determines the approach to clinical teaching?

These authors return to the discussion of Experiential Learning in Chapter 2. The same basis of teaching is utilized by faculty in all of the examples, but different emphases are discussed. They are influenced by the development of the student, the site of the clinical experience, the experience of nursing staff, the objectives of the course, and the placement in the curriculum. In their adaptation to all the variables facing faculty and students, the reader is offered suggestions for facing her or his own situation, and permission to make adaptations.

Example 1
Teaching Research in the Clinical Area

Susan R. Colgrove, Nancy Schlapman, and Constance Erpelding

The following is an example of using experiential learning to teach an introduction to nursing research course to three registered nurses working toward their B.S.N. degree. The dean approached a faculty member, who was actively involved in research at a clinical setting, to teach the course over the summer while she was engaged in research at the site. Since there was a long-established relationship between the faculty members and the clinical site, research was occurring at the time of the course, and staff at the site were very open to students, it was an excellent opportunity for students to learn research. It was thought that a clinical research experience for beginning students would make a traditionally difficult and boring topic more interesting and understandable. The faculty believed that combining theory with clinical application would illustrate both the ideal and real aspects of clinical research. By being actively involved, the students would be exposed to the relationship between theory and practice.

The experiential learning methods utilized in this course were group discussion, structured activities (study guides), and clinical work (participation in the research process at the setting). Methods included seminars (no formal lectures were used), and guest speakers from the nursing faculty and the research setting. Classes took place at the university, the clinical setting, and the library.

The course was taught during an eight-week summer session. The class was divided into a theory component (24 hours) and a clinical component (24 hours). A syllabus, developed by faculty at the University of Wisconsin College of Nursing, served as the guide for the course and presentation of theory content.[1] Objectives for the course and study guides from the syllabus were used to help students focus their readings and identify key issues. However, not every aspect of the syllabus was covered equally. Emphasis was placed on topics of importance to students and issues relevant to and/or occurring in their clinical experiences. Too often, time spent on topics in lecture may not reflect their incidence in practice.[2] The purpose of the course was to introduce students to the basis of nursing research, to familiarize students with basic terminology, purpose of research in nursing, influence of research, research design and methods, ethical and legal issues, and beginning critical reading of research reports. The course objectives were as follows:

- Demonstrate an understanding of research process as it relates to nursing.
- Demonstrate an understanding of the relationship between research and theory.
- Demonstrate a beginning competency in critical reading of nursing research.
- Describe the role of the nurse in research.
- Describe the purpose of selected research designs and data collection methods.
- Demonstrate a beginning competency in the use of American Psychological Association's (APA) writing style.[3]

The required texts for the course were as follows:

American Nurses Association. *Human rights guidelines*. Kansas City.

American Psychological Association, 1993. *Publication manual of the American Psychological Association*. 3rd ed. Washington, DC.

College of Nursing, University of Wisconsin, Oshkosh. 1992–1993. *Introduction to nursing research*, 74–230. University of Wisconsin, Oshkosh, College of Nursing.

LoBiondo-Wood, G., and J. Haber. 1990. *Nursing research: Methods, critical appraisal and utilization*. St. Louis: Mosby-Year Book, Inc.

In addition to the above texts, each student received a copy of the proposal for the research under study at the setting, and the human subjects information submitted to the internal review board at the university related to the research. These documents became the basis for combining theoretical and practical aspects of research during discussions and were the protocols used at the research site.

This course could easily be taught by one faculty member. However, because of other responsibilities, two faculty members split the responsibilities of the course. During the first meeting, Stage 1 and Stage 2 of Burnard's model for combining experiential learning and andragogy were accomplished. During the first class, faculty reviewed the course objectives as prescribed in the syllabus, explained the organization of the course, discussed faculty and student roles, and reviewed the research going on at the clinical setting. The students discussed their nursing expertise, their expectations for the course, and their learning needs. Together a timetable was negotiated between the faculty and the students. This was divided between theory and clinical research practice. Both faculty and students were very flexible, and topics changed based on what was happening at the setting and student issues.

The theoretical portion of Stage 3 followed the course outline and student needs. Students identified very little knowledge of nursing research, and none had used it in their practice. Students were expected to come to class having completed the study guide in order to participate in class discussions. Answers to these questions were found in the required texts. The study guide questions served as one source for class discussions. Following are a few examples of study guide questions from the course syllabus:

- What is the significance of research in nursing?
- What are some of the various sources of human knowledge? Give an example of each.
- What is meant by scientific research? Is it the same as nursing research?
- Why is nursing research important for clinical practice?
- What is "theory"?
- How are theory, research, and practice related?[4]

Initial classes presented basic information about research and the research process. They were held at the university and at the clinical setting. A tour of the setting and discussions with clinical staff and faculty helped the students see the connections among practice, theory, and research. The research proposal served as the guide for class discussions related to research purpose, research questions, review of the research, use of theory, methodology, data analysis, discussion, and implications of research. Discussions also centered on student questions about what is meant by scientific research, the main concepts of nursing research, what was nursing theory, and how it was tied to the research process. By combining the study guide questions with the actual research proposal, understanding of the importance of research, the steps in the research process, terminology, and design of research became very clear because they were connected to a real research project. Students could see every aspect of the research process in action through the proposal and at the research site. Because the faculty member was active in the research, credibility and practical experience were not issues.

One early class was held in the library. Students had identified a lack of knowledge about nursing journals and use of the library. At the library students were helped to identify and find scholarly nursing journals and to find topics and authors using CINHAL. At this time discussion centered around these R.N. students' use of research in their current practice, where research ideas originated, the importance of research to improve practice, and the meaning of refereed journals. The use of the APA format for writing papers was also discussed at this time, and students were shown the format through the use of articles from nursing journals. Students remained in the library to explore topics of interest to them and to begin to look for a research article they would like to critique.

As the students learned about samples, discussions centered around the sample they were working with at the setting. This included the difference between a population and a sample, probability and nonprobability sampling, and how the sample at the setting was obtained. Also brought into discussion was human subjects approval. Students reviewed the document and approval format at the university. In addition, they reviewed and discussed the consent form, and legal and ethical issues related to research and human subjects.

Students were involved in interviewing residents at the site regarding their satisfaction with the nursing home, and mailed interviews to family members of residents. After reading about the different approaches to data collection and answering study guide questions, interviewing was discussed at length. Role-play was used to demonstrate and practice interviewing techniques. Discussion also centered on patient rights, timing of interviews, confidentiality and privacy, and validity and reliability of instruments. When interviewing began, we did inter-rater reliability by observing each other—faculty as well as peers—and comparing scores. When we all were scoring subjects equally, students were assigned five subjects to interview over a two-week period. Class discussion following this experience was full of examples and questions that centered around the interviews. Students were prepared for discussions and actively involved. Because the group was so small, everyone quickly became comfortable with one another and the faculty members. The group worked together as colleagues.

The students were responsible for every aspect of the mailed interview. They helped prepare the interview and consent form for mailing, put the list of subjects together, addressed and stuffed envelopes, and developed a checklist for returned interviews. Much of this was done independently by the students. Discussion related to mailed interview data combined theory related to clarity of interview questions and instructions, coding forms, reading level of forms, and consent to participate. Because the faculty were at the site, many times informal discussion went on with individual students.

After data collection was completed, students were introduced to data entry and the use of the computer. Two students had very little computer experience and the third was very knowledgeable. The experienced student assisted the faculty member in giving individual instruction to the other students. Coding of data and basic principles of LOTUS were explained to the students. Students were assigned data to enter and came to the clinical site at preset times to enter data either with the instructor or the student familiar with this process. After they felt comfortable they entered data unassisted, and a faculty member checked their work. The students worked on data entry for about two weeks. They were excited about their work and recognized quickly the tedious aspects of data entry and the importance of accuracy by subjects and researchers in completing interviews and questionnaires.

A requirement of the course was a research critique. Early in the course, students were encouraged to select a research article of interest to them. The article was reviewed with the faculty to ensure that it was at a level that the student could understand and review critically. At this point in time class discussions had been focused on research designs, true and quasiexperimental designs, samples, reliability, and validity; levels of measurement of data; and basic descriptive statistics. These topics, along with previous discussions, study guides, and references in their syllabus on writing a critique, gave the students the basic information on critiquing a research article. Students had several weeks to write the paper, and faculty support was available to review their progress. Prior to class, the students received a copy of the article the others were to present. Students presented the papers orally, and the other students raised questions and issues. All members of the group participated, and much discussion was created, because the students were familiar with each other's articles.

Qualitative research was covered by a guest faculty member, who discussed this form of inquiry—its purpose, methodologies, rigor, credibility, transferability, and dependability. The speaker then presented her research regarding survivors of cancers who had used alternative therapies. The students were all interested in the topic and discussion about the method she used, selection of the sample, the problems she encountered, and her findings. Students and faculty were seated around a table and slides were shown. Because the group was small, it was easy for all the members to be involved in the discussion. Students also learned how to put together a presentation and again saw the research process in action.

Students were evaluated on their class participation, research critiques, completion of interviews, data entry, and work done with the mail-out questionnaires. No written examinations were given.

Student Evaluation of the Learning Experience

Students gave the following *advantages* of this learning experience:

- hands-on learning; doing, rather than lecture
- independent nature of the clinical portion, making it easier to fit the class into a student's working schedule
- independence required of the student, requiring motivation
- small group formation, allowing for more individual help
- sharing of expertise and experiences
- student preparation required before going to class or to the clinical portion (But it seems like less work than typical lecture course, and you remember more.)
- nonthreatening environment

Students gave the following *disadvantages* to this type of learning experience:

- short time period, allowing students only a brief, cursory view of research, not enough to see the whole picture
- threatening environment; the course moved quickly, and a basic understanding of the topic seemed necessary to participate
- much flexibility and independence required

NOTES

1. College of Nursing, University of Wisconsin, Oshkosh, *Introduction to Nursing Research 74-230* (Oshkosh: 1992–1993), 1–57.
2. D. McCaugherty, The Use of a Teaching Model to Promote Reflection and the Experiential Integration of Theory and Practice in First-Year Student Nurses: An Action Research Study, *Journal of Advanced Nursing* 16 (1991):534–543.
3. Ibid.
4. Ibid.

SUGGESTED READING

Gueldner, S.H., et al. 1993. The undergraduate student as research assistant: Promoting scientific inquiry. *Nurse Educator* 18, no. 3:18–21.

Example 2
Teaching Critical Care in the Intensive Care Unit

Christine Berding

Since the inception of intensive care units in the late 1960s, critical care nursing has grown into a well-defined specialty. A wide knowledge base and great proficiency at highly technical skills are needed, with the essence of critical care nursing lying in the decision-making process of gathering appropriate information, making judgments, and establishing priorities. These critical thinking abilities are very difficult for the student to master in an area where a life-or-death decision may be needed in only a moment's time.

Experiential learning methods can be tailored nicely to teaching the concepts and goals of critical care nursing. According to Reilly and Oermann,[1] learning varies with the experience of each learner, due to differing perceptions and meanings of events in the environment. They believe that experiential methods recognize the importance of perception and insight in learning. Critical thinking is fostered by the direct experiencing of events through the utilization of problem-solving skills associated with client care and staff/peer relations.

Preceptorship has generally been recognized as the optimum method for educating students and new nurses in the ICU setting. However, difficulties arise when there is limited access to senior staff because of numbers or scheduling problems. Other challenges may present themselves, such as having multiple preceptors with varying levels of proficiency and competence, increasing the responsibilities of an already overburdened preceptor, and instructing individuals with differing degrees of knowledge. The use of Burnard's model[2] of experiential learning methods presents an excellent framework for teaching critical care nursing in the ICU.

Self-assessment of knowledge and skills by the student, combined with faculty direction of objectives from the syllabus or orientation package, constitute the first stage of Burnard's model of experiential learning. This information is then utilized to develop a timetable (Stage 2) with theoretical and clinical components that guide the student through the learning process. The timetable must be flexible to meet the various needs of individual learners. It is similar to the concept of critical pathways being used in many institutions today. In Stage 3, theoretical components best suited to the learner and appropriate clinical assignments are identified.

As stated earlier in this chapter, theoretical components may be presented by traditional methods such as lecture, reading assignments, presentations, and self-study. Written assignments are also valuable in that they provide students with an opportunity to reflect on their experiences, thus promoting critical thinking skills. Written assignments may be given in many forms, including nursing care plans, case studies, teaching plans for the client, and experiential diary/learning logs.

Reilly and Oermann[3] describe experiential diaries and learning logs as a means of recording experiences by a dialogue with self, the student noting his or her feelings, reactions, attitudes, perceptions, and activities. This allows students to reflect on their experiences and derive personal meaning. In an area as highly charged with critical activity and intense emotion as the ICU, the experiential diary would give the novice an excellent opportunity to express and understand the feelings experienced from day to day. With the large volume of new skills and learning experience encountered daily, the learning log provides an excellent means of recording information for the timetable developed in Stage 2.

In experiential learning, clinical assignments provide the student with the opportunity to learn the relevance of theory when applied to practice. Discussions are directed by the students, giving them an active role in learning by and from their experiences. Problem-solving and decision-making skills with clients, as well as with other professionals, are enhanced.

In the critical care setting, it is important for clinical assignments to be made with a gradual increase in client acuity, according to the comfort level and skill of the student. At the completion of a clinical experience, a postconference provides students with the benefits of sharing new experiences. Staff also need to have input at this time. Their expert interpretations of experiences provide valuable learning tools for the student.

Stage 4, evaluation methods, consists of feedback from peers, verbal feedback from instructors and staff, written reports, personal objectives, and evaluation of the timetable. This should be done informally on a weekly basis, and formally at midterm and end of term. At the end of term, the student should also provide a formal evaluation of the instructor.

The concept of a written timetable allows the student, instructor, and preceptor (if there is one) an opportunity to plan strategies for meeting goals on a weekly basis. With goals clearly delineated, there is no question regarding outcomes to be accomplished, thus reducing stress on the student and staff. There should be no more questions such as "Just what exactly can the student do?" arising halfway through the term!

The timetable addresses the drawbacks of not having enough senior staff for precepting, and having varying levels of experience among preceptors and students. Each staff member working with the student will know where the student is in the learning process. The timetable will also assist in identifying current skills and experiences required by the student.

Experiential learning permits empowerment of students and assists them in assuming control. They develop a positive attitude toward themselves and toward their critical thinking abilities. Connolly and Brenner[4] list the above as attributes of critical care nurses. They also include characteristics such as drawing on life experiences, valuing self-learning, learning best by doing, and preferring informal environments. These are all features of experiential learning, which is tailored nicely to teaching the concepts and goals of critical care nursing.

NOTES

1. D.E. Reilly and M.H. Oermann, *Clinical Teaching in Nursing Education*, 2nd ed. (New York: National League for Nursing, 1992).
2. P. Burnard, *Learning Human Skills: An Experiential Guide for Nurses* (Oxford, England: Heinemann Nursing, 1990).
3. Reilly and Oermann, *Clinical Teaching in Nursing Education.*
4. M.A. Connolly and Z.R. Brenner, *Critical Care Education in the Service Setting: Building a Curriculum for Excellence* (Atlanta: National Teaching Institute of the American Association of Critical-Care Nurses, 1994).

SUGGESTED READING

Goldrick, B., et al. 1993. Learning styles and teaching/learning strategy preferences: Implications for educating nurses in critical care, the operating room, and infection control. *Heart Lung* 22, no. 2:176–182.

Moser, D.K., and S. Coleman. 1992. Recommendations for improving cardiopulmonary resuscitation skills retention. *Heart Lung* 21, no. 4:372–380.

Example 3

Teaching Family-Centered Care to Junior Nursing Students

Astrid Hellier Wilson

For the last four decades family-centered care has been evolving in nursing.[1] The theoretical underpinnings of family-centered care revolve around the notion that the family is a system and symbiotic relationships are present. When a child is hospitalized, consideration must be given to the needs of the other family members when planning care.[2] Therefore, family-centered care is crucial in the acute pediatric setting.

The pediatric setting can be overwhelming to beginning nursing students because of the complexity of family-centered care and the movement away from caring for an adult hospitalized patient. Frequently nursing students perceive themselves as lacking skills in the growth and development of children at different ages, lacking personal interactions with children, being fearful of caring for children, or identifying their patients with their own children. Nursing faculty are challenged with the task of decreasing student anxiety and assisting students to utilize the family members when determining care for pediatric patients.

The undergraduate course *Caring for Pediatric Populations*, taught at the School of Nursing in the College of Health Sciences at Georgia State University, has one objective that states: "Upon successful completion of this course, the student will be able to apply knowledge of developmental theory and family-centered care when providing nursing care to children and adolescents." Essential to the success of the experiential learning method is the environment in which learning occurs. One setting that enables faculty to meet the course objective and utilize the experiential learning method is the Scottish Rite Children's Medical Center, Wilbur and Hilda Glenn Hospital for Children. The philosophy of the department of nursing at this institution is based on the mission of the medical center and focuses on excellence in the delivery of nursing care as defined by the family, the nurse, and the department. Beliefs related to the family, the professional nurse, and the nursing environment are contained in Exhibit 27–1. The staff nurses at the institution are excellent role-models for nursing students in providing family-centered care to pediatric patients.

The ideal clinical setting and collaboration among nursing staff members, faculty, and nursing students provides the opportunity for students to have a positive learning experience. One innovative strategy to decrease initial student anxiety is setting a pace that enables students to become comfortable in a new, complex, clinical setting. Clinical assignments are made weekly, with clear expectations of the students' responsibilities. The students' responsibilities are increased over the eight-week course, culminating in total family-centered care. During the hospital orientation a written handout is provided to students to facilitate their clinical learning (see Exhibit 27–2).

The weekly student assignments are posted on the unit and the staff nurses assigned to the students are reminded of the students' responsibilities. The written student responsibilities are a clear form of communication among staff nurses, faculty, and nursing students. Examples of weekly assignments are found in Exhibit 27–3.

Exhibit 27–1 Beliefs Related to the Family, the Professional Nurse, and the Nursing Environment

THE FAMILY

We recognize that each child and family is unique and is deserving of individualized care.
We promote optimal health by:

- Supporting communication and collaboration between the family and the health care team.
- Educating the child and family based upon their learning needs.
- Encouraging continuity of care.

We respect the child and family's right to privacy, confidentiality and their own personal values.

THE PROFESSIONAL NURSE

We recognize the specialized role of the pediatric nurse as a child and family advocate, as the primary care coordinator, and as an innovator basing nursing practice on established standards of care.
We promote professional and institutional commitment by:

- Encouraging the nurse to assume responsibility and accountability for personal and professional practice.
- Supporting active involvement in participative management.
- Providing an atmosphere that encourages peer and team support, and open communication.
- Promoting a positive image of nursing.

We respect that the health care environment is rapidly changing and that nursing is instrumental in its strategic success by:

- Initiating innovative problem-solving and strategic planning.
- Demonstrating fiscal responsibility and resource allocation.
- Promoting physical and emotional well-being by recognizing and managing personal and professional stressors.

THE NURSING ENVIRONMENT

We recognize the need to maintain a competitive compensation and benefit package which will assist in recruiting and retaining committed nursing staff.
We promote professional development by:

- Supporting academic and continuing education in order to maintain and enhance nursing practice.
- Developing an environment conducive to risk-taking and problem-solving.
- Educating nursing staff concerning fiscal and resource allocation issues.

We respect the unique contribution nursing makes to our community by sharing our knowledge of family centered care, child safety, wellness, parenting/child development and the role of the professional nurse.

Source: Reprinted with permission from Scottish Rite Children's Medical Center.

Exhibit 27–2 Facilitation of Students' Clinical Learning

GEORGIA STATE UNIVERSITY
SCHOOL OF NURSING
STUDENT CLINICAL SCOTTISH RITE PCA 2 EAST
CLASS HANDOUT

To facilitate your learning prior to coming to the clinical setting the following information must be obtained. If you are having difficulty on Monday obtaining the data, please contact me.

- Interact with the assigned patient and parent(s) to obtain data related to formulating nursing diagnosis.
- Complete the information on the CHILD/FAMILY DATABASE FORM.
- Look up and review all patient drugs and bring drug cards to the unit.
- Check the patient's drug drawer to determine the form of the medication, i.e., pills, liquid, and how you will administer the drug to the patient. For IV drugs, check the form the drug is in, i.e., powder that needs to be reconstituted, or already mixed, and then check the IV administration chart to determine how many ccs are needed and how long to run the medication.
- Write out a discussion of the normal anatomy and physiology and the pathophysiology related to the medical diagnosis on database form.
- List and prioritize nursing diagnoses using a family-centered approach to the nursing process.
- Complete an individualized nursing care plan for two diagnoses.
- Make an hourly schedule from 7:00 AM to 11:30 AM indicating the nursing care you will provide.

The students are able to concentrate on the weekly student focus because they have limited nursing responsibilities from week one to week five. During the first five weeks there is time for students to become adjusted to the demands of collecting data and formulating care plans with a family-centered focus. Students soon learn that family members are valuable resources in planning and implementing care for pediatric patients. It is the primary care giver who can inform nursing students about the best way to gain cooperation from the patient through knowledge of how the patient likes to take his or her medications, special feeding techniques, and even the growth and development of the child. The gradual method of taking on total family-centered patient care also helps to build confidence in beginning nursing students because they can be successful without being overwhelmed.

Both student and staff nurse evaluations of the method have been positive. Staff nurses have noted that the method enables the student to gain confidence, knowledge, and skills. At the end of the course students seemed surprised at how

Exhibit 27–3 Examples of Weekly Clinical Assignments

STUDENT CLINICAL ASSIGNMENTS PCA 2 WEST
FIRST WEEK

DATE: Tuesday, 1/18 and Wednesday, 1/19
TIME: 7:00 AM - 12:00 NOON, Post Conference 11:30 AM
FACULTY:

STUDENT FOCUS 1/18: ORIENTATION TO HOSPITAL AND UNIT

STUDENT RESPONSIBILITY ON PCA 2 WEST:
Students will read handout materials prior to class and participate in both hospital and unit orientation. Attire: Lab coats over street dress

STUDENT FOCUS 1/19: ASSESSMENT AND DOCUMENTATION

STUDENT RESPONSIBILITY ON PCA 2 WEST:
8 AM Vital Signs/AM Care (Bath, Bedchange)/Monitor and Record PO INTAKE HOURLY/ Monitor and Record OUTPUT HOURLY/Assist RN assigned to patient in monitoring and recording IV FLUIDS/Perform patient assessment and chart findings/Observe and assist nurse performing procedures/Sign off with completed flow sheet with nurse & faculty prior to post conference.

STUDENT: PATIENT/ROOM #:

****

STUDENT CLINICAL ASSIGNMENTS PCA 2 WEST
SECOND WEEK

DATE: Tuesday, 1/25 and Wednesday, 1/26
TIME: 7:00 AM - 12:00 NOON, Post Conference 11:30 AM
FACULTY:

STUDENT FOCUS: ASSESSMENT, DOCUMENTATION, PRN MEDICATIONS

STUDENT RESPONSIBILITY ON PCA 2 WEST:
8 AM Vital Signs/AM Care (Bath, Bedchange)/Monitor and Record PO INTAKE HOURLY/ Monitor and Record OUTPUT HOURLY/Monitor and record IV FLUIDS/Perform patient assessment and chart findings/Observe and assist nurse performing procedures/Administer PRN MEDICATIONS ONLY THIS WEEK/Sign off with completed flow sheet with nurse & faculty prior to post conference.

STUDENT: PATIENT/ROOM #:

continues

Exhibit 27–3 continued

STUDENT CLINICAL ASSIGNMENTS PCA 2 WEST
THIRD WEEK

DATE: Tuesday, 2/1 and Wednesday, 2/2
TIME: 7:00 AM - 12:00 NOON, Post Conference 11:30 AM
FACULTY:

STUDENT FOCUS: ASSESSMENT, DOCUMENTATION, PRN AND PO MEDICATIONS

STUDENT RESPONSIBILITY ON PCA 2 WEST:
8 AM Vital Signs/AM Care (Bath, Bedchange)/Monitor and Record PO INTAKE HOURLY/ Monitor and Record OUTPUT HOURLY/Monitor and record IV FLUIDS/Perform patient assessment and chart findings/Observe and assist nurse performing procedures/ADMINISTER PRN AND PO MEDICATIONS ONLY THIS WEEK/Sign off with completed flow sheet with nurse & faculty prior to post conference.

STUDENT: PATIENT/ROOM #:

****

STUDENT CLINICAL ASSIGNMENTS PCA 2 WEST
FOURTH WEEK

DATE: Tuesday, 2/8 and Wednesday, 2/9
TIME: 7:00 AM - 12:00 NOON, Post Conference 11:30 AM
FACULTY:

STUDENT FOCUS: ASSESSMENT, DOCUMENTATION, IV MEDICATIONS

STUDENT RESPONSIBILITY ON PCA 2 WEST:
8 AM Vital Signs/AM Care (Bath, Bedchange)/Monitor and Record PO INTAKE HOURLY/ Monitor and Record OUTPUT HOURLY/Monitor and record IV FLUIDS/Perform patient assessment and chart findings/Perform and/or assist nurse performing procedures/ADMINISTER IV MEDICATIONS ONLY THIS WEEK/Sign off with completed flow sheet with nurse & faculty prior to post conference.

STUDENT: PATIENT/ROOM #:

****

STUDENT CLINICAL ASSIGNMENTS PCA 2 EAST
FIFTH WEEK

DATE: Tuesday, 2/15 and Wednesday, 2/16
TIME: 7:00 AM - 12:00 NOON, Post Conference 11:30 AM
FACULTY:

continues

Exhibit 27–3 continued

STUDENT FOCUS: ASSESSMENT, DOCUMENTATION, ALL MEDICATIONS

STUDENT RESPONSIBILITY ON PCA 2 EAST:
8 AM Vital Signs/AM Care (Bath, Bedchange)/Monitor and Record PO INTAKE HOURLY/Monitor and Record OUTPUT HOURLY/Monitor and record IV FLUIDS/Perform patient assessment and chart findings/Perform and/or assist nurse performing procedures/ALL MEDICATIONS/Sign off with completed flow sheet with nurse & faculty prior to post conference.

STUDENT: PATIENT/ROOM #:

****

STUDENT CLINICAL ASSIGNMENTS PCA 2 EAST
SIXTH, SEVENTH, AND EIGHTH WEEKS

DATE: Tuesday and Wednesday
TIME: 7:00 AM - 12:00 NOON, Post Conference 11:30 AM
FACULTY:

STUDENT FOCUS: TOTAL FAMILY-CENTERED PATIENT CARE

STUDENT RESPONSIBILITY ON PCA 2 EAST:
8 AM Vital Signs/AM Care (Bath, Bedchange)/Monitor and Record PO INTAKE HOURLY/Monitor and Record OUTPUT HOURLY/Monitor and record IV FLUIDS/Perform patient assessment and chart findings/Perform appropriate procedures/ALL MEDICATIONS/Sign off with completed flow sheet with nurse & faculty prior to post conference.

STUDENT: PATIENT/ROOM #:

much they had learned, and became more confident in their role as professional nursing students because of the positive role-models of family-centered nursing care and the contributions of family members.

NOTES

1. K.A. May and L.R. Mahlmeister, *Maternal and Neonatal Nursing Family-Centered Care*, 3rd ed. (Philadelphia: J.B. Lippincott Co., 1994).
2. C.L. Betz, et al., *Family-Centered Nursing Care of Children*, 2nd ed. (Philadelphia: W.B. Saunders, 1994).

Chapter 28

Issues in Clinical Teaching: Cautionary Tales for Nursing Faculty

Patricia Christensen

"My patient doesn't have an apical pulse!" declared the sophomore nursing student to her instructor. "Really?" the wary instructor asked as she and the student headed toward the patient's room. Once at the bedside of a smiling, very alert elderly woman, the student indicated to her clinical professor the spot where she was attempting to auscultate the heartbeat—at approximately the level of the small intestine. "You said we should listen one inch below the nipple line," she said as she indicated the area of the sagging breasts.

This is just one of the hilarious anecdotes reported by a nursing faculty member who has been teaching for more than 20 years.[1] "I could write a book" can be heard around the table of the faculty lounge in most nursing schools. Nursing students are nowhere a greater challenge than when they attempt to demonstrate their newfound knowledge in the clinical area on real, live patients. Thankfully, most of the mistakes of students do not have dire consequences, but the supervision of students raises issues that are of concern. Long gone are the days when a doctor told a patient—and the patient bought the story—that her shaved head was "part of her treatment," this after a horrified student nurse discovered that she had prepped the wrong patient for a craniotomy! This true story illustrates how far accountability for mistakes has come. Patients today would not accept that story—nor should they.

In the dynamic environment of clinical teaching, issues and events will arise unexpectedly. While no one can accurately know all eventualities, it is wise for nursing faculty members to be aware of, and plan for, student clinical errors and problems. Presented here are vignettes of clinical situations—all true—that may prove useful to faculty members to explore as they venture forth with neophyte nurses-to-be.

CASE HISTORY 1: PROTECTION OF PATIENT SAFETY

Approximately three hours into a busy clinical day on an obstetrics unit, Rhonda, a junior nursing student, approached her clinical instructor. "I don't feel so good," Rhonda said. "I have this fever and my neck is all swollen." "What?" her instructor exclaimed, "What are you doing here with a fever?" "I didn't want to miss a clinical day. You said we should make sure to meet all our clinical objectives," the student responded. The student was immediately sent home and the patient reassigned to a staff nurse. The clinical instructor reported the incident to the nurse manager and finished the clinical day. The faculty member had practically forgotten the incident when, two days later, the student called and reported, "Guess what? I have the German measles." The faculty member thought back on the patient this student had cared for on that day. With a sickening feeling, she remembered that the student had cared for the *only* antepartal patient on the unit—a patient in early pregnancy with hyperemesis gravidarum. What if the student had infected the pregnant woman? Immediately, the faculty member called the patient's doctor and reported the ghastly coincidence. After a quick check of the patient's file, it was established that the patient had already been immunized for rubella, so there was no further cause for concern.

Today, with students required to show proof of immunizations, this particular case probably would not occur. But still, students can report to the clinical area with a wide array of possible infectious processes. For example, a common coldsore can infect a newborn with herpes virus, which can prove deadly to the baby. With clinical time at a premium at most facilities, the students are frequently warned not to be absent for clinical days. Clinical absences can mean the loss of valuable experiences and faculty scrambling to make up labs at semester's end. While no faculty member would suggest that a student come to clinical sick, a message can be sent by faculty that clinical days are so valuable that students had better not miss them. A student, often conscientious and not wanting to miss valuable clinical time, may under-report or minimize an illness.

CASE HISTORY 2: THE STUDENT NURSE UNCOVERS A SCANDAL

Helen, a senior nursing student in her last semester before graduation, was attempting to complete the assignments for the nursing management practicum. As part of her requirements, she had to assess an organizational unit independently, including leadership style, structure, strengths and weaknesses of the unit, and so forth. She had been assigned to a community long-term facility, where she also worked as a patient care technician part

> time. The student was having difficulty completing the assessment because she had become aware of some very disturbing incidents that were occurring at the nursing home, and she was unclear how to handle them. Serious suspected problems such as patient abuse, employees reporting to work inebriated, and inadequate supervision of licensed personnel were among the concerns of the student. In her clinical conference, the student reported her suspicions to her clinical instructor. The instructor cautioned the student to report only her observations and not to draw conclusions, but nevertheless the instructor was concerned. When the student submitted her final report on the facility, the instructor was aghast to read what the student had reported. While the student had, in some instances, reported naive conclusions, there was no doubt that the student had also made some very astute observations of real problems—suspicious bruises on elderly arms, the smell of alcohol on an employee's breath, and the absence of licensed personnel at certain times. Armed with this information, the faculty member requested a conference with the dean of the nursing school to discuss the legal and ethical responsibilities of the student, the instructor, and the school in this case. Likewise, the dean was alarmed, and deemed it imperative to include the university's attorney in the conference. After careful consideration, the attorney determined that most of the damning information in this case had been obtained while the student was an employee of the institution, not as a student. Therefore, the school's responsibility lay in urging the student employee to report her suspicions to her supervisor. This the student did with very unsatisfactory results—denial by the supervisor of any trouble and an accusation that the student was mistaken. The student subsequently resigned from that nursing home; no further attention was given to her suspicions. The nagging doubt remained, however, in the minds of the student, the instructor, and the dean—were patients in that facility at risk, and what should have been done?

This case illustrates the real dilemma faced by nursing faculty members when students observe reportable conditions—things such as child abuse and neglect—but which the nursing instructor does not witness. Do the faculty member and the school of nursing have a responsibility to report these cases? All states have laws that govern reportable incidents by health professionals, and it is incumbent upon faculties to explore these issues. Consultation with the state board of nursing, the state department of social services, and the university attorney may be indicated in these cases.

CASE HISTORY 3: SAFEGUARDING OF NURSING STUDENTS

> In the community health course, junior nursing students were assigned to various agencies within the health department, and assigned as well to visit

homes of families in the community. Many of the homes were in poor, neglected, crime-ridden areas. All students had been cautioned about safety concerns while in dangerous neighborhoods and were encouraged to go in pairs on their home visits. The instructor took turns going with each student, but for most of the semester, the students had to make their home visits without the instructor.

Nursing student Rebecca was assigned to a new, single mother and her infant in a government housing project. On the scheduled home visit day, Rebecca was unable to arrange to visit with another student and so proceeded to the client's home alone. While walking toward the new mother's apartment, the student's progress was impeded by a group of young black men who were loitering around the project. As Rebecca attempted to make her way down the walkway, the five young men made lewd and suggestive remarks to her. Eventually, the men surrounded the student but did not touch her. The remarks included, "Hi, Baby, whatchoo doin' here?" "Can we help you?" "Man, you are some chick." The student attempted to retain her composure, but she later stated that she was very afraid. With as much confidence as she could muster, she told the group that she was a nurse and she came to take care of Ms. Wilson's baby. As she spoke, she continued to walk toward her client's home. She was able to reach the client's apartment and complete her assessment of the newborn, but she dreaded returning to her car. She wanted to call her instructor, but the young mother did not have a phone. Rebecca waited in the apartment until the young men moved on, and then made a quick walk to her car and sped away. While she was unhurt, the episode was very unsettling for her, and later for her instructor, whom she told at the clinical conference.

This encounter was reported to the program director and the dean, and a committee was formed to study the issue of student safety in the community health course and to formulate policies and procedures to deal with these potential problems. Among the recommendations were that students were never to make home visits alone. Each student must be accompanied by at least one other student, public health nurse, or the instructor. Additionally, students and faculty were issued beepers so their whereabouts could always be determined.

Student safety is a major issue on college campuses today. Families have the right to expect that their son or daughter will be safe while at that school. Nursing students—especially in community health courses—are often exposed to environments such as the one described above. It is incumbent on the schools of nursing to take extra precautions while students are out on clinical experiences. Not only are students in unsafe neighborhoods, they are often en route in other students' cars and vans. Insurance coverage must be adequate to cover all eventualities. There must be a system in place to ensure that students and the school are adequately served in the area of student safety.

CASE HISTORIES 4 AND 5: STUDENTS AS POLICE

Nursing professionals, including students, are often confronted with situations where liability for reporting to authorities is unclear. For example, where is the line between child abuse and discipline as understood by parents and nurses? Is a smack on a child's face by a parent, in the presence of a nurse, child abuse or the parent's usual mode of discipline? Situations like this can and do arise in the course of clinical experiences. The following two vignettes may serve to illustrate some examples.

Case History 4

Betty, a senior nursing student, was assigned to a welfare mother and her two children for home visits as part of the requirements for the child health course. She was to make a series of visits to assess the children's growth and development, their immunization status, and other aspects of primary care.

In the state where Betty practiced, it was unlawful for women to receive welfare benefits if they were living with, or being supported by, a man in the house. Welfare fraud had become a major issue in the state, and all abuse of the system was to be reported. Betty, on several of her visits, observed a young man, who was reported by the mother to be the father of her children, playing with and caring for the children. Betty also observed that the father kept his clothes and personal effects in the trailer he shared with the young family. The dilemma that confronted Betty was, should she report this case? Betty consulted with her clinical instructor and together they attempted to analyze as many aspects of this case as possible, with the over-riding question being, what was best for these children? On the numerous occasions that Betty had been at the home, she had observed the father interacting lovingly with his children and providing much-needed help with their care. Betty did not ask directly, nor was it ever mentioned by the parents, the exact circumstances of the man living with the family. The two small children appeared to be benefiting from the relationship, and it appeared that the family badly needed the consistent financial support of welfare. A central question appeared to be, should nurses be part of law enforcement? Was this a case of fraud or a matter of client confidentiality? After careful consideration, it was determined by Betty and her instructor to just leave well enough alone and not report that the children's father probably lived in the home. This was a case where the nurse did not feel it to be her responsibility to report a suspected violation of policy or law. Would the situation have been different if the children were not being cared for as well?

Another case of a student nurse in a difficult clinical situation shows a different perspective.

Case History 5

> Philip, a senior nursing student, was assigned a single-parent family in his community health course. In the home lived a 22-year-old mother, a three-year-old girl, and an infant boy six months of age. Also, it appeared that different men lived with the mother occasionally. Philip found the public housing apartment to be extremely dirty and untidy on all occasions when he made home visits. The children were often hungry and poorly dressed, but no one had observed the mother or the various men abusing the children, nor were they left alone. Frequently, however, no one would answer the door when the student knocked. One Sunday morning, the clinical instructor read in the paper that the woman who was Philip's client had been arrested for prostitution and was suspected in the death of a man who had come to the apartment for sex. After verifying that, indeed, the woman reported in the paper was the children's mother, the question arose, was there an obligation to report possible child neglect? After careful consideration, the student and the clinical instructor decided that, in this case, it would be prudent to report to the social services authorities that the children needed further evaluation of the home to be safe from abuse and neglect.

Both of these cases illustrate the need for careful analysis of each case individually. Most families, especially poor ones, have very complex relationships that can either harm or enhance the well-being of children. If nurses are seen as agents of law enforcement, they may lose the confidence and rapport that has been fostered over many years of public health tradition. More important, if nurses are not trusted, poor, vulnerable families may lose the care that they so desperately need.

CASE HISTORY 6: THE INCOMPETENT STUDENT

> Eleanor, a second-semester junior student, was the daughter of a trustee of the university where she attended nursing school. She appeared to be an average student in her class work, but her clinical skills were incompletely assessed. In her first two years of clinical courses, her final evaluations reflected that she had met the objectives, but lacked confidence and was reluctant to ask for assistance. Eleanor was very open about being the daughter of a trustee, and made numerous remarks about her influential father and their discussions of her nursing school experiences.

> One clinical day in her parent-child course, Eleanor was assigned to a young woman in labor. All students had been assigned readings and audio-visual aids to see before they attempted patient care in the hospital. The objectives for that clinical laboratory were to provide comfort measures, to assess the progress of labor, to provide psychological support, and to observe and report any possible signs of complications. While the patient was also assigned a staff nurse, that staff nurse was very busy that day and did not stay in the room with the patient at all times. About four hours into labor, the fetal monitoring strip of the unborn began to show decelerations (slowing heart rate), and on several occasions the mother stated that she felt "faint and dizzy." Eleanor, who was in the room alone with the patient for approximately 20 minutes, did not assess the fetal monitoring strip, take the vital signs of the mother, or report to the nurse or her instructor what the patient stated. On entering the labor room, the instructor immediately observed the slow fetal heart rate and promptly turned the mother on her side and took her blood pressure. Within a few minutes, the fetal heart rate was within normal limits and the mother was comfortable. Her blood pressure, which had been 90/48 when the instructor entered the room, rose to her baseline reading of 128/78. On interviewing the student about the situation, it became clear to the instructor that Eleanor lacked even basic judgement and knowledge about the relationship among vital signs, patient well-being, and indicated nursing actions. Somehow, through copying other students' and published care plans and being quiet and unobtrusive, Eleanor had progressed through two years of clinical courses with minimal clinical skills. The question lingered in the instructor's mind, had other clinical faculty been intimidated—perhaps unconsciously–by the student's father's influence in the university? On careful evaluation, it was determined by the instructor that Eleanor would receive a failing grade for the clinical course.
>
> When the student was informed of her grade, she stated that she thought it was unfair and said, "I'll tell my father." After several conferences with the program director and the dean, it was determined that since the student had passed other clinical courses and was allowed to progress in the program, she was entitled to extra tutoring and could not be failed at that time. Vast amounts of faculty time were spent in extra tutoring for Eleanor. After she graduated with her class, Eleanor took the NCLEX exam on two occasions and failed both times.

In subsequent faculty discussions, there was always the issue lurking: Should this student have been allowed to progress and graduate? In an effort to ensure that a similar situation did not occur, stricter and more objective clinical evaluation methods were instituted. These methods included objective written clinical exams as well as tests of performance. In addition, a policy was adopted that did not permit progress in the program after a clinical failure. Also, an early warning system of identifying and reporting students at risk for failure was instituted.

GUIDELINES FOR FACULTY

While problems such as the ones reported here are unpredictable, clinical nursing faculty members would be wise to consider some contingency plans for the unexpected. One of the most important considerations in protecting the student, the patient, and the school is open communication. An ongoing and supportive relationship between the school of nursing and the respective state board of nursing is essential.[2] Additionally, an open communication line with the university attorney (or an attorney consultant) can provide essential legal guidance. Paramount in these relationships is the need for immediacy in replies. Often, situations will occur that demand an answer quickly. Relationships must be forged on a trusting basis that allows for on-the-spot consulting.

Another dimension of open communication centers on informing students of their rights and responsibilities while in attendance at the school of nursing. A student handbook is often an avenue for such information. A written account, such as a handbook, can serve as a contract for students. A student handbook should be specific enough to be useful, but not so specific as to hamstring the school in a changing environment. For example, it is not possible—or desirable—to attempt to list every eventuality that may occur. Pertinent information can be catalogued under headings such as "Uniform Policy," "Student Illness in the Clinical Area," and "Student Safety in the Clinical Area."

Another avenue of student information can be a complete and mandatory student orientation. There is often a need to convey information to students that is more fluid and changing than can be covered in a handbook—for example, the location of an agency, parking, contact persons in the clinical area, and so forth. In many cases, having students sign for written information can form a "contract of understanding." Under no circumstances can school officials assume that students have essential information on entry into the program or course. A certain amount of redundancy in student expectations for each course is to be expected.

The National League for Nursing, and program nurse consultants at all state boards of nursing, can provide guidance to schools on the formation of student policies and handbooks. It is advisable to have policies and handbooks pilot tested and read by students, faculty, and parent groups for clarity and meaning before officially disseminating them to students and faculty. A legal opinion on policies is also advised by this author.

In the dynamic environment of clinical teaching, events will occur that are unpredictable and troublesome. While no one can accurately know all eventualities, it is wise for nursing faculty members to be aware of, and plan for, student clinical errors and problems. The careful and judicious formulation of student policies and handbooks, and open and ongoing communication with students, faculty, state officials, and legal consultants will diminish the chances of dire consequences arising from student mishaps.

NOTES

1. L.A. Rooda, Surviving Two Decades of Nursing Students, *Journal of Nursing Jocularity* 4, no. 1 (1994):26–30.
2. B. Kellogg, Program Nurse Consultant, South Carolina Board of Nursing, August, 1994.

Part VII

Futuristic Techniques

This part's strategies leave the world of known facts to seek inferences, probable and possible knowledge that may still exist in the future. It is an entirely new experience for student and faculty facilitator, who have always concentrated on existing knowledge, to open themselves to creatively anticipate the future.

The other techniques that have been discussed are based upon a great deal of previous knowledge, and therefore are perhaps most appropriate to the advanced student. However, the tree of impact strategy, at least, has been used with unexpected success with beginning graduate students in an issues class. Perhaps readers will find earlier applications for the other strategies as well.

Chapter 29

Delphi

Beverly Henry

DEFINITION AND PURPOSES

The *Delphi* technique is a mechanism for soliciting expert opinion. It was developed in the 1950s by Helmer and Dalkey at the Rand Corporation in Santa Monica, California. The technique involves extracting informed intuitive opinions from a panel of experts in a field of inquiry. In a Delphi, face-to-face discussions are replaced with repeated questionnaires and feedback to a panel of experts in the form of statistical summaries.

The purpose of a Delphi is to obtain the most reliable consensus of opinion possible using a series of questionnaires. Another purpose is sharing individual divergent perspectives and highlighting differing theoretical views, semantic interpretations, and factual differences.[1] The goal in a Delphi is to establish efficient and effective communication among individuals who may be geographically separated. A typical schedule of Delphi activities is as follows:

1. Develop the broad Delphi questions.
2. Brainstorm for preliminary ideas.
3. Select panel of experts.
4. Develop, test, and distribute round 1 questionnaires.
5. Analyze responses from round 1.
6. Develop, test, and distribute round 2 questionnaires.
7. Analyze responses from round 2, and distribute and analyze round 3 . . .*n* questionnaires.
8. Prepare research, policy, and implementation reports.[2]

THEORETICAL RATIONALE

Professionals from many fields are found in health care organizations. One way of participating in decision making about the future is by using a technique in which experts communicate but avoid the potentially problematic group dynamics and psychological distractions typically accompanying open-forum discussions.[3] A Delphi provides individuals who have high levels of expertise with an opportunity to participate anonymously in decisions using controlled interactions and is the method of choice where medium- or long-range forecasts are needed.[4] Helmer notes, "Expert opinion must be called on whenever it becomes necessary to choose among alternative courses of action in the absence of an accepted body of theoretical knowledge that would clearly single out one course as the preferred alternative."[5]

In health care much existing knowledge is pretheoretical. Experts participating in a Delphi may draw on existing theory in tangential fields, but primarily they bring to a Delphi the benefit of their intuitive insights.

CONDITIONS

A Delphi is the method of choice when a few voices in a field may dominate existing thinking about a subject. In a Delphi the influence of highly vocal individuals is minimized through the use of questionnaires and written feedback to all experts in the form of aggregated summaries.

The following three conditions are critical for the completion of a Delphi.

1. adequate time to formulate questions and analyze data
2. availability of participating experts who are skilled in written communication
3. availability of participants who are motivated to persist through a number of Delphi iterations, popularly called Delphi rounds[6]

Studies using the Delphi are time consuming. A considerable number of days, weeks, or months may be necessary to carefully formulate questions, distribute questionnaires, and analyze responses. It is best if a minimum of two months is budgeted for completion of a Delphi exercise.[7]

In addition to thinking about the amount of time available to conduct a valid and useful Delphi, consideration should also be given to the resources available to generate well-constructed questionnaires containing unambiguous questions. A high level of mathematical sophistication is not a requirement for a Delphi.

Minimal quantitative and computer capabilities are needed to calculate descriptive statistics and tests of reliability. Well-done Delphi studies do, however, require the input of investigators capable of assessing reliability and validity in new innovative ways.

At least five skills are developed when a Delphi technique is used as a learning activity. *First*, students develop oral and written communication skills by presenting the project to potential participants, formulating letters of request, sending memos to experts who may be overlong in responding, and developing research reports.

Second, use of a Delphi enhances students' facility with critiques of the literature. The technique calls for analyzing existing theory, formulating Delphi items that are contextually and semantically valid, and delineating positions based on previous scientific findings that are coherent, intelligent, far-sighted, and useful.

Third, a Delphi fosters development of group facilitation skills. Brainstorming among subgroups prior to the implementation of a Delphi to enable investigators to develop the most appropriate broad research question a Delphi will address requires an understanding of group interaction and creativity.

Fourth, use of a Delphi enhances students' understanding of research methods and highlights the usefulness of skills needed to develop questionnaires and perform content analysis in which pattern identification and clustering are paramount.

Fifth, a Delphi is useful for developing students' facility with statistical analysis. Although mostly descriptive statistics are used, development of interquartile ranges, analysis of statistical differences among participating groups, and probability calculations to determine degrees of consensus are often necessary.

TYPES OF LEARNERS

Beginning and intermediate-level researchers may benefit most from using the Delphi technique. Individuals in both the academic and work settings can conduct Delphi exercises. A Delphi in health services organizations is especially useful for long-range forecasting of needs and markets.[8] Time is the most expensive resource needed. Access to statistical software and personal computers is also necessary. Consultation may be required, particularly for development of a statistical model of consensus.

USING THE METHOD

Preparing to conduct a Delphi requires, first, that considerable time be spent thinking about the broad question that will be addressed. Statement of the question is the key to a successful Delphi project. Questions like the following should be asked:

- Why are we interested in this kind of study?
- What information is needed in the field that is not now known, that is of both a theory-building and problem-solving nature?
- How will the results of a Delphi seeking to elucidate important concepts, questions, and solutions influence future decisions?[9]

To respond to these questions, brainstorming procedures, as noted, may be used in conjunction with a Delphi in the early stage as a means of stimulating participants' creativity and productivity.

Selection of experts is the second most critical aspect of preparing for a Delphi. When thinking about the experts who should be selected, the first question is what kinds of experts are needed, given the purposes of the Delphi and the research questions being addressed. Second, information about the qualifications of experts should be sought and evaluated. Information about expertise that should be collected includes the following:

- kind and quality of professional experience
- number, kind, and quality of publications
- estimated status in respective field
- extent of participation in profession
- degree of accuracy about previous predictions[10]

These data are available in professional journals, reports from governmental and private foundations, and membership and editorial lists.

Those who are interested in the problems addressed by a Delphi may also nominate experts. Nominations may be sought on an individual basis, by telephone survey, or by attending national professional meetings.[11] Attending national meetings, presenting the purposes and goals of a Delphi, and soliciting nominations, after having described nomination criteria, are valuable learning activities. In preparing to implement a Delphi, faculty and students alike should budget sufficient time for developing the questionnaire, pretesting, and piloting. Access to computer software packages for statistical analysis and for statistical consultation also should be acquired in the preparatory phase.

The role of faculty members and students in a Delphi is contingent on whether a faculty member or student is the primary investigator. In either case, common elements and responsibilities include the following:

- critical analysis of theory development in the field
- careful and thorough review of previous key studies that have been reported using the Delphi and of critiques of the Delphi technique by its originator, particularly by Olaf Helmer
- careful thought about questions related to reliability and validity
- preparation for the generation of position and policy papers that will result from the study

POTENTIAL PROBLEMS

With advanced planning, many of the problems that can accompany a Delphi will be avoided. Adequate review of the theoretical and research literatures in the field for which a Delphi is to be used will reduce the likelihood of not choosing the finest experts—those capable of making valid predictions and formulating useful responses. Helmer notes that an expert's assessment of his or her own relative competence in an area of inquiry is correlated highly enough with actual levels of expertise to be a useful aid in selecting experts.[12]

An additional problem that should be anticipated has to do with attrition of experts once they agree to participate. H. Blohm and K. Steinbuch note that because a Delphi is anonymous there is the danger that participants may not feel adequately challenged.[13] A way of alleviating this problem and strengthening the motivation of experts to be highly committed, creative, and involved is to provide them with sufficient information concerning the critical nature of the problems being addressed in the Delphi, as well as information about the obligations of respondents.

Example
A Delphi Study of Research Priorities*
Beverly Henry

This example describes how students can facilitate a Delphi using an interdisciplinary panel of experts. The *National Nursing Administration Research Priorities Study*[14] illustrates possible learning activities. Two major purposes of the study were to develop and rate definitions of *nursing administration research* and to generate priority research questions for the field.

At initiation of the study, faculty held informal preliminary brainstorming sessions with students to talk about (1) empirical investigations reported or currently being conducted in nursing, (2) the choice of research studies to be undertaken given the theoretical limitations in the field, (3) the problems practitioners faced, and (4) research that would most likely be useful in the medium and long ranges.

Experts who participated in the study represented two generic fields, nursing and hospital administration. Decisions in health care are made by people from a number of fields. The opinions of individuals with expertise in economics, management, and the health sciences, at a minimum, are needed for development of effective policy decisions that are sensitive to the needs, expectations, and budgets of consumers of health services.

In the study, faculty and students contemplated the following with respect to experts:

- Which categories of health care professionals are most essential for nursing administration research—research typically cutting across several disciplines?
- Which individuals in the fields of nursing and health administration are most knowledgeable and motivated?

A number of mechanisms were used to solicit nominations of highly respected individuals. First, students, faculty, and project consultants attended and participated in a major national council meeting. At the meeting, time was allocated for presentation of the problems that would be addressed by the Delphi, for

*The study that provides the example described in this section was supported by the U.S. Department of Health and Human Services (Division of Nursing, Bureau of Health Professionals, Health Resources and Services Administration, Public Health Service) and by the National Center for Nursing Research, National Institutes of Health and under grant number RO1 NU 08085; *National Nursing Administration Research Priorities.*

determination of the eligibility of criteria for selection of experts, and for solicitation of nominations. In addition, the round 1 Delphi questionnaire was critiqued. After the meeting, follow-up letters soliciting additional nominations were developed and mailed to all members of the council. Students and faculty then sifted through the names of nominees to determine which candidates best met the eligibility standards.

Letters of invitation and the round 1 questionnaire were then sent to potential Delphi panel members (see Exhibit 29–1). All correspondence developed for the study was also assessed for attractiveness, conciseness, and technical correctness. Many of the rules for business and scientific writing were adhered to for the correspondence.

Round 1 Analysis of Experts' Responses

As Delbecq and colleagues note, the round 1 Delphi questionnaire can take on several forms, but typically, one or two items are set forth as statements or questions, particularly if round 1 is a preparatory round as in this study.[15] An open-ended questionnaire asking experts to describe the nursing administration research that needed to be done according to highest priority was used in round 1. In addition, each expert was asked to complete a self-rating scale, a panel-of-profile form and a consent form, and to rate 12 definitions of nursing administration research. Excerpts from the round 1 questionnaire used in the nursing study are in Exhibit 29–2.

Before the round 1 mailing, students assisted with pretesting each of the documents included in the mailing and recommended changes in content and format. In the process, they raised questions about the number of anticipated responses, the treatment of collected data, and the time that would be used analyzing responses and developing questionnaires for subsequent Delphi rounds. Discussions like these were as useful for faculty as they were for students.

Before analysis of responses began, students also participated in decisions about how to encourage respondents, once they had agreed to participate, to persist for the duration of the Delphi. They recommended some "dunning" procedures over others. Telephone calls and postcard reminders were ruled out in favor of formal, follow-up letters encouraging continued participation.

Responses from all experts to the open-ended questions in round 1 were analyzed by first developing lists of all the responses, then printing the responses on separate cards, categorizing cards by like content, then labeling the categories of ideas submitted using key concepts from the responses as category headings. Reviewing responses and the accompanying discussions between investigators and students about category headings, the classification of responses, and

Exhibit 29–1 Cover Letter of Introduction and Instruction

Dear __________:

You have been nominated by members of the Council on Graduate Education for Administration in Nursing to participate in a study to determine national research priorities for nursing administration.

Nursing administrators and nursing administration faculty are asking for an interdisciplinary perspective to determine the field's research priorities. Persons like yourself—administrators and faculty in the fields of nursing, education, and health administration—were nominated to assist in the development of these priorities through participation in this Delphi study, "National Nursing Administration Research Priorities."

According to your colleagues, you are in a strong position to identify and prioritize areas for nursing administration investigations. Clearly, the field of nursing administration is replete with investigatable problems. Judgment about high-priority research problems, based upon the extensive experience and national perspective you possess, are needed.

Specifically, as a participant in this project, you are asked to provide us with

1. your ratings of a list of definitions of nursing administration research (rounds 1–3).
2. specific research questions (round 1) and your assessment of their priority, value, and impact on patients' and nurses' welfare (rounds 2 and 3).
3. information about nursing administration research you may know of that is currently underway (round 2).

We plan to initiate three Delphi rounds. Providing the information needed in each round will take approximately one hour. This is round 1. Rounds 2 and 3 will occur in November and January.

Copies of final reports will be given to you as they are generated. Although an honorarium cannot be provided, your participation, with your permission, will be acknowledged in all reports.

Your skills, expertise, and background uniquely prepare you to provide us with the information needed to address the purposes of the study. We hope you are willing to participate. Please signify your response by completing and returning the questionnaire in the envelope provided.

Thank you in advance for considering this request. We look forward to your response and to working with you. If we can be of assistance please phone us.

Sincerely,

Source: Courtesy of Beverly Henry and Linda Moody.

Exhibit 29–2 National Delphi Study: Nursing Administration Research

Round 1 Questionnaire

Part 1

The following definitions of nursing administration research were developed by the study monitor team and project consultants, with input from members of the Council on Graduate Education for Administration in Nursing. From the randomly ordered list below, rate from 1, not useful, to 7, extremely useful, how helpful each definition is in providing a conceptual framework to guide and conduct nursing administration research.

(Check *one* response for each definition.)

List of Definitions:

Rate the usefulness of each of these definitions.

	Not Useful						*Extremely Useful*
1. Nursing administration research concerns itself with scientific inquiry related to management of nursing personnel and the quality of care delivered to clientele.	[1]	[2]	[3]	[4]	[5]	[6]	[7]
2. Nursing administration research is the scholarly investigation of human and/or organizational responses to health and resource problems.	[1]	[2]	[3]	[4]	[5]	[6]	[7]

Part 2

Please list *five* researchable questions regarding the field of nursing administration that you think are of top priority.

Question 1: ____________________

Question 2: ____________________

Source: Courtesy of Beverly Henry and Linda Moody.

classification theory was useful for improving students' knowledge of content analysis and of categorization as a data reduction mechanism.

Round 2 Questionnaires

For many weeks following development of the categories, the study team was heavily involved in formulating the final research questions that would be prioritized in subsequent Delphi rounds. Working individually and in small groups, investigators and interested students undertook two tasks:

1. editing original questions submitted by experts who had had similar ideas
2. developing new questions by combining a number of ideas that had been submitted into single research questions

The second task involved using for the questions the largest number of key ideas described or suggested in the original contributions submitted by the panel of experts. At this stage of the study, students improved their understanding of reliability and validity in qualitative research and developed additional skill at formulating questionnaires. Assessment of the round 2 questionnaire format was based on the criteria in these four questions:

1. Are items easy to understand and identify from round 1?
2. Is there a section in the questionnaire where comments can be shared?
3. Are instructions for participation clearly stated?
4. Is the questionnaire clear enough and of a length that can be completed in a reasonable period of time?

In this phase of the study, students also learned a great deal about the research topics national experts thought were of highest priority. Comparing the experts' responses to trends in health and nursing as reported in the professional and popular media enabled students and faculty to have informed discussions about the contribution of various projects to theory development and problem solving. Conversations in which faculty and students talked about what the experts were recommending as the most important research topics were also immediately useful for students, many of whom were in the process of formulating thesis or dissertation proposals.

Analyzing Round 2 and 3 Questionnaires

In the nursing administration Delphi, returned round 2 questionnaires were analyzed to determine the median score of the rating of each definition and research question and the interquartile range. In round 3 the interquartile range of responses obtained in round 2 were depicted for each item, and experts were asked once again to indicate their opinion of the usefulness and importance of each item by reconsidering and revising their previous opinion. The experts were also asked to comment briefly on their rating of any item if their response fell outside an interquartile range.

Students reviewing the round 2 and round 3 questionnaires were as interested in the median scores and ranges achieved for each item as they were in the experts' arguments and comments. Arguments developed by experts justifying their extreme responses provided students with insight into the perspectives of key thinkers that many times do not appear in professional journals. The dialogue about divergent ideas enlarged students' world views and improved their understanding of the complexity of the problems they could anticipate when doing their own research.

In analyzing responses in round 3, students were also asked to assess why convergence, as represented by a shrinking interquartile range, had or had not occurred for each of the items in the questionnaire. Where convergence did not occur, answers to the following questions were sought:

- Was the language used in an item ambiguous?
- Where more than one key variable was used in a single research question, was the over-riding theme of the question undecipherable to the experts?
- If convergence did not occur, did opinions polarize?
- Were there separate, identifiable schools of thought with respect to a particular research topic?

Research, Policy, and Implementation Reports

Questions like these and others concerning differences, or the absence of differences, in responses among groups of respondents involve students in discussions important for their intellectual development as beginning researchers. Participating in decisions about the kinds of reports that should be prepared and the content of reports addressing varying aspects of a Delphi also enlarges students' understanding of data analysis; the nature of research reports developed as manuscripts; the policy implications of research projects for individuals, organizations, professional groups, and governments; and implementation plans. Reviewing drafts of manuscripts and presentations enhances students' knowledge of the mechanics of the Delphi method and of the research process.

This learning technique has been used with graduate nursing students to dual purpose—to introduce the place of intuitive thinking into the realm of factual knowledge, and to teach an accepted research approach. This technique has been used to the added benefit of bringing new knowledge into the field of nursing.

NOTES

1. O. Helmer, *Looking Forward: A Guide to Futures Research* (Beverly Hills, Calif: Sage Publications, Inc., 1983), 134–135.

2. A. Delbecq, et al., *Group Techniques for Program Planning: A Guide to Nominal Group and Delphi Processes* (Glenview, Ill: Scott, Foresman & Co., 1975), 84.

3. C.R. McLaughlin, et al., Management Uses of the Delphi, *Health Care Management* (Spring, 1976):51–62.

4. D.M. Georgoff and R. Murdick, Manager's Guide to Forecasting, *Harvard Business Review* 86, no. 1 (1986):110–120.

5. Helmer, *Looking Forward*, 56.

6. Delbecq, et al., *Group Techniques*, 84,

7. Georgoff and Murdick, Manager's Guide to Forecasting, 120.

8. Delbecq, et al., *Group Techniques*, 87.

9. Helmer, *Looking Forward*, 58–59, 150–152.

10. H. Blohm and K. Steinbuch, *Technological Forecasting in Practice* (Westmead, England: Saxon House, 1973), 15.

11. B. Henry, et al., Research Issues for Nurse Administrators, *Series on Nursing Administration* 1 (1988): 155–176.

12. Helmer, *Looking Forward*.

13. Blohm and Steinbuch, *Technological Forecasting*, 15.

14. Henry, et al., Delineation of Nursing Administration.

15. Delbecq, et al., *Group Techniques*, 84.

SUGGESTED READING

Barton, A.J. 1994. Data needs for decision support of chief nurse executives. *Journal of Nursing Administration* 24, no. 4 (suppl):19–25.

Campostrini, S., and D.V. McQueen. 1993. Sexual behavior and exposure to HIV infection: Estimates from a general-population risk index. *American Journal of Public Health* 83, no. 8:1139–1143.

Clarke, H.F., et al. 1993. Public health nurses' vision of their future reflects changing paradigms. *Image: Journal of Nursing Scholarship* 25, no. 4:305–310.

Cronin, S.N., and V.B. Owsley. 1993. Identifying nursing research priorities in an acute care hospital. *Journal of Nursing Administration* 23, no. 11:58–62.

Crotty, M. 1993. Clinical role activities of nurse teachers in project 2000 programmes. *Journal of Advanced Nursing* 18, no. 3:460–464.

Dailey, A.L. 1988. Faculty consensus at a multi-campus college through Delphi. *Community/Junior College Quarterly of Research and Practice* 12, no. 1:21–26.

Dailey, A.L., and J.C. Holmberg. 1990. Delphi: A catalytic strategy for motivating curriculum revision by faculty. *Community/Junior College Quarterly of Research and Practice* 14, no. 2:129–136.

Duffield, C. 1993. The Delphi technique: A comparison of results obtained using two expert panels. *International Journal of Nursing Studies* 30, no. 3:227–237.

Georgoff, D.M., and R.G. Murdick. 1986. Manager's guide to forecasting. *Harvard Business Review* 86, no. 1:110–120.

Helmer, O. *Looking forward: A guide to futures research.* 1983. Beverly Hills, Calif: Sage Publications, Inc.

Kurtzman, J. 1984. *Futurcasting*. Palm Springs, Calif: ETC Publishing.

Leape, L.L., et al. 1992. Small-group judgment methods for determining resource-based relative values. *Medical Care* 30, no. 11:NS28–39.

Martino, J.P. 1983. *Technological forecasting for decision making*. New York: North Holland.

Murray, J.P. 1992. The department chairperson: The confessions of a researcher turned practitioner. Paper presented at the National Conference on Successful College Teaching and Administration. Orlando, Fla. March 1–4.

Noble, K.A. 1992. An international prognostic study, based on an acquisition model, of degree philosophiae doctor (Ph.D). Unpublished doctoral dissertation, University of Ottawa.

Nugent, K., et al. 1993. Facilitators and inhibitors of practice: A faculty perspective. *Journal of Nursing Education* 32, no. 7:293–300.

Ptaszynski, J.G., and J.L. Morrison. 1989–1990. Applying the ED QUEST planning model in a school of management: A case study. *Planning for Higher Education* 18, no. 1:65–78.

Snyder-Halpern, R. 1994. An assessment taxonomy for designing nursing research programs. *Western Journal of Nursing Research* 16, no. 1:81–93.

Williams, P.L., and C. Webb. 1994. The Delphi technique: A methodological discussion. *Journal of Advanced Nursing* 19, no. 1:180–186.

Zadinsky, J.K., and J.H. Boettcher. 1992. Preventability of infant mortality in a rural community. *Nursing Research* 41, no. 4:223–237.

Chapter 30

Scenarios

Martha H. Bramlett

DEFINITION AND PURPOSES

The term *scenario* has its origins in drama, where it meant the story or outline of a play and more recently of a screenplay.[1] In studying the future, a scenario can be defined as a hypothetical outline or story proposing future events or trends.[2] Whether written in narrative or matrix form, the scenario is based on real facts and logic.[3]

A narrative scenario, such as in the example, is the prediction written in story form. In matrix form, alternative possibilities are placed in matrix squares. If a grand scenario has been developed, then the most probable future may be designated with percentages or lines within the squares.

Scenarios may vary in scope, dealing with a single issue or many. They are generally used to deal holistically with many aspects simultaneously. Additionally, they can be either the projections of a single individual or the combined estimations of a panel of experts.[4]

The purpose of a scenario can vary. Some are written for entertainment or for satisfying curiosity about future directions. Alternatively, scenarios can be used to determine alternative futures for use in planning.[5]

THEORETICAL RATIONALE

Present-day scenario building is credited to Herman Kahn of the Rand Corporation and think tanks. Perhaps Hollywood's proximity gave Kahn the idea to script the future for planning, scene by scene like a writer would write a movie. The scenario took facts, projected them into the future, and then looked back over the intervening years at what happened. A type of scenario, the tree of impact, is described in Chapter 31.

CONDITIONS

When planning for the future, scenarios can be used in several ways. They are useful in defining trends that are probable but still subject to molding, as well as trends that are possible and open to influence. They are also useful for defining trends that are either possible and subject to influence or probable but not amenable to alterations.[6] By defining these trends, individuals or groups can alter their plans to accommodate trends that cannot be altered and plan ways to exert influence to modify trends.[7]

Scenarios also provide an interesting teaching technique. In developing the scenario, the student must first research the background information and must then analyze that information in order to develop the scenario. Finally, the student can look at the trends predicted and develop possible methods for influencing those trends.[8]

Scenarios can be utilized with a variety of topics. Topics to be examined can be either narrow or broad in focus. However, scenarios are particularly useful when a holistic approach is desired.[9] Although scenarios are based on fact, the exercise gives an opportunity for the student to use imagination in forecasting.

TYPES OF LEARNERS

As a teaching technique, scenarios can be utilized in either individual or group situations. The technique is more suitable for the learner with higher-level thinking skills because it requires not only accumulation of information, but also synthesis, analysis, and formulation.[10]

RESOURCES

The resources required for this technique vary with the topic. To obtain the full benefit of imagination in scenario building can be very time consuming. Shorter exercises can be devised to use part of the process. It is also helpful to have experts in the area of investigation available for student consultation.[11] The activity can be performed in independent study or in a classroom set up for group activity.

USING THE METHOD

A topic must first be selected. The learners then acquire information on past trends related to the topic. This can be accomplished either individually or through class activity.[12]

A good way to develop a list of possible alternatives within a topic is through brainstorming.[13] After developing lists of possible events, small groups can be randomly assigned possible future events.[14] Each group then creates one or more alternate scenarios using the possibilities. In doing this all participants should use the same perspective, looking back from the same future year. Some groups may introduce completely new possibilities.[15]

After all small groups develop their scenarios, the results are shared. The class as a whole can then evaluate and discuss the alternative scenarios. The class should evaluate the plausibility, desirability, and malleability of various scenarios. Finally, the class may elect to present the final combined alternative scenarios to a panel of experts who will each determine which alternative they consider the most likely. By combining the responses of each expert, various alternatives are designated as most likely. The final step creates a grand scenario.[16]

The faculty has a dual role. First, the faculty is content consultant, giving the student direction in acquiring necessary information. The other faculty role is as a process consultant, helping students to develop analytical, brainstorming, and group process skills.[17]

The student is encouraged to give free reign to the imagination. Fact gathering is used here only to begin. The special contribution to learning scenarios is the creative component. The students can think of themselves as temporary members of the think tanks of the businesses that are involved in the topic of their study. After the period of creativity, the work becomes critical analysis, and entails responsibility for group work.

POTENTIAL PROBLEMS

A major problem in using the scenario technique is in the scope of the topic selected. If the scope is too narrow, the scenario can be simplistic and not exhibit the holistic potential of the technique. If, on the other hand, the scope is too broad, the technique can be cumbersome and awkward.[18]

The example is a typical scenario, the product of extensive research and analysis by a graduate nursing student. As extensive background information is needed to develop a scenario and/or a grand scenario, this strategy is most appropriate for advanced students.

Example
A Nursing Department on Hos-Space
Elaine J. Allanach

The scenario can be a useful method for monitoring a student's understanding of course curriculum. In this example, a graduate student in nursing administration has used a scenario as a paper. The assignment was to define a new nursing service department through the use of a scenario. This student set the scenario to occur in the future and in space. "Hos-Space" was a hospital designed to care for the basic and general needs of space indigents. This is an excerpt from that paper.

Hos-Space: Purpose and Goals

Clarity of an organization's purpose and goals is necessary not only in the beginning stages of existence, but also to maintain its viability.[19] Because of the inherent limitation of space, we were required to carefully define the major purpose and the *necessary* supporting goals and objectives. In the case of Hos-Space, the actual environment as well as the social and cultural environment defined our purpose: To provide a healthful environment in which ill indigents may regain normal functioning of body and mind. Our goals were to

1. provide a living environment with a mean rotational acceleration velocity of one-third to one-half that of Earth mean surface gravitational acceleration (32.174 feet per second);
2. provide a clean, utilitarian living space for the patient to encourage restoration of body processes through moderate exercise, nutritious food, stepped mental activity, and counseling services; and
3. provide basic life-saving services such as fluid and electrolyte replacement, short-term computerized organ system assistance, and tissue-regeneration services not to exceed ten cubic centimeters per 24-hour period.

The beginning objectives were extrapolated for each goal. Goal number one had only one objective: to obtain a reasonably priced gravitational space station that could function with as small a human crew as possible. The second goal's objectives were dependent on the configuration of the obtained space station, as to what tasks had to be done in order to make the necessary structural changes.

Goal number three had three objectives: (1) set up a fluid and blood banking laboratory, (2) obtain and calibrate a computerized body diagnostic and organ assistance module, and (3) obtain and activate a tissue regeneration incubator with generalized cell cultures.

Goals of the Project

Restoration of the patient's body processes was the goal of the project. The management model used was an integrated nursing and management process model by Stevens.[20] Consideration was given to goals, processes, structures, resources, and controls.

This project, Patient Services Management, accounted for the daily operational direct work of Hos-Space. Because this project had the potential of being very broad, with many issues of concern, Martha Rogers's Science of Unitary Man was chosen as a unifying force.[21] This encourages a holistic view of the patients and staff within the organizational environment. Outcome goals become less important, both in patient care and management, than network processes.

The acausality of the relationship between the nurse and the patient is also recognized, as is the constant evolutionary or helical nature of the nurse–patient, Hos-Space–patient, and Hos-Space–nurse field interaction, consistent with the Rogers framework. The causal, discrete medical model of assessment, planning, implementation, and evaluation is not utilized. Instead, the nurse engages in a process of inter-relationships based on perceptions of the nurse-patient network.

Using the network process and Rogers's Science of Unitary Man in the administration of nursing services required in the project also disannulled the concept of outcome goals. Outcome goals were viewed as manifestations of a suspect causality. Instead, the view of management was an ever-developing relationship among individuals, individuals and their work, and individuals and the organization of Hos-Space. Behavior was thought to be a reflection of people's assessment of what they could do within their situation or network to make it livable, to become competent, to gather rewards, and to maintain their self-respect. Behavior was neither predefined nor predestined. Kantor has made the point that while people recognized their dependence on the network, their behavior was more often to seek independence than competence, rewards, and self-respect.[22]

The written philosophy of the Patient Services Management Project did center around the value placed on the "actualized worker."[23] Our philosophy maintained that when the staff was encouraged to grow, the patients too would be encouraged to heal and grow. The relationship between this philosophy statement and the objective of Hos-Space was clear: a healthful environment was not possible without creative growth of all individuals, both staff and patients.

The goals of the Patient Services Management Project were as follows:

- Design and maintain the 15 modular patient care living spaces in a manner conducive to patient health restoration.
- Design individualized exercise programs for patients based on nursing needs assessment.
- Maintain a nutritious food supply for patients.
- Design individualized mental activity or education programs.
- Provide individual and group counseling directed toward healthy planning for the future.

When considering methods for attaining these goals, it became very clear that there was indeed a synthesis between nursing and management.[24] The goals were not limited to the traditional definition of nursing. There was a considerable overlap into the fields of physical therapy, dietetics, social work, and the clergy. Yet it seemed logical for nursing to reintegrate these areas—as a pendulum swings, so does nursing. Given the limitations of space and personnel, this did seem to be the trend in off-Earth nursing practice anyway.

Structures of the Project

Functions and Standards

Drucker noted that there were four kinds of functions: "result-producing activities, support activities, hygiene and housekeeping activities, and activities of top management."[25] For each of the project goals, the functions had to be identified. This is the point where the abstract became the concrete.

Once the functions were identified, jobs could clearly be assigned, whether to humans or to robots. It also became clear where more staff was needed. It was found that recovering patients could perform particular jobs, when the jobs were consistent with the patients' needs for mental and physical activity.

Departmentalization and Committee Organization

As noted above, Hos-Space began as a series of projects in which the eight of us served as project leaders or members. Once operations became routine, projects reverted to departmental designations. I became the director of the Patient Services Department.

One of the physicians, Craig, became the director of Life Saving and Emergency Services, while Bruce, the senior computer specialist, became director of Environmental Management. While these were relatively unnecessary designations among the eight of us, as patients began to come to us, and other staff members joined us, we found it necessary to designate "the leaders." Ultimately, I became the CEO of the operation, when members of the original eight moved on to other stations and programs.

Committees were appointed when the types of decisions that needed to be made were ongoing and it was believed that a group decision would be advantageous. The first committee to be appointed was, believe it or not, the Menu Planning Committee. Eating serves many purposes for space dwellers: nutrition, emotional satisfaction, socialization, religious imagery, relaxation, reward, and psychological safety, to name a few. Poor menu design could be a major roadblock to life, much less useful life, on a space station.

Assigning, Staffing, and Scheduling

Once the functions were defined, assignments were made according to who could best do the job among those willing to do it. Because of the small size of Hos-Space, the number of staff and working patients never became large enough to bureaucratically make assignments. Group participation was the norm. Scheduling of monitoring activities, such as patient monitoring, environmental monitoring, or guidance-system monitoring, was attained through negotiation. Systems monitoring held great survival value so nobody balked at taking a turn.

Policies, Procedures, and Practices

It was noted many years ago that all organizations have to survive in a changing environment, yet find ways of doing so without changing the essential character or objective of the organization.[26] Policies are reflective of decisions that are made in regard to strictness of adherence to organization purpose versus survival, multiplicity versus singleness of purpose, and narrowing versus broadening of objectives.

Policy making at Hos-Space was participative, and occurred in relation to perceived problems. This generally occurred at the lowest level needed to reach an acceptable conclusion. Thus, the maintenance procedure was defined and written by Joe, the robotics engineer, as were maintenance procedures. The policy related to the schedule of day lighting and night lighting involved all eight of the original staff, and was renegotiated whenever two or more people requested reconsideration.

Because of the value placed on the development of the staff as individuals in their own right, it was expected that the usual conflicts of space living be handled between the people involved. Every attempt was made to not "policy and procedure" every aspect of life and work on Hos-Space.

Areas where standardization of procedure were implanted were on those processes and systems that impacted on the survivability of Hos-Space. Life support procedures and life threatening procedures were codified, such as how to exit Hos-Space for outdoor work, how to maintain the crops, and bacterial and viral colonization control. Even so, procedures were open to change to ensure that the safest and most up-to-date information was integrated.

The Executive Role

As the years passed, and members of the original eight went on to other things, I became the CEO of Hos-Space. In many ways, this was a different role. Even as director of patient services, it still seemed to be a collegial relationship. Yet, when new people came in, they perceived these positions in a more hierarchical relationship. Leadership became more important.

A leader cannot exist without followers. People are the focus of getting tasks accomplished. Fuszard said it so well: "Marketing of health care will have no material to market if the health care workers are not motivated to produce quality care."[27] I had a dream—a true adhocracy in a health care organization—always at the back of my mind.[28] We came very, very close to it, at the inception of Hos-Space. But to survive, we had to grow, and growth meant the end of the adhocracy dream. But, my role as a leader still needed to reflect that dream, or I would not have been true to myself. I did view myself as "an enactor of policy decisions made at the lower levels" implicit in the use of quality circles[29] and Theory Z.[30]

Heider made a comment that I hung on my wall: "The wise leader is not collecting a string of successes. The leader is helping others to find their own success. There is plenty to go around. Sharing success with others is very successful. The single principle behind all creation teaches us that true benefit blesses everyone and diminishes no one.[31]

NOTES

1. R.B. Heydinger, and R.D. Zentner, Multiple Scenario Analysis: Introducing Uncertainty into the Planning Process, in *Applying Methods and Techniques of Futures Research*, ed. J.L. Morrison, et al. (San Francisco: Jossey-Bass, Inc. Publishers, 1983), 52.

2. I.H. Wilson, Scenarios, in *Handbook of Futures Research,* ed. Jib Fowles (Westport, Conn: Greenwood Press, Inc., 1978), 225.

3. J. Kurtzman, *Futurcasting* (Palm Springs, Calif: ETC Publishing, 1984), 44, 55.

4. Ibid., 55.

5. Wilson, Scenarios, 227.

6. Ibid.

7. Kurtzman, *Futurcasting*, 45.

8. D.L. Kaufman, *Teaching the Future: A Guide to Future-Oriented Education* (Palm Springs, Calif: ETC Publishing, 1976), 123.

9. H.A. Linstone, Recent Projects: Introduction, in *Futures Research, New Directions* by H.A. Linstone and W.H.C. Simmonds (Reading, Mass: Addison-Wesley Publishing Co. Inc., 1977), 191.

10. Wilson, Scenarios, 228.

11. Kaufman, *Teaching the Future*, 123.

12. Ibid.

13. Ibid., 124.

14. Kurtzman, *Futurcasting*, 45.

15. Kaufman, *Teaching the Future*, 125, 126.

16. Kurtzman, *Futurcasting*, 45.

17. Kaufman, *Teaching the Future*, 123.

18. Wilson, Scenarios, 225.

19. M.P. Charns and M.J. Schaefer, *Health Care Organizations: A Model for Management* (Englewood Cliffs, NJ: Prentice Hall, 1983).

20. B.J. Stevens, *The Nurse as Executive*, 3rd ed (Gaithersburg, Md: Aspen Publishers, Inc., 1985).

21. M.E.Rogers, *An Introduction to the Theoretical Basis of Nursing* (Philadelphia: F.A. Davis Co., 1970).

22. R.M. Kantor, *Men and Women of the Organization* (New York: Basic Books, Inc., 1977).

23. M. Sinetar, The Actualized Worker, *The Futurist* 21, no. 2 (1987): 21–25.

24. Stevens, *The Nurse as Executive.*

25. P.F. Drucker, *Management: Tasks, Responsibilities, Practices* (New York: Harper & Row, 1973), 532.

26. D. Katz and R.L. Kahn, *The Social Psychology of Organizations*, 2nd ed (New York: John Wiley & Sons, Inc., 1978).

27. B. Fuszard, Theory Z, in *Self-Actualization for Nurses: Issues, Trends, and Strategies for Job Enrichment*, ed. B. Fuszard (Gaithersburg, Md: Aspen Publishers, Inc., 1984), 83–89.

28. B. Fuszard and J.K. Bishop, "Adhocracy" in Health Care Institutions?, in *Self-Actualization for Nurses: Issues, Trends, and Strategies for Job Enrichment*, ed. B. Fuszard (Gaithersburg, Md: Aspen Publishers, Inc., 1984), 90–99.

29. Stevens, *The Nurse as Executive.*

30. W.G. Ouchi, *Theory Z* (New York: Avon Books, 1981).

31. J. Heider, *The Tao of Leadership* (New York: Bantam Books, 1986), 161.

SUGGESTED READING

Campinos-Dubernet, M. Spring 1992. Meeting the challenge of trained skilled workers: French strategies. *Training and Development: French Dimensions* 7.

Ducci, M.A. 1991. Financing of vocational training in Latin America. Discussion paper no. 71. Geneva: International Labour Office.

Hodgson, V., et al., eds. 1989. Information technology-based open learning—A study report. Occasional paper InTER/12/89. Lancaster, England: Economic and Social Research Council, Lancaster University.

House subcommittee on elementary, secondary, and vocational education. 1993. Hearings on H.R. 1804—Goals 2000: Educate America Act. Washington, DC: U.S. Government Printing Office, Serial No. 103-17.

Impact assessment and forecasts of information and telecommunications technologies applied to education and training. 1992. Vol. II. Main report and issues analyses. Brussels: Commission of the European Communities.

Knop, S.A. 1991. As the baby boom ages—Adult participation in postsecondary education, 1960–2010. Boulder, Colo: Western Interstate Commission for Higher Education.

Markley, O.W., ed. 1991. *Preparing for the future of the workplace.* Vol. II: Analytical studies. Austin, Tex: Texas State Higher Education Coordinating Board, Division of Community Colleges and Technical Institutes.

Reddings, R.E., et al. 1991. Cognitive task analysis of prioritization in air traffic control. McLean, Va: Human Technology, Inc.

Chapter 31

The Tree of Impact

Richard L. Sowell

DEFINITION AND PURPOSES

The *tree of impact* is a shorthand analysis of the possible consequences of a policy decision or event. This technique does not provide an in-depth analysis. It only looks at the relationship among options. The tree of impact provides an overview of possible relationships as the consequences of alternative futures are developed. It is important to realize that this technique provides a view of possible alternative futures, but does not tell the future. The technique is a method of helping the futurist determine where, when, and how significant elements of change can occur. It also helps the futurist understand the logic of specific systems of change.[1] The tree of impact is also referred to as a futures wheel,[2] or a relevance tree.[3]

The purpose of this strategy is to provide an overall framework that organizes ideas or actions, and subsequent consequences over time. The technique provides a method by which the impact an idea might have on the future can be simulated. Additionally, this technique provides a method that readily organizes the large number of diverse ideas that can arise from group discussions or brainstorming sessions. The construction of a tree may be desirable to accomplish any of the following:

- structure the problem
- identify the system alternatives
- identify the possible impact of the focus problem
- help evaluate the impact of various approaches to the focus problem
- identify decision makers

- identify possible action options for decision makers
- present results[4]

This technique, when used with students, gives the student the opportunity to interact with a large volume of knowledge through preclass preparation and in-class participation. It furthers the logical application of knowledge to anticipate the long-term consequences and interactions of ideas.[5] Once initiated through classroom participation, it can serve as a guide for more in-depth study by the student. Each branch of the tree can serve as the focus of further investigation and analysis as the student works toward the alternative future that is determined to be most appropriate or desirable.

THEORETICAL RATIONALE

The theoretical foundation for the tree of impact is brainstorming. Brainstorming is based on the free-flowing generation of ideas within an innovative and non-restrictive atmosphere. This technique employs not only the application of knowledge in problem identification and problem solving, but creativity and intuitive insight as well.[6] Such an approach is designed to overcome the tendency for absolute patterning of thought identified by Edward de Bono in 1971. De Bono stated that the mind develops patterns from early acquired knowledge and then filters out all new information that does not fit that pattern.[7] The innovation and free association of brainstorming helps overcome obsolete patterning, allowing the acquisition of new modes of thought.

This teaching strategy, as derived from brainstorming, acts to organize the ideas that are generated. It provides a visual frame of reference for the session that can further stimulate the participants' imagination and provide insight into crucial elements as possible points of impact or consequence. The tree, as an organized overview of alternative futures, is supported by Clark and Cole as a model of value in that it provides simplification and structuring of potential realities.[8]

CONDITIONS

The use of this method is based on the need for a group or individual to

- anticipate the long-term consequences and interactions of current events or trends,

- foresee the long-term results of present policies and actions,
- compare the possible long-term consequences of other options or alternative futures, and
- identify the elements of alternative courses of action and potential opportunities for intervention before undesirable consequences are realized.[9]

This teaching-learning technique is used when innovation, creativity, and flexibility are desired in an approach. This method is particularly well suited for use in viewing complex trends and alternative futures that are subject to contradictory pressures, change, and duplication. The construction of the tree is a versatile technique that can be adapted to a variety of situations. It is especially valuable for nursing staffs planning for future technology, or studying issues that have an impact on nursing.

In the brainstorming, any consequence may be proposed by any group member as the branching of the tree is developed; once a consequence is proposed it is included as part of the developing tree. This process is a quick and free-wheeling approach to problem solving that encourages innovation.

Since the tree of impact can be used in conjunction with the beginning or final stages of the Delphi survey, guidelines for choosing topics of interest, as well as expert panel members, are often the same.[10] Because an in-depth presentation of such guidelines is provided under the Delphi technique, these guidelines will not be repeated in this section.

A modification of the technique can be used as the final stage of the Delphi technique, serving to further narrow the focus elements obtained from the Delphi survey to something more specific. In contrast to the application of the tree within brainstorming, the rules for developing the tree in this procedure are essentially reversed.

In developing the tree, any group member may propose a consequence related to the determined focus concept, but every other member of the group maintains potential veto power over inclusion of that consequence. To be included in the tree as a consequence or event, the item must receive the group's unanimous approval.[11] In this manner the results of a Delphi survey can be narrowed and critical elements examined in-depth. The results of this approach do not allow for the richness of unrestricted individual input found in brainstorming, but they make more accurate the probabilities of the resulting outcome consequences.

The tree of impact technique can also be used to provide schematic representation of the critical points of interest for future scenario development. While it is not as comprehensive as the scenario technique, it does have the advantage of providing a precise visual representation of the critical information found within a futures scenario.[12]

It is important to remember that the lines used to form the branching of a tree of impact do not necessarily represent a cause-and-effect relationship. Rather they signify a relationship that may or may not represent a time sequence, depending on the guidelines provided for the specific tree being developed. This ability to develop individualized trees makes this technique applicable in a wide variety of situations and settings.

The objective of the tree of impact technique is to free the learner from the restrictions of old knowledge patterns and develop an innovative method of viewing potential futures. The technique incorporates elements of creative problem solving, including fact finding, problem finding, idea finding, and acceptance finding.[13]

The learner goes from an examination of what is or has been to an exploration of what might be. From this perspective the learner is able to develop modes of critical-thinking and decision-making skills that permit attainment of the goal of determining what will be.[14]

This method of learning facilitates flow of ideas from both individuals and groups that can be logically ordered into a meaningful system of understanding. However, the learner must be aware of the principle of "counter intuitive"—that is, events that seem to defy common sense and logic.[15] The learner must guard against constructing faulty alternative futures by not considering the possibility of the occurrence of such counter-intuitive events. Such a situation challenges learners to look beyond themselves and use their mental abilities to their fullest.

TYPES OF LEARNERS

This technique can be used with any individual or group who has knowledge of the focus topic or who has access to such knowledge. This technique is particularly suited for adult learners who are able to apply knowledge gained from life experiences to the exercise. The construction of a tree stimulates the informed learner or expert by providing a fast-moving exercise that provides opportunity for short-term feedback in viewing potentially long-term consequences or trends.

RESOURCES

The tree of impact technique can be used within various types of futuristic programs. Such futuristic programs include the following:

- The academic futuristics program—within this setting the tree of impact is employed in an educational context to teach individuals about futurism and the use of techniques that are used to predict alternative futures. Construction of the tree is designed to develop the learners' skill in creative thinking. The learner usually cannot implement the results of the exercise.[16] The exercise teaches the student how to identify critical factors and analyze their impact.
- Strategic planning program—such strategic planning usually takes place within the work setting. Strategic planning allows organizations to develop strategies to meet organizational goals. The tree of impact is an important tool in developing alternative futures as strategic planners explore the consequences of various ideas and actions. In this situation, results are often put into action, so predicting the future significance of trends is a major part of the organizational planning process.[17] Strategic planning would be aided by this process, for example, when studying environmental trends that would impact on a proposed ambulatory care unit.
- Personal futuristic program—here an individual or group uses the predictive technique in developing alternative futures from which the desirable can be chosen. The chosen future may be implemented in whole or in part by devising relevant action plans.[18] The participant, for example, can test consequences of pursuing a master's degree in nursing as opposed to a degree in education or business.

The most important resource required in the development of a tree of impact is the participants' time. However, the time investment can be limited by the number of participants in the sessions and the time allotted for each accomplishment. The development of a tree should be a fast-moving process that involves a limited number of sessions of no more than approximately an hour each. This time limit keeps the process fresh and spontaneous.[19]

The actual equipment needed to implement the technique consists of a flip chart or chalk board and a marker with which to draw. However, in the educational setting, adequate library resources must be available so that student participants can investigate topic areas as part of their preclass preparation.

USING THE METHOD

The initial step in implementing the tree of impact technique is preparation. The individual or group wishing to use this approach must first determine the topic of interest.

Second, they must establish specific objectives to be achieved by use of this technique. For teaching, topics of interest should be chosen that are familiar to both the instructor and students; once the steps of the technique are mastered, the strategy may then be applied to more complex or unfamiliar problems.

Once the topic of interest and exercise objectives have been established, the third step is information gathering and synthesis. When the tree of impact technique is used with a group of experts, this step may include activities such as review of present knowledge, analysis of recent events and trends, or investigation of new technology. However, when the technique is employed in teaching, the scope and time commitment of preclass preparation will most likely be more extensive. It is critical that the students familiarize themselves with the topic area before participating in the class exercise. Student preclass preparation should include the following:

- review of historical developments in the topic area[20]
- past examples of logical and counter-intuitive trends or events in the topic area[21]
- identification of critical factors or elements related to the topic[22]
- present knowledge in the topic area[23]
- opinions of experts in the area[24]
- other topic areas that will potentially have impact on the topic area of focus

The implementation of the technique can begin once the participants have acquired the necessary knowledge base. The rules related to specific trees should be clearly stated and enforced. The group leader or instructor is responsible for ensuring that participants understand the technique and the specific guidelines for this particular exercise. The guidelines may be adjusted regarding use or nonuse of a time relationship in developing branching; an individual or unanimous group approach to inclusion of proposed consequences; or the time allowed each participant in the construction process. By clearly stating and adhering to the exercise guidelines, the exercise procedure will be kept on target and arguments and misunderstandings will be prevented.[25]

After the guidelines for the exercise are established, the actual tree of impact is constructed. The tree is built from the central topic statement by initially adding a single row of consequences related to the topic statement. Each of these first-row consequences serves as a focus as other related consequences are added to the tree. In this manner each level of the tree becomes more complex while serving as a focus.

The tree development occurs as each group member provides a consequence or impact event in turn. Each proposed consequence may or may not be included in the tree's development, depending on the guidelines established for the exercise. In either case the next participant proposes an item. A group member who is unable to contribute an item for the specific branch under consideration passes, and the process continues with the next participant. This process is continued for the time allotted for the exercise or until the desired level of investigation is reached.

The construction of a tree can be simple or quite complex. When broad topics such as racial issues are explored, there is often duplication and contradiction among various branches of the tree.[26] This is to be expected and may be desirable. It is often necessary to indicate relationships both vertically and horizontally between the elements of various branches of the tree, as the complexity of the topic issue is explored.

When completed, the tree of impact provides immediate feedback to group participants. However, it also provides the basis for further analysis of specific elements identified during the exercise. The developed tree can serve as the foundation for further refinement of trends or events, and be the inspiration for constructions of still other trees of impact.

Example
Plotting the Future of AIDS
Richard L. Sowell

The development of the tree of impact described in this example was undertaken as part of the coursework for a graduate-level course in sociopolitical issues. The goal of the course was to examine forces that have an impact on the nursing profession as well as the larger health care system. The overall learning objective emphasized the use of futurcasting techniques as a method of examining alternative futures that may evolve from present events or trends. The objectives were specifically that, upon completion of this exercise, the student would be able to

1. define the tree of impact technique
2. evaluate the purpose of the technique as a tool for planning
3. identify incidents in which the technique would be appropriately used
4. analyze the advantages of the tree of impact technique over other futurcasting techniques
5. discuss the steps necessary to fully initiate and develop a tree of impact
6. apply the technique to a selected topic of interest to develop a method of viewing alternative futures
7. defend the role of the tree of impact as a method of generating further research and analysis within a study area
8. defend the importance of exercise guidelines as a means of individualizing the technique to meet specific situational objectives

The initial step in the exercise was selection of a focus topic, acquired immunodeficiency syndrome. AIDS was especially suited for the exercise because the issues surrounding this health care issue are complex, yet familiar to the group.

The topic provides adequate challenge for students at the graduate level as they implemented the tree of impact technique within a learning setting. To assist the student in obtaining needed knowledge during the preparatory phase of the exercise, a reading list was provided. The student was required to read a minimum of seven articles from the list before participating in the exercise. The following terminology was necessary:

1. Tree of impact
2. Futures wheel
3. Relevance tree
4. Consequence
5. Branching
6. Relationship linkage
7. Futurcasting
8. Counter-intuitive
9. Topic of focus
10. Alternative futures
11. Futurist
12. Creative problem solving
13. Trend
14. Academic futuristics
15. Strategic planning
16. Personal futuristics
17. Impact
18. Panel of experts
19. Delphi survey
20. New knowledge

The exercise in which the actual tree was constructed took place near the end of the academic term. The student consequently had adequate time to obtain an understanding of the futurcasting techniques, as well as knowledge in the topic area to be explored. The exercise was conducted in a classroom setting with all members of the sociopolitical class. Rules for the exercise were established by the group prior to beginning the exercise. It was determined that the overall goal of the exercise would be to construct a tree of impact that would organize the many diverse issues related to AIDS. This approach was designed to provide a logical framework for viewing the topic issues, and to help predict the potential impact of specific events in the future. It was determined that the branching links developed among concepts and events in this exercise would not signify actual cause-and-effect or true relationships. Rather these links would indicate only that the items were related within the framework.[27]

During the initial phase of the exercise four subtopics related to AIDS were determined by the group: (1) public action, (2) HIV infection, (3) education, and (4) research. These were to help focus the exercise despite the broad scope of the AIDS topic.

Once the four subtopics were identified it was clear that each of these concepts formed the center of a new individualized tree of impact under the broad topic of AIDS. The initial level of the framework was constructed to reflect this situation (Figure 31–1) and the exercise proceeded.

At the second level of the exercise, group members were able to propose a consequence for any of the four trees of impact being developed from the subtopics. All proposed consequences were included in the branching process as the exercise progressed through the various levels of the technique, and the overall outcome is shown in Figures 31–2 through 31–5.

The tree developed during this exercise features examples of both duplication and contradiction.[28] The concept of "life style change" was identified as a potential consequence within both the HIV infection and education subsystems. Likewise, both an increase and decrease in the number of AIDS cases was predicted by different branches of the research subsystem. The inter-relationship among the elements of the developed overall system gives insight into the topic issues, and adds to the tree's ability to provide an adequate framework with which to view the future. The beginning student may be encouraged to know that when this exercise was conducted, several of the proposed consequences were not seen as likely by most participants. Such a consequence was the development of zero-negative dating clubs, included within the education subsystem. However, since this tree of impact was constructed such organizations have become reality. In this instance the technique was successful in predicting the future.

This particular exercise was concluded with the construction of the tree depicted in Figure 31–6. However, this end product has the potential for generating further analysis of this topic as items or systems identified in this exercise are further explored using futurcasting techniques. Figure 31–6 shows how the consequence of "increased profit from AIDS related products" can become the topic of focus of a new tree of impact.

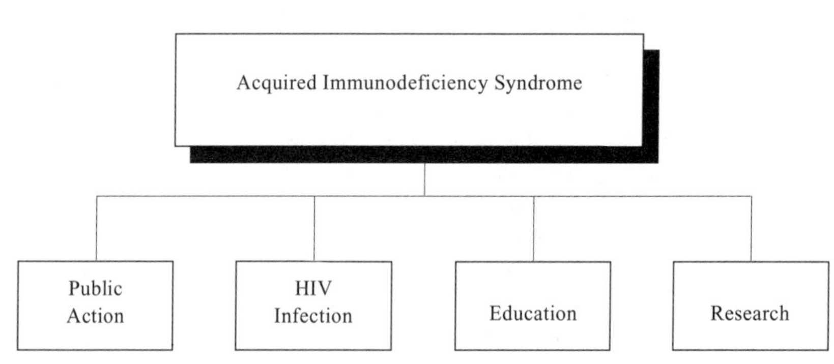

Figure 31–1 Initial Framework for the Tree of Impact for AIDS Developed During the First Phase of the Exercise

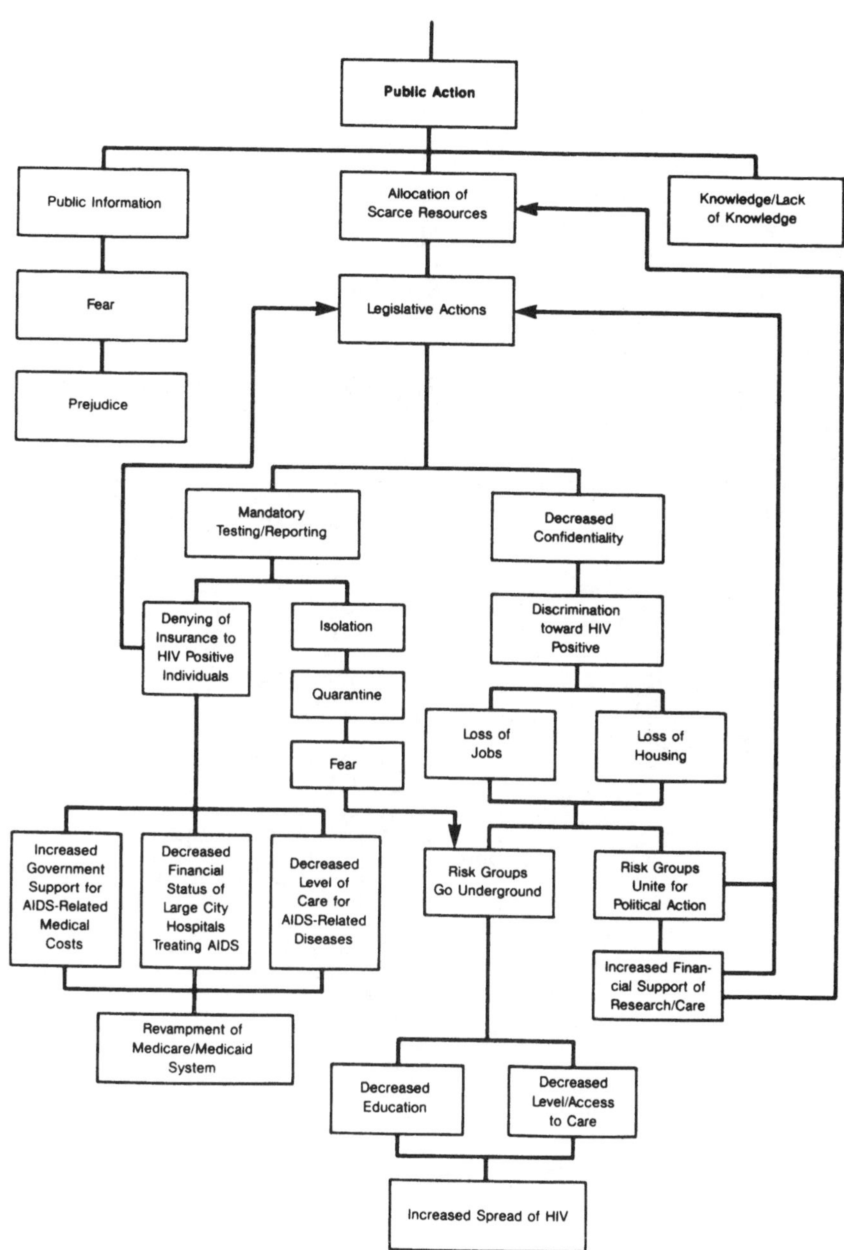

Figure 31–2 Public Action

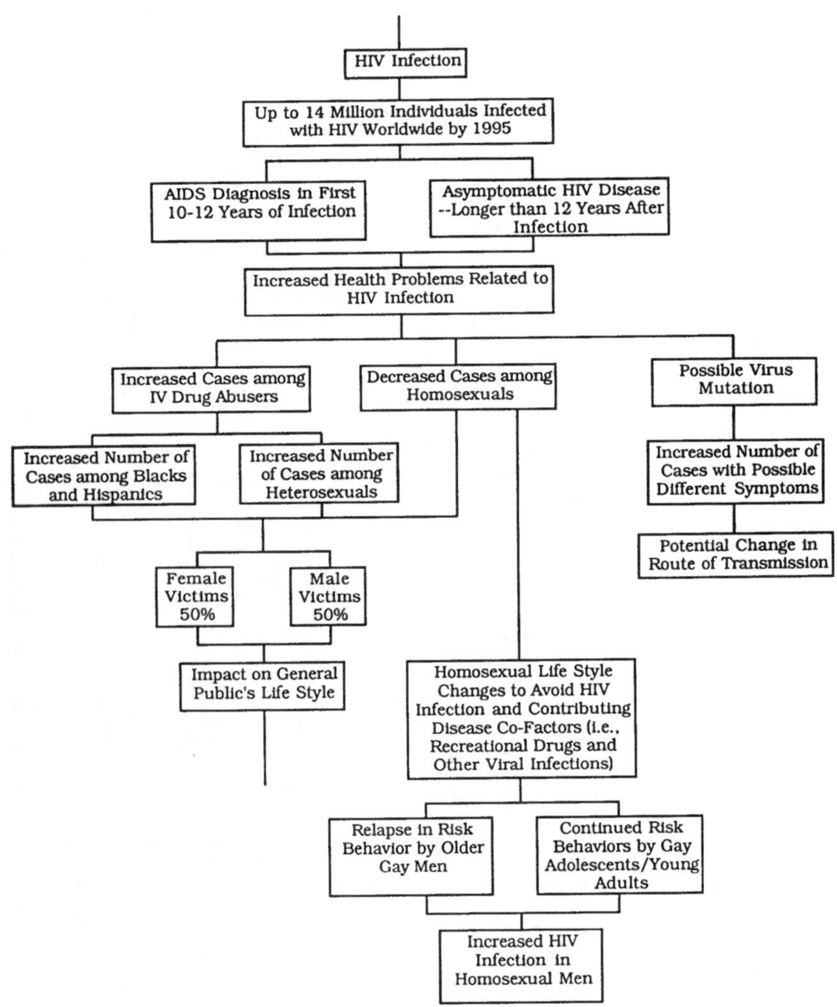

Figure 31–3 HIV Infection

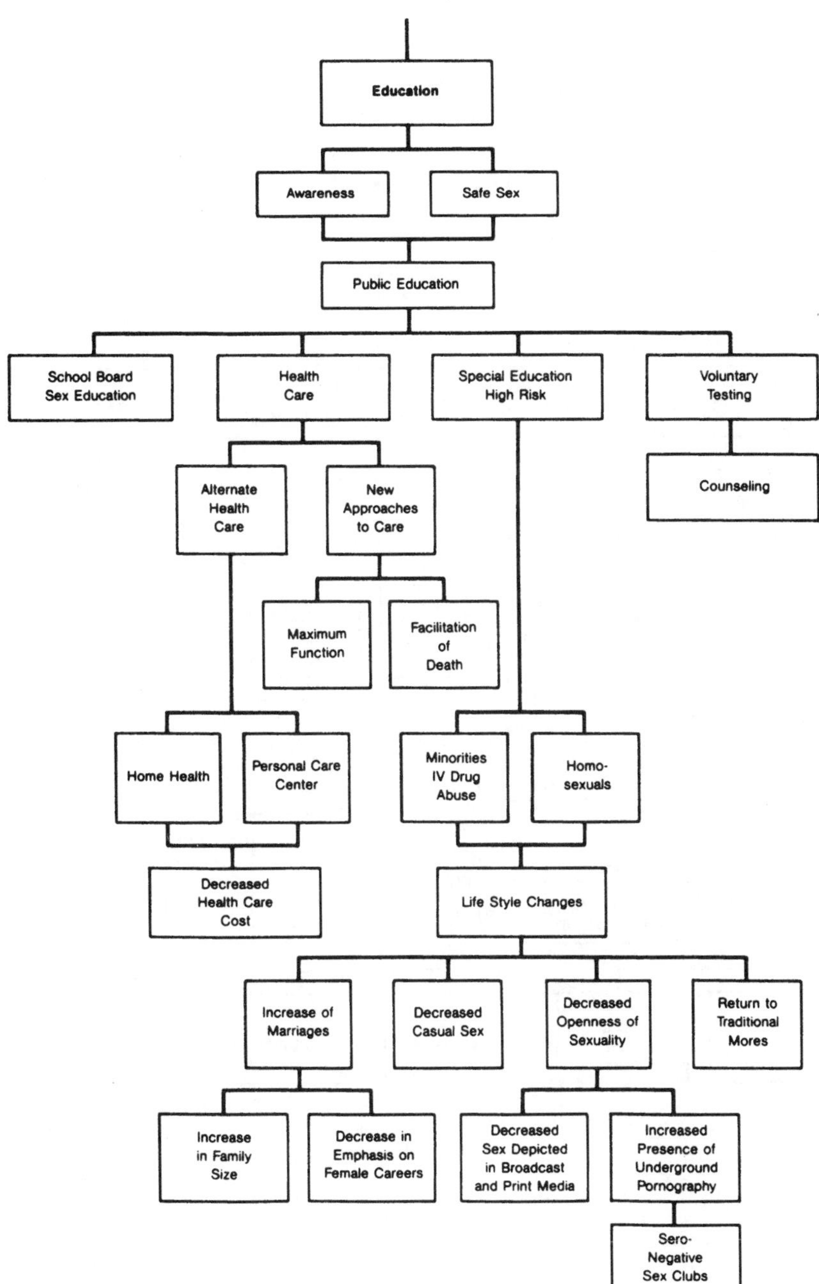

Figure 31–4 Education

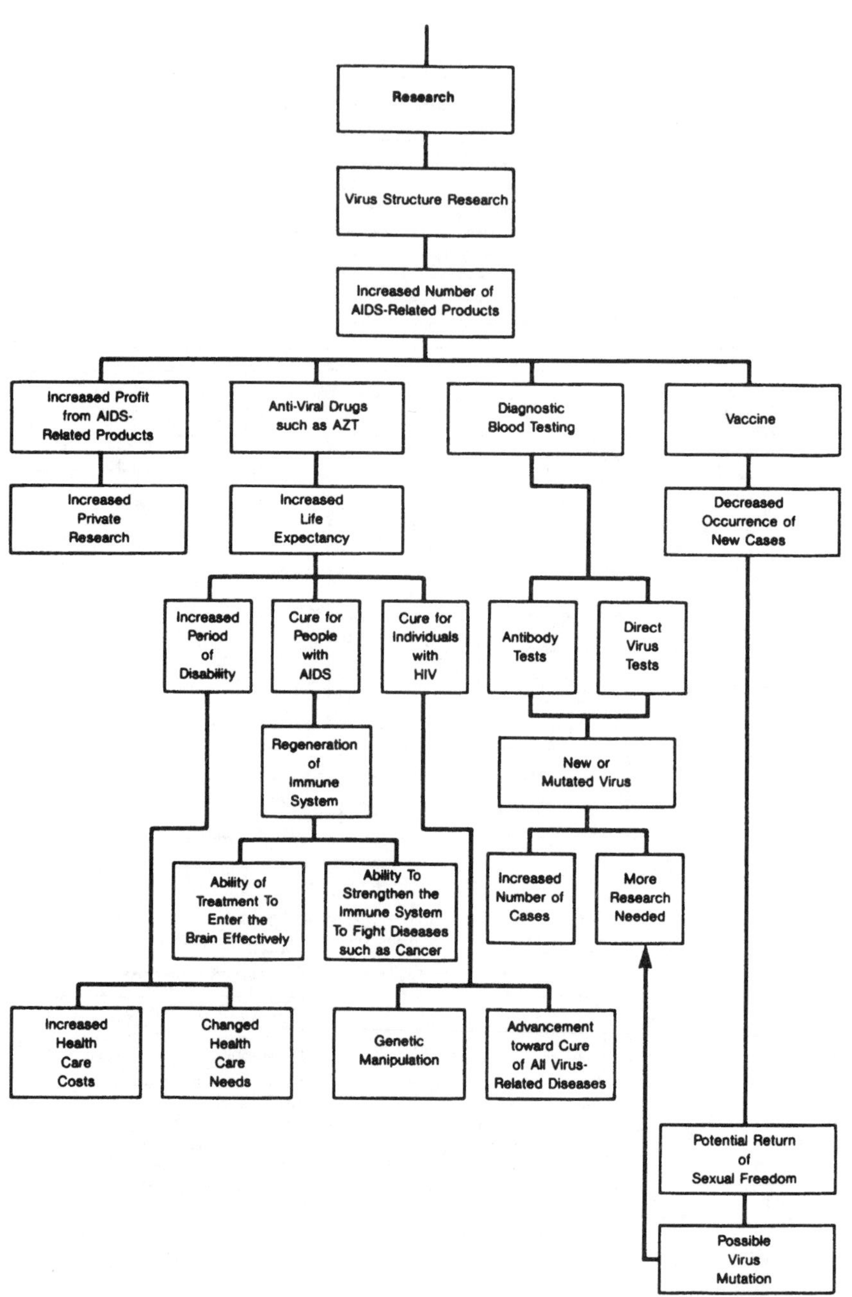

Figure 31–5 Research

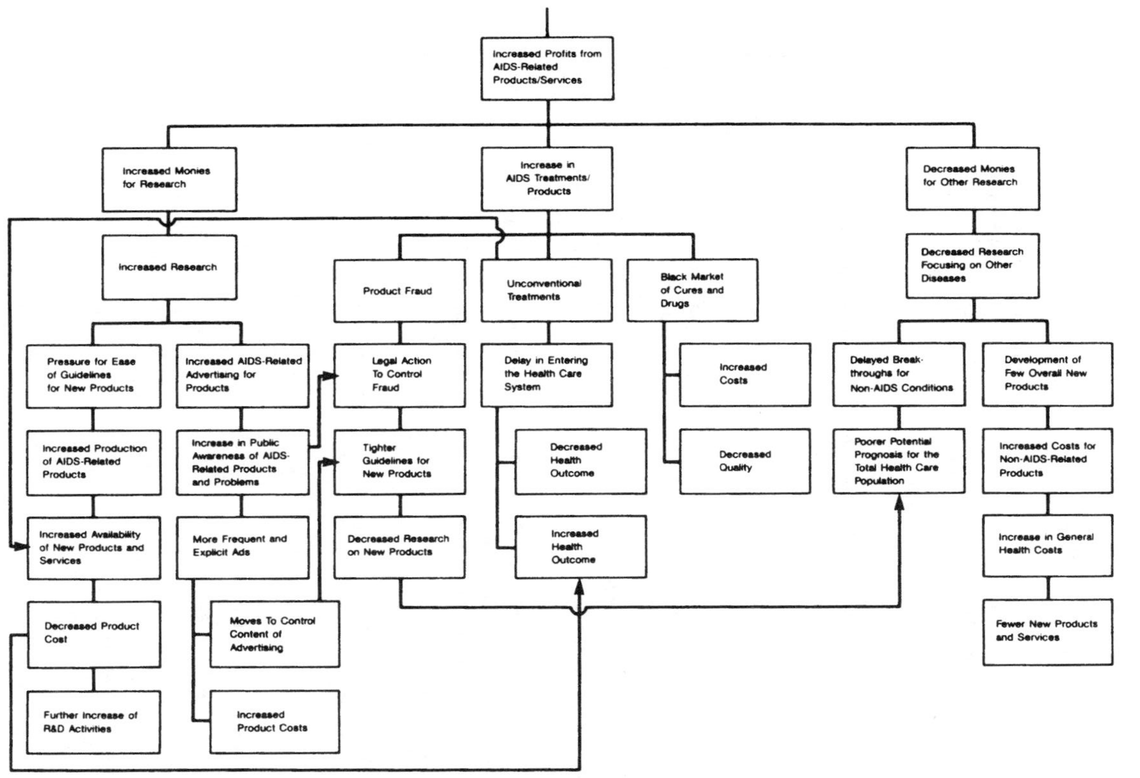

Figure 31–6 Tree of Impact for Further Analysis of a Specific Consequence Generated during the Initial Learning Exercise

NOTES

1. J.J. Kurtzman, *Futurcasting: Charting a Way to Your Future* (Palm Springs, Calif: ETC Publishing, 1984), 29.
2. P.H. Wagschall, Judgmental Forecasting Techniques and Institutional Planning: An Example, in *Applying Methods and Techniques of Futures Research*, ed. J.L. Morrison, et al. (San Francisco: Jossey-Bass, Inc. Publishers, 1983), 44.
3. J.F. Coates, Technology Assessment, in *Handbook of Futures Research*, ed. J. Fowles (Westport, Conn: Greenwood Press, Inc., 1978), 408.
4. Ibid., 415.
5. J.M. Richardson, Jr., *Making It Happen: A Positive Guide to the Future* (Washington, DC: U.S. Association for the Club of Rome, 1982), 19.
6. Coates, Technology Assessment, 417.
7. J.S. Mendell, The Practice of Intuition, in *Handbook of Futures Research*, ed. J. Fowles (Westport, Conn: Greenwood Press, Inc., 1978), 150–154.
8. M. McLean, Getting the Problem Right—A Role for Structural Modeling, in *Futures Research: New Directions*, ed. H. Limestone and W.H.C. Simmond (Reading, Mass: Addison-Wesley Publishing Co., Inc., 1977), 149.
9. Richardson, *Making It Happen.*
10. Wagschall, Judgmental Forecasting.
11. Ibid.
12. I.H. Wilson, Scenarios, in *Handbook of Futures Research*, ed. J. Fowles (Westport, Conn: Greenwood Press, Inc., 1978), 234.
13. S.J. Parnes, Learning Creative Behavior: Making the Future Happen, *The Futurist* 18, no. 4 (1984):30.
14. Ibid., 32.
15. Kurtzman, *Futurcasting*, 33.
16. Parnes, Learning Creative Behavior.
17. Ibid.
18. Ibid.
19. Wagschall, Judgmental Forecasting.
20. Kurtzman, *Futurcasting.*
21. Ibid., 33.
22. Coates, Technology Assessment, 415.
23. Kurtzman, *Futurcasting.*
24. Ibid.
25. Wagschall, Judgmental Forecasting.
26. Ibid.
27. Kurtzman, *Futurcasting.*
28. Wagschall, Judgmental Forecasting.

SUGGESTED READING

Fowles, J. 1978. *Handbook of futures research*. Westport, Conn: Greenwood Press, Inc.

Kauffman, D.L., Jr. 1976. *Teaching the future*. Palm Springs, Calif: ETC Publishing.

Kurtzman, J. 1984. *Futurcasting: Charting a way to your future*. Palm Springs, Calif: ETC Publishing.

Limestone, H., and W.H.C. Simmond. 1977. *Futures research: New directions*. Reading, Mass: Addison-Wesley Publishing Co., Inc.

Morrison, J.L., et al. 1983. *Applying methods and techniques of futures research*. San Francisco: Jossey-Bass, Inc. Publishers.

Part VIII

Homemade Strategies

Many other teaching strategies are available to faculty. Perhaps the homemade strategies are the most effective, for they are developed by faculty for a special student population and a specific purpose. Some of the gaming examples could fit here as well under simulations.

The purpose of this chapter is to stimulate the creativity of the faculty member to use materials already in the surroundings, materials that will be immediately relevant to the student. Faculty already have this ability, as can be seen by the sprouting of pertinent comic strips on bulletin boards and office doors the day after they appear in the media. Students, too, need stimulation to transfer knowledge from classroom to the real world, by associating current events with classroom content.

Chapter 32

Analogies, Metaphors, and Other Fun Strategies

Barbara Fuszard

Many of the teaching strategies used by faculty members are homemade, but nonetheless effective. A cartoon, a line in the paper, a memo tickles one's fancy, and the thought comes, "This would be an ideal example of. . . ."

Highest praise goes to two teachers who broke the ice with a new class of junior nursing students the first day of nursing practicum with a lesson on removal and application of ted hose that no one will ever forget. One faculty member sat on the edge of the desk in the front of the room wearing culottes and ted hose. As the other faculty member started the record "The Stripper," the first faculty member silently raised a ted hose leg and slowly began to roll it down.

An exchange of memos gave a good example to be used to illustrate the concept of bureaucracy. A letter to the editor of "In-House News," the institution's newsletter, stated:

> I have noticed that some of the references to faculty members in "In-House News" have asterisks before the faculty names. When I checked on this, I found that the asterisk meant the faculty member was a member of the School of Graduate Studies. This letter is to inform you that twelve of us nursing faculty were recently appointed to the graduate faculty, and yet the asterisks are not preceding our names in your newsletter. I would be happy to send you a list of the faculty group, or you could get it from the Dean of the School of Graduate Studies. I hope this will solve "The Case of the Missing Asterisks."

The editor responded:

> Re: "The Case of the Missing Asterisks"
>
> The only way I know for sure that someone is a member of the School of Graduate Studies is if his name appears in the biennial college catalog with an asterisk. As the catalog was published this year, and the names of your

faculty members were not asterisked in that publication, I will have to wait two years until the new catalog is published. Thank you for your interest in "In-House News."

Webster defines *analogy* as something resembling something else in some ways, whereas otherwise they are unlike. *Metaphors*, says Webster, are compressed similes, a likeness or implied comparison, or an analogy. Analogies are offered in nursing, such as the analog model, which uses analogy "for explaining something by comparing it to something else."[1]

Analogies and metaphors were collected over a period of time, and then used as a final examination in a management course to determine whether students could generalize and transfer knowledge. Some examples follow.

"The head nurse, a very broom of a presence, swept the place clean with a look."—Margaret Lee Runbeck. What type of leader would you say this head nurse is? Why?

"Tell me thy company, and I will tell thee what thou art."—Cervantes, *Don Quixote*. What sociological concept explains this statement?

"To the timid and headstrong everything is impossible because it seems so."—Scott. What motivation concept speaks to this? Explain.

"The mission of the U.S. is one of benevolent assimilation."—William McKinley, in a letter (1898). To what management concept is McKinley speaking? Explain.

"When the cat's away, the mice will play."—English Proverb. Explain the motivation theory that contradicts this statement.

"They can because they think they are able."—Virgil, *Aeneid*. How do you explain this statement?

"'Rights' often seem more important to him than food. Sometimes it is necessary to remove the food to restore the sense of values."—Unknown. Please relate the above quotation to a motivation theory you have studied.

A tiny museum in Jefferson, Texas, contained this letter from Sam Houston, which offers excellent examples of leadership and motivation content:

Executive Department
Washington, May 14, 1843

c/o Col. Joseph C. Eldredge:

Sir—You will, with as little delay as practicable, proceed to the Comanche nation of Indians. You will have charge of your accompanying escort. Thomas S. Jorrey, Esq., will accompany you as Indian Agent;

together with Jim Shaw and John Conner, two Delawares with such as they may think proper to take with them, for the protection and security of their outfit and other goods. Shaw will go direct so as to approach the Comanches in the most direct manner.

You will take with you two prisoners—"Wm. Hockley" and a Comanche girl.

Should you meet with the Comanches agree ably to the appointment which the chief made with Shaw; you will restore the prisoners to him, and make him such presents of the goods sent for that purpose as your discretion may suggest.

The accompanying talk you will communicate to him through Shaw and Conner, and impress upon his mind that the presents made to him are the gifts of friendship but not the offerings of fear. You will also impress him as far as possible with the pacific policy which the administration is now pursuing in relation to the Indians. You will tell him that the same man is not the Chief of Texas at this time who was when their chiefs were killed at Bexar and that he looks upon such things with abhorrence—that both parties are to forget all past injuries, and that for the future we are to be friends. Also, that the chief who made war with all the Indians in Texas has left it and will never return again to bring trouble upon them.

When they make peace, they shall come to our trading houses where they will find friends, but not enemies. Tell them that I expect them in early August, when the moon is full, at the Great Council to be held at Bird's Foot on the Trinity—which will be ninety-four days from this date.

Tell the chief that I expect he will send runners to all the tribes of the Comanches with talks of peace, and to say to them that the tomahawk is buried—that there is to be no more blood in the path—that no more horses are to be stolen—and that I wish the head chiefs of each band to attend at the council.

You will tell him to bring all the prisoners which they have of ours to the council, and that their prisoners shall be there also. As proof of it, I send him two of theirs without ransom.

If the Comanches have been deceived by our people, they will never again be told falsehoods. The same chief who sends this talk made a treaty with the Comanches at Houston, and whilst he was chief, it was not broken. It was broken by bad men; and the whites as well as the Comanches have had much trouble and sorrow since that time. Let us forget our sorrows and live like brothers. There is room enough for the Comanches in the prairies. They shall hunt their buffalo, and the white man shall not harm them. When they come to the white men in peace, they shall be met as brothers, and trouble will no more come amongst us.

I have not sent the chief the uniform coat and the four men which he wished for hostages. When he makes peace, and comes to see me, I will give him his uniform coat, and will make him presents such as one brother would give to another who had come on a long journey to see him.

I am sure he will believe my talk. The Delawares will tell him that I am a friend to the red men—that I have grown up amongst them, and have lived with them since I have been a man. I have never told a red man a lie; nor have I ever turned away from my friends. When I take him and his people by the hands, I will never turn away from them; but while they keep peace and treat us as brothers I will always be their friend and never forget them. Nor shall the wind scatter my words.

You will keep a diary of all important incidents that may occur, and such observations as you may deem worthy of record, on your tour. Should an opportunity be afforded, you will communicate to this Department such facts as you may deem important for its information.

You will not fail to have such of the Comanche chiefs at Bird's Foot as practicable. You will inform them that no more presents will be made till a firm peace is established between the red and white men; also that the place where the Council is to be held is so far from the settlements that it will be impossible for the whites to get provisions there. As this is a council to make peace, the whites will not be prepared to afford such supplies, as they would be if they had had peace. When we shall have made peace, and our brothers meet us in council, it will be near our people, when we will have plenty to give them to eat.

You will have to exercise a discretion in relation to many matters that may arise. I would suggest the propriety of advising at all times in case of the slightest difficulty, with Shaw. His being an Indian, acquainted with all their diversity of character as well as with the different nations, will enable him to devise the best means possible for surmounting obstacles which may be interposed to the object of your mission.

I have the honor to be
Your ob[t] serv[t]
Sam Houston
Supt. Indian Affairs

This letter gave rise to the following review questions and assignments.

1. What was Sam Houston's overall leadership style?
2. Draw an organizational chart including positions for all those mentioned in the letter, as appropriate.
3. List two types of power Sam Houston possessed as evidenced in this letter.
4. What steps of the decision-making process did Houston delegate to Eldredge?

The faculty member asked one student, "How would you feel about an assignment to face this angry group of Indians?" The student answered: "I would rather face the Indians than go back to Sam Houston and tell him I didn't." This student understood Sam Houston's letter well!

Humor has a permanent place in the classroom, for relieving tension and changing negative attitudes, for removing the distancing between faculty and student, and for promoting retention.[2] Comic strips and cartoons are fertile fields for content.

Finally, pictures, pictures from anywhere. Newspapers, books, even coloring books are good sources of pictures. In the middle of a long workshop, a different kind of break was introduced: a whole group of overheads that referred to topics that had been discussed thus far. The following examples (Figures 32–1 through 32–4) were taken from that group, showing that teaching adults is, can, and should be, fun.

This book, for those who teach, in Margareta Styles's words, this "exquisite, exhausting, obsession"[3] called nursing, draws to a close. It is intended to offer the "exquisite" joy of teaching to the faculty member, who so often also feels the "exhausting" aspect of the obsession of teaching.

Thirty-two strategies were discussed and illustrated, alternatives to the lecture method, alternatives for the adult learner. The strategies each emphasize some aspects of adult learning principles, develop critical thinking abilities, and thus prepare the adult learner for a future of life-long learning. A teacher-facilitator can offer no more to students of nursing.

Figure 32–1 What Is Happening Here? *Source:* Reprinted from *Executive Library: Looking into Nursing Leadership*, p. 12, with permission of Leadership Resources, Inc., Merrifield, Virginia.

Figure 32–2 What Is Happening Here? *Source:* Reprinted from *Executive Library: Looking into Nursing Leadership*, p. 3, with permission of Leadership Resources, Inc., Merrifield, Virginia.

Figure 32–3 What Is Happening Here? *Source:* Reprinted from *Executive Library: Looking into Nursing Leadership*, pp. 6–7, with permission of Leadership Resources, Inc., Merrifield, Virginia.

Figure 32–4 What Is Happening Here? *Source:* Reprinted from *Executive Library: Looking into Nursing Leadership*, p. 17, with permission of Leadership Resources, Inc., Merrifield, Virginia.

NOTES

1. R. deTornyay and M.A. Thompson, *Strategies for Teaching Nursing*, 3d ed (New York: John Wiley & Sons, Inc., 1987), 21.

2. B.E. Puetz, *Contemporary Strategies for Continuing Education in Nursing* (Gaithersburg, Md: Aspen Publishers, Inc., 1987), 114.

3. M. Styles, at the Annual Scientific Session of the New Zealand Nurses Association, 1987.

Part IX

Afterword

Although lecture bashing did not occur in this text, a faculty member who believes strongly in the lecture method offered to provide rationale for the continued use of this teaching strategy as an Afterword to this text. Thus these pages close with

LECTURE IS NOT A FOUR-LETTER WORD!

Chapter 33

Lecture Is Not a Four-Letter Word!

Barbara C. Woodring

INTRODUCTION

Perhaps it is fortuitous that the chapter related to one of the oldest known instructional methods, the lecture, appears at the conclusion of this text. This is somewhat reminiscent of the Scriptural admonition of the last being first and the first being last! Some, however, may believe that this discussion was placed last because it is the least important. That is incorrect!

During the preceding chapters the reader has been introduced to some innovative teaching strategies recently added to the higher-education arena. During the evolution and development of these strategies the lecture has been relegated to the status of second-class citizen—at least so it appears in the literature. It has become trendy to "lecture bash," to describe our colleagues who openly espouse the use of lecture techniques as old-fashioned and out of step with educational trends. To many, the term *lecture* has been added to their list of unspeakable four-letter words.

However, in practice, the lecture format is alive and well. Regardless of the negative overtones that surround it, the lecture remains the most frequently utilized teaching method in the repertoire of educators. In this chapter we explore the reasons for the long-term popularity of this teaching strategy and how to make its use more acceptable.

DEFINITION AND PURPOSES

By definition the lecture is a method of presenting information to an audience. It was the singular approach used prior to the invention of the printing press, when only the scholars had access to hand-written information sources. Learners would gather around the master-teacher and take notes related to what he or she said. The lecture remained the common mode of transmitting information until printing resources made books affordable to the learners.

It would appear that when students were able to purchase their own textbooks, methods of presenting knowledge should have changed. Interestingly, change has occurred very slowly. Today, with textbooks and study helps galore, lecture remains a very commonly used technique. It is suggested that there are two major reasons for this: (1) most current educators learned via the lecture, and it is well known that individuals will teach as they were taught unless they make a specific effort to alter their techniques; and (2) the lecture is the method that is safest and easiest to prepare, while allowing the educator most control in the classroom. Some of the more common advantages and disadvantages of using the lecture method are listed in Table 33–1. Whatever the rationale, there still can be very positive outcomes achieved by using the lecture, especially when the lecture and lecturer are well prepared.

THEORETICAL RATIONALE

Probably few lecturers take the time to contemplate the theoretical basis of the practice, since the technique existed prior to identification of theoretical bases. The lack of a theoretical or organizational framework may be a reason the technique is perceived by learners as disorganized and often difficult to follow.

Today, however, there are a variety of philosophical and theoretical processes from which the teacher may derive a basis for lecture. Two common approaches are communication and pedagogical theories. The theories supporting effective communications should be well understood by nurse educators, and for that reason they are not discussed here. Pedagogical theory is not as well understood and is addressed briefly.

Over the past few decades graduate nursing education has focused on clinical specialization rather than educational processes, resulting in only a limited number of current nursing faculty members having a strong background in educational and pedagogical theory. This alone may indicate why the use of innovative teaching strategies has occurred so slowly within nursing education. Pedagogical theory loosely refers to educating the chronologically or experientially young or immature. A major tenet of pedagogy lies in the fact that someone exterior to the learner decides who, what, when, where, and how information will be taught; the learner becomes a passive recipient of knowledge. In the historical rigidity of the teaching of nursing based on the medical model, this approach has worked well. When used in this context, the lecture establishes the teacher as the one in command, the source from whom answers come.

Recently there has been a shift in both age and experiential background of traditional college students, causing educators to question the appropriateness of

Table 33–1 Advantages and Disadvantages in Using the Lecture

Advantages	*Disadvantages*
• Permits **maximum** teacher control • Presents **minimal** threats to students or teacher • Able to enliven facts and ideas that seem tedious in text • Able to clarify issues relating to confusing/intricate points • Teacher knows what has been taught • Lecture material can become basis of publication • Students are provided a common core of content • Able to accommodate larger numbers of listeners • Cost-effective student: teacher ratio 20–200:1 • Economy of time: teacher can present content in much less time than to elicit from students • Teacher controls the pace of presentation • Reward for teacher who becomes known as an expert in specific area/topic • Encourages and allows deductive reasoning • Enthusiasm (role-model) of teacher motivates students to participate and learn more • Can present the newest information available	• Attempt to cover too much material in given time • An easy teaching method, a far less effective learning strategy • 80% of lecture information is **NOT** recalled by student 1 day later and 80% of remainder fades in 1 month • Presumes that all students are learning at the same pace • Not suited to higher levels of learning • Classes tend to be too large for personalized instruction • Creates passive learners • Provides little feedback to learners • Student attention wanes in 25–30 minutes • Teachers attempt to teach all they have learned in a lifetime about a subject in 1 hour • Inhibits development of inductive reasoning • Poorly delivered lecture acts as a disincentive for learning • Viewed by students as a complete learning experience; feel lecturer presents all they need to know

the pedagogical methods so long held dear.[1] In response, educators such as Knowles[2] and Kidd[3] introduced the concept of andragogy. The concepts previously utilized in teaching the young (pedagogy) were adapted and applied to "mature" learners.

Those who ascribe to andragogical theory treat the learner as an adult who brings a variety of rich, valuable experiences into every learning situation. Table 33–2 illustrates the comparison of andragogy and pedagogy within the educational process. After studying Table 33–2, it becomes apparent that the teacher must know as much as possible about both the learners and the topic

Table 33–2 Comparison of Characteristics: Andragogy - Pedagogy

Characteristic	*Pedagogy*	*Andragogy*
Concept of learner	• Dependent • Passive learner • Needs someone outside self to make decisions about what, when, and how to learn	• Independent/autonomous • Self-directed • Wants to participate in decisions related to own learning
Role of learners' experiences	• Few experiences; given little attention • Narrow, focused interest • Focuses on imitation	• Wide range of experience—not just in nursing—which impacts life/learning • Broad interest—likes to share previous experience with others • Focus on originality
Readiness to learn	• Determined by someone else (society, teachers) • Focus on what is needed to survive and achieve • Tends to respond impulsively	• Usually in the educational process because they have chosen to be • Wants to assist in setting the learning agenda • Tends to respond rationally
Orientation of teaching/learning	• Looks to teacher to identify what should be learned and then provide the information and process to learn it • Focuses on particulars, concerned with the superficial aspects of learning (grades, due dates) • Needs clarity/specificity • Evaluation of learning done by the teacher or society (grades, certificates)	• Teachers are facilitators providing resources and supports for self-directed learners • Evaluation is done jointly by teacher, learner, and sometimes by peers • Likes challenging independent assignments that are reality based • Tolerates ambiguity

before deciding upon the teaching strategy to be used. When lecture is used in the andragogical context it is accompanied by other teaching methodologies, such as lecture-discussion, lecture-practice (demonstration), lecture-computer link, lecture-video integration, and/or interactive lecture, including small group interaction and/or question-answer segments. Students become active learners when the lecture technique does not stand alone. Lecture, in and of itself, is not a bad or inappropriate approach to teaching. It may be the most effective method when dealing with large groups; however, like any other strategy, it is more effective when not used as a single, exclusive technique.

Eble, in his text *The Craft of Teaching*[4] suggests that the lecture should be thought of as a discourse—a talk or conversation—not an authoritative speech. As a discourse, the lecture can then be viewed as part of the art or craft of teaching. As such, lecturing becomes a learnable skill, a skill that improves with practice.

TYPES OF LEARNERS

The lecture can be used effectively with learners from a variety of developmental and cognitive levels. In fact, that is one of the most positive aspects of this method—a teacher may, on a moment's notice, alter the depth, sophistication, and level of the material to be presented based on the responses of the learners. This assumes that the teacher has command of the subject matter, as well as the flexibility to alter the content and teaching plan (this level of flexibility probably will NOT exist with novice educators, or the first time new content is presented). Combining the lecture with the pedagogical approach to teaching/learning is especially useful in basic/beginning courses in a sequence, as well as orientation to a new clinical area or agency. Novice learners of any age tend to prefer the structure of pedagogy. The more mature and secure teachers and learners become, the more they enjoy the flexibility and challenge of integrating andragogical concepts into the lecture format.

RESOURCES

The major resource needed to utilize the lecture technique effectively is **you**, the lecturer. Presenting an informative and interesting lecture is a craft and a learnable skill. Since the speaker is the key element for this strategy, the following points are presented to help polish presentation skills.

• Conveying *enthusiasm* is the key element in presenting an effective lecture. Enthusiasm is contagious and is demonstrated by facial expression and excitement in voice, gesture, and body language. A lack of enthusiasm on the part of the speaker is interpreted by the listener as a lack of self-confidence, lack of knowledge, a disinterest in the learner, and/or disinterest in the topic. If you do not have an effusive personality, practice adding a smile and small hand gestures to each lecture. Once this is comfortable, add other interactive methods.

• Know the *content*. Even a structured lecture will not hide the insecurity of being unprepared/underprepared.

• Use *notes*. The use of notes is generally the option of the speaker; however, to avoid the distress of losing the train of thought or incorrectly presenting complex information, use some type of notes. For ease of handling, record the notes all on the same size paper or card (most useful are four-by-six- or five-by-seven-inch note cards or 8-by-11-inch sheets of paper). Sequentially number each card/page. This is a great asset should you drop them or have a fan or air conditioner blow away your note cards. The depth and contents of lecture notes should fit the lecturer's comfort level (use anything from a skeletal outline to a full manuscript). Notes should be double-spaced with major points highlighted so the eye can easily pick up a cue when needed. While the use of notes is perfectly acceptable, the reading of notes is NOT. Rehearse as long and as often as needed so the lecture will appear spontaneous and enthusiastic and will be completed within the given time frame.

• *Speak* to an audience of 200 as if they were a single student. Speak clearly and loudly enough to be heard in the back of the room. The use of a microphone may be necessary if you are in a large room or auditorium. Always use the microphone if there is any doubt that the speaker's voice will not be heard in the last row. It is sometimes helpful to have a friend sit in the back and signal if the speaker's voice is not being heard during the presentation. The use of a small clip-on microphone is preferable to using a hand-held or stationary microphone because it allows the speaker to move away from the podium and it frees one's hands to handle notes. If a microphone is to be used, the speaker should arrive in the assigned room early enough to try out the equipment and regulate sound levels.

• *Make eye contact*. Select someone in each corner of the room with whom to make eye contact. Slowly scan the audience. Smile at familiar faces. Review information related to the process of group dynamics. That review may come in handy.

• Use creative *movement*. Movements of the speaker's head and hands in gesturing should appear natural, not forced. Be careful when standing behind a podium, do not grip the sides tightly with your hands or lock the (shaky?) knees. This causes a circulatory response that could cause the speaker to faint. Occasionally step away from the podium and toward the listeners (this conveys an attitude of warmth and acceptance). Avoid distracting mannerisms (pacing, wringing hands, clearing throat, jamming hands into pockets).

• The use of a stage or *podium* places an automatic barrier between the speaker and the listeners. This gulf needs to be bridged early and often during the lecture. Suggestions for bridging the gulf: (1) use note cards rather than a manuscript—they are more portable and allow freedom to move away from the podium on occasion; (2) step away from behind the podium, especially if you are shorter than the podium! The audience does not wish to see a "talking head"; (3) walk *toward* the listeners—this is interpreted as a sign of warmth and reaching out to the audience; (4) address the right half of the audience and then the left half. Do not turn your back to either side of the audience; (5) if the group size allows, call on someone by name, or name an individual familiar to the lecturer and the participants; (6) use hand gestures to accentuate words, but be careful not to overdo this; and (7) if given the opportunity to be seated on a stage/platform, be aware of the eye level of the audience. Should anyone seated on a platform feel the need to cross legs, he or she should cross them at the ankles.

• Create a *change of pace*. An astute lecturer is constantly assessing the audience and reading its signals, indicating agreement/disagreement with what has been said or exhibiting an expression of misunderstanding. Another signal is being given when listeners begin having side conversations or are squirming in their seats. These signals call for intervention, response, or change of pace by the speaker. The change of pace can be as simple as turning off the overhead projector (the sound and changing light pattern will cause the listener to refocus attention on the speaker, away from the visual); shifting the focus from the speaker to a handout; using a humorous example; altering the tone or inflection of voice; or dividing into small groups for a brief discussion or taking a "stand and stretch" or a few-minutes' class break. Keep this rule of thumb in mind: an individual's optimal attention span is roughly one minute per year of age up to the approximate age of 45 (e.g., a five-year-old has a five-minute attention span; a 25-year-old, 25 minutes). Therefore, plan a change of pace or break according to the average age of your listeners. This author's favorite saying, "The mind can only absorb as much as the seat can endure," is a fairly valid guideline.

• Finally, hand out a skeletal outline only if this will help the learners identify key points. Emphasize principles and concepts. *Do not* copy charts, graphs, etc. from the learners' texts. Handout information should supplement the lecture. The lecture should *not* be a rehash of the learners' textbook. If handouts are used, they should be clear and contain a limited amount of information so the learner is not overwhelmed. Handouts printed on colored paper stand out and are more likely to be read than those printed on white paper.

Several publications that may be of assistance in keeping lecture material fresh are *The Teaching Professor*, a monthly newsletter from Magna Publications; *Change*, a monthly publication of the Association of Curriculum and Development; and the Sage Publications *Survival Skills for Scholars* series.

USING THE METHOD

The best time to begin the planning of a lecture is at the end of the previous one. The ideas to re-emphasize are fresh in the presenter's mind, as are the questions raised by the students. The speaker can recall what worked, what didn't, and how change can best be employed. (This is also the best time to write exam questions.) However, most lecturers are not so fortunate, and preparation is often relegated to a very brief time prior to the presentation. In order to present an effective lecture, the speaker needs to plan time to prepare specifically for two crucial time periods: the first five minutes and the last five minutes.

During the first five minutes of the lecture, two significant things are occurring: (1) the speaker lays out the objectives and expectations she or he has of the audience, and (2) the audience decides whether it trusts the speaker to produce what was promised and whether it is interested enough to invest its energy to follow the presentation. In the last five minutes the speaker has to make a link between what has been taught and what will be used by the learners in their life or practice. Thus, each lecture needs to be carefully planned and presented with an introduction (first five minutes), conclusion (last five minutes), and a well-organized body (the remaining amount of time allocated for the lecture).

Lecture Introduction (First Five Minutes)

"There is too much material to be covered within the time allocated, but I'll do the best I can." From a teacher's point of view this is always true, but this should *never be said to the audience*. If a lecturer opens a presentation with this statement, he or she has already conditioned the listener to expect a less-than-topnotch presentation. Once this statement has been made, the lecturer will have difficulty regaining the full attention of the listener; therefore, eliminate that statement from your repertoire. Instead, begin by identifying what the learner should gain from this lecture—state the objectives in clear, pragmatic, achievable terms. Then make a solid connection with the listeners by using an example of how the information can be (or has been) used in practice or life in general. Outline the three or four key concepts that will be addressed and use the expertise and clinical experience of the speaker to provide some background for this lecture. Conclude the introduction by establishing an open atmosphere. This can be accomplished by posing a question, making a bold statement, using a controversial quote, using humor, or using a visual aid or cartoon. The better one knows the audience, the easier and more successful this introduction becomes.

Body of Lecture

Like the human body, the body of the lecture is divided into specific parts. Begin with the definition of concept or principles; illustrate them with pragmatic, personal examples; and unfold the expectations and provide closure by helping the students incorporate the new ideas into their cognitive structure (this last phase may be used in the conclusion—last five minutes).[5] The body is the part of the lecture in which the speaker conveys the critical information the learner needs to know. It is well organized, with smooth transitions between topics. Before launching into the body of content, the ground rules should be outlined (e.g., "Because of the nature of the presentation, I will handle all questions at the end of class; we have two hours together today, so we'll take our first break in about 55 minutes").

It is during the body of the lecture that the speaking/presentation style is most evident. The following tips plus the suggestions made in the resources section of this chapter will enhance one's presentation style.

Lecture Conclusion

The lecture needs a definite ending. Closing a notebook, running out of time, or dismissing the class is *not* an acceptable conclusion. An effective communicator knows that any interaction deserves a closure. The lecture is not an exception. By focusing the learners' attention during the last five minutes of class, the lecturer is able to establish finality. A good conclusion will tie the introduction and the body together in a manner similar to the abstract of a well-written paper.

The well-developed objectives that were used as a portion of the introduction can be reiterated, assuming that they have been accomplished. The conclusion should also contain a review of the key points or topics covered and allow time for elaborating, amplifying, and/or clarifying issues presented. The lecturer must resist the temptation to present new information during the conclusion. Offering suggestions related to the application and transfer of knowledge may be helpful to the listeners. Using this approach allows the learner quickly to rethink the content, stimulate continued interest, and consider further action. The students then leave the lecture hall feeling that they have accomplished certain objectives and understood specific content.

POTENTIAL PROBLEMS

Nothing is perfect. As with any teaching method or strategy, problems exist with the use of the lecture technique. A key question to be answered is, "What is it that makes lecture and lectures unattractive?" During the last ten years, this author has taught graduate courses in which teaching methods and strategies were analyzed. Each year, students were asked the above question, and each year student responses were consistent. The most frequently repeated negative characteristics of lecture/lecturers focused on the person, NOT the method. Examples of these negatives and some suggestions for improvement are found in Table 33–3.

The remainder of this section is devoted to negative perceptions, which are more generic than the characteristics in Table 33–3.

Student Boredom

Educators face an incredible challenge different from that of our predecessors—how to obtain and retain the attention of the "Nintendo generation"—a generation of learners who are accustomed to fast-paced, action-packed, colorized entertainment at the flick of a switch. To compensate for this situational dilemma and still utilize the lecture technique effectively, the teacher should experiment in combining advanced technologies with the lecture in the classroom. Two examples are the in-class use of a computerized notebook to correlate data from the textbook and record the supplementary information presented via the lecture, or the use of the computer link that transmits and projects data from the computer screen to the video screen at the front of the classroom. This allows the lecturer to interject computer-generated charts, graphs, diagrams, and up-to-the-minute research findings into the lecture. An additional possibility is the assignment of out-of-class computer-assisted instructional programs (such as ADAM or subject-disease-specific learning packages) to complement the lecture.

Institutional Blocks

There are blocks that exist within every institution. The timing of class offerings is not to be overlooked. Traditionally, teachers have disliked teaching and students have disliked attending classes offered at 7:00 or 8:00 A.M. No one likes getting up that early! But some very unscientific study done by this author found that students, in general, dislike attending the first class of the day regardless of the time it is taught! Classes taught immediately after lunch are

Table 33–3 The Perceived Negative Factors Related to Lecturing

Negatives	*Suggestions for Improvement*
Disorganized or hard to follow Lack of outline or outline too detailed	Prepare and follow brief outline for each lecture.
Wears clothing that is distracting; lacks professional appearance	Dress as a professional role-model. (If you don't care about wearing stripes and plaids together, enlist the help of a colleague you consider to be a professional.)
Lack of facial expression Monotone voice (nervous, shaky voice) Lack of enthusiasm	Audio- and/or videotape one of your lectures; analyze it and establish some goals for improvement; then view it with a friend or colleague to support your decisions for change.
Won't take eyes off notes Reads the lecture material	Practice your lecture in front of a mirror, or videotape it. Practice until you know the main points by memory. Use only as many written notes as absolutely essential. Write yourself cues in the margin (smile—walk—relax!)
Often sits behind podium to lecture (referred to as the "talking head," since that is all that students see!)	Don't stand behind a podium unless you are six feet tall, ask for a shorter, lower lectern or table.
Uses no visual aids or visuals of poor quality	Teachers tend to put too much information in small print on slides and overhead transparencies. Ask your librarian, media center, or learning center for assistance in preparing visuals.
Lacks knowledge of educational principles; doesn't acknowledge that adult learners like to participate	Review techniques for keeping adult learners engaged. See references by Cross, Kidd, Knowles.
Inconsiderate of learners' needs—doesn't give breaks	Implement planned change-of-pace activities.
Distracting habits or characteristics: pacing; staring out windows; playing with objects (paper clips; rubber bands; change), using nonwords (ah, um) and repetitious phrases (you know, like . . ., well ah)	Use a videotape of your lecture to identify repetitive habits. Repositioning hands or holding note cards may help the "nervous hands" problem. Make a list of alternate words that could be substituted for the frequently repeated pet term. Nonwords are a verbalization that allows your speech to catch up to what your brain is thinking. Becoming aware of the use of nonwords may or may not be all you need to eliminate them; when they occur, stop, take a deep breath, and then go on.

considered "sleepers," since blood leaves the brain and moves to the gastrointestinal tract. Classes taught late in the afternoon or early evening are bad because the students and teachers are tired. Well, try as we may, short of one-on-one teaching, we will never find the perfect time to have class. Speakers must make their presentations stimulating and motivating at any time of the day!

Another institutional barrier to be considered is the number of students proportional to the size of the classroom. Lecturers are often placed in small, crowded classrooms with large numbers of students, and vice versa. Often, geographical relocation of desks/tables can ease this problem. Figure 33–1 depicts some alternative seating arrangements that facilitate the presentation of lecture and enhance listener attention.

Negative Press

The faculty member who consistently lectures may be subjected to student-generated negative comments, such as "This class is so boring, all he does is lecture"; "It's awful, she reads to us right out of her book"; or "I can't learn to think critically if all she does is lecture!" In fairness, it is generally not the method, but the teacher who is at fault. Try to break this negative stereotype by acknowledging that the situation has existed in the past; in order to correct it, introduce at least one additional teaching method (e.g., discussion, video, question-and-answer, role-play) into each lecture session. This will increase student interaction and should increase student satisfaction as well. In addition, you will have gained listeners' respect because you have acknowledged their feelings and made an overt effort to respond to them.

Knowledge Retention

This problem must be addressed. Although those of us who enjoy using the lecture method hate to admit it, research has proven that 80 percent of information gained by lecture alone is not recalled by students one day later, and that 80 percent of the remainder fades in a month.[6] However, research has also shown that the more the learners' senses (taste, touch, smell, vision, hearing) are involved in the learning activity, the longer and the higher the volume of knowledge retained.[7,8] Therefore, it would appear that if equipment were passed around to illustrate a point (touch, sight), or a video clip was inserted into the midst of the lecture (sight, hearing), or any other active learning process were introduced, the student's knowledge retention would increase.

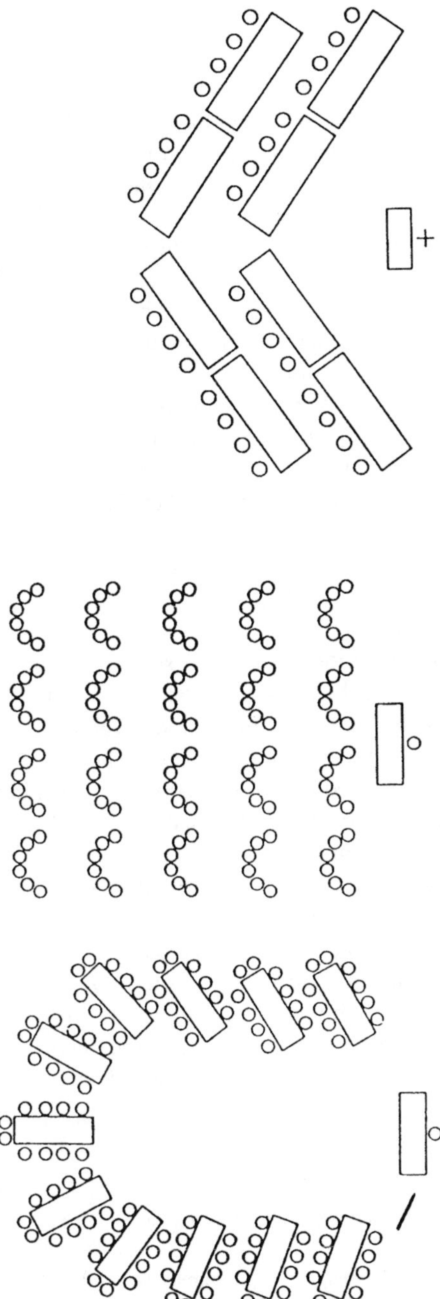

Figure 33–1 Alternate Seating Arrangements To Maximize Communication

EVALUATION

It is imperative that an evaluation of the lecture/lecturer be completed in a timely manner. The most useful time is at the completion of the lecture. This need not be a laborious task. Ask the listeners to respond to a few specific questions and then allow them to provide additional comments in an anonymous format. This is especially helpful for the novice lecturer. The evaluation process should aim to provide constructive criticism and comments for improvement. (The author utilizes this technique with graduate students. They may make any comments they wish; however, a negative comment cannot be made without offering a suggestion as to its resolution). If this evaluation technique is used frequently, the learners become accustomed to it. The process can be completed in as little as five minutes. Often, speakers are so interested in assessing whether the course objectives have been met that they forget to evaluate the means by which they were met. Lecturers will not improve without suggested change; suggested change can best be obtained by a planned evaluation method.

CONCLUSION

Presenting an effective lecture is more than simply standing in front of a group and verbalizing information. The lecturer must take into consideration the learner's abilities and learning style, the cognitive and developmental levels of the learner, the stated objectives of the class, and the individual objectives of the learner. The lecture should be divided into three major segments: introduction (five minutes), body, and conclusion (five minutes). Each section should be planned and presented in an organized manner, *never* "off the cuff." The prepared lecturer will be *considerate, credible,* and *in control* (not to be mistaken for rigidity).

A number of factors will enhance the presentation of a lecture, but none is more important than genuine enthusiasm. The lecture should *not* be considered a secondary teaching strategy. In many situations it is the most appropriate methodology to be used. To elicit the best results, the lecture should be accompanied by at least one of the other effective strategies discussed in this text.

NOTES

1. B. Flood and J. Moll, *The Professor Business: A Teaching Primer for Faculty* (Medford, NJ: Learned Information, Inc., 1990), 43–95.
2. M. Knowles, *The Modern Practice of Adult Education: Andragogy versus Pedagogy* (New York: Association Press, 1970).
3. J.R. Kidd, *How Adults Learn* (New York: Association Press, 1973).

4. K. Eble, *The Craft of Teaching* (San Francisco: Jossey-Bass, Inc. Publishers, 1982).

5. R. deTouryay and M. Thompson, Teaching by Lecture, in *Strategies for Teaching Nursing*, 3rd ed., ed. R. deTouryay and M. Thompson (New York: John Wiley & Sons, Inc., 1987), 95–110.

6. Flood and Moll, *The Professor Business*, 48.

7. M. Gullette, Leading Discussion in a Lecture Course, *Change* (March/April 1992):32–39.

8. K. Roberts and H. Thurston, Teaching Methodologies: Knowledge Acquisition and Retention, *Journal of Nursing Education* 23, no. 1 (1984):21–26.

SUGGESTED READING

Baird, M., and M. Monson. 1992. Distance education: Meeting diverse learners' needs in a changing world. *New Directions for Teaching and Learning* 51:65–76.

Boice, R. 1992. *The new faculty member.* San Francisco: Jossey-Bass, Inc. Publishers.

Cooper, J., et al. 1994. Cooperative learning in the classroom. In *Changing college classrooms*, ed. D.A. Halpern, 74–87. San Francisco: Jossey-Bass, Inc. Publishers.

Cross, K. 1981; reprinted 1993. *Adults as learners: Increasing participating and facilitating learning.* San Francisco: Jossey-Bass, Inc. Publishers.

King, A. 1994. Inquiry as a tool in critical thinking. In *Changing college classrooms*, ed. D.A. Halpern, 13–38. San Francisco: Jossey-Bass, Inc. Publishers.

Myers, C., and T.B. Jones. 1993. *Promoting active learning: Strategies for the college classroom.* San Francisco: Jossey-Bass, Inc. Publishers.

Powers, B. 1993. *Instructor excellence: Mastering the delivery of training.* San Francisco: Jossey-Bass, Inc. Publishers.

Schroeder, C. 1993. New students—New learning styles. *Change* (Sept–Oct):21–26.

Vella, J. 1994. *Learning to listen, learning to teach.* San Francisco: Jossey-Bass, Inc. Publishers.

Index

A

B

C

H

I

J

K

L

O

P